NEW PUBLIC MANAGEMENT

New Public Management

The transformation of ideas and practice

Edited by
TOM CHRISTENSEN and PER LÆGREID

Ashgate

Published by
Ashgate Publishing Limited
Gower House
Croft Road
Aldershot
Hampshire GU11 3HR
England

Ashgate Publishing Company
131 Main Street
Burlington, VT 05401-5600 USA

Ashgate website: http://www.ashgate.com

British Library Cataloguing in Publication Data
New public management : the transformation of ideas and practice
    1. Public administration 2. Public administration - Case studies 3. Civil service reform 4. Civil service reform - Case studies
    I. Christensen, Tom, 1949- II. Lægreid, Per
    351

Library of Congress Control Number: 00-109569

ISBN 0 7546 3212 1

Printed and bound in Great Britain by MPG Books Ltd, Bodmin, Cornwall

Contents

Contributors

Tom Christensen is a Professor at the Department of Political Science, University of Oslo. In his research and teaching he is concerned with civil service and public reform, based on instrumental and institutional theory. He has published numerous articles and books on these topics. His recent publications include studies of administrative structures, culture and governance.

Anders Forssell is a researcher at the Stockholm Center for Organisational Research (Score) and a lecturer at the Stockholm School of Economics. His main research interests are organisational change, reform theory and administrative practices in the public sector. He has several publications on these subjects.

Robert Gregory is an Associate Professor of Public Policy and Administration at the School of Business and Public Management and the School of Political Science and International Relations, Victoria University of Wellington, New Zealand. He has written widely on state sector reform and on public policy-making theory and organisational behaviour.

John Halligan is a Professor of Public Administration at the University of Canberra and Convenor of Research Degree Programs in Public Administration/Management. He has published extensively in the fields of public-sector reform and public management in Australia and New Zealand and more generally in the OECD countries. His main teaching fields are public administration/management and issues in governance.

Synnøve Jenssen is an Associate Professor at the Department of Political Science, University of Tromsø. Her research and publications have centred on three themes: dimensions of rationality in local politics, the modernisation of local government and the conditions for local democracy.

Per Lægreid is a Professor at the Department of Administration and Organisation Theory, University of Bergen and a research leader at the Norwegian Research Centre in Organisation and Management (LOS-centre). He has published numerous books and articles, especially on public administration, administrative policy, organisational reform and institutional change. His recent publications includes studies of organising political institutions.

Martin Painter is an Associate Professor at the Department of Government and Public Administration, University of Sydney. His research interests are in the fields of political institutions, public policy and public management. His recent work has been on multi-level governance, intergovernmental relations and federal systems.

Paul G. Roness is a Professor at the Department of Administration and Organisation Theory, University of Bergen and a Senior Researcher at the Norwegian Research Centre in Organisation and Management (LOS-centre). His main fields of interest are organisational change, administrative reforms and state employees' unions. He has published several books and articles on these subjects.

Kerstin Sahlin-Andersson is a Professor of Management at Stockholm University and a research leader at the Stockholm Center for Organisational Research (Score). She is also affiliated to the Department of Business Studies at Uppsala University. She has published books and articles about the global spreading of organisational models and standards, organisational changes in the public sector, and the organising of large projects.

Hans Robert Zuna is a Research Fellow at the Department of Political Science, University of Oslo. His main field of interest is administrative reforms, with a special focus on devolution and corporatisation in the public sector.

Preface

This book examines the dynamics of comprehensive civil service reform in Norway, Sweden, New Zealand and Australia. During the past 15 years, New Public Management has evolved into a new international administrative orthodoxy. This book challenges the globalisation thesis, which maintains that NPM is spreading fast around the world and generating convergence between civil service systems. We argue that administrative reforms are transformed by a complex mixture of environmental pressure, polity features and historical and institutional contexts and that this transformation implies substantial divergence and organisational variety and heterogeneity. There is therefore a need to look behind the new NPM orthodoxy and to develop a more differentiated view of the problems of governing the public sector.

Three forms of transformation of NPM are studied in this book. First, the transformation of the reforms themselves, which is examined by focusing on NPM reform processes, ideas and content. Second, the transformation of administrative systems – i.e., the effects of NPM reforms on political-administrative control, organised interests, policy capacity and governmental culture. Third, the transformation of theory and the implications of NPM for reform theory and democratic ideas.

There are a number of individuals and organisations to whom we owe our thanks. A first acknowledgement goes to our network of colleagues and friends who share an interest in institutional change, comparative public administration and public sector reform. We particularly wish to thank Joel Aberbach, Mark Considine, Dag Runar Jacobsen, Reginald Mascarenhas, Knut Mikalsen, Walter W. Powell, Harald Sætren, Roger Wettenhall and Lois R. Wise for comments on various sections of the book.

The idea for this book was conceived during a study tour to Australia and New Zealand. Special thanks therefore go to our hosts at the Centre for Research in Public Sector Management at the University of Canberra, at the Department of Government and Public Administration at the University of Sydney and at the School of Business and Public Management at Victoria University of Wellington.

Special thanks are also due to Maila Solheim for excellent technical assistance in supervising the preparation of the manuscripts, to Melanie Newton for very competent language assistance and to Marjoleine Hooijkas Wik who compiled the indexes.

We are also grateful for generous financial and administrative support from the Norwegian Research Council, the Swedish Council for Research in the Humanities and Social Sciences, the Norwegian Research Centre in Organization and Management, Stockholm Center for Organizational Research, the Scandinavian Consortium of Organizational Research at Stanford University, the Department of Administration and Organizational Theory at the University of Bergen and the Department of Political Science at the University of Oslo.

Oslo/Bergen, July 2000

Tom Christensen and Per Lægreid

1 Introduction

TOM CHRISTENSEN AND PER LÆGREID

A Transformative Perspective

Until the end of the 1970s the Scandinavian welfare state, with its large public sector and close co-operation between the state and organised interests in society, was regarded as exemplary. Sweden was the archetype for this successful Scandinavian model (Lægreid, 1999a). This is no longer the case. Twenty years later reform agents are looking 'down under' for inspiration. New Zealand, in particular, with its emphasis on rolling back the state and its confrontational policy style, represents the new model for organising a modern public sector, and New Public Management (NPM) is the new administrative orthodoxy (Olsen, 1997a).

This book is about NPM-related reforms in Australia, New Zealand, Norway and Sweden over the past two decades, with special emphasis on reform of the central civil service apparatus. The administrative reforms are studied from a transformative perspective. First, we focus on the transformation of NPM-related reform ideas and argue that the content of NPM varies from country to country. Second, we analyse to what extent the NPM reforms have transformed the state apparatus in the four countries studied. Third, we discuss to what extent these comprehensive administrative reforms might change the model of democracy in this kind of political-administrative system. We argue that the institutional dynamics in the transformations can best be interpreted as a complex mixture of environmental pressure, polity features and historical institutional context. These factors define how much leeway political leaders have in making choices about NPM reforms – i.e., they both further and hinder reforms following complex patterns.

NPM is seen in this book as a global reform movement that has occurred over the past two decades. It is inspired by a particular set of economic theories and normative values whose main focus is on increasing efficiency. Some of its main characteristics are increased market orientation, devolution, managerialism and the use of contracts and it has led to a transformation of the public sector in many countries (Boston et al., 1996). However, the process of reform has not been the same everywhere. In some countries there might be a strong element of diffusion of NPM ideas from outside, whereas in others the reform process might be more a result of national or local initiatives that have subsequently acquired a NPM label. Thus, the spread of NPM is seen as a complex process, going through different stages and packaged in different ways in different countries, with each country following its own reform trajectory within a broader NPM framework. NPM imposes constraints on reforms of the civil service, meaning that some reforms are more likely than others, and one NPM-inspired reform may potentially open doors for other, similar reforms. We do not see NPM either as having a specific starting point or as a neat package of reform elements following a specific path or having a specific destination.

One school of thought regards the implementation of NPM primarily as a response to external pressure. This environmental determinism (Olsen, 1992) can be of two kinds. In the first instance a country may adopt internationally based norms and beliefs about how a civil service system should be organised and run simply because these have become the prevailing doctrine. NPM has its origins in certain Anglo-Saxon countries and international organisations, like the Organisation for Economic Co-operation and Development (OECD) where a kind of reform myth has taken hold, become ideologically dominant and diffused all over the world (Czarniawska and Sevón, 1996; Meyer and Rowan, 1977; Scott, 1995). This diffusion process may imply isomorphic elements – i.e., it may create pressure for similar reforms and structural changes in many countries (DiMaggio and Powell, 1983; Scott, 1998). Isomorphism can be seen as a deterministic, natural process engendered by common dominating norms and values. In the second instance, NPM may really be seen as the optimal solution to widespread technical problems – i.e., it may be adopted to solve problems created by a lack of instrumental performance or by economic competition and market pressure. In this instance NPM reforms are adopted not because of their ideological hegemony but because of their technical efficiency.

Another view of NPM holds that reforms are primarily a product of the national historical-institutional context. Different countries have different historical-cultural traditions and their reforms are 'path dependent', meaning that national reforms have unique features (Krasner, 1988; March and Olsen, 1989; Selznick, 1957). The reform roads taken reflect the main features of national institutional processes, where institutional 'roots' determine the path followed in a gradual adaptation to internal and external pressure. This view stresses institutional autonomy and internal dynamics. The greater the consistency between the values underlying the reforms and the values on which the existing administrative system is based, the more likely the reforms are to be successful (Brunsson and Olsen, 1993).

A third view emphasises that different countries have different constitutional features and political-administrative structures and these factors go some way to explaining how they handle national problems and reform processes (Olsen and Peters, 1996a; Weaver and Rockman, 1993). The main features of the polity, the form of government and the formal structure of decision-making within the political-administrative system may all affect a country's capacity to realise administrative reforms.

Within the constraints spelled out political leaders have varying amounts of leeway to launch and implement NPM reforms via administrative design and an active administration policy. Their identities and resources (March and Olsen, 1995) and capacity for rational calculation and political control (Dahl and Lindblom, 1953) are to a great extent constrained by environmental, historical-institutional and polity features. Thus, adaptation to external pressure is not only about environmental determinism but may also have intentional elements connected to the actions of the political-administrative leadership, the professions or consulting firms that 'certify' certain 'prescriptions' or reforms, or represent systematic 'double-talk' or 'hypocrisy' (Brunsson, 1989). Conscious national handling of internationally inspired reforms can, however, also lead to the imitation of only selected reform elements instead of whole reform packages (often labeled 'institutional standards' within organisational fields) and as such create variation between countries (Røvik, 1996). Furthermore, political ability to control reform processes can be affected by polity and structural factors enhancing capacity and attention for political leadership or hindered by negotiation processes or by a lack of compatibility with historical-institutional norms (Brunsson and Olsen, 1993, pp. 5–6; Christensen, 1995; Christensen and Peters, 1999, pp. 8–9). Such conditions will probably also make political-administrative systems more vulnerable to pressure for reform from the environment.

This book looks primarily at the dynamic relationship between the reform features described in the three views stated and asks how much political leeway they offer. International reform trends like NPM have global potential, but they can also be transformed in the diffusion process when they encounter national contexts, so that they are not only seen as myths without behavioural consequences (Meyer and Rowan, 1977; Røvik, 1998). While nationally based reforms have unique features, they are also influenced by international trends; and, as the examples of Australia and New Zealand show, they also have the potential, in turn, to influence these trends. We will not discuss this latter aspect, however.

While we accept that international actors are important for spreading NPM reform ideas around the world and that they exert strong normative pressure, we see the diffusion process more in terms of a transformation of NPM and the civil service. This means that the main reform ideas, solutions, methods of implementation and practice or effects coming from outside change when they encounter different political-administrative and historical-cultural contexts. Such transformation may reflect a lack of compatibility between reform content and national institutional norms and values (Brunsson and Olsen, 1993, pp. 5–6). A kind of 'editing' of reform ideas takes place as they are put into operation and come face to face with existing national ideas and practice (Røvik, 1996; Sahlin-Andersson, 1996) or else a reform 'virus' manages to penetrate a country's administration only after a certain period of time (March and Olsen, 1983; Røvik, 1998).

The focus of this book is quite specific – it examines not just the transformation of NPM and its main ideas as such, but the transformation of the civil service after being exposed to NPM over two decades. We label this the transformation of practice or the effects of NPM reforms. This transformation may be related to changes in the attitudes and thinking of central actors in the public sector or to changes in patterns of influence and decision-making behaviour. These effects can be directly connected to the core of the reform intentions and elements, together with efficiency effects, but there may also be side-effects or unintentional consequences that are of interest. We focus primarily on internal effects, those taking place inside the executive – the political leadership and the civil service – but there are also external effects, more directly related to other national actors, societal groups and public opinion in general. We will also touch upon the wider implications of NPM – namely, how NPM eventually changes our thinking and political models.

Main Research Questions

The main research questions covered in the book are:

1. What is the dynamic relationship between the diffusion of NPM as a global reform wave and the more nationally based NPM-related reforms in the four countries studied? To what extent and in what way are the central NPM ideas transformed when facing different national contexts?

Are the national reform processes characterised by similarity in the organisation and content of reforms (more specific reform elements) or by the variety engendered by differences in environmental, cultural and political-administrative contexts?

2. In what way and to what extent has NPM transformed practice and affected political control, patterns of influence and the relationship between central actors, or indeed decision-making processes more generally? Has the main effect been a systematic undermining of political control or has NPM increased efficiency and strengthened political control? Does reform divergence – whereby the four countries are consistently and cumulatively moving in different directions as a result of NPM reforms – stem from differences in environmental factors, national political-administrative and cultural features, with New Zealand and Norway at the two extreme ends of the spectrum? What are the effects of the NPM reforms on the relationship between central political-administrative actors and societal groups? Have the NPM reforms produced major side-effects in the countries studied?

3. What are the broader implications of NPM? How and to what extent are NPM-related reforms transforming our models of democratic systems? Can traditional democratic models meet the challenge of NPM?

A Profile of the Book

How can we relate our study to research traditions and other reform studies? The book is mainly inspired by an international research tradition in public administration that is theoretically informed and empirically oriented and combines political science theory and organisation theory (Christensen and Lægreid, 1998c; March, 1998; Olsen 1988c). The study is more in a governance tradition, attending to political constraints, than in a managerialist tradition (Ingraham, 1996). The latter tradition, however, has a more prominent role to play in the theories driving the NPM reforms and as such is also relevant.

There are three distinctive aspects to this study of the transformation of NPM and the civil service. First, in outlining, discussing and applying a transformative perspective its orientation is generally theoretical and explores the main theoretical components mentioned above. Its purpose is thus more to develop and illustrate a number of theoretical concepts using comparative empirical examples than to cover a broad range of systematic comparative reform data.

Second, the book is chiefly concerned with the transformation of practice or the effects of NPM, and in that respect it fills a gap in our knowledge about reforms. Most reform studies concentrate on process features, such as formal changes or the content of reform programmes, or else focus on effects in broad ways using aggregative statistics. Our approach is a more qualitative one and focuses closely on the central political-administrative actors and their decision-making behaviour.

Third, the book gives comparative examples from four countries – Australia, New Zealand, Norway and Sweden. New Zealand and Australia have been highlighted as countries where extensive NPM reforms have taken place during the last two decades. In Sweden, by contrast, the perception is that there has been a lot of talk about reforms but, in comparison to the Anglo-Saxon countries, a much less coherent reform programme has been carried out and less dramatic effects have been reported. Norway has been portrayed as a much more reluctant reformer, and NPM seems to be more of a marginal phenomenon there with less impact. Thus, in terms of the ideas, the reform process and the effects, the application of NPM has been quite different in each of these countries. Attempts to explain why this should be reveal that the four countries have similar statist traditions and similarities in the development of their welfare states and in the traditional importance of corporatist features but differing environmental factors and differently structured central political-administrative systems (Christensen, 1995; Christensen and Lægreid, 1999a). One particularly interesting feature is that the NPM-related reforms were initiated by Labour parties in all four countries, but they chose different reform paths, probably because of differences in environmental and national contexts.

An Outline of the Chapters

The book consists of an introductory chapter, three parts and a concluding chapter. In Chapter 2 Tom Christensen and Per Lægreid outline two broad models of governance, as a background for understanding modern public reforms. These are the 'sovereign state model', in which a centralized state upholds collective values; and the 'supermarket model', where the state is a market-oriented, efficient supplier of services, catering primarily to the needs of individual consumers and clients. It then goes on to discuss the content of

NPM, especially its hybrid character and inconsistency, and how this content varies in the countries studied. Third, a transformation perspective on NPM is outlined and discussed, emphasizing the relationship between environmental factors on the one hand and national, political-structural and historical-cultural factors on the other hand. Scores for these independent variables in the four countries are also suggested. Fourth, our model of analysis and general transformation hypotheses are outlined, followed by a section discussing comparative method in relation to our study.

Part one of the book concentrates on the transformation of NPM reforms by focussing on the ideas and the process aspects. In Chapter 3 Kerstin Sahlin-Andersson views NPM reforms in a global context. Her thesis is that alongside each country's own 'local' version of reform, global templates for reform have also been produced. She asserts that the amount and type of attention that reforms in countries like Australia and New Zealand receive internationally is in itself an effect of the reforms and may also transform NPM and be reflected in 'local' reforms.

The chapter discusses three different types of global reform trends: the first is the nationally based – i.e., when countries come up with the same reforms and solutions independently of one another simply because they are facing similar problems. The second type is the internationally based, where NPM can be seen as a set of ideas travelling around the world that are imitated and diffused through the action of reformers. The third type is the transnational, where a number of different agents mediate reform ideas and experiences between and within countries in a less co-ordinated way.

Chapter 4, by John Halligan, identifies and analyses the key process questions involved in reforming the public sector in OECD countries, comparing Australia, New Zealand, Norway and Sweden. It clarifies three questions concerning the reform process – the nature of the reforms at the system level, the character of reforms and the components of the reform processes – and also discusses approaches to reform and different styles and strategies. In comparing the four countries Halligan contrasts old and new reform styles.

The second and main part of the book deals with the transformation of the administrative systems. It forcuses on the practice and the effets of NPM through such means as contracts; devolutions; corporatization; and management on political-administrative control; state employee unions; policy capacity; and governmental culture. Chapter 5, by Tom Christensen and Per Lægreid, is a broad discussion of the effects of NPM on political control. Using a transformative perspective and a discussion of process features in the four countries, the focus is first on the hybrid character of NPM with regard to the economic and managerial elements. There then follows a discussion of different elements of devolution and their effects on political control. The extensive use of contracts brought about by the reforms is also discussed as well as how this feature, combined with devolution, eventually changes the leadership role from one of culturally based responsibility to one of instrumentally based accountability. The chapter concludes by showing how there has been a general decrease in political control, albeit with a certain amount of variation between the countries studied in how NPM is transforming political control and leadership roles.

In Chapter 6 Hans Robert Zuna describes the effects of corporatisation in New Zealand and Norway on the relationship between enterprises and the political authorities concerning autonomy, political influence and control. Do these reforms give enterprises more room for manoeuvre and is this compatible with a continuous focus on political influence and control? Within a transformative framework, different organisational and constitutional arrangements, together with differing cultures, are expected to create national variation.

Following the reforms, state-owned enterprises in New Zealand are all formally controlled by the minister of finance and a minister of state-owned enterprises in the same department, while their Norwegian counterparts are still controlled by the sectoral ministries and are expected to take account of both political and commercial considerations. Non-commercial interests in state-owned enterprises, often meaning collective political interests, must be paid for in New Zealand. The general effects of the more extensive use of state-owned companies in the two countries indicate that political control is decreasing compared with the former system. Interestingly enough, actual control of companies in New Zealand seems to be more active but also more narrowly focused on commercial objectives. Political control and influence in Norway is passive concerning political and commercial aspects, and companies have increased their autonomy in all matters following devolution.

In Chapter 7 Per Lægreid makes a comparison of the development and the use of new contract system for chief executive administrative leaders in New Zealand and Norway. The leadership contract system in New Zealand started out in a more radical way than the Norwegian and was later extended, while the Norwegian one has been further restricted over time. The system in New Zealand is more formal and more performance- and incentive-based, while the Norwegian one is more limited and provides less scope for wage inequality.

A survey of the effects of the systems shows both similarities and differences: both systems have produced real pay increases and increases in internal wage inequality; both countries have had problems attracting people from the private sector through the contracts systems, and salary increases lag behind those in the private sector; and both countries have also had problems specifying goals and measuring performance. The new contracts system in Norway seems to have changed little in the relationship between political and administrative leaders, a relationship based largely on shared values, mutual trust and responsibility. In New Zealand chief executives now have greater policy discretion and more emphasis is put on managerial accountability, but there are also problems of ambiguity and lack of trust.

The state employees' unions were an important factor in the reforms in most of the four countries. In Chapter 8 Paul G. Roness analyses the extent of union involvement in the reforms and the impact this has had on the unions. While the union confederations and national unions seem largely to have been passed over by reformers in New Zealand, many of the Australian reforms were in part made possible or influenced by the participation of the unions. In Norway and Sweden there were some differences in how the union confederations and their national unions reacted to the reforms and in the effect this had. The discussion emphasises the importance of the historical legacy of the unions and their relationship to the Labour parties.

The second theme of the chapter analyses the extent to which the reforms affected the unions themselves. While union density has been markedly reduced in New Zealand and Australia, membership has been quite stable in Norway and Sweden. In New Zealand and Australia the reforms seem generally to have weakened the unions, while in Norway and Sweden they appear to have maintained their position, though the union confederations and to some extent the national unions as well have lost out to local branches. The discussion emphasises the importance of the characteristics of the reforms.

'Policy capacity' is an elusive concept but refers in Chapter 9, by Martin Painter, to the effectiveness of the policy-making process, as distinct from the effectiveness of the outcomes of a policy. It is distinguished from policy responsiveness, which is a measure of the effectiveness of day-to-day political control over policy. Have managerialist reforms enhanced or diminished policy capacity and/or policy responsiveness? The implications of managerialist public sector reforms for policy capacity and policy responsiveness are explored and potential effects and side-effects in different phases of the policy cycle are discussed. Particular attention is paid to the effects of reforms that impinge directly on the central policy machinery and processes. Examples and detailed case material are drawn from housing policy-making in the intergovernmental arena and in the context of Commonwealth budget cabinet decision-making in Australia to argue that, while responsiveness may be enhanced, policy capacity may be threatened by recent trends. These arguments and examples are then discussed in a comparative perspective.

Chapter 10, by Robert Gregory, assesses the impact of NPM on New Zealand's central government administration some ten years after the establishment of the two main legislative pillars of public sector reform, the State Sector Act 1988 and the Public Finance Act 1989. As commentators have observed, New Zealand implemented NPM ideas in a more comprehensive and theoretically coherent manner than virtually any other country, with the possible exception of Britain.

Most of the academic commentary on the New Zealand experience has presented a favourable view of the reforms, which have been credited with transforming a traditionally bureaucratic system of governmental administration into a more vibrant, flexible, and efficient system much more focused on the achievement of policy results than on the (mere) maintenance of administrative process. Now, however, certain strains are appearing in New Zealand's governmental system, some, if not all of which seem to have their origins in the reformist determination to transform the public sector in the image of private management, as if there were few essential differences between the two.

In particular, this chapter argues that in New Zealand a 'mechanistic' as opposed to 'organic' approach to public sector change has largely failed to distinguish adequately between the ideas of responsibility and accountability in government administration, has lowered public trust in the integrity of government officials and has resulted in a need for a new synthesis between more traditional conventions of public service trusteeship and the managerial imperatives of NPM. The relevance of these arguments is then discussed in relation to the effects and implications in the other three countries.

The third part of the book focuses he implications of NPM reforms on reform theory and democratic models. In chapter 11 Anders Forssell discusses what happens when the Scandinavian reform theory meets NPM reforms in Sweden. He tells a story of the Swedish road to NPM and discusses the question of loose coupled reforms. His argument is that the general idea of market reform works as a selection mechanisms for more specific reform means. Chapter 12, by Synnøve Jenssen, discusses some of the changing conditions of representative democracy in the era of NPM. A central question raised is how the ideas of modernisation and renewal of the public sector are challenging the democratic aspects of politics. NPM is in fundamental ways changing the structure, role and management of the public sector, but are these ideas adequate for coping with the challenge that political and administrative institutions will face in the future? The normative perspective is that the main goal of modernisation should be to strengthen political co-ordination and democratic influence.

Two different views on politics and democratic processes are outlined: a liberal market perspective, underscoring the instrumental and private character of politics, which involves compromises and aggregation between atomised actors with opposing interests; and a forum perspective, which emphasises integrative features, public discourse and deliberative aspects. The chapter then discusses more generally how the renewal has handled various aspects of democracy, especially the relationship between politics and administration. Some main themes are discussed, such as the market as an effective regulator, the new individualism, problems of political integration and the problem of political autonomy.

In the concluding chapter Tom Christensen and Per Lægreid reflect on some of the main insights gained from the transformation of NPM and the civil service in the four countries analysed with a special focus on the democratic aspects of NPM and the question of accountability. The future of the civil service in the new millennium is also discussed on the basis of these insights. We ask whether one will see a continued development of NPM-inspired reforms, a revival of traditional administrative structures and values or an increasingly complex and hybrid civil service.

2　A Transformative Perspective on Administrative Reforms

TOM CHRISTENSEN AND PER LÆGREID

Introduction

When studying administrative reforms in the public sector it is important to stress the distinctiveness of public administration and the uniqueness of civil service systems (Pollitt and Bouckaert, 2000). A discussion of administrative reforms in public organisations should address two main issues(Lægreid and Roness, 1999). First, based on the ideas of representative democracy, the conditions for governing by political leaders and the effect of administrative reform on political governance are particularly relevant. Second, public reform processes and administrative apparatuses have specific structural features which distinguish them from other types of reform process or organisation. Public organisations are an integral part of the political-administrative system which encompasses a complex ecology of actors, tasks, beliefs, principles, interests, resources and rules. In a multi-functional civil service, reformers may not merely maximise a simple set of goals and considerations but are obliged to compromise between partly conflicting objectives and values. This implies that we cannot expect one single model of governance and autonomy to apply to all government agencies in all situations. The Weberian model, which is based on a fairly simple notion of both the external and internal structure of public administrations has been challenged by administrative reforms during the past twenty years. The external organisation is no longer dominated by the administration's legal subordination to the political leadership and the internal organisation is no longer dominated by a strict hierarchy and rules. Hierarchy, law, and rule-bound behaviour have been supplemented by a variety of other features introduced by the New Public Management (NPM) movement (Christensen and Lægreid, 1998c).

The debate about NPM-reforms has in many countries centred on two different views of democracy and the role of the state, reflected in cleavages between political parties. It has also lead to a division in the scholarly community between those emphasising a governance tradition, preoccupied with political constraints, and those adhering to a tradition of managerialism, encompassing economic and management elements (Ingraham 1996). The first part of the chapter will outline these models and cleavages. The second part will discuss the content of NPM ideas and reforms, examining them for internal consistency and looking at which elements have been used in the four countries studied. The third part outlines a transformative perspective on the processes and effects of NPM. It refers to three main explanatory variables – the environmental, the cultural and the political-administrative. We look at how different countries score on these variables and relate them to some general hypotheses. The chapter concludes with an outline of the model of analysis and some considerations of comparative method.

Models of Governance: The Sovereign State and the Supermarket State

A traditional view in the countries studied is that democracy and political-administrative control are defined according to the 'parliamentary chain' and the mandate given to political leaders through the election channel (Olsen, 1978 and 1983). In elections the people select representatives to political bodies, executive power is based on the political majority in these bodies and the executive has at its disposal a neutral civil service with a wealth of professional expertise, which prepares and implements public policy, including reforms. This perspective of the role of the bureaucracy is still relevant, as some of the most comprehensive surveys of the civil service ever made (studies of the civil service in Norway over a period of twenty years) show (Christensen and Egeberg, 1997; Christensen and Lægreid, 1998a; Egeberg, 1989b; Lægreid and Olsen, 1978).

Olsen (1988a) labels this model of governance 'the sovereign, rationality-bounded state', meaning a centralised state with a large public sector in which standardisation and equality are prominent features. The model emphasises the collective and integrative features of the political-administrative system, the common heritage and the role of the citizen (March and Olsen, 1989). Thus, Dahl Jacobsen (1960) sees the role of the civil service in such a state as complex, having to take into consideration many decision stimuli and premises that are ambiguous and inconsistent. These considerations are related to political control, to decision effectiveness and responsiveness and to professional competence and also to *Rechtsstaat* values and other elements (Christensen, 1997; Egeberg, 1997). This complexity is said to enhance the flexibility and political sensitivity of civil servants and is therefore perceived as more of a strength than a weakness (Christensen, 1991).

According to this state model, change and reform processes in a political-administrative system are hierarchical and dominated by political and administrative leaders – i.e., the processes are closed and have an exclusive group of participants (Hood, 1998a, p. 73; March and Olsen, 1976 and 1983). Leaders score relatively high on rational calculation or conscious organisational means-end thinking (Dahl and Lindblom, 1953, p. 57). They have relatively unambiguous goals, based on a range of information and decision premises, and are supposed to know which reforms will solve pressing problems (Simon, 1957).

This traditional model has been supplemented by a variety of others (Olsen, 1988a; Peters, 1996a). One can paint a picture of

> ... a public administration integrated into complex political and societal networks of organized interests and clients... (characterized by) a complex interplay between competing logics, loyalties and influences, demanding more elaborate models of decision-making and change than assumed by the Weberian ideal model... (Christensen and Lægreid, 1998c, p. 148).

Olsen (1988a, pp. 241–242) labels one alternative model of democracy and political-administrative control 'the supermarket state'. This model presumes that the government and the state in general have a service-providing role, with an emphasis on efficiency and good quality, and views the people as consumers, users or clients (Hood, 1998a, p. 98). In this model the hierarchy is in a sense turned upside down – i.e. rather than the state controlling society on the basis of a democratic mandate from the people, society controls the state more directly through market mechanisms. Taken to its extreme this model implies that if governmental units do not produce satisfactory services at a low price they should be abolished or downsized. Such units are not there for their own sake and must demonstrate their raison d'être.

The supermarket state primarily attends to economic values and norms, meaning that other values and considerations from the centralised state model must be downgraded, making this model more one-dimensional (Nagel, 1997, p. 354). Furthermore, public reform processes are primarily a result of changes in market processes and user demand and hence very much environ-mental-deterministic in nature (Olsen, 1992).

Administrative reforms, according to this model, appear to be apolitical or even anti-political in nature (Frederickson, 1996, p. 268). Thus, political bodies and politicians tend to be seen as almost illegitimate actors who obstruct efficiency. It is obviously more preoccupied with the state at the street level and sees the centralised state as overloaded and inefficient at the central level (Boston et al., 1996, p. 8, p. 11; Gustavsson and Svensson, 1999, p. 47). What it lacks is a perspective on the relationship between the influence of voters or citizens on politicians through the election channel, on the one hand, and their more direct influence on public bodies as clients and consumers on the other. Nor is it particularly preoccupied with the importance of resources in providing public services and products or with possible bias of political significance.

Nevertheless, the model does contain some elements of an alternative view of democracy – namely, a direct, individually oriented democracy with economic overtones, even if this aspect is not well developed. It is not easy to see how atomised actors making choices in a market can participate in creating a stable and responsible democratic system. And their potential to influence services is also ambiguous and debatable.

To sum up, the supermarket state seems to represent a one-dimensional view of the public sector, where the economic factor predominates, while the society-controlling state is far more preoccupied with a complex balancing of different and legitimate considerations.

The two state models presented have normative-political implications, traditionally associated with a left-right spectrum. Socialist and social democratic parties have defended the sovereign state model, while conservative and liberal parties have supported the supermarket state model in a more or less clearly pronounced manner in different countries (Nagel, 1997, p. 354). The attitudes of interest groups have also followed the same cleavage, exemplified historically by resistance among trade and civil servants unions associated with the labour parties to the supermarket model (Castles, Gerritsen and Vowles, 1996a; Jacobsen, 1996; Lægreid and Roness, 1998). But a movement in electorates towards the right during the last twenty to twenty-five years has led to a breakthrough of the supermarket model. Thus, even social democratic parties have come to accept elements from this model, seen by some as highly controversial but by others as a political necessity, or as a 'third way' (Giddens, 1998), and probably resulting generally in a wider implementation of NPM. It is worth noting that a clear majority of EU countries now have social democratic governments, often with a Blair-like profile.

This political-normative debate about the development of the public sector has been accompanied by a parallel debate among scholars around the world. Some economists (mostly those associated with the new institutional economics school) and management scholars have pointed to the inefficiency of the public sector and called for a leaner and more efficient state (Boston et al., 1996, pp. 16–40). And they have been activists in reform processes, both as producers of models and ideology and as entrepreneurs in the civil service, as exemplified in New Zealand (Goldfinch, 1998). At the same time, representatives from the social sciences, like political scientists, and to some extent humanists, have defended a public sector model based on collective and institutional arguments. Citing Herbert Simon (1957) one can say that the value-anchoring of professional groups, not only the actual or factual connections they emphasise, has been in conflict.

Few countries have adopted all the elements of the sovereign state model or accepted uncritically the major principles of the supermarket state in their reforms, suggesting a discussion about how these could or should be blended and synthesised. The potential exists for a transformation of systems and roles that combines evolutionary change, as indicated by the traditional sovereign model, and the revolutionary change prescribed by the supermarket model (Greenwood and Hinings, 1996). Such a combination draws on both global models of NPM and local versions (Røvik, 1998). So what are the characteristics of this new hybrid? How can political-democratic control be secured under more market and management and, conversely, how can the sovereign state be modified by these market elements? Is this a question of structural or cultural change or a combination of both? How does this affect and transform the roles of central politicians and administrative/institutional leaders and what are the wider democratic implications?

Since the 1980s the international tendency in administrative reform has been a neo-liberal one, encompassing managerial thinking and a market mentality. The private sector has become the role model, and public administration has come to be seen as a provider of services to citizens who were redefined as clients and consumers. These reform trends have weakened the sovereign state model and enhanced the supermarket model. These new administrative doctrines came to be known collectively as New Public Management. We will now outline some of the main features of NPM. First, we describe the common ideas behind NPM; second, we give an account of the tensions within the NPM concept; and third we discuss how the content of NPM varies across the countries studied.

Main Features of New Public Management

New Public Management is a label for recent administrative reforms first used by Hood (1991). Thus, it is important to emphasise that reform agents did not use this term when they launched administrative reforms in the 1980s and early 1990s, even if the content of those reforms was later classified as NPM. This means that reforms that today are seen as NPM-reforms might have started out as part of a national administrative policy. In contrast to general change processes, reform always entails deliberate change. For a reform to be labelled NPM it must constitute an intentional effort by central political-administrative actors to change the structure, processes or personnel of the public sector and it must contain some of the elements outlined below.

The Primacy of Economic Norms and Values

The main feature of NPM is its emphasis on economic norms and values – i.e., the concept and the related reform wave and reform programmes are in this respect one-dimensional. This ideological dominance, whereby many traditionally legitimate norms and values in the public sector are seen solely in economic terms, makes the conflicts and tensions between different norms and values more evident (Boston et al., 1996, p. 354). In NPM this dominance is also connected to strong, and not always well-founded, opinions about how economic norms and values have certain effects on other considerations, for instance that emphasising efficiency implies changes in the formal organisation of the public sector, in procedures, in the expertise needed and in its relationship to the private sector.

When NPM reforms are said to be typically theoretical, as in New Zealand, this often means that economic theories dominate. Examples are public choice theories, principal-agent models and transaction cost models (Boston et al., 1991; Boston et al., 1996, pp. 17–25). In these models relations between actors in the political-administrative system are seen as strategic games between rational actors who intend to make the political-administrative system more efficient, streamlined, and consistent (Boston et al., 1996, p. 3; Evans et al., 1996). Such economic models seem to regard the ambiguous goals, complicated formal structures and composite cultural norms of a complex civil service as signs of 'disease' and not as fundamental distinctive features of the public sector. At the same time, critics of such models emphasise that this way of thinking is simplistic and plays down the importance of public sector ethics and institutional-cultural constraints and that it has not proven as fruitful as anticipated when confronted with everyday life in the public sector. NPM, with its economic performance and market focus, sees other values and considerations embedded in the civil service as more or less unproblematic and not generally threatened or negatively affected by the efficiency and economy focus of NPM (Olsen, 1997b). In this book this view is challenged in a discussion of the effects and implications NPM-reforms have for political-democratic control of systems.

Here we will primarily discuss how the dominance of economic thinking in the public sector, as represented by NPM, is connected to changes in the structure, procedures and culture of political-administrative systems. A main question is how these reform elements affect the political-democratic control of systems and what the implications are.

The Hybrid Character of NPM

Even if NPM espouses economic values and objectives, the concept is loose and multifaceted and offers a kind of 'shopping basket' of different elements for reformers of public administration (Hood, 1991; Pollitt, 1995). The main components of NPM are hands-on professional management, which allows for active, visible, discretionary control of an organisation by people who are free to manage; explicit standards of performance; a greater emphasis on output control; increased competition; contracts; devolution; disaggregation of units; and private sector management techniques. Ferlie et al. (1996) distinguish between four different NPM models: the efficiency drive, downsizing and decentralisation, in search of excellence and public service orientation. NPM promises to integrate these themes, linking efficiency and accountability together (Minogue et al., 1998).

Tensions arising from the hybrid character of NPM, which combines economic organisation theory and management theory, have been noted by Aucoin (1990), Hood (1991) and Yeatman (1997). These tensions result from the contradiction between the centralising tendencies inherent in contractualism and the devolutionary tendencies of managerialism. The first set of ideas comes from economic organisation theory, which includes public choice and principal-agent theory, and focuses on the primacy of representative government over the bureaucracy (Boston et al., 1996). A lesson from this paradigm is that the power of political leaders must be reinforced against the bureaucracy. This concentration of power requires attention to centralisation, co-ordination and control, and contractual arrangements are a main device to attain that goal. The question, however, is how well this instrument fulfils this goal.

The second set of ideas comes from the managerialist school of thought, which focuses on the need to re-establish the primacy of managerial principles in the bureaucracy (Kettl, 1997). This concentration on enhancing the capacity of managers to take action requires attention to decentralisation, devolution and delegation. NPM is thus a double-edged sword which prescribes both centralisation and devolution.

Our interpretation is that NPM may lean somewhat more towards devolution than towards centralisation when combining the managerial and contractual elements. Managerialism points in the direction of more devolution, while the centralising tendency in contractualism is not altogether clear-cut. Contractualism also favours increased competition, potentially undermining central, hierarchic control (Kerauden and van Mierlo, 1998), and can potentially enhance the influence of administrative leadership at the expense of political leadership. On the other hand, there might be an element of centralization in managerialism – i.e. by increasing the power of ministries and their political advisers in the corporate planning process (Painter, 1987). In addition to the intrinsically hybrid character of the NPM concept, additional hybrid features often arise as a result of mixing NPM with elements of traditional public administration, which often happens in practice (Christensen and Lægreid, 1998a).

NPM generally relies to a large extent on a combination of micro-economic theory and managerialism, and many of the most important and problematic reform elements, such as the relationship between public managers and elected officials, reflect the potential tensions in the way these are combined. Through devolution and contracting NPM has sought to separate policy-making more clearly from policy administration and implementation. Policy-makers make policy and then delegate its implementation to managers and hold them accountable by contract. Below we will discuss whether this represents a well-balanced change in the four countries studied.

NPM Diffusion: Convergence and Divergence

According to the Organisation for Economic Co-operation and Development (OECD) (1995, 1996a) NPM represents a global paradigm change concerning the control and organisation of public service. We question this convergence thesis and argue that the cases of Norway and New Zealand mainly illustrate the divergence of public sector reforms. Even though countries to some extent present their reforms in similar terms and support some of the same general administrative doctrines, closer scrutiny reveals considerable variation (Cheung, 1997; Hood, 1995a; Premfors, 1998). Pollitt and Bouckaert (2000) distinguish between four groups of NPM reformers: the maintainers, the modernisers, the marketisers and the minimal state category. Australia and New Zealand fit the marketiser group for part of the period in question, but during Howard's 1996 Liberal government in Australia and the 1990 National Party government in New Zealand, they moved towards the minimal state category. Sweden is put mainly in the moderniser group, but has occasionally ventured into the marketiser category, while Norway supposedly started out as a maintainer but has moved towards the moderniser group.

Our argument is that Norway has been a moderate and reluctant reformer, scoring low on contractualism and competition and moderately on devolution. New Zealand is a radical and aggressive reformer, scoring high on devolution, contractualism and competition. Australia is somewhere in between but significantly closer to New Zealand than to Norway, using contracts at the upper federal and state levels and structural devolution and competition to a slightly lesser extent. Sweden is significantly closer to Norway than to Australia and New Zealand, scoring moderately on contractualism and high on devolution and decentralisation.

In Australia and Sweden, and to some extent in Norway, there was a strong demand by state agencies for increased local autonomy and greater flexibility, partly to enhance cost efficiency, but also motivated by other considerations. Government reformers preached the need to '*let* the managers manage' more than to *make* the managers manage, even though both elements were embedded in the managerialist model, especially in Australia (Kettl, 1997). Through devolutionary arrangements, managers were to be given much discretionary power and be free to manage. Reformers believed that managers knew the right thing to do but that existing rules, procedures and structures created barriers to them doing so. The idea was that letting managers focus on the problems that had to be solved and giving them the flexibility to solve them produced organisations that could adapt faster and governments that worked better (Aberbach and Rockman, 1999). They concentrated on administrative decentralisation, improving the skills of their managers through training and reshaping the civil service system to encourage better performance. Accountability systems were established and the performance elements were strong but not based on contracts to the same extent as in New Zealand.

The adoption of the discourse of management by the Australian public service in the 1980s can be seen as a cultural revolution (Yeatman, 1987) and even in Norway administrative and political leaders have begun to talk about public service more in management terms. The background for such tendencies is somewhat different in the two countries. Australia was more pre-occupied with clear-cut political and administrative roles as an instrument to weaken the bureaucracy, while in Norway this question seems to be seen more as a practical task of increasing the capacity of political leaders, while under-scoring the fact that political and administrative leaders do have shared norms and values. Australia was also preoccupied early in the reform process with changing the central financial management, inspired by private actors (Guthrie and Parker, 1998).

In the 1980s Australia used NPM more pragmatically than New Zealand, and in Scandinavia the pragmatic approach to NPM was even more evident. In Australia, unlike New Zealand, the managerialist wave preceded the marketisation and contracting one (Considine and Painter, 1997; Davis, 1997). But the two countries have become more similar in the 1990s through the greater emphasis Australia has put on market elements – competition, contracting out and privatisation (Halligan, 1998, p. 157; McIntosh et al., 1997; Wettenhall, 1998a). One should add that both Australian Capital Territory (Canberra) and Victoria are pretty similar to New Zealand in their reform profiles.

New Zealand has aggressively pursued a philosophy of '*making* the managers manage' (Kettl, 1997, p. 448). The only way to improve government performance, the reformers believed, was to change the incentives of government managers by subjecting them to market forces and contracts. Top managers were hired on fixed-term contracts, rewarded according to their performance and could theoretically be sacked if their work did not measure up. Individual work- and performance-contracts replaced the rule- and process-based civil service system. This hard-edged contractualism, first used in New Zealand and later in Australia (Schick, 1998), seems to have cultural problems in becoming adopted in Norway. Performance agreements may displace the old ethics of trust and responsibility, with accountability for results expected from each leader and executive officer, making the relation-ship more instrumental and less culturally oriented. Contract-like agreements have even been extended to policy advice, so that ministers can opt to obtain information and ideas from private consultants and other external sources (Boston et al., 1996, pp. 122–125). In New Zealand this is partly due to the fact that ministers have few political advisers.

Even if many observers place Sweden and Norway in a common Scandinavian category as hesitant and moderate NPM countries (Dunleavy, 1997; Naschold, 1996; Pollitt et al., 1997), patterns of administrative reform do differ from one country to another (Klaussen and Ståhlberg, 1998; Lægreid and Pedersen, 1999; Schwartz, 1994). Halligan (1998) puts the Scandinavian countries in a middle group when comparing the extent of NPM reforms in the OECD countries, but with significant variation within this sub-category: Sweden is classified as an active reformer but Norway as a reluctant one. Olson et al. (1998) have studied the new finance management systems in the public sector in eleven countries and conclude that there have been major changes at all levels in Sweden. Hood (1996a, p. 274), too, argues that Sweden scores high on the NPM scale. Via a comprehensive process of devolution and local autonomy Sweden has gone far in the direction of a fragmented public administration and the slogan *renodling* (purification) has emerged as a core element in its administrative policy (Premfors, 1999). On the other hand, Sweden has also been characterised as a cautious mover in public sector reforms during the 1980s. Even if Sweden is moving towards greater devolution, a stronger productivity focus and a greater focus on citizens as consumers, traditional democratic values still continue to influence public sector reforms to a greater degree than in many Anglo-American countries, and the Swedish reform strategy has been described as dualistic (Ferlie et al., 1996; Lægreid and Pedersen, 1999; Premfors, 1999). Sweden has responded to pressure from administrative reform in a way that combines change with stability (Bergström, 1999) and is seen as retaining a social responsibility model (Fudge and Gustavsson, 1989) as opposed to an extreme market and efficiency model.

To understand these differences in scope, scale and intensity in the way the four countries have adopted NPM reforms and their effects and implications, we now turn to a transformative perspective on administrative reform.

A Transformative Perspective on Administrative Reform

Main Theoretical Features

One way of looking at NPM is to see it as a label applied retrospectively to a set of administrative reforms initiated through an active administrative policy or emerging from the bottom up through sector-specific or agency-specific initiatives (Lægreid and Pedersen, 1994). NPM can also be interpreted as a modernisation concept or prescription conceived and spread by international reform entrepreneurs, being absorbed into national political-administrative systems and having a profound impact on attitudes and decision-making behaviour (Røvik, 1996, 1998). An environmental deterministic view (Olsen, 1992) would stress that NPM is a collection of reform ideas that have survived selection processes and therefore shown their strength. But there is still some ambiguity here: the deterministic pressure from the environment might mean that these reforms are really the most effective and efficient ones; but it might also mean that NPM is a myth or fashion that has gained ideological dominance as the most appropriate reform package and is simply being used to increase the legitimacy of the political-administrative system (Brunsson, 1989; Meyer and Rowan, 1977; Painter, 1988).

We will argue that public reform processes, such as those related to NPM, are not characterised by a simple adjustment to current international administrative doctrines but must be understood from a transformative perspective. By this we mean that the institutional dynamics in this kind of reform process can best be interpreted as a complex mix of environmental characteristics, polity features and historical-institutional context. A transformative perspective emerges when we combine internal and environmental reform features to explain why NPM may have different content, effects and implications in different countries (Christensen and Lægreid, 1999a). External reform concepts and programmes are evidently filtered, interpreted and modified by a combination of two further nationally based processes. One is the national political-administrative history, culture, traditions and style of governance, which have developed in an evolutionary manner; the other is national polity features as seen in constitutional and structural factors.

These factors place constraints on and create opportunities for purposeful choice, deliberate instrumental actions and intentional efforts undertaken by political and administrative leaders to launch NPM-reforms through administrative design and active national administrative policy (Olsen, 1992; Olsen and Peters, 1996a). They can both further and hinder actions, and we ask whether they work in any systematic and cumulative way or are combined in complex patterns. A transformative perspective denies both the optimistic position that wilful political reform actors have full, comprehensive insight into and power over reform processes and the fatalistic position that they have no possibility of influencing reforms through political choice (Lægreid and Olsen, 1993; Lægreid and Roness, 1999; Olsen, 1992). Instead, the transformative perspective offers an intermediate position. Political leaders are assured a degree of manoeuvrability but their influence is constrained by environmental factors, polity features and historical-institutional context. The transformative perspective adds complexity to our understanding of administrative reform processes and this makes the story less elegant, though more realistic.

At one extreme, international environmental pressure to adopt NPM reforms may have profound effects on national systems if they are simultaneously furthered by the political-administrative leadership and are compatible with historical-cultural traditions. At the other extreme, environmental pressure for reform may produce few changes and effects if political and administrative leaders consciously try to stop or avoid the reforms owing to their lack of compatibility with traditional norms and values and nationally produced reforms (Brunsson and Olsen, 1993). These extremes correspond, respectively, to a decontextualisation process – which emphasises where environmental change concepts and internal needs match – and a contextualisation process, which stresses the uniqueness of national systems and the lack of compatibility between their values and norms and externally produced reforms (Røvik, 1996).

In reality it is likely that when externally generated reform concepts and processes are transferred to national political-administrative systems, they are more complex and have more varied and ambiguous effects and implications than the extremes outlined above. In practice political leaders can use certain elements of externally generated reforms or try to redefine ambiguous reform elements in a national context in order to match instrumental goals and national culture. Or they might deliberately manipulate the reforms as myths and symbols, pretending to implement them, but actually having little intention of doing so, and try to further their legitimacy through double-talk or by separating talk, decisions and actions (Brunsson, 1989). In yet another scenario political leaders might accept the reforms, leaving their implementation to administrative leaders and thus allowing for adjustment and editing to fit institutional-cultural features (Røvik, 1998; Sahlin-Andersson, 1996).

The effects of NPM-related reforms on political control can, given the potential complexity shown by the transformation perspective, point in different directions. Politicians may intend to retain or strengthen their power and control by consciously using the reform wave instrumentally or symbolically or both. But they may also lose control by accepting reform elements that undermine their leadership, either intentionally or because, under pressure to reform, they do not understand the effects and implications of reforms or they misconceive the cultural implications. Alternatively, the effects of NPM reforms on political-democratic control may be related to how administrative and institutional leaders define or redefine their roles and implement reforms.

National Variety

The transformative perspective focuses on external environmental dimensions and internal cultural and polity dimensions for understandingthe ideas behind the reforms, their content and practice and the effects experienced and achieved through NPM. Using these dimensions, we will discuss potential and experienced effects in the four countries selected – i.e., the effects theoretically expected and the empirical results actually obtained – and how these are related to the variation in reform context and reform content.

Environmental characteristics raise questions about turbulence and insecurity that create a need for substantial changes in the public sector or lead to the adoption of international myths of modernity. Apparently New Zealand and, to a somewhat lesser extent, Australia felt that they were in economic crisis in the early 1980s, and that made it easier to press for comprehensive civil service reforms aiming at rolling back the state (Evans et al., 1996). Sweden, too, experienced a fiscal crisis, but it came later and was not as strong as in Australia and New Zealand. The answer in Sweden was to modernise the state and to make it more efficient rather than to minimise it.

The economic crisis in New Zealand was compounded by a need for reform that had built up but not been dealt with during the years that Muldoon was prime minister (Bollard, 1994, p. 90; Massey, 1995, p. 31). The economic reforms had to include the state sector, which represented a large share of GDP. One possible effect was to strengthen market control at the expense of political control. The pressure from the environment was defined as deterministic, in a kind of 'worst case scenario' thinking. In Australia, for example, it was argued that without major surgery, Australia would end up as a banana republic (Campbell and Halligan, 1992, p. 92; Melleuish, 1998, p. 80). In addition, being a member of the family of Anglo-American or English-speaking countries may have made it easier for Australia and New Zealand to imitate or build on some reform elements from the United States and Britain (Castles, 1989; Halligan, 1998; Hood, 1996a). In Norway there was no obvious economic crisis that could legitimate comprehensive public reforms, and the cultural distance to Anglo-American reform elements was greater.

The first of the internal dimensions potentially explaining reform processes and effects is the cultural-institutional traditions – i.e., the norms and values that characterise the political-administrative system (March and Olsen, 1989). The historical-institutional context in Norway and Sweden is characterised by a strong statist tradition, homogeneity in norms, mutual trust between political and administrative leaders, equality, incremental changes, the balancing of many considerations, a de-emphasis on economic factors in the civil service and a policy style of peaceful co-operation and revolution in slow motion, all of which suggests that NPM will be implemented more slowly, reluctantly and in a modified form (Christensen, 1997; Christensen and Lægreid, 1998b; Christensen and Peters, 1999; Olsen, Roness and Sætren, 1982).

The neo-liberal flavour of the NPM reforms challenged the traditional core concept of a good public sector, as it had become institutionalised in Norway and Sweden over decades. There was a cultural incompatibility between international criticism of the public sector and the Scandinavian model of an interventionist and planning state. This state, with a large public sector under tight political control, was viewed as a suitable means for promoting the common good (Olsen, 1996).

New Zealand is also a relatively small country, building on some of the same values as Norway, with the state as a collective vehicle for popular action; but it is probably more polarised and culturally heterogeneous and its statist tradition has weakened since the 1980s (Boston et al., 1996, pp. 10–11; Castles, 1993, p. 17). This leaves us with a somewhat mixed picture: on the one hand, long-term cultural incompatibility with NPM and on the other, a system that in a short-term perspective is becoming more receptive culturally to NPM reforms.

Australia also has a statist tradition, but it is larger, federative and more heterogeneous, with much more varied cultural traditions and a greater degree of tension between political and administrative leaders, making it more likely that certain parts of the system will be compatible with NPM-oriented reforms. In contrast to Norway, mistrust characterised the relationship of the Labour governments in Australia and New Zealand with their civil servants for periods of the 1970s, even though both countries traditionally had relatively close links between the two groups (Mascarenhas, 1990). This does not, however, mean that in Australia this mistrust is lower at the end of the 1990s than it was twenty years earlier.

In contrast to the public interest culture and confrontational style of the Anglo-American reform movement vis-à-vis interest groups, the Norwegian and Swedish policy style was traditionally more legalistic and *Rechtsstaat*-oriented and was distinguished by co-operation and mutual understanding

(Christensen, 1997; Pollitt and Bouckaert, 2000). Traditionally, Norway and Sweden have been described as archetypes of a corporate-pluralistic state (Olsen, 1983); but in fact traditional co-operative, corporatist arrangements and close links between the labour parties and the trade unions were also politically important in Australia and to a lesser degree in New Zealand. These corporate elements began to weaken in Sweden in the late 1980s (Rothstein and Bergström, 1999).

The second internal dimension, the polity features, is also different in the four countries. The two-party Westminster system used in Australia and New Zealand makes the forceful implementation of reforms more likely than in Norway and Sweden, where the multi-party system and minority governments tend to result in negotiations and parliamentary turbulence (Campbell and Halligan, 1992, pp. 5–6; Christensen and Peters, 1999). Especially in New Zealand control potential has been substantially related to a unitary form of government, a unicameral parliament, a strong executive and tight party discipline in parliament (Boston et al., 1996, pp. 43–50). In addition, the Westminster system probably also offers more opportunity for strong political leaders to act as reform entrepreneurs than the multiparty-system in Norway and Sweden, with its formally weaker prime minister, even though it is also argued that their power is dependent on the collective power of a concerted cabinet (Slotnes, 1994). In contrast to the other three countries, Australia has a federative system. Federalism may modify features of the Westminster system and implies parallel systems that both compete with and imitate one another, thus leading to substantial variety and a greater possibility of reform from below rather than from above. But even within the unitary state model there is are significant differences between the highly centralised New Zealand state, on the one hand, and, the strongly decentralised structures in Norway and Sweden on the other.

One difference between Norway and Sweden is that Norway's model of ministerial administration is based on the principle that a minister can be held responsible for any decision made by the part of the administration he controls. The Swedish model, with its independent central administrative agencies, is based on an organisational split or dualism between the government ministry and the agencies. Swedish administrative authorities are subordinated to the government as a whole and not to a particular minister. These differences between the Norwegian and Swedish forms of administration are quite considerable (Lægreid and Pedersen, 1999; Petersson, 1994). One implication is that the Norwegian reform process might be more segmented and sectorised, while the Swedish might be dualistic with a stronger cabinet but also more independent central agencies. But compared to New Zealand and Australia, the Norwegian and Swedish models of governance have weak centres of government and delegate more authority for policy and administrative reform to departments and agencies (Lindquist, 1999).

Combining the three sets of independent variables in the transformative perspective may highlight some variety among the countries. New Zealand has taken the most dramatic reform path because of a combination of an economic crisis and elective dictatorship (Mulgan, 1992), while the cultural tradition makes the journey less understandable and more problematic in some ways. For example, popular support for a new election system, seen by many as a reaction to the reforms, currently makes further comprehensive reform more unlikely, because of more parties and turbulent coalition conditions (Levine and Roberts, 1997, pp. 25–33). In Australia the NPM reforms started out against a background of tension and conflicts between political leaders and the civil service and experimentation with reform in some states, forcefully led by the prime minister as a political entrepreneur (Campbell and Halligan, 1992). But the road taken was a more cautious one than in New Zealand, because of greater heterogeneity and corporatist features. This is even more true in Sweden, where the process of public management reforms has been incremental but continuous since the early 1980s. The 1980s were characterised by a renewal of the public sector and efforts to bring it closer to the public, while in the 1990s the emphasis moved towards increasing organisational autonomy and making public expenditure savings, a development intensified by the financial crises of the early 1990s. In Norway NPM reforms started late and when they did get off the ground it was in an incremental and reluctant way, because of low cultural compatibility and relatively weak political-instrumental power, which made civil servants more important change agents than political leaders (Christensen, 1997; Christensen and Lægreid, 1998b).

When discussing the trade-off between political governance and administrative autonomy, it is important to distinguish between the process of changing the system itself and the new system in operation. One possible paradoxical implication is that, while the reform process in New Zealand and Australia seems to be under strong political control, the new system may in practice have weakened political control in favour of administrative autonomy. In contrast, the Norwegian reform process was more under administrative control, but the implemented reforms have probably weakened political control to a lesser extent. The same applies to a great extent to

Sweden. One way of understanding this paradox is by using a transformative approach.

Model of Analysis and General Hypotheses of Transformation

Studies of public reforms like NPM have traditionally had different foci or attended to different aspects. One distinction to mention is the different levels studied. In this book we primarily combine studies on macro and meso levels – i.e., we focus both on general features of the political-administrative systems in the four countries and on certain groups of political and administrative actors. But we also use results from the micro level to support arguments on the other levels. Examples of this are the results of surveys of the civil service in Scandinavia or analyses of entrepreneurship in Australia and New Zealand (Campbell and Halligan, 1992; Christensen and Lægreid, 1998a).

Effect and Process Studies

There are two approaches to studying administrative reforms: process studies and effect studies (Egeberg, 1984 and 1989b). The main focus in this book is on the transformation of practice – i.e., on the effects and implications of reforms. This is a much less studied topic than the process of reform, probably because it is more problematic. Little has been invested in evaluating the effects of NPM reforms, both as regards fulfilling the major goal of efficiency and as regards the effects on other goals, such as political governance, partly because this is not an easy task (Peters and Savoie, 1998). There seems to be relatively little evidence that the application of reform strategies based on NPM actually leads to uniform and desired results. The effects and implications of NPM are often assumed or promised but not well documented. They are hard to measure and much debated: relations between cause and effect are contested, indicators of efficiency and effectiveness are often elusive, side-effects are hard to trace and the methodology used in evaluating NPM is often insufficient (Hesse, Hood and Peters, 2001; Kerauden and Van Mierlo, 1998; Olsen, 1996; Pollitt, 1995; Pollitt and Bouckaert, 2000). Even in Australia and New Zealand, after years of supposedly successful reform, much of the evidence on outcomes remains anecdotal and difficult to verify (Minogue et al., 1998).

Taking NPM as a point of departure for studying effects of reforms is potentially interesting because of the paradoxes and puzzles it throws up.

First, even though some believe the ideas of NPM are consistent, we have shown that NPM actual contains potential inconsistencies. Second, even though one can argue that NPM seems to represent a global trend and exerts very strong international pressure on national political-administrative systems, our view is that national structural and cultural features influence the implementation process and effects, thereby retaining diversity. And third, NPM is a set of ideas but also a set of more specific instruments and programmes brought in to solve problems with the existing ones (Miller, 1994; Power, 1997). We will analyse how these instruments and programmes are related to the ideas of NPM, how they may vary between countries and how they affect political control. The links between a) NPM ideas and programmes b) specific NPM methods and measures and techniques and instruments and c) the experience these methods and techniques yield in practice as well as their implications can be more or less close (Lægreid and Roness, 2001).

There seems to be a tendency in the reform literature to infer too easily from process to effects. One example of this can be seen in the basis of the convergence hypothesis – i.e., the notion that the spreading of NPM is a global trend of a deterministic character whose implementation and effects correspond to the main ideas in NPM and are the same all over the world (OECD, 1995, 1996a). This approach underestimates the ambiguity of reform ideas and the problem of linking reform ideas, reform programmes and real change without going into the mechanisms whereby ideas are transferred and the importance of national contexts.

Another example is the assumption that similar reform programmes and formal reform changes made in different countries must produce the same effects, a thesis which ignores the cultural context (Osborne and Gaebler, 1992). A third example is the assumption that the actual effects of NPM will correspond with the stated goals of politicians and top administrative leaders in statements or policy documents – i.e., increased political control and efficiency. We would like to look behind such statements and find out what happened after the reforms were implemented – i.e., the period of the reforms at work.

NPM is an ambiguous set of reforms. Its ideas may be adopted in a different way in every country: accepted fully, modified and edited or mostly denied access. Alternatively, reform ideas may be initiated locally or nationally and subsequently acquire an NPM label. Furthermore, the formal decisions about the content of the reform package may be modified and changed during the implementation process, producing even greater variation.

When we talk about effects we mean what is actually achieved in the administrative apparatus after the implementation process has been completed.

We try to handle some of the problems with evaluating effects by combining theoretical ideas and empirical studies. Using as a background the process, content and implementation of reforms, we discuss both potential and experienced effects of NPM reforms on political control. We analyse the effects of NPM-like reforms on the political-administrative decision-making system in the four countries, discuss whether the main pattern of influence in these countries has changed as a result of NPM and put the reforms in a broader political-democratic context. There are two main categories of effects: intra-executive effects and intra-polity effects. Intra-executive effects includes such things as possible changes in how political and administrative leadership roles are defined and in the relationship between them following the reforms; and whether there is a real devolution of authority to lower levels and institutions in the governmental structure and, if so, whether this might be tilting the balance of influence towards economic and commercial arguments and signals. Intra-polity effects concern the relationship between the civil service and some of the main actors in the environment, such as parliaments, interest groups or international actors.

Our analysis of effects faces a general methodological problem, namely, that of distinguishing between the effects of NPM-like reforms and those of other reforms or more gradual changes in the civil service. Further difficulties are presented by the contrafactual problem and the problem of ambiguous and multiple ends and internal contradictions within the NPM movement (Pollitt, 1995). Our way of coping with this is to specify both the potential effects drawn from the theoretical perspective and the experienced effects based on the formal and other changes made as a direct result of NPM.

The main goals of NPM are to enhance efficiency and make the political-administrative system work better – through more political 'frame control' and managerial autonomy, more transparency, more use of devolution and contracts, etc – without changing much the pattern of influence in the political-administrative system. In this book we focus on the effects on political control – i.e., we attend more to the questions of governance (Ingraham, 1996). We do not test the efficiency hypothesis but we do look at possible increases in the importance of economic decision-making premises and discuss whether the focus on efficiency in NPM has some important side-effects that influence political control. Efficiency questions are of course important, because in NPM reforms they have a tendency to overshadow political-democratic considerations, and they are disputed because efficiency is difficult to measure and evaluate.

A focus on effects presupposes insight into the process of reform. The processes are resulting in the changes that are meant to produce certain effects and are constraining decision-making processes in different ways. One type of process study focuses on different driving forces or central actors in the international environment who participate in shaping or spreading the reform message (Lerdell and Sahlin-Andersson, 1997). Examples here are studies of international standardisation and the spreading of similar reform ideas between countries and sectors (Brunsson and Jacobsson, 1998; Meyer, 1994; Naschold, 1996; Olsen and Peters, 1996a). Another type analyses what characterises the reform process once the national features of reforms have been laid down. These generally analyse the tension between national attempts at political-administrative control and conflicts and confrontations between different national actors, adaptation to international administrative-policy trends and adaptation to national administrative traditions and cultures and they often show that the reform process is characterised by different combinations of these factors (Christensen and Lægreid, 1999a; Lægreid and Pedersen, 1996; Lægreid and Roness, 2001).

A third type of process study analyses the content of public reforms. This implies a preoccupation with what characterises the vision, the problems and the solutions that are the basis of a reform – i.e., what norms and values they represent and what type of effect they are supposed to have (Olsen, 1991, 1993). A fourth type of process study focuses on the implementation of administrative policy. This is the process of translating general comprehensive administrative policy programmes into specific working programmes and actual changes. The attempt to put reform ideas into practice can result in a transformation of the original design, and implementation studies point to the complexity of the reform process. All these types of process analysis are relevant in this book, for they cover how the main NPM reform ideas are transformed during this process.

Model of Analysis

Our general model of analysis is outlined in Figure 2.1. The main explanatory factors in a transformative perspective are, as already outlined, environmental factors, polity features and national-administrative culture. These factors may transform NPM reform ideas. Through a complex mix of external economic and ideological factors, internal polity features and national administrative policy and national historical-institutional context the NPM reforms are transformed through a 'creolisation' process. Reform ideas and solutions are partly affected by situational factors, either through the import of popular administrative doctrines from outside or as a response to domestic economic problems, but they are also initiated locally and through an active national administrative policy constrained by polity features and administrative culture and tradition. And these factors also have a major impact on the implementation process. The result is a hybrid, whereby each country develops its own variant of NPM. The transformation of NPM reforms is studied in a global context (Chapter 3) and a comparative context (Chapter 4). To what degree political control over the NPM reform process is constrained by the influence of civil service unions in the four countries is discussed in Chapter 9.

Second, the national administrative apparatuses are transformed by the NPM reforms. By this we mean the achievements or effects that eventually accrue from the process of reform (Pollitt and Bouckaert, 2000). The final result of reforms is difficult to identify. Even if new administrative structures, processes and procedure exist after the reforms, it is often difficult to know how closely they can be attributed to the reforms (Pollitt, 1995). Thus, we will discuss the transformation of the administrative apparatus both as a result of NPM reform and as a more direct consequence of environmental factors, polity features and historical-institutional context. This is done in Chapter 9, for instance, where the effects on policy capacity are discussed. We will use rather loose terminology when focusing on things like experience, practice and implications; and we will distinguish between potential and actual achievements and internal and external achievements. The implications of devolution, contracts and corporatisation on political control are the main focus in Chapters 5 and 6; the effect on political responsibility is also addressed in Chapters 7, 9 and 10. These chapters also discuss the internal effects on accountability, policy capacity, administrative culture and recruitment. The more external effects of NPM reforms on civil service unions are addressed in Chapter 8.

Third, we will discuss to what extent the NPM reforms and changes in the administrative apparatus might transform our reform theory and models of democratic governance. In Chapter 11 a Scandinavian reform theory focussing on a loose coupling between talk and action is modified, and in Chapter 12 the market model of NPM is contrasted with a forum model and the normative implications of these models for standards of evaluation are discussed.

Figure 2.1 A model of transformation

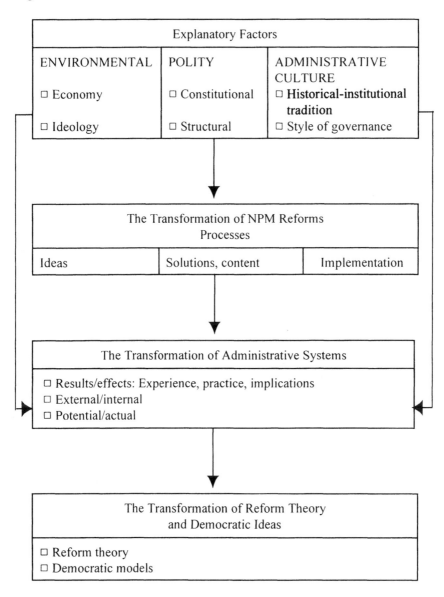

General Hypotheses of Transformation

As a general frame of analysis in this book we can group the theoretically based expectations into two main hypotheses. A hypothesis of *convergence* indicates that the transformation of NPM-related reforms and the transformation of the administrative apparatus creates the same type of features through processes and effects in the countries studied. Such a hypothesis might assume that all the countries have the same strong environmental pressure to attend to, whether the pressure comes from the technical or the institutional parts of the environment, and therefore the same type of reform content. To this we could add the assumption that national features, whether they are structural or cultural, are similar and reinforce the effects of the environment.

A hypothesis of *divergence* – the one the book is based on – emphasises that NPM ideas are transformed to produce a different variant in each of the four countries and that differences between their administrative apparatuses become ever greater as a result of reforms, because external and internal conditions point cumulatively and systematically in different directions (Hood, 1998a). This implies that environmental pressure, the content of the reforms, the polity factors and the cultural constraints are all different and that the independent variables reinforce each other. This hypothesis assumes that NPM is transformed in different ways when it travels and is confronted with unique and differing contexts when entering different countries and becoming adopted inside these countries.

These general hypotheses could also be modified by a looser coupling between NPM-reform and practice. This means that there might be a convergence in NPM-reforms without convergence in administrative systems or vice versa and that there might be greater divergence in administrative reforms than in administrative practice. The analyses in this book will primarily be of a general nature, without going into details about different sectors, levels or institutions, so we will mainly use the convergence and divergence hypotheses as our frame of reference.

Our Approach

This book is preoccupied with how different internal, national and external contexts are of relevance for explaining the transformation of NPM. We will compare administrative reform processes, effects and implications within each country over time and also compare different countries. It is a comparison of a limited number of cases and this approach allows more for analytical than for statistical generalisation (Yin, 1994). Our aim is more to illustrate theoretical arguments that permit the construction of general statements than to engage in strict theory testing.

Even if the comparison between the four countries is not done in a systematic manner in each chapter, our approach is based on a general distinction between the methods of difference and similarity. This distinction is connected to different research strategies in comparative analysis, the most similar systems design and the most different systems design (Lijphart, 1971 and 1975; Przeworski and Teune, 1970; Smelser, 1973).

The *most similar systems* strategy compares systems that are similar on as many dimensions as possible except for the explanatory variables of theoretical interest and the dependent variable – i.e., in our case the process, effects and implications of reforms (Frendreis, 1983; Lijphart, 1971). The aim of this method is to find as few independent variables as possible that clearly vary among the cases studied and can therefore explain the variation in the dependent variable.

There are obvious features of this strategy in our book if we consider the theoretical perspectives and variables outlined above and take into account that we are doing a longitudinal analysis. Based on a hypothesis of divergence, the dependent variables – i.e., the process, effects and implications of reform – will vary among some of the countries studied, for example New Zealand and Norway. Most of the countries will have some independent variables that traditionally are quite similar, like parliamentary features, welfare state features, types of labour party, a statist tradition, the structure of the civil service, administrative-cultural traditions, corporatist traditions, etc. So what can then vary and explain the differences between the countries in the dependent variables? We can look at this question in two ways combined: one is traditional differences in structure and culture, like the fact that New Zealand and Australia have a Westminster-type system whereas Australia has a federal system. Another is to focus on how the reforms as such lead to differences in independent variables. Above we have indicated that there are differences in the international environments – such as more obvious economic crises in Australia and New Zealand than in Norway and to some extent Sweden – but also differences in connections to concept entrepreneurs internationally. And Australia and New Zealand have made more substantial changes in formal structures, like comprehensive structural devolution, than the other two countries as well as changes in their political-administrative culture. One important job is to narrow down this selection of variables to the really crucial ones.

The *most different systems* strategy deviates from the most similar systems design by selecting systems that do not differ on the dependent variable and then trying to eliminate as causes all independent variables that differ between the systems (Przeworski and Teune, 1970). The aim here is to find as few independent variables as possible that are similar in different systems and can therefore explain the similarity in the dependent variable.

There are also elements of this strategy in our study, especially if we attend to a hypothesis of convergence and redefine some of our independent variables. The question then is how we eventually may explain similarities in the dependent variables – i.e., that the reforms are moving the countries in the same direction of management and market effects. Concerning the environmental variable one can argue that even though there are differences in the economic crises experienced, all of the countries will experience rather strong deterministic pressure from the international concept entrepreneurs, making them more similar in their reactions to the reforms and their effects. If we move on to the polity variables, there are some obvious differences between the countries – historically between their labour parties and conservative/liberal parties and also between their civil service systems. But the reforms have changed this in many ways: labour parties are more open to management and market reforms now than before, and the civil service systems have undergone some of the same structural devolution, making the countries more similar in effect. In addition, civil servants in these countries seem to have developed more similar attitudes towards the reforms over time, making it easier to implement changes and change their decision-making behaviour.

One basic problem with both the most similar and most different system strategies is that they have inherent limitations in generalisability. Frendreis (1983) therefore proposes a *mixed system* research strategy that combines the two. In a mixed system strategy the systems/cases will vary along both the independent and dependent variables, thereby allowing for a variety of comparisons to be made. This mixed design is, in essence, the type of research we undertake here. As outlined, there are differences between the four countries, but there are also important similarities.

The comparison of different political-administrative systems is often done synchronically on a general, macro level. This type of comparison can be expanded in at least two ways. One is to analyse the development of the relationship between the central variables over time, in our case, for example, whether the relationship between political and administrative leaders changes as a result of the reforms. Thus, it is not only the national systems but their characteristics at different points in time, as well as the dynamics by which they change, that are the subject of analysis.

We argue that there is a co-evolution between reform and system variables (Lægreid and Roness,1999). The environmental factors, structural features and administrative culture influence the content, implementation and effects of the NPM reforms, which, in turn, may have an impact on the environment, structural changes and administrative culture. Thus, in a dynamic reform process NPM reform is both a dependent and an independent variable.

Another comparative strategy is to combine inter-national and intra-national studies (Lijphart, 1975), whereby sub-national units within one country are the subject of analysis. One can try to connect intra-systemic differences to inter-systemic variations (Linz and de Miguel, 1966; Rokkan, 1966).

Our study has elements of a mixed system strategy in the ways indicated. We are primarily interested in whether the reforms have features that make the working of the political-administrative system in the four countries more or less different as such, but we are also preoccupied with the development over time. In this respect the study is both *synchronical* and *diachronical* in its method – i.e., we both study contemporary relations between the variables and analyse their historical development (Frendreis, 1983).

THE TRANSFORMATION
OF ADMINISTRATIVE REFORMS
- NPM IDEAS AND PROCESSES

3 National, International and Transnational Constructions of New Public Management

KERSTIN SAHLIN-ANDERSSON

How Extensive Are Reforms and How Extensive Are the Effects? Layers of Explanations

New Public Management (NPM) is a label used both to define a general trend towards changing the style of governance and administration in the public sector and to describe a number of reforms that were carried out in several countries during the 1980s and the 1990s. New Zealand and Australia have been highlighted as countries where extensive NPM reforms have been implemented. In Sweden, it is said, there has been a lot of talk about reforms, but in comparison to the Anglo-Saxon countries, a much less coherent reform programme has been carried out and less dramatic effects have been reported. In contrast, Norway has been portrayed as a much more reluctant reformer where NPM seems to be more of a marginal phenomenon with less impact.

The fact that we find similar reform attempts in Australia, New Zealand, Norway and Sweden – four countries on opposite sides of the globe – indicates that NPM is a global trend. While most studies of this trend cover only the countries of the Organisation for Economic Co-operation and Development (OECD) (and many studies are based on OECD data), similar reform attempts have been reported from a number of other countries around the world (OECD, 1999a; World development report, 1997). Several countries have embarked on the same reform path, yet their approach to reform and the results of these reforms differ. Why have they embarked on the same reform path and why do approaches and results differ?

The evolution of NPM into a more or less global trend, where similar reforms have been pursued, more or less simultaneously, in a number of countries, provides students of such reforms with convenient opportunities for making comparisons. Most explanations offered in the literature, however, say little about whether we should expect reforms that are part of such a global trend to be different and to yield different results to reforms that are more unique to single countries. One may ask whether it makes a difference if national reforms are part of a global trend, how such a trend develops and how national reforms and global trends are related.

Even though accounts of NPM normally portray the trend as one with extensive international and transnational elements, explanations for the extent, shape and effects of reforming are generally sought on the national level. If it is true, as I am claiming here, that NPM is a trend that is for the most part internationally and transnationally formed, then more elaborate explanations are called for, explanations that go beyond the national level when analysing differences and similarities. In addition to similarities and differences in national context, we may also find reasons for similarities and differences between reforms as we follow the spread of NPM and find out how and why reform ideas have been circulated and mediated between countries. In this chapter I outline three types of global trend and show how each of them offers a layer of additional explanations for the similarities and differences between NPM reforms.

Three Types of Global Trend

How do we identify a trend? Usually when we observe similar phenomena appearing in different settings. Any given trend may, however, have developed in a number of different ways. Here I will distinguish between three types of trends, using as a criterion the way in which national reforms are related both to each other and to the evolving global trend.

The first type of trend is nationally based and results when a number of countries pursue similar reforms at the same time but independently of each other. The reason why countries reform in similar ways may be that they face similar problems and have developed similar ways of solving them. The way in which individual reforms have been designed and developed and the national contexts of these reforms may explain similarities, but also differences between them. In a world with extensive contacts between countries, such trends are actually quite unlikely. It seems more reasonable to assume that trends will come about as a result of some kind of interaction among reformers.

The second type of trend is internationally formed. Reformers do not act only in an isolated national context but learn from each other, imitate each other, react to each other and present their reforms to each other. The trend is a consequence of a set of ideas travelling around the world (Czarniawska and Joerges, 1996). In order to understand how such a trend emerges and what explains the extent, shape and effects of reforming, one needs to look closer at how and why countries have followed each other and what impact this has had on the design and development of reforms in different settings. In other words, relations between reformers in different countries may account for what shape the trend takes. Thus, we may explain similarities and differences between countries by looking at how countries imitate and learn from each other and how ideas and experiences are transformed as they move from one country to the next.

The third type of trend is transnationally formed. In addition to reformers, there are a number of observers and mediators of reform ideas and experiences, such as researchers, international organisations, consultants and publications. They produce and provide information and comparisons, report on and propose initiatives for change and act as arenas for the exchange of experience, ideas and ideals. They assess reforms and publish guidelines for how to reform. These mediators do not only report about and transport ideas and experiences between reformers. They turn their attention to certain reforms and they produce information about some reforms, but not others and when doing this they also direct others' attention to certain reforms which may then be seen as prototypes which countries direct their attention to and try to follow. They also frame ideas and experiences, transforming them in the process, and they teach countries how to reform (Finnemore, 1996). Thus, parallel to and interwoven with national reforms, more or less global templates for reform have been produced by the many observers, assessors, researchers and, not least, international organisations tracking the reforms. The trend thus takes the form of a kind of transnational network where similarities and differences between countries partly follow from the way reforms are reflected and constructed by the many mediators of ideas – such as researchers, international organisations, consultants and the media – that are perceived to constitute a world society with a certain culture and structure (Boli and Thomas, 1999; Meyer et al., 1997).

When characterizing the trend as transnationally formed I want to emphasize the importance of transnational mediators and how they form templates and prototypes outside the national context. Another important feature of transnationally formed trends is that the reform ideas may enter a national state administration at a number of different levels. Circulated ideas need not only be adopted by central administrators and politicians who then initiate national reforms. This is especially true as the public service – as a result of decentralization, devolution and reforms which have strengthened the identity and autonomy of local units – in several countries has become reconstructed as a kind of polycentric network consisting of many separate organizations (Brunsson and Sahlin-Andersson, 2000; Hood, 1996b; Martin, 1995; Stewart and Walsch, 1992; Åkerstrøm Andersen, 1995).

It is reasonable to assume that most global trends come into being partly through more or less independent national initiatives, partly through a process of international mimicry and partly through transnational construction and circulation of prototypes and templates, though it may not always be easy to distinguish these three processes empirically. In fact we may seldom see pure examples of any one of these three types of trend. Rather, a global trend is likely to combine elements of all three, albeit with varying emphases. I would like to use this typology of global trends to show where explanations for differences and similarities between reforms may be found. The point I want to make is that while NPM is a trend which can be described as nationally, internationally and transnationally formed, most explanations found in the literature are nationally based. This disproportionate focus on national settings may miss some of the more fundamental dynamics of the reform processes. Hence my argument that additional layers of explanations should be considered. Below I will elaborate on these three types of global trend and on the explanations they offer for differences and similarities between NPM reforms. Because my claim here is that national explanations dominate the literature, while international and transnational aspects of the NPM-trend should be more attended too, in the overview below I will just give a brief overview of some nationally based explanations, while I spend somewhat more space to elaborate on internationally and transnationally based explanations to differences and similarities between NPM reforms.

Nationally Formed Public Management Reforms

Most reports on NPM reform processes either concern one country or are structured as comparisons between countries. From such studies we learn how reforms have been initiated in a national context and how this context may explain the outcome of the reforms.

Extensive overviews of public management reforms are published regularly by the OECD's Public Management Committee (PUMA). Here similarities in reform attempts have mostly been attributed to similarities in the problems that countries face (OECD, 1993, 1995, 1999a). As countries face similar problems, it is argued, they have reformed, and ought to reform, along similar lines. The differing results, on the other hand, are attributed to differences in the design, focus and degree of coherence of the reforms. New Zealand has repeatedly been described as a country where consistent and extensive reforms were initiated, while the reforms pursued elsewhere were less coherent and less revolutionary. New Zealand is also repeatedly cited as the country that shows the most dramatic changes in its public management.

Several studies have gone beyond comparisons between reform initiatives and have developed more contextual explanations for similarities and differences between NPM reforms in different countries. Differing constitutional arrangements (Olsen and Peters, 1996a), administrative systems (Christensen and Lægreid, 1999a; Hood, 1995a), reform traditions (Pallott, 1998) and cultures (Christensen and Lægreid, 1999a) account for differences in governments' motives for launching reform, what opportunities are available to them and what changes such reforms lead to. The dynamics connected with changing political majorities are further explanations for why some countries have reformed more dramatically than others and why their approaches have been different (Mascarenas, 1990). Other studies have suggested that the economic situation and varying types of economic control explain why some countries have reformed more than others and why reforms have led to more dramatic effects in some countries (Olson et al., 1998).

In this section I have given a brief summary of some explanations found in the literature have shown that the design as well as the results of NPM reforms are shaped by differing national context. National explanations, which are those most commonly found in the literature, portray reforms as nationally constructed and nationally implemented. Similarities and differences are explained by national particularities. Such explanations have contributed extensively to the understanding of these reforms, and extensive studies of reforms in different contexts have led to conclusions that what is appropriate to do in one context may not be possible or suitable in another context (World development report, 1997). Such nationally based explanations may, however, seem too limited when considering how NPM has evolved into a trend. Interaction between the reform initiatives in different countries is not taken into account in such explanatory models. To these nationally focused explanations may be added other types of analyses that more explicitly take into account that NPM is an internationally and transnationally formed trend.

Internationally Formed Public Management Reforms

Processes of imitation have driven several NPM reforms (Olson et al., 1998; Røvik, 1996, 1998; Sahlin-Andersson, 1996) and organisational and admini- strative changes more generally (DiMaggio and Powell, 1983, 1991; Sevón, 1996; Westney, 1987). Sometimes such processes of imitation are evident when reformers make open reference to each other. Often, however, we find few direct references but many indirect and less visible links between reformers. Countries learn from each other, they imitate each other and, with reference to similar problems, they launch similar reforms. However, in the transfer of ideas from one country to another, these same ideas are trans- formed. Thus, even when reforms follow from processes of imitation, the content, shape and scope of such reforms differ.

When focusing on how ideas travel between countries rather than on what happens to them once they have been adopted, three types of explanation may be relevant. First, by establishing who imitates whom and why, we can explain why some countries have reformed more than others and why reforms differ in shape, scope and focus. Second, some aspects of reform seem more likely to be imitated than others and some 'types of reform' seem more likely to be imitated than others. If one examines the process of imitation, it becomes clear how and why some aspects of reform are imitated while others are not. Third, ideas and experiences are formed and transformed as they are transferred. Even though certain national experiences and practices are frequently referred to in writings and talks about NPM, it is not the practices and experiences as such that diffuse but their representation and presentation. Thus, in order to explain similarities and differences between reforms that result from the process of imitation, we need to learn how the presentation and representation of reform ideas and experiences are shaped and transformed as they circulate.

Who Imitates Whom?

Uncertainty has been shown to drive imitation (DiMaggio and Powell, 1983); more specifically, when organisations are uncertain about their own experi- ences, or when their earlier development and activities are questioned, they turn to others for experiences and models to imitate (Sahlin-Andersson, 1996; Sevón 1996). The public sector was questioned in many Western countries during the 1980s, especially in those facing fiscal problems, and these countries turned to other countries and other societal sectors for experiences and models to imitate.

NPM is most elaborated in Anglo-Saxon countries. Great Britain, New Zealand and Australia, and to some extent USA, were early reformers who were later imitated (Laughlin and Pallot, 1998). Imitation took place earlier and was most common among countries with similar cultures and languages. These early reformers are also the countries where reforms have been most extensive and thorough, partly, of course, because the reforms have been in progress for a longer period of time. Other countries, such as Sweden, followed, and later, countries such as Norway, Switzerland, Germany and France pursued similar, but less thorough reforms (Laughlin and Pallot, 1998; Lüder, 1998; Musselin, 1997).

The diffusion of reforms seems to follow a similar pattern to that of other processes of imitation. Actors within a field tend to imitate the more prestigious and well-known actors, but also those they identify with (DiMaggio and Powell, 1983, 1991; Sevón, 1996). Developments and reforms in Anglo-Saxon countries – I am thinking primarly of the UK and US – receive a lot of attention around the world, and thus reforms carried out in these countries can be expected to be more likely imitated than reforms initiated in less 'well-known' countries. In addition, countries that are viewed as similar and whose administrations are structured in similar ways may be more ready to imitate each other than countries where this is not the case. Furthermore, we can expect that as one country has imitated another country earlier, it may continue to imitate the same country. Thus habit as well as perceived similarities play a role in the process of imitation.

Keeping all these explanations in mind it is not surprising that the NPM-trend first spread among the Anglo-Saxon countries, then followed countries who identified themselves with and were closely identified by others as in one way or another similar to these early reformers. Similarities between Sweden, New Zealand and Australia have been pointed out earlier and Sweden has, in terms of language and culture if not in terms of administrative structure, often kept close contacts with Anglo-Saxon countries. In contrast countries such as Germany and France are far more distant – in identity terms (for a discussion on this see Olson et al., 1998). Furthermore, reforms initiated in one part of Scandinavia are often taken up by other Scandinavian countries. Scandinavian countries have been shown to imitate each other in many areas, a repeated imitation which may be explained by their similarities in languages, common history, similarities in how public sector is structured; but also following from earlier imitation and ongoing collaborations, and the formal structures for collaboration among these countries which have been formed over the years (cf. for example Jacobsson and Sundström, 1999; Lægreid and Pedersen, 1994).

Which Types and Aspects of Reforms Are Imitated?

Even when countries imitate each other, they do not imitate everything. Some reforms seem to be more readily imitated than others, and some aspects of reform seem to be imitated more than others. Change – and movement – receives more attention than no change (Bateson, 1979; Sevón, 1996). Hence, reforms which are described as bringing with them dramatic changes can be expected to be more likely to be imitated than less dramatic or incremental changes or non-changes. Moreover, models that are 'packaged' so that they can 'be transported' are more easily imitated (Røvik, 1998, forthcoming; Strang and Meyer, 1993). More precisely, it has been shown that ideas which are associated with the dominant and celebrated values of modern society, such as science, rationality and efficiency, diffuse better than those imbued with other values (Meyer, 1996; Røvik, 1998, forthcoming). Furthermore, ideas that are associated with or seem to originate from settings that have displayed some type of success spread more easily than those that are associated with less successful models (Røvik, 1998, forthcoming; Sevón, 1996). The much referred to and imitated New Zealand reforms have been described and argued for in theoretical terms and in terms of dramatic changes. The theoretical framing has meant that the reforms have appeared as much more consistent – and more rational – than for example Australian and Swedish reforms which have appeared more incremental (OECD, 1999a; Olson et al., 1998).

Reforms, or indeed models in general, are not, as DiMaggio and Powell (1991, p.29) phrased it, 'imported whole cloth'. Rather, certain aspects of a model or reform may be imitated while other parts are ignored. In her study of the modernisation of Japanese society during the Meiji period, Westney (1987) showed that unique Japanese forms of public service and public administration were built through the imitation of well-known Western societal institutions. When the Western models were imitated, some aspects of them were left out and others were added. This was partly a result of a conscious decision to imitate only certain aspects of an administrative system that had evolved elsewhere, partly because some practices and models may not have been fully understood or were impossible to imitate, and partly because imitated models were mixed with other models and national traditions. Similarly, when following the travels of reforms from New Zealand to other OECD countries, some aspects of the reforms have been imitated and others not. Management principles and new ways of measuring were among those aspects of the reforms that have been subject to widespread imitation, while the more fundamental restructuring of the public sector and the economy in general did not seem to be imitated to the same extent (OECD, 1995). A simple way to describe this is to say that things that are easiest to imitate are also those that tend to be most imitated.

Reforms are usually argued for in terms of positive consequences (Brunsson and Olsen, 1993). Some common arguments behind the NPM reforms were that they would result in more efficient public operations, increase the transparency of the administration and make managers accountable – and more accountability would lead to improved service, increased attention to clients' wishes and needs, and better performance (Boston et al., 1996). In line with such arguments one might have expected that late reformers would follow in the steps of early reformers, as the consequences of the early reforms became evident. However, even though writings about the reforms are widespread and extensive, it is not easy to find systematic reports on the effects of these reforms. What is more, NPM reforms were imitated and spread at such a rapid rate that it was in any case too early to assess their consequences when the reform attempts were imitated. Thus, we cannot conclude that it was the consequences of the early reforms that led to their imitation. Instead, it was the plans and initiatives that were imitated, for plans circulate more easily than effects and they are often dramatic, announce change and are formed in such a way that they are possible and attractive to imitate.

What was imitated then was not the whole package of NPM, but certain aspects and parts thereof. The term NPM had not even been heard of when some of the reforms and procedures began to be imitated in the 1980s. The term NPM was first used by Christopher Hood in 1990, when he compared changes in the style of public administration in the OECD-countries during the 1980s. Hood (1990) observed a number of reforms that had been carried out and found similarities. This motivated him to place these reforms under the same heading, but he also noticed that countries had reformed differently. Thus, while there were enough similarities to warrant a common heading, as has been emphasised time and again, NPM is not a coherent and consistent reform model. Instead, NPM has been described as a group of ideas (Hood, 1991), variations on a theme (Hood, 1995a) or a cluster of ideas (Olsen and Peters, 1996a; Power, 1997).

Originally NPM was not the name of package of reforms to be implemented but was retrospectively used as a label to describe reforms that had already taken place, and the application of this label did not stop the reforms developing further. This is even true for the New Zealand reforms, often described as the most coherent set of reforms and sometimes presented under the rubric 'The New Zealand model' (Boston et al., 1996). Originally the reforms in New Zealand were designed, in part, as a model for dramatic change, inspired by public choice theory, agency theory and transaction-cost economics (Boston et al., 1996). A closer look at the reform process, however, reveals that the reforms were not actually designed all at once as a coherent package. In New Zealand, as elsewhere, one reform led to another (Boston et al., 1996; Pallot, 1998). Thus, the model was constructed as the reforms proceeded.

When grouping a set of reforms and procedures under the heading of NPM, several writers have emphasised the theoretical and ideological underpinnings of these reforms and the ways of governing advocated. The reforms are said to mark a paradigmatic shift (Aucoin, 1990). What is common to all NPM reforms is that their ideas have been borrowed from the conceptual framework of private sector administrative practice (Power, 1997) and the reforms have been described as a marriage between two different streams of ideas: managerialism and agency theory (Hood, 1991). These characterisations point to the programme of the reforms, as Power (1997) formulated it.

When characterising NPM in terms of its programmes, Power built on a useful distinction, taken from Rose and Miller (1992), between, on the one hand, programmatic or normative elements of a certain practice and, on the other hand, its technological or operational elements (similar distinctions have been used, for example, by Bäckström, 1999 and Blomgren, 1999). While the programmatic element refers to the ideas, aims and objectives of a certain practice, the technological element refers to the concrete tasks or routines of which this practice consists.

While the programmatic character of NPM has often been stressed in the academic literature, it may not always be as clear in practice. Even though recent reforms in the public sector, retrospectively seem to have marked something of a paradigmatic shift, with a changed identity for the public sector, this may not always have been the reformers' intention (Brunsson and Sahlin-Andersson, 2000). While NPM's programme has been extensively discussed and analysed in academic writings, when the reforms were initiated in practice, the programme behind these techniques was not always visible or explicit, but the technical elements, such as the introduction of new accounting systems, documentation instruments, pricing systems or hiring and payment procedures, were discussed and introduced in terms of their technical elements.

Studies of organisational reforms have suggested that the link between the programmatic and technical elements of a given practice may be loose and may change over time. Bäckström (1999) showed that organisational arrangements which were introduced in the 1970s to bring more democracy into the workplace (his studies concerned organizational development projects in the private sector industry) were reintroduced in the 1990s, but this time framed in terms of efficiency and competition. Bäckström concluded that not only were techniques and their accompanying ideology loosely coupled, but the ideology seemed to change more easily over time than the techniques.

Some techniques, however, seem clearly connected to a certain program, even when such a program is not explicitly announced as the reform is being launched. Reformers may have been attracted by a certain technique or tool, discovering only later that this technique presupposed certain programmatic ideas. Vrangbaeck (1999) analysed just such a reform process in the Danish healthcare system, calling it a 'Trojan horse.' The reform, a system of customers choice, was conceived and argued for in technical terms, but when it was implemented it changed the logic of the whole operation. New comparisons, frames of reference, assumptions and overall objectives were invoked by the newly introduced techniques (see also Blomgren, 1999).

Accounting arrangements are at the centre of the NPM ways of governing, and the introduction of more business like forms of accounting have been pointed out as some of the more prevalent and central NPM reforms (Olson et al., 1998). Sweden, as well as New Zealand and Australia, now have more or less complete systems of accrual accounting on all levels of government. When tracing the introduction of accrual accounting in the Swedish public sector, however, Olson and Sahlin-Andersson (1998) showed that the first elements of more business like forms of accounting were introduced in Swedish local governments already in the 1920s. Since then the system has gradually been extended, elaborated and added to so that in the late 1990s accrual accounting had been diffused across levels and sectors in Swedish society; where similar standard charts of accounts are used in private and public organizations alike. When tracing this development it becomes clear that in different periods different objectives lie behind the request for an elaborated accounting; at different phases in this development, the techniques have been attached to differing programmes or normative elements. Moreover, since the forming of accrual accounting in the Swedish public sector evolved over such a long period of time, in a highly incremental process, these reforms do not seem as readily to attract others' interest and to be imitated to the extent as the more revolutionary, concentrated and more distinctively theoretically programmed New Zealand accounting reforms.

The examples above suggest that programmes do not always drive techniques – sometimes it can be the other way round, whereby techniques are developed or imported and open the way for programmatic changes. This, of course, is not unique to the development and circulation of NPM. A similar observation has been made about scientific developments. While scientific advances are often described as more or less paradigmatic shifts marked by great discoveries and new theories, in fact they are not necessarily theoretically driven. Rather, the parallel processes of experimentation, the development of new tools and techniques and general theoretical developments combine in a more ecological fashion to produce new scientific insights (Fujimura, 1996; Galison, 1997).

The distinction between programme and technique suggests that when studying a global trend we need to look closer at what is being spread, how it is being spread and by whom. When tracing how NPM has evolved into a global trend we will discover that not only have different but related reforms been pursued in various places, but also that when the NPM label, ideas and tools are circulated they may be combined differently at different stages of the process and in different places.

How Are Ideas Transformed When They Are Transferred?

Reformers may learn about reforms to imitate through written reports, on short visits during which they are given talks about a country's experience with reforms, or more indirectly when consultants or researchers tell them about change initiatives elsewhere. Thus, what is spreading is not practice as such, but accounts of this practice. Models, ideas and experiences are presented and represented in various ways as they are circulated, most commonly in the form of written presentations or in oral communication. In previous studies I pointed to the forming and transforming of such presentations as a vital aspect of the circulation of ideas and described it as a kind of editing process (Sahlin-Andersson, 1996, 2000). The distance between the supposed source of the model and the imitating actor provides scope for translating, filling in or editing the model in various ways. The way in which such editing is done may help to explain why countries following the same reform path do so in such different ways.

Written texts are often subjected to editing, not only once but repeatedly, and texts are edited differently depending on the context in which the editing is done and the use that the writer sees for the text. Through the process of editing, an idea may be formulated more clearly and made more explicit, but reformulation may also change not only the form of the text but also its focus, content and meaning. So if we view the circulation of ideas as a process of editing, we can see how and why ideas are transformed when they are transferred from one place to another.

If we trace the path of a circulated model we see that such editing is circumscribed by the context in which it is done and that the process exhibits a certain pattern. Usually both written and more implicit rules or conventions guide such editing. I have termed these 'editing rules' in order to imply that they are derived from the context in which the editing takes place, that they restrict the process of representing and retelling and that they are only to a limited extent explicit and should be understood as 'rules which have been followed'. In following the paths of concepts and models I have discerned three sets of editing rules: they concern context, logic and formulation.

As an experience is accounted for and transferred from one setting to another, overly unique and country-specific aspects of the reforms are discarded. As practices are accounted for and turned into models these practices are disembedded from the country-specific and time-specific contexts. They are distanced and disconnected from time and space and rendered generalisable (Czarniawska and Joerges, 1996; Giddens, 1990). In this way the models are made available for others to imitate or adopt (Greenwood et al., 1998; Røvik, 1998).

Stripping models of their national context takes place in several steps. It may start when countries report on their reforms. They may want to shape their presentation in a way that will make their reforms interesting to others, disregarding those aspects of the reforms that seem too unique and too time- or country-specific and emphasising those that seem to be general and generalisable. Further editing is then done by those who mediate ideas, experiences and models, and again when the model is adopted in a new setting.

The NPM trend can be said to have started with, or have a background in, the reforms that were carried out in Britain during the Thatcher era. At that time such reforms were seen as highly political and ideological. Such a feature may restrict the reforms' potential for diffusion – those who adhere to a different ideology are not likely to adopt them as models. Over the years, however, the ideological element of the reforms has been de-emphasised and they are instead described and argued for in terms of expertise. One type of NPM reform has been concerned with what has often been described as deregulation. In a number of publications on such reforms issued by the OECD's public management committee (see below for more on this) the expression 'right regulation', rather than deregulation, is used. This change of terms was deliberate in an attempt to keep ideology out of the discussion and instead to argue for the reforms in terms of expertise (Lerdell and Sahlin-Andersson, 1997). There are of course different opinions, expressed in the literature, about the extent to which NPM presupposes a specific ideological program. The example given above suggests, however, that repeated efforts have been made by OECD and others to de-emphasise the ideological element in their accounts of the reforms.

As NPM has become a trend, its ideas have come to be regarded as universal and as applicable everywhere, regardless of the special circum- stances of different countries. Procedures have been generalised in the sense that they state how organisations in general should be managed, controlled and structured. They have been made apolitical in the sense that they are defended on the basis of expertise rather than ideology and presented as free from ideological considerations (Boston et al., 1996; Hood and Jackson, 1991). This brings us to the second set of editing rules.

A second set of rules concerns logic. As initiatives and effects are pre- sented the logic of the story is often reconstructed. Developments may acquire a more rationalistic flavour. Causes and effects tend to be clarified, effects are presented as resulting from identifiable activities, and processes are often described as following a problem-solving logic. Attention may be paid to a certain aspect of a development, while other aspects are omitted or erased. I noted above that plans tend to circulate more easily than effects. As these plans are circulated, however, they are often described as if were they effects – plans are interpreted as accounts of how reforms have proceeded (Sahlin-Andersson, 2000). In the course of the editing, accidental or coincidental circumstances are removed, as are aspects of reforms and their effects which cannot be explained and accounted for in simple terms. The models that attract the interest of other countries and that are deemed to be worthy of imitation are those whose implementation seems possible in another setting. Thus, models and reforms that are imitated are those that are presented as planable, and the editing procedure may involve emphasising or ascribing intentions, actors, procedures and effects to an observed and presented development. As procedures are imitated they are often described as models. As experiences in one place are edited into a model they tend to be rationalised and scientised (c.f. **Strang and Meyer, 1993**).

Even though the NPM-reforms in all countries have evolved over time, where one reform has led to another, when these reforms have been told about and accounted for they have been described in much more consistent and coherent terms, as pre-packaged, and with clear intentions. Another example of how national procedures are edited into transportable models is found when one follows the flow of the idea of independent agencies. As part of its recent reforms of the public sector, Britain planned to reform its ministries and agencies. Inspired by principal-agent theories, a model was proposed that would make agencies quite independent of ministries. The idea was that, if politics and public service could be more clearly separated, the executive capability of the agencies would increase. When designing this reform the British went to study Sweden, where a system of independent agencies has been in place since the 17th century. So while the restructuring of British agencies was clearly framed in NPM terms, reference was made to Sweden as an example that had been followed. This thus came to be known as a 'Swedish model', with the result that Sweden then started to regard its own, centuries-old system of independent agencies in NPM terms! This is not only an example of how followers make leaders (Edelman, 1988) but also of how pointless it is to look for the origin of an imitation process– for values and **meanings are generated in the process of diffusion (c.f. Bourdieu, 1977).**

A third set of editing rules concerns formulation. As reform initiatives and their effects are presented and represented, they acquire labels and may also be dramatised as they are told in a certain kind of language. These accounts acquire certain formats, or stated differently, they are formed into narratives of certain genres (Czarniawska, 1997). Concepts, categories, proto-typical examples, counter-examples, references, and ideological frameworks are used to structure, narrate and make sense of a certain procedure or to draw others' attention to a certain development. In the editing process various techniques may be packaged under a common heading, or they may be repackaged under a different heading than they had before. The programme behind certain techniques can be made more or less visible, and in some cases, as described above, techniques can even be ascribed a different programme (Bäckström, 1999; Blomgren, 1999; Brunsson and Sahlin-Andersson, 2000; Vrangbaeck, 1999).

The definition of NPM is general rather than specific. What is more, it is sometimes argued for and defined not as a new form of governing, but rather in terms of what it is not– i.e., the old public administration and bureaucracy.

This feature is most clearly captured by the word 'new', which signals that it is a way of managing that breaks with previous traditions. Even though parts of what is today included in NPM is not particularly new – in relation to previous ways to administer the public services or in relation to theories and principles for management that have been taught in business schools and practiced in business (Furusten and Lerdell, 1998; Jacobsson and Sahlin-Andersson, 1995) – when circulating these models under the heading of NPM, this label clearly signals a break with the past and the introduction of something new. The emphasis of the 'new' attracts attention, and makes the reforms interesting for those who want to break with previous traditions. As the public sector was being questioned in many western countries in the late 80s, reforms that so clearly signaled a break with the past and the introduction of something new attracted a lot of interest.

In what way, then, does the editing follow a rule like pattern? As reforms and experiences are accounted for and narrated, they need to be framed and presented in familiar and commonly accepted terms in order for them to make sense to the reader or listener. Thus, national experiences and reforms tend to be presented to others in terms of existing templates, examples, categories, scientific concepts, theoretical frameworks and widespread classifications that are familiar. These concepts, references and frameworks form the infrastructure of editing and they restrict and direct how the accounts are given. In such a way widespread and well-known classifications may be used to sort out what is being told as accounts are delivered and transferred (c.f. Bowker and Star, 1999).

Concepts, ideologies, examples and interests are not the same everywhere. Examples and ideologies that dominate one setting, and may be taken for granted in this setting, may be unknown or unpopular in another setting. The infrastructure, and thus the editing rules, differ between situations and contexts. For example, in settings dominated by certain ideologies or interests, accounts may be framed and formed by certain normative and ontological assumptions. This specific infrastructure determines the editing of ideas and experiences. Each context in which the editing of models and experiences takes place may be regarded as an editing infrastructure. We may thus describe the process as one of recontextualising experiences and models. When using the term editing I want to emphasise that this recontextualization may change the formulation as well as the meaning and content of experiences and models. As ideas change over time, we may expect later reforms to differ from earlier reforms.

In this section I have suggested that explanations for differences in the shape and scope of reforms among countries that have embarked on the reform path may be found not only by comparing reforming countries with each other but also by following how NPM ideas flow and how they are constructed and transformed as they flow. The analysis shows the importance of previous relations, attention structures, processes of imitation and editing and also timing. As ideas change over time, we may expect later reforms to differ from earlier reforms.

Transnationally Formed Public Management Reforms

Despite the comparative lack of knowledge regarding the effects of the NPM reforms, a number of guidelines have been circulated – via the media, consultants, researchers and, not least, international organisations – on how to reform, and models of best practice have been disseminated. Australia, and to an even greater extent New Zealand, have often been pointed to as examples for others to follow or to learn from. As a result, these countries have attracted tremendous attention from various international bodies as well as from representatives of other countries. For example, in the 1990s Swedish media have written quite extensively about New Zealand models, and also in papers issued within the public administration New Zealand was often mentioned as a model to follow, as a comparison with which Swedish reforms and experiences were compared, and, less often, accounted for as a model that Sweden should not follow (for example Henriksson and Svensson, 1998).

When describing the circulation of reform ideas and experiences in terms of editing processes, above I pointed to the importance of the observers and mediators of such ideas and experiences. A number of observers of reforms – such as researchers, consultants, media and international organizations – mediate information about these reforms, and more generally about ways of governing and managing, and as they mediate such information they edit it in ways described in the previous section. They focus on certain examples and direct others' attention to them. They describe initiatives and ideas and as they describe them they frame their observations in certain ways, they provide comparisons and analyse what they see. Sometimes they assess and evaluate national reforms; they draw more normative conclusions from what they observe, and thus set standards for what is good, bad, necessary or unimportant. This indicates that global reform trends to a large extent are constructed and pursued transnationally, by these mediators and editors of ideas and experiences. Many such mediators and editors are not representing any specific country, but they cut across and transcend national boundaries. In such a way global trends are transnationally constructed.

In this section I will focus on one important mediator and editor of NPM ideas – OECD's public management committee (PUMA) – and I will use this international organisation as an example to show three aspects of the transnational construction of NPM. First, I will exemplify how international organisations edit and circulate ideas. Second, I will discuss how countries have reacted to and adopted such circulated accounts and assessments. And third, I will suggest why international organisations take on the role of editors and circulators.

Before turning to these issues, I will briefly present the organisation – PUMA – on which this section mainly focuses. PUMA was formed in 1990 as an OECD committee. PUMA stands both for the Public Management Service and the Public Management Committee. The committee directs the work of PUMA and consists of representatives of the OECD member countries. The work programme is carried out by the Public Management Service in collaboration with appointed experts. The committee meets twice a year at the OECD, where decisions are taken on PUMA's focus of activity and programme. At its meetings the committee also discusses subjects and reports prepared by the secretariat and various working groups. Participants share their experience and information about what is happening in their own national administrations. Aside from committee meetings, PUMA organises groups of national representatives in a number of areas, and each group arranges working meetings, symposia, seminars, etc. These are administered by the secretariat, which also prepares and follows up activities by producing documentation and publishing reports, as well as in other ways. PUMA is thus an important mediator and editor of NPM ideas.

International Organisations as Producers of Templates and Prototypes

In previous studies the OECD has been described as an information system (Sjöstedt, 1973), a harmonising agent (Harrison and Mungal, 1990), an active disseminator of ideas and ideals (Olsen and Peters, 1996a), and a driving force and creator of national ideas and ideals (Finnemore, 1992; Mörth, 1996). International organisations such as the OECD play an important role in directing attention to specific countries, specific phenomena and specific aspects of developments; they codify, compare and categorise reforms and changes. In other words, they are important editors of reform ideas and experiences (Sahlin-Andersson, 1996, 2000). More specifically, OECD's Public Management Committee – PUMA – has been identified as an important mediator, proselytizer and editor of NPM ideas.

Such editing was done as PUMA collected, summarised, compared and assessed information about reforms in the member countries. PUMA regularly perform surveys of Public Management Developments. While the background and context of public management reforms differ between countries and between reforms in individual countries (Hood, 1995a), they are put into a common framework as they are collected and presented in publications issued by PUMA. Presentations are usually organized in the same way for all countries so as to permit comparison. Promising attempts at reform are described in aspects that seem relevant for implementation. Often the reports would include a number of key indicators that summarize the reforms.

In a report entitled 'Governance in transition: Public management reforms in the OECD countries' (1995) PUMA issued an extensive overview of reforms in their member countries. The entire report emphasized reforms. Here specific countries were pointed out as examples to follow. In addition, direct references to the reform attempts in specific countries were made in the form of excerpts from statements by representatives of the member countries on certain reforms. Repeatedly, it was emphasized that even though public management reforms have been inspired by 'best practice' in the private sector, 'in the public sector they are, in many respects, journeys into unknown territory' (p. 27). It was also said that 'there is no single model of reform; there are no off-the-shelf solutions' (p. 25). Thus, it was important continually to follow up and evaluate what had been accomplished. The final and summarizing chapters, however, downplayed the differences and uncertainty; they presented a reform agenda which embodied the principal features of the national reforms. The agenda consisted of recommendations and normative pronouncements on how government should be reformed. Differences among countries were said to reflect differences in emphasis and rate of national reform, but the direction and the main content of the reforms were claimed to be similar from country to country and also to be the right (and only) way to go. Reforms and experiences were generalised and assembled as a reform agenda or policy package, and a common logic and common explanations were ascribed to the reforms. The reforms were described and justified as responses to a common set of problems facing all OECD countries, and they were labelled as a coherent and consistent package.

This packaging – which was done not only by PUMA but also by researchers, consultants, the media and others in the many publications and reports that have been written about these reforms – took place after some of the more significant reforms referred to had already been initiated. The Anglo-Saxon countries had been reforming for a decade and some aspects of what was now included in the presented reform package were arrangements and changes of much older origin, but they were now presented as a more or less coherent package. This package was then used as a basis for comparing and assessing countries.

The term packaging may give the impression that this international organization's treatment of the ideas and experiences does not affect the ideas and experiences themselves, they just bundle them together in certain ways. But, as I have described above, what is circulated are presentations, not the ideas themselves. Consequently, when packaging, it is not only the form of these ideas that changes but the content as well. This further suggests that it may not be easy to distinguish between form and content; changes in form may well imply changes in content (Czarniawska, 1997).

PUMA provided normative models or examples – prototypes – for how to improve and reform the public sector. These prototypes were presented as a series of recommendations, together with instructions on how to implement them, and they sometimes referred to how a reform or reform package had been carried out in practice in a particular country. In the PUMA publications New Zealand has repeatedly been pointed out as an example to follow – a prototype for successful reforms. In addition, PUMA formed and used templates: sets of concepts and criteria that were used to present, compare and assess reforms. In relation to the coherent and consistent reform template with which PUMA compares reforming countries, Sweden and earlier, to a more limited extent, Australia, were shown to be – and partly criticized for being – much more incremental reformers.

While some reports point to specific examples, others give a more general overview and summary of the reforms in the OECD countries. In the report 'Syntesis of reform experiences in nice OECD countries' (OECD, 1999a) a more generalized picture of reforms is given. No specific countries are mentioned, instead expressions such as 'some countries', 'a few countries' and 'most countries' are used. Here, what is produced, is a scheme or a template with which single countries may be compared and assessed. When packaging reforms, and issuing prototypes and templates, the international organization edits national stories of reforms according the editing rules concerning context, logic and formulation that I described above. As shown below, countries seem likely to follow, or at least respond, to the issued prototypes and templates.

Reformers as Followers of Templates and Prototypes

PUMA does not issue binding rules and has no authority to do so. Still, PUMA, and many other international organisations, have had a major impact on how certain areas of activity have been defined and organised in national states. Finnemore (1992, 1996) has analysed a number of such processes. One of her studies concerned national research policies. Between 1955 and 1985 a large number of countries developed a national research policy and set up central bodies in charge of it. Finnemore differentiated between demand- and supply-based explanations for this trend. By demand-based she meant that special government units were created in response to a demand within the country. However, she found few examples of demand-based national research policies. Instead, countries were 'taught' by international bodies – such as the OECD and UNESCO – that all modern countries urgently and unquestionably needed to have a national research policy under the super-vision of a central unit. This is one example of international organisations as designers and disseminators of prototypes for countries to follow, and of templates with which countries can be compared and assessed. International organisations may provide countries with solutions and general recommen-dations as well as with meanings or programmes to be ascribed to such policies, and they direct countries' attention to certain other countries iden-tified as originals, prototypes or successful examples.

A number of statements in one recent publication from the OECD, where reform experiences from nine OECD countries were synthesized, supports the conclusion that reforming countries not only learn from each other but also follow prototypes that are issued transnationally (OECD, 1999a) and present and view their reforms in terms laid down by transnationally formed templates. This report described PUMA and other international organisations as having inspired and pushed countries to reform.

> Even where a country lacked economic imperatives to reform, and had the luxury of not doing so, reputation-conscious governments, sensitive to unfavor-able comparisons with others, initiated albeit moderate change. Alternatively, reform-minded governments or individual ministers championing reform were able to use rankings to raise awareness and build a critical mass to support reform agendas (OECD, 1999a, pp. 4–5).
>
> In some countries, the influence of the international bodies such as the OECD and especially thinking on 'New public management' might have been stronger than the effects of administrative traditions and culture (OECD, 1999a, p. 15).

Here the OECD is portrayed as an important circulator and shaper of models – a trend-setter (c.f. Abrahamson, 1996) which 'reputation-conscious' governments may follow. This is not to say that the models originated in the OECD itself. The OECD report referred to above is, like most PUMA reports, based on countries' own accounts of their reforms. What international organisations do is collect information, compare countries and analyse developments, and they edit them into prototypes. They generalize individual examples and put them into the common template.

Again we can see that it is not easy to identify an original model for a trend that later spread, for the trend as well as the models being spread are actually formed as they pass through the transnational network. Reports both from one of the most eager reformers, New Zealand, and from one of the more reluctant reformers, Norway, show that in both cases transnationally formed templates were reflected in national reforms and these reforms were inspired by transnationally formed prototypes. In one of its country reports New Zealand stated that

> The thinking of officials and key politicians was greatly influenced by intellectual developments internationally, particularly from academics and international organisations such as the World Bank, the International Monetary Fund and the OECD (OECD, 1999b, p. 8).

Norway, the country least inclined towards reform among the four being analysed in this book, used a more distant language in its report, talking about force, competition and little involvement rather than about strong effects and influence. But it also clearly pointed to the impact of international bodies– international organisations as well as consultants – on its national reforms. 'The inspiration from the 'New Public Management' was maybe stronger than from administrative traditions, administrative culture and historic associations engraved in the Norwegian welfare state' (Strømsnes, 1999, p. 7).

What is illustrated in the quotations above is the interaction between reforming countries and an international organisation. The international organisation not only gives an account of what is happening in countries in terms of reform, but also encourages countries to reform and provides arguments for reforming further. What is displayed here is a global trend which has formed not only from interaction between states, but also from interaction between states and international organisations. A global trend is therefore formed and pursued transnationally. National reformers learn from international organizations what is appropriate to do, they may aquire certain values, norms, ideals and ideas and they may use international organisations to argue the need for reform and to motivate their own governments to take measures. International organisations, in turn, provide arguments for why further reforms are needed.

While the label 'NPM' earlier was generally found in the academic literature as a way of making sense of and finding more general patterns in the extensive process of reforming in OECD countries, its use has since become more widespread and the term has been adopted by observers and by reformers themselves. Indeed, NPM has become the most widely used label for the cluster of reforms that have been pursued by OECD countries and others during the last few decades, and there are signs that the label itself motivates actors to reform or at least it is used to argue for the need to reform further. Thus, as NPM is described and perceived as a package, it provides a strong argument for countries to add one set of reforms to another – in order to complete the 'package' – once they have embarked on the reform path.

In March 2000, the most recent plans for reforming the Swedish national budget were presented by one of the advocates of this particular reform for a group of scholars and civil servants. In his presentation this reform advocate argued that this reform was a typical NPM reform and a natural continuation of earlier NPM reforms which had been launched in the Swedish state administration during the 1980s and 1990s. The planned budget reform was described as a way to 'complete the reform path embarked on' and to 'fill the reform package'. As the NPM reform package has been circulated and become more widely spread, there seems to be a tendency to view countries or organizations that have adopted parts but not all of the 'package' as less coherent (OECD, 1999a) and 'incomplete' (c.f. Brunsson and Sahlin-Andersson, 2000). Thus, describing NPM reforms as a 'package' may in itself be a way of driving countries further along the reform path.

PUMA not only issues policy recommendations for how to reform. It also identifies certain countries as successes and others as less successful examples (OECD, 1995, 1999a). New Zealand has repeatedly been described as a success story when it comes to public sector reforms. Australia is also often regarded as a successful case, while reports on Sweden have been more critical. The relative allocation and attraction of attention is an important aspect of transnationally driven reform processes. International organisations have helped to direct the world's attention to New Zealand and Australia, and representatives from all levels of government have travelled to these countries from the northern part of the globe to learn how to reform. In 1998, representatives from the national audit office in New Zealand told us that they had groups of international visitors almost every week who wanted to learn about the reforms. Not only the most reformed and well known units receive visitors, but it seems as though a number of delegations find an interest in the country as it is written about in media and they pay attention to what is going on throughout the administration. From such visits a number of parallel processes of imitation and increased interaction may follow. Such processes lead to convergence between countries, but it also means that attention is directed to certain countries and to certain aspects of reforms, and this may explain differences between reforming countries and account for processes of transformation.

The attention that reforms get from international organisations is not only seen as a sign of success by foreigners but is also taken as reassurance by the reformers themselves that they are on the right track. As pointed out above, relatively few comprehensive reviews and evaluations of the effects of NPM reforms have been done. The tremendous attention that New Zealand and Australia received from the rest of the world, however, signaled to these reformers as well as to their domestic and foreign audiences that they were on the right track.

So far, when describing reforms I have not specified in detail who the reformers are. When describing countries as reformers, this may give the impression that reform ideas are adopted by central administrators and politicians who then initiate national reforms. Many reforms inspired by widespread NPM, however, have been adopted and pursued by actors at rather low levels of the state hierarchy. Moreover, in some countries several different but related models have been pursued at the same time in different parts of the administration. Different kinds of modern quality-control models, for example, have been adopted in different parts of the Swedish healthcare system. One study showed that at least three different such models were used at the same time in one hospital (Erlingsdottir, 1999). The actors– politicians, administrators, and professionals – adopted different models and they had learned about these models through different transnational networks.

Another example of how new reform ideas were adopted first, not at the top, but at lower levels of the administration is the introduction of new forms of accounting in the Swedish public administration (Olson and Sahlin-Andersson, 1998). The accounting system in the Swedish public sector was first reformed on the local level, through local experiments but also through local governments imitating each other and through collaboration between these governments and university professors specialising in accounting. The university professors here served as mediators and editors of experiences and ideas taken both from the Swedish private sector and from other countries. It was only much later that the accounting system was reformed on the state level. These reforms were clearly inspired by transnationally spread proto-types, but they also contained elements of imitation of the practice of local and regional levels of the Swedish administration. Such processes of transnational reform may lead to great variations not only between but also within countries.

Why Do International Organisations Circulate Templates and Prototypes?

In the section above I have described how PUMA played an important role both as a disseminator and as a more active constructor and circulator of templates and prototypes. What then are the dynamics that drive international organisations to engage increasingly in this process? In analysing this we need to look closer at the conditions under which these kinds of international organizations work, and how their way of organizing and working may be understood. There are a number of organisations whose task, like PUMA's, it is to produce and provide information and comparisons, report and propose initiatives for change, and act as arenas for exchange of experience, ideas, and ideals. Among the many international organisations that have emerged during the last century, there are a number of this kind – organisations intended as arenas where people from different countries can share each other's ideas and experience. John Meyer has used the term 'others' to capture the specific features of such international organisations and their activities (Meyer, 1994, 1996) and to distinguish them from organisations that are assumed to pursue their own interests and policies, and which are held responsible for their actions.

> Others, in this scheme loosely derived from George Herbert Mead, do not take active responsibility for organizational behavior and outcomes. They discuss, interpret, advise, suggest, codify, and sometimes pronounce and legislate. They develop, promulgate, and certify some ideas as proper reforms, and ignore or stigmatize other ideas... (Meyer, 1996, p. 244).

When analyzing and assessing local initiatives or when issuing recommen-dations, international organisations argue not in terms of their own interests but in terms of what is best for the countries in question; they formulate their advice and models in terms of expertise, not in terms of interests (Jacobsson, 2000). However, even though international organisations may present themselves as neutral arenas of interaction, they are not any more neutral than other organisations are. International organisations not only co-ordinate and mediate interests and ideas but, like all other organisations, they influence and shape the activities that take place under their auspices (Finnemore, 1996; Mörth, 1996). How an organisation conducts its operations depends on its environment and on what it has to do to be considered important and worth dealing with. The latter determines the way an organisation obtains legitimacy and resources.

The number of international organisations, intergovernmental as well as non-governmental, has increased dramatically during the post-war period (Boli and Thomas, 1999). With this development international organisations have become more important intermediaries of ideas and experiences and important providers of templates and prototypes for countries to follow. This increase in the number of international organisations has also meant increased competition between international organisations. National actors are not obliged to pay attention to them and participate in their activities, but these organizations have to compete for attention, legitimacy and resources. PUMA, just like other organisations, seeks to attract attention and resources in order to survive. Its legitimacy has been questioned ever since the committee was formed and thus it has to show that it is useful for the member states and it has to show some type of results. Disseminating prototypes and templates widely and maintaining relations with the reforming member countries are ways for PUMA to maintain the attention, legitimacy and resources needed to continue operations. This quest for attention and legitimacy seems to have led to three developments. First, the type of activities engaged in has continuously broadened. The 1999 statement of the chair stated:

> ...while the future members will no doubt continue to need what might be termed 'traditional public management support', there should be a discernable shift in PUMA's work towards broader issues of governance...

Second, PUMA has sought to broaden the geographical scope of its activities. Among the directions for the future work of the committee were (also metioned in the same statement of the chair, 1999): '...developing capacities for more coherent and globalised policies; (and) delivering on policy commitments in a changing world...'

Third, as a way to ensure continuous support, the committee seeks to become more clearly policy oriented in order to play a central role in forming and reforming NPM. A glance at the list of publications from PUMA supports this conclusion. While publications during the first part of the 1990s consisted of overviews, surveys and summaries, in the last few years it has published a number of reviews and assessments of single countries, and its reports define best practice, success criteria and the like. This shift in focus towards clearer policy recommendations and a more normative and evaluatory role, more generally as well as towards individual countries, may be the result from a development where NPM has become a well known concept and agenda. Lots of reforms are carried out and reported under this heading. The number of research projects and report and writings more general has grown enormously. And a number of international organizations – not only OECD, but also for example the World Bank, IMF and EU – are reporting on and emphasizing the importance of NPM. With this development NPM has developed into a field of expertise with a number of experts – many of them connected to international organizations. The emerged groups of experts displays many characteristics of an epistemic community (Haas, 1992) and with this development a widespread agreement and understanding has emerged concerning what forms of governance are good and bad, right and wrong, appropriate and possible, which reforms to recommend, and what outcomes to expect. When being able to issue more firm recommendations and assessments PUMA may also be viewed as producing results that are useful for the members. Assessments and normative statements attract members attention, and activate their involvement in the organisation's activities. Producing norms and models for others to follow and reviewing and evaluating its members' reforms seemed to be one way for PUMA to maintain its legitimacy as an independent and neutral arena and at the same time yield the results needed to obtain resources and support from its environment. Thus, constructing NPM prototypes and templates is a way for an international organisation to compete with others for resources, legitimacy and attention.

In this section I have shown how global trends are formed transnationally, via a process of interaction between reformers and international organisations, and I have discussed in somewhat more detail the role played by PUMA in turning NPM into a global trend. The implication is that in order to explain the development and effects of NPM reforms one needs to analyse what role the international organisations play in the process: how they mediate and edit information about the reforms, how they interact with reformers and what their interests in evaluating and pursuing reform ideas are.

Conclusions

As an increasing number of countries around the world have reformed along similar lines, NPM has evolved into a global trend. Comparative studies reveal that even though the reforms display great similarities – to the extent that we can talk about a trend, or a reform path – because the reforms have been initiated differently, and because national contexts differ, the effects of the reforms have not been the same everywhere. In this paper I have argued that even though such studies may explain why certain effects follow or do not follow from the reforms, these studies do not explain why and how NPM became a global trend. What is missing is a demonstration of the transformation dynamics that this trend displays between countries and over time. I have suggested that the NPM trend has evolved nationally as well as internationally and transnationally. Analysis of how the reforms have been shaped internationally and transnationally reveals processes of convergence – we see how and why NPM evolved into a global trend. Furthermore, such analysis shows how the reforms, as well as their effects, are not only shaped nationally but also through processes of imitation and reflection between one country, parts of its administration and another. Furthermore, reforms are shaped as a product of interaction between national reformers and transnational mediators and editors of such reforms. Analysis of how NPM has evolved internationally and transnationally not only portrays convergence but also provides us with explanations for the transformation of reforms – differences that emerge over time and between countries.

To conclude, I will briefly return to the four countries. With this brief account I just want to point to a few examples of differences and similarities between the countries, in order to indicate how the national, international and transnational trend in combination shaped reforms and their effects. Australia, New Zealand, Norway and Sweden faced quite different situations in the 1980s, which lead them to put more or less emphasis on reforms. Australia, New Zealand and Sweden all faced severe fiscal crisis, even though this came later in Sweden than in the other two countries, and the New Zealand crisis was experienced as even more severe than the ones experienced in the other countries (OECD, 1999a; Olson et al., 1998).

The New Zealand reforms were not only extensive, but were also framed in theoretical terms with expressed expectations for far reaching consequences. The small and comparatively centralized New Zealand, with a previous history of extensive and revolutionary reforms could reform in a coherent and revolutionary way (Pallot, 1998). As the New Zealand reforms have become know throughout the world, and many countries have been inspired by them and imitated them, the New Zealand reforms have become known as a model (c.f. Boston et al., 1996). The coherence and consistence has been reemphasized over and again as the reforms have been packaged into a model. The international and transnational attention paid to New Zealand led to further attention and imitation, and to further reforming.

Australia and Sweden, with more decentralized structures – and in the case of Sweden's accounting reforming, a history of more incremental changes – did not follow such coherent paths, at least not initially. Australia started to reform in a more pragmatic and incremental way. However, as Australia increasingly caught international attention and the Australian reformers were compared with others, and as they learned about the trans-nationally spread NPM templates and prototypes at least some parts of Australia have reformed much more extensively and coherently, and they have based their reforms more in theoretical terms and in terms that we recognize from the widely spread template (OECD, 1999a).

The Swedish reforms have been even more incremental. While certain parts and aspects of the administration were extensively reformed other aspects of NPM did not meet any enthusiasm in Sweden (see Forssell, this volume). As was the case in Scandinavia in general, there was initially widespread skepticism regarding the more market oriented aspects of NPM (Christensen and Lægreid, 1999a).

At this time, Norway, which in contrast to the other countries did not experience a fiscal crisis, did not see as strong needs for reform and they were skeptical of the NPM reforms more generally (Christensen and Lægreid, 1999a).

These are examples of how differences in the design of reforms and the nation's economic situation, administrative structure and earlier history of reforms resulted in the shape and effect of reforms, and these explanations point out how differences between reforms follow from differences in national initiatives and national contexts. When following process of imitation we could point to further explanations to differences between countries. Some aspects of the reforms have been more easily imitated than others, and the nature of reforms change as the ideas travel around the world.

We could also see that similarities among countries follow from such processes of imitation. As NPM has become increasingly known as a global trend, comparisons, assessments and evaluations have been performed by the many observers of such reforms. I have given examples of how the OECD collected information about reforms in the member countries, and how they, based on this information, have formulated a template with which countries then have been compared and assessed. Even though many close observers of the reforms find local variations, when the national reforms have been reported and accounted for they are described in terms of a widespread template. As NPM has been packaged and spread there are not many alternatives around for those who want to reform and search for ideas to be inspired by and to imitate. Even though the reforming decisions are nationally taken, with the editorial activities of transnational mediators, such as PUMA, prototypes have been formulated that have turned out to be available, attractive and appropriate to follow. Moreover, as transnational observers argue for certain prototypical ways, and they regard those who follow the templates to be on the right track it is not surprising if countries tend to follow such prototypes and templates.

While we can still easily point to a number of differences among OECD countries – in terms of economic situation, administrative structure, reform-tradition and political structure – most OECD-countries have picked up at least some aspects of NPM. Australia, New Zealand, Norway and Sweden displayed quite dramatic differences in the late 1980s and early 1990s concerning how they talked about governing public service and how they tried to reform the public sector. Today, differences are not as dramatic, they all refer to NPM reforms and they all talk about further reforms along the same trac. As a result of the transnational processes reforming countries have been given great possibilities and incentives to converge – and to pursue similar reforms.

4 The Process of Reform in the Era of Public Sector Transformation

JOHN HALLIGAN

Introduction

This chapter identifies and analyses key questions pertaining to the process of reform in OECD public sectors. It pays particular attention to two pairs of countries: Australia and New Zealand, with their variant of the Anglo-Saxon tradition; and Norway and Sweden, representing the Scandinavian tradition. They offer a nice contrast between four countries in the process of reform, two of which have overwhelmingly embraced a New Public Management (NPM) paradigm, one of which has partially taken on NPM – straddling the old and the new – and a fourth, Norway, which has sought to accommodate NPM within a traditional paradigm.

The current era of public sector reform is distinguished by the high level and impact of systemic change, which for many decades was incremental and ad hoc. One explanation for this may be that reform mechanisms and approaches to the reform process have become more effective. Does this mean that new types of reform require distinctive types of process? If so, what are the attributes of a successful reform process (success being defined in terms of change accomplished rather than by normative judgements about the quality of the reforms)? How do these processes differ from those of the past? Where do they lead us? What opportunities do they present? And what costs and constraints do they involve?

Analysing Reform Processes

If we are to address these questions, three issues must first be clarified: the nature of reform at the system level, the character of reform and the components of the reform process. Under a transformative perspective, reform processes can be analysed in terms of external and internal factors that influence and shape them, but here it is the internal effects that are most relevant. This chapter concentrates on the national and internal aspects of the reform process, while Chapter 3 primarily dealt with the external and international context.

Reforming Complex Public Service Systems Over Time

One distinguishing transformative feature of the current era is that significant reform has occurred. A second feature, closely related to the first, is that the character of reform in many contexts is rather different to that previously experienced. Three things in particular distinguish it from reform in the past: it is complex, it is comprehensive and it consists of multiple stages and elements in programmes designed to be implemented over time.

Much of the literature on organisations focuses on change in a specific agency. Where public service systems are under consideration, however, several arenas of reform and a number of organisations of different types may be involved. Furthermore, the public sector is multi-level, comprising a core public service within the central (or federal) government, a broader public sector and possibly similar distinctions replicated at the regional level. The national public sector may well be designated as the reform arena, increasing the layers of complexity.

If reform is comprehensive it implies both multi-agency and multiple reforms, features that are associated with complex transformative reform contexts. Comprehensive reform involves greater complexity and is more likely to lead to 'garbage-can' processes (Brunsson and Olsen, 1993, p. 26).

Analysing complex and lengthy reform processes also presents a number of other challenges. If the reform cycle is depicted in terms of a simple policy model we find that identifying the reform process may be difficult if it is not conveniently distinctive and clearly promulgated and implemented. In addition, with reform programmes that extend over time, more than one reform cycle may be apparent.

Types of Reform

Administrative change has traditionally been recognised as a constant feature of organisational environments and has been regarded in terms of adaptation to the environment. In the public sector, this has typically involved the expansion of activities and the organisations which provide them and has normally been incremental, piecemeal and based on a department, ministry or other type of agency. There is a lack of coherent and sustained strategy or direction in their application and implementation.

What is different in the current reform era is the presence of at least three major orders of reform. These involve questions of both scale and substance: the magnitude of change is greater, but there is also a qualitative dimension because the substance represents a fundamentally different way of doing things. Two less extensive but nonetheless significant orders of reform are specialised reform (significant reform types, such as corporatisation or decentralisation); and sectoral reform of a policy field (e.g. health) or of a major system component (e.g. local government or the outer public sector). Comprehensive reform means that a range of reforms are introduced that affect most aspects of the functioning of a public service or public sector or both. This large-scale reform may of course encompass various specialised and sectoral reforms (Halligan, 1997b).

These distinctions correspond with those reported by Dunphy and Stace (1990): two forms of incremental approach (fine tuning and incremental adjustment) and two forms of transformative approach (modular and corporate). It should be noted that these categories are defined in terms of organisational change, which may present some difficulties because of the differences between a focused organisation and a multi-organisational public sector.

The aforementioned types of reform can be adapted for classifying reform in OECD countries. In practice, at least four main types can be identified:

- *The hesitant reformer*: Implementation of some principles but essentially old-style (or in slow transition) with a reliance on adaptation and incrementalism on a sectoral basis (e.g. Norway).
- *The specialist reformer*: The focus is on one or more distinctive types of reform (all four countries at some point).
- *The ambivalent reformer*: There is a commitment to general change, but cross-cutting pressures (or inertia) mean that implementation is mixed (Sweden; Australia up to 1986).
- *The comprehensive reformer*: Makes a major commitment to reform, employing a range of reform types at system level (Australia and New Zealand).

The majority of OECD countries have not reformed comprehensively but generally fall into some variation of the first three categories (Halligan,

1997b; Pollitt and Bouckaert, 2000). The language of comprehensive reform may be there, as in the case of Norway, but not the results (Brunsson and Olsen, 1993; Christensen and Lægreid, 1998b; Lægreid and Roness, 1999). This pattern is not confined to the public sector. Dunphy and Stace (1990), for example, reported that only one quarter of the private and public organisations that they surveyed had achieved corporate transformation, while fewer than two-fifths had achieved modular transformation (see also Kotter, 1995 on the mixed results of companies).

Elements of the Reform Process

Process covers a number of elements used to develop, initiate and implement reforms, including several of those raised here. These include structure, the use of frameworks and leadership or reform style. Reform content – or the nature of specific reforms – is an integral element of process, but since it has been examined at great length elsewhere (Pollitt and Bouckaert, 2000) it will not be further considered here. The structure of the reform process may consist of a series of reforms over time that occur in multiple stages that may be either incremental or transformative.

A related element is the character of reform or how reform is organised and given coherence. The relationship between the elements is acknowledged through some sort of framework or organisational doctrine, which provides a coherent set of ideas for influencing and establishing action and reference points.

Stages in the Process

The stages of the reform process can be depicted in several ways. One approach is to examine the sequence of reforms and their relationships. For an Australia-New Zealand comparison, see Halligan 1997a; also Pollitt and Bouckaert 2000 on trajectories. Another is to identify the significant developmental stages in the reform process. The initial stage will normally involve a grand announcement of a reform programme or significant reform, followed by a series of other, not always distinctive, phases in which new reforms are launched and implementation and institutionalisation proceeds. The cycle may also be repeated in a lengthy reform process, with seemingly endless variations at the agency level.

Delineating the stages, or even the official reform programme, may not be straightforward. What J. Power (1994, pp. 3–4) describes as the 1980s style of reform was formally initiated with the publication of *Reforming the Australian Public Service* (Australian Government, 1983), a statement he depicts as 'somewhat oracular in tone, its length was short, its tone instrumentalist and its scope sharply delineated, being restricted to just three topics'. While it 'provided an essential authorising framework for the plurality of reforms which were to follow, it did not...provide the public with a clear outline of the shape of the reforms ahead' (pp. 9–10). There continued to be difficulty in identifying what was formally regarded as reform because of the lack of a single (or even just two) official sources of reform. The major review, the Task Force on Management Improvement (1993, p. 6), described the reforms as 'a combination of broad policy objectives, long-term strategies and specific one-off or ongoing changes acted upon in all parts of the APS'. Academic observers pointed to the lack of a 'solid philosophical or theoretical basis' (Painter, 1988, p. 2).

Having acquired a rudimentary Financial Management Improvement Program in the early 1980s, the Australian central reformers put together a set of management reforms through a process that involved several strategic interventions of varying significance punctuated by more incremental and less public activities that supported and extended them (Halligan, 1996).

All of this points to the significance of stages in a linear reform programme. In Australia and New Zealand, the reform programme extended over several stages, and its success depended upon review, refinements and consolidation. Britain also illustrates this point, because each major reform (e.g. privatisation, executive agencies, charters etc) signaled a new stage and became emblazoned on international thinking.

Reform Approaches and Styles

Two key dimensions of reform management are reform or leadership style and external direction. The reform process can be bottom-up and consultative, even collaborative, or top-down and directive.

Reform Style

Various reform styles may apply at different times or stages in a complex reform process. Dunphy and Stace (1990), for example, focus on four styles: two participative (collaboration and consultation) and two coercive (directive and coercive). A number of studies (e.g. Dunphy and Stace, 1990) note the constraints imposed on achieving extensive reform where a pronounced participative style is an important part of the process.

Mascarenhas (1996a, p. 207) focuses on technocratic and political approaches, reflecting two broad schools distinguished by March and Olsen (1989): one derived from orthodox administrative theory, involving the administrative design of structures and procedures to facilitate bureaucratic efficiency and effectiveness; the other, realpolitik, which regards administrative structures as a product of interests and reform as a political issue. Mascarenhas recognises that the actors involved may extend well beyond the reforming institution when it comes to public organisations and systems: 'a political strategy adopts uncontrolled public involvement or participation, while a technocratic strategy adopts a more controlled public involvement' (1996a, p. 217).

Australia provides an interesting contrast to New Zealand because it employed a 'political or consensus model' involving gradual education and achieved through existing institutions. Because public service reform was an election issue, *Reforming the Australian Public Service* (Australian Government, 1983) was used for public consultation (including public servants). 'As a result not only was the reform package firmly based on prior studies of the problem, it also enjoyed considerable support from both the public service and political parties' (Mascarenhas, 1996a, p. 217).

New Zealand's approach, described as a technocratic strategy, was not a product of an election manifesto, a review or prior consultation but had a more confrontational character. The implementation strategy of the main architect, Roger Douglas, sought to overcome vested interests by advocating 'speed and clarity of objectives...for overcoming such obstacles...Accordingly, the government entrusted responsibility for reform to a small group which established informal links with key advisers' (Mascarenhas, 1996a, pp. 209, 217).

While New Zealand may be the archetypal 'coercive' case, Prime Minister Margaret Thatcher in Britain provided the role model for later directive reformers internationally. 'The Thatcher government...employed a confrontational and ideological style, making its era a traumatic one for the career civil service and the trade unions' (Brunsson and Olsen, 1993, pp. 30–31; March and Olsen, 1989).

Brunsson and Olsen (1993, p. 30) contrast Britain with Nordic countries in terms of reform styles and how they handled conflict:

> In the Nordic countries, where there was a commitment to consensus, conflict was avoided. This was particularly so where opponents claimed that reform

proposals broke with the post-World War II development of the welfare state and raised constitutional questions.

Comprehensive reform is not about a single document or stage. Mascarenhas was writing very much about initial reform in Australia, and the process changed at later stages and was sometimes more conflictual and less consultative. In practice, such reform involves moving between stages and styles. There are intermediate cases which have combined directive elements at certain points in the reform process with some provision for consultation.

External and Internal Direction: The Role of Politicians and Central Agencies

In disaggregating the processes we need to distinguish between the system designers – those operating in central agencies with responsibility for cross-service change – and the key line operatives, those who test and experiment with applications at the agency level, although we cannot deal directly with the latter here.

Central agencies are part of the internal apparatus, but often function as detached drivers of change. There is much evidence of the blocking capacity of entrenched central agencies to initiatives of reformers who sought change that conflicted with convention – e.g., moving from input to output budgeting (Halligan and Power, 1992; Painter, 1987). In Norway, the political weakness and low standing of relevant agencies and their location within a polycentric model for the organisation of reforms worked against progress (Brunsson and Olsen, 1993; Christensen and Lægreid, 1998b; Lægreid and Roness, 1999, p. 315).

Once converted to a new approach, however, the central agency becomes a most potent driver of change (Campbell and Halligan, 1992). The best known case of the reform era is the New Zealand Treasury. The key reforms were derived from the rigid application of public choice and related theory, first articulated by this agency and, indeed, explicitly termed the 'Treasury's framework'. For much of the reform period, the Treasury maintained policy advocacy of its preferences and intolerance of alternatives (Boston et al., 1996, p. 4; Gregory, 1998c).

The role of external direction has been identified as one significant factor in reform generally (Dunphy and Stace, 1990) as has the need to develop policy largely outside key institutions if fundamental change is intended (Martin, 1998). The primary element is likely to be the political executive: the more significant the reform, the more likely politicians as well as officials are to be involved. The conventional wisdom once regarded the lack of political support and the failure of politicians to sustain their commitment to reform as key factors in reform failure (March and Olsen, 1989). There is evidence that major change requires the intervention of politicians and that politicians have been actively seeking to play a more active role in reform (Aucoin, 1990; Halligan, 1994; Halligan and Power, 1992).

The political executive can be the key factor in the success of major reform, at least at certain strategic points in the reform process. The reasons for this are obvious: fundamental change means a new paradigm and approaches and inevitably some new leadership. The existing senior public service is unlikely to support change of this order if it undermines their positions and values. Contrariwise, where governments are divided and reliant on special interests for support, or on lack of tenure in office, they face greater obstacles to achieving change.

Of all the strategic instruments, the use of political appointments as a means of obtaining leverage over a public service is one of the most important. The four countries under consideration have not sought to rely heavily on such appointees, favouring instead a mixture of selective appointments and conventional reform methods. There is, however, some variation in the approaches adopted by each country.

The non-implementation of Australian proposals in the 1970s was attributed to the neglect of political factors. The development of appropriate mechanisms centred on the increasing use of ministerial advisers and avoiding isolated changes in strategies for strengthening political control (Wilenski, 1986). The enhancement of the political executive's power proceeded through several phases and resulted in a set of political mechanisms for influencing and directing the public service, but the package remained incomplete until governments embraced managerialist approaches to enforcing and maintaining control (Halligan and Power, 1992). Australia continued to rely heavily on tight political control to sustain reform, whereas New Zealand, which had initially emphasised the role of political advisers, resorted to the principles of its well-known model as the basis for driving reform until recently (Halligan, forthcoming).

The combination of external (key politicians) and internal (key civil servants) direction is highly potent, but it is most formidable where change is driven by such things as a financial agenda shaped by economic factors and an organisational mission, such as decentralisation that derives from management mantra.

Revisiting the Direction of Reform

Bottom-up and top-down are best regarded as either polar points on a spectrum in which there are intermediate cases (Pollitt and Bouckaert, 2000, p. 90) or as components of a hybrid or contingent approach (Thompson and Sanders, 1998).

It has long been established that participation may not enhance reorgani-sation (Mosher, 1967). Recent research indicates that bottom-up may work under particular circumstances and for specific tasks (Peters, 1998a; Thompson and Sanders, 1998). System-wide reform directives must be implemented through agencies and at different levels within them, providing scope for a mixture of processes (e.g., the US National Performance Review used devices such as the reinvention labs to encourage 'the incremental, flexible and experimental development of changes and their implementation' Rainey, 1998a, p. 165).

The application of this type of process element has been clear in recent times: the top-down approach has been clearly identified with the active reformers. Comprehensive reform generally involves first-order reform (Hall, 1993) and invariably must be top-down or directive. In contrast, second- (and third-order) reform is usually applied at the micro or organisational level, where greater collaboration is likely and therefore the bottom-up approach more appropriate. However, the bottom-up approach can be highly important in the intergovernmental reform process, where delivery-led reform involves sub-national systems. Specific types of reform are likely to be involved, particularly those which incorporate participatory elements. A recent list of approaches to implementation predictably gives quality initiatives as the example for bottom-up (Bouckaert, 1997, p. 470).

Initially, then, reform is likely to be implemented from the top down, using a directive approach. Over time, however, as individual agencies become responsible for implementation and seek to institutionalise reform at the middle and lower levels, bottom-up or hybrid elements will probably become more common.

Reform Strategies

Rationality and Reform Strategies

Reform agendas imply that a strategy is involved. The idea of change strategies as premeditated and controlled also suggests rational approaches to change. There are some fairly universal principles that can be drawn from reform experiences.

One limitation of using the term 'change strategy' when talking about reform – and one which emerges clearly from the complex and dynamic transformative contexts outlined – is the implication that change can be readily managed. Whereas this may be the case with a single agency or private sector firms, it is far more difficult in a complex public sector that is subject to a changing political environment. The differences between these two levels makes the universal application of the work of observers such as Dunphy and Stace difficult. There is also the question of the utility of change strategies. The organisational literature seeks 'a way of portraying how much change an organization needs to restore fit' [with the environment] (Dunphy and Stace, 1990, p. 71). If we are confined to simple distinctions between a cluster of characteristics that may or may not be present, then classifying change strategies as incremental, modular or corporate may not mean very much.

How the reform process in practice brings rationality to design is illuminating. Two devices for imparting rationality are integration through a framework and modes of rationalisation.

Integration Through Frameworks

The need to define a framework has been important in countries carrying out comprehensive reform, such as Australia and New Zealand. Elsewhere, forging a new model through some form of framework has been part of the rhetoric of reform but in practice has failed to materialise. Relying on declarations of intent is old-fashioned in an age when action (i.e., reform activity) is what counts. Sweden engaged in 'too much talk and too little action' in both major phases of reform (Premfors, 1998, pp. 15–2), a feature even more evident in Norway (in contrast to its two Nordic neighbours, Finland carried out a comprehensive review of its reforms: Pollitt et al., 1997).

The process of major change is more likely to result from a period of fairly steady change over time, with adjustments made on the basis of experience and contingencies. There are different tasks to perform in moving to, working through and implementing reform. A distinction can be made between changes that contribute to the development of a new paradigm, including facilitating processes of change, and those which serve to implement the new framework, including the employment of new techniques to support the framework (Halligan, 1996; Halligan and Power, 1992).

Reform by Design or Faith?

In the past, the reform process typically featured an inquiry that reported to the government. In Australia this was the Royal Commission on Australian Government Administration (1976) and in New Zealand, the 1962 Royal Commission. The commission also has a long tradition in Scandinavia (Arter, 1999).

The broad pattern seems to involve the decline of certain mechanisms and the increasing use of others. The Royal Commission (the more prestigious body along with the commission of inquiry, which had a statutory basis and special powers) was dispensed with in New Zealand after a 1988 inquiry, 'whose lack of success may have generated the perception that such inquiries are not effective for policy development'. But committees of inquiry, particularly ones that reported to the minister, continued to exist (Easton, 1994). The use of the public commission for policy formulation has declined in Norway, with internal task forces taking the lead (Lægreid and Roness, 1999, p. 314). Australia also favoured various types of task force, but under political direction and not confined to public servants, and cross-departmental mechanisms driven centrally (e.g. the Management Advisory Board).

Because of the impossibility of rationally planning on a comprehensive scale, great advances require faith – a belief in the 'great leap forward'. Some of the main reforms of the 1980s involved leaps into the unknown and were driven more by faith than evaluated experience. The New Zealand model, fabricated from economics but lacking a sound basis in organisational and political reality, was the most ambitious case (Scott, 1996). It is now acknowledged to have failed to take into account the unpredictable influences of the plitical environment.

Style of Discourse

Major initiatives also heightened the need for subsequent rationalisation, with the role and commitment of key players being of supreme importance. In Australia, following their appointments, respectively, as secretaries of finance and prime minister and cabinet, Michael Keating and Mike Codd assumed responsibility for and became closely identified with the main strands of the reform programme in the late 1980s: Codd with restructuring and with overall management direction; Keating with financial management and managerialism in general. Both responded to the critiques of the programme and maintained campaigns to sell and justify the changes (Codd, 1991; Keating and Holmes,

1990). Similarly, in New Zealand Graham Scott, who went from his position as head of Treasury to become an international consultant, continued to argue the case for the mid-1980 reforms (Scott, 1996).

John Power (1994, p. 1) makes the Lindblomian observation that 'the intellectual quality of any discourse on public service reform is of much less policy significance than the shape of the interactions through which the discourse takes place'. Where discourse is confined 'to small, closed professional elites intent on the reform of their own practices', the result will be retrospective, often rationalising pre-existing commitments. Where there is wide and public canvassing of options prior to finalising commitments, prospective policy can be developed.

The traditional response since Haldane was that of the lawyer's: 'reform should be preceded by a formal inquiry (often a royal commission) which would as a matter of course invite submissions from interested parties'. Power terms this type of process prospective policymaking. Following the gathering and review of evidence, the sequence involves making recommendations – hence prospective – and only then are decisions made and implementation proceeds (1994, pp. 1–2).

The Task Force on Management Improvement observed that the 1970s represented the decade of inquiries into public service reform and the 1980s that of public service reform, but the relationship between the two decades remained unclear (J. Power, 1994, p. 3). In contrast, reform era processes distinguished by an emphasis on the traditional mode were 'replaced by a more retrospective mode of policymaking'. The examples of this retrospective mode included the *The Australian Public Service Reformed* (1993), issued by the Task Force on Management Improvement, which provided both an evaluation and progress report and pointers to further agendas.

Overview of New Reform Processes

Several distinctions can be drawn between traditional processes and those of the reform era. The traditional processes were more likely to be consensual and to feature the public service. The 'new style' of process is top-down, conflictual and involves major commitment to ideas and concepts that may be untested, certainly in new contexts. Table 4.1 shows some differences between the old and new styles. It cannot cover the full range of variation, owing to the complexities of long-term systemic reform mentioned earlier. Reform processes in New Zealand, for example, provide the strongest examples of decision-making by a secretive elite and the exclusion of interests from policy processes as prescribed by public choice theory, but in contrast to traditional practice, which was more participative.

Table 4.1 Old and new styles of process

Dimension	Old style/Traditional	New style
Direction	Top-down and bottom-up	Top-down
Mode	Consensual or consultative Compromise and bargaining	Conflictual Directed
Process	Public process/Broadly based	Private process/ Narrow elite
Character	Incremental, sectoral and cautious	Comprehensive, systemic, faith in bold ideas
Key advisers	Internal public service advisers	Private sector advisers Ministerial advisers
Implementation	Centralised (decentralised in Scandinavia)	Decentralised
Review mechanisms/ Reform initiatives	Commission of inquiry	Task force Ministerial
Review of reform initiatives	Not applicable	Quasi-independent review Parliamentary review
Stance	Reflective	Active/instrumental

The drive to implement and therefore validate the reforms may impair the capacity to reflect on them. For reform to be successful, it must involve high commitment and focus. This precludes reflection that is in conflict with the fundamental direction of change. Reflection is more likely with lower orders of reform that do not threaten the fundamental tenets of the emerging paradigm. Sustaining both commitment to reform and reflection on it appears to be difficult at the system level and may therefore be associated with different stages.

The relationship between the intensity of change and reflective capacity is important. At certain points in the reform process both Australia and New Zealand apparently lost much of their ability for reflection as the reform machine moved relentlessly on. However, as Olsen (1996) makes clear, the entrenched Norwegian system is not particularly good at learning from experience either.

Perhaps not surprisingly, the divergences between the old and new styles, while explicit, are not as great as they appear at first sight. Traditional reform was also inclined to be top-down. The new reform approach is often less coherent and planned at the outset than it might appear retrospectively or once it has been fashioned into a 'framework'. There remains scope for negotiation and variation during implementation, but the major principles are fixed. Similarly, the limits to learning apply to most countries and approaches. In Norway, for example, 'the consensus was so strong that few found it necessary to *study* the effects of alternative forms' (Olsen, 1996).

To look at the variations in the aptitudes of countries to engage in 'new-style' reform we need to return to the other major dimension of the trans-formative approach. In Sweden, and particularly Norway, there has been a problem with reform direction. In Norway, it was 'difficult for reformers to document precisely what the reform needs are, to formulate clear goals, and to say exactly what is to be accomplished' (Olsen, 1996, p. 198). The Swedish cabinet (and broader labour movement) was unable to reconcile the divergence between three reform positions at the time of the first major attempt at reform (Premfors, 1998, p. 150).

The weak centres of government under the Norwegian and Swedish models have been important (see Chapter 2). Norwegian 'administrative policy' was largely a product of 'processes and events in numerous institutional arenas, rather than the result of a coherent, comprehensive strategy' (Olsen, 1996). The existence of a coalition government in Sweden meant that the Swedish experiment with comprehensive reform was subject to inter-party deals, something not unknown in Australia and New Zealand but not so potent, but it was still more 'action-prone' than the Norwegian government. Norway's 'communal political culture' is based on compromise and bargaining (Christensen and Peters, 1999, p. 156; Olsen, 1996).

Finally, Sweden's highly decentralised system had historically always been a significant feature, even before NPM emerged in the 1980s. So much of the state is concentrated at the local level that there is not much to managerialise (Lane, 1997; Premfors, 1998).

The Costs of the Reform Process

Moving a complex administrative machine requires large investments of time, resources and energy. Reformers invariably underestimate the length of time it takes for major reform to take hold, particularly since they are normally pursuing multiple objectives which place conflicting demands on those affected by implementation. Moving from a tradition that valued permanence and durability to one that espouses the short term and change has important implications for the reform process.

One consequence of the commitment to continuous change is the transience of much reform. A lesson is that success with major reform does not remove the need to change echoing one of the lessons of popular management – e.g., Osborne and Gaebler 1992; Crainer 1997 – that the reported cases of excellence and reinvention experienced short lives. Comprehensively reformed systems have continued to evolve rapidly: a decade after the new approaches to public management took shape in the 1980s, both the Australian and New Zealand administrative systems have been substantially replaced by a different type of framework.

The transient nature of reform is a product of the failures and limitations of implementation and even more so of the contagion of change ideology ranging from the drive to bring about continuous improvement from day to day to the compulsion of new governments to leave their mark by introducing change.

Other costs, including transaction costs, may also be high. The New Zealand drive to achieve full accountability for results had its price, for 'the contractual model goes further than managerial reform in demanding accountability in the public secto ...it exacts a substantial cost for achieving efficiency in output production'. The demands of accountability overloaded departments with substantial costs that escalated as the requirements increased and required far more resources than previously (Schick, 1996, pp. 26, 83–4).

The importance of rhetoric and symbols in reform is well established (March and Olsen, 1989). However, just as they are essential in launching major reform, so they continue to be necessary in extended reform processes to justify continuing action. The implementation of comprehensive reform inevitably appears to require, in particular, asset sales and dramatic cuts in public service employment in support of politicians' pursuit of short-term budgetary and fiscal objectives as visible indicators of change (e.g. the 'budget surplus').

Ultimately, the question of costs is an imponderable. The unpredictable dimensions of organisational change are well documented (March, 1981) and the unintended consequences of ambitious reform processes have been increasingly examined (e.g. Gregory, 1998c; Halligan, 1997a). However, such costs cannot be explored here beyond noting the effects in New Zealand on the quality of economic policy advice, the legitimacy of the system of government and the long-term durability of the radical reforms which by 2000 had become vulnerable (Bayliss, 1994; Goldfinch, 1998). Moreover, there are a number of problems in evaluating reform processes, and the debate over the effects of reform continues (Boston, 2000; Halligan, 1997a; Pollitt and Bouckaert, 2000).

Conclusion

The reform process presents distinctive challenges for large public administrations comprising multi-organisational systems. Translating approaches developed at the organisational level to a broader public sector can present difficulties because of the transformative complexities of the larger system. There are limitations on the rational approaches advocated in the organisational literature, particularly with model development that is not sufficiently grounded empirically.

If reform initiatives of the past failed during implementation, it would appear that more recent successful reform is generally the result not of a specific activity or a single plan but rather of a series of actions that may add up to a coherent programme. There is now considerable evidence to suggest that in complex organisational contexts major reform occurs in a series of stages where both external and internal factors have a role to play (see Chapter 2). The reform process typically involves major initiatives followed by more incremental change and implementation.

The relationship between reform style and reform results (degree of reform) is direct: reform involving significant departures from tradition requires particular styles (directive and possibly conflictual). There are significant differences between old-style and new-style processes but also, as might be expected, some interesting similarities. The experiences of the Scandinavian and Antipodean countries reflect differences in the reform process that can be accounted for by state traditions and other factors of the transformative approach.

THE TRANSFORMATION
OF ADMINISTRATIVE SYSTEMS
- EFFECTS OF NPM

5 New Public Management – Undermining Political Control?

TOM CHRISTENSEN AND PER LÆGREID

Introduction

Political-administrative systems in Western democracies are based on a complex and often ambiguous set of norms and values related to political-administrative control, codes of professional behaviour, due process and government by rules, democratic responsibility, public service ethics and participation of affected groups (Olsen, 1997a). This complexity of multi-functional modern civil service systems has in the last two decades been challenged by New Public Management (NPM), a reform wave spreading fast around the world, which offers a universal economic model of governance and efficiency and which will potentially have a major and similar impact on public organisations wherever it is applied (Røvik, 1996 and 1998).

In this chapter we concentrate on one set of effects and implications of NPM – namely, the effects of devolution and contracts – two of the central reform elements – on political control at the central level. In order to do this we combine theoretical ideas and empirical studies. Against the background of reform content and reform processes, we ask whether the reform wave may undermine democratic control by politicians over the civil service, over public enterprises and over public decision-making processes.[1]

Some main questions are: Can NPM be seen as a consistent reform furthering a decrease in political control and increasing administrative influence and institutional autonomy? Or is NPM an inconsistent reform package with elements pointing in different directions – i.e., with some elements undermining political control and others strengthening it? What are the consequences for decision-making processes of paying greater attention to economic considerations and values? Does devolution undermine the potential for political control and does contracting cause political-administrative relationships to be based more on individual accountability and adaptation strategies than on collective, political responsibility?

To illustrate our discussion we will contrast some reform features in three countries – Australia, New Zealand and Norway – without intending to compare these countries in any broad or systematic way.[2] The empirical basis in the case of Australia and New Zealand is extensive reviews of existing studies of reforms, and interviews and meetings with researchers and civil servants. The data from Norway is taken from various sources, including intensive reform studies, but one main element is a large survey done in 1996 of 2,500 respondents in executive positions and above in the central civil service (Christensen and Lægreid, 1998a).

Transformation, Hybridisation and Ambiguity

As discussed in Chapter 2, NPM is seen by some as a one-dimensional and global concept characterised by consistent ideas, but our analysis is more based on the growing scepticism about this (Hood, 1995a and b; Rhodes, 1999). We see the content of NPM as consisting of potential inconsistencies, a tension between centralizing and decentralizing economic ideas. But NPM could also be seen as consisting of more specific instruments and programs, brought in to solve problems with old ones. There is therefore also a tension on a more specific level within the concept between elements of central political-administrative control and local administrative and institutional autonomy. We hightlight this tension by focusing on two main features of NPM: reform measures intended to bring about more autonomy through devolution; and reform measures intended to enhance centralised control through various kinds of contracts. The relationship between political control and administrative/institutional autonomy is discussed with regard to the question of accountability and responsibility, with the aim of summarising some of the main possible negative and positive effects of NPM on political governance.

It is evident from our discussion in Chapter 2 that NPM is hybrid, complex and inconsistent, both in its main ideas and in its more specific reform instruments (Aucoin, 1990; Yeatman, 1997). It was shown that the three countries studied chose to combine different theoretical and practical elements of NPM in their reforms, meaning that the degree of hybridisation varied, a feature that makes an analysis of the effects on political governance more rewarding. New Zealand experienced a more theoretically oriented reform wave, with more intensive use of most NPM elements, while Australia started out with a more pragmatic and reluctant approach to devolution and focused on the centralising elements, a feature that changed in the 1990s. In the 1980s Australian managerialism was dominated by importing modern theory of firm and business practice into the public sector. Market arguments and contractualism gained more currency later. Norway has dragged its feet over reform for all of the past two decades, showing another type of tension and hybridisation – i.e., between old and new administrative doctrines– which was stronger in Norway than in the other two countries (Christensen and Lægreid, 1998a).

The basis for seeing the effects of NPM as an inconsistent reform wave is both the content of NPM as such and specific features of the reform process in the three countries. As discussed in Chapter 2, we regard both the process and effects of reform from a transformative perspective. This perspective emphasises that global reform ideas change when they spread, especially when they meet and meld with national cultural and polity features. Variety in environmental conditions and national contexts help to explain the discretion of political leaders in undertaking reform and therefore the variety in reform content, process and effects (Brunsson and Olsen, 1993; Cheung, 1997; Olsen, 1992; Olsen and Peters, 1996a).

It was the combination of an internationally related economic crisis in both countries and political entrepreneurship that made Australia and New Zealand embark on substantial reform processes in 1983/84, and in both cases the reforms were initiated by labour governments (Campbell and Halligan, 1992). But they chose somewhat different paths concerning the speed, scope and content of civil service reforms, with New Zealand adopting a more aggressive, sweeping and headlong approach, while Australia initially chose a more gradual and consensus-oriented style, though this weakened over time (Castles et al., 1996a; Mascarenhas, 1996a). Australia started early on the NPM path but moved more slowly. This was explained by cultural traditions and a political structure related to Australia's corporatism and federalism. The New Zealand reform path was defined by a combination of elective dictatorship and deep economic crisis (Mulgan, 1992). In Norway the reforms (which took place mainly while the Labour Party was in power) started later and proceeded in a more reluctant way, though they picked up speed in the mid-1990s; but they were still rather limited by New Zealand standards (Lægreid and Roness, 2001; Olsen, 1996). This was due to the absence of an economic crisis, strong state and corporatist traditions, parliamentary turbulence, and other factors.

Devolution: More Autonomy and Power for the Managers?

Devolution can take many forms, but one main idea is to strengthen the discretionary power of managers and give subordinate levels and agencies more autonomy (Grønlie and Selle, 1998; OECD, 1996b). Devolution is different from political decentralisation, where authority is delegated to elected representatives (Pollitt, Birchall and Putnam, 1998). A distinction can be drawn between two types of devolution, both of which we discuss. Managerial devolution entails empowering managers, separating political and administrative functions, or separating administrative functions within the same organisation. Structural devolution entails a transfer of authority down-wards in the hierarchy between different organisational forms, either between existing organisations or to new subordinate governmental organisations. When discussing how strong the devolution element in NPM is in the three countries studied it is important to be aware that they started out from very different positions. New Zealand was in the early 1980s a relatively centralised country while Norway was more decentralised (Pollitt and Bouckaert, 2000).

Separating Political and Administrative Functions

The economic way of thinking in NPM points to an almost generally accepted axiom in certain circles: that it is more efficient to separate political and administrative functions than have them integrated, as traditionally has been the case in most countries (Boston et al., 1996, p. 4). The argument is that a division between these functions makes it clearer that they are different functions with different actors – that the politicians should set the goals and the civil servants implement the policies. It is also often connected to the idea of decentralisation – namely, that decision-making should be moved closer to customers and clients, though it is unclear whether this should apply only to the less important administrative decisions. New Zealand, for example, has modified an integrated model, where ministers and top civil servants strive for a co-operative relationship that recognises their joint interests, into a purchaser/producer model where political and managerial roles are more clearly institutionally separated. This is most evident for the non-core institutions like State Owned Enterprises and Crown Entities.

One argument in favour of a sharper division between politics and administration is that an integrated solution makes politicians vulnerable to influence and pressure from civil servants, that civil servants threaten to invade the political sphere and that a stricter separation of functions makes it easier to control the civil service. This was the background to the reform in Australia in the early 1980s (Campbell and Halligan, 1992). By hiving off parts of the civil service, political control from a distance was to become less ambiguous and more effective. An additional argument was that such a separation would increase both political control and administrative discretion at the same time, creating better policies and services in the public sector.

A discussion of the effects of separation of functions for political control pinpoints many different arguments. First, very few practitioners or re-searchers would argue that politicians and civil servants should do the same job. But that said, there are many ways to define their functions, from bureaucrats-turned-politicians at one extreme to apolitical, technocratic civil servants at the other (Christensen, 1991). Second, it is not easy to accept that a differentiated solution will maximise the influence of both politicians and the civil service. Instead, one could forcefully argue that formal organisational changes always tilt the pattern of influence in one direction or the other. This is also one reason why public reorganisation processes are often characterised by conflict (Christensen and Lægreid, 1998c).

Third, the one central difference between an integrated and a segregated solution is that the former combines potentially tight control of the civil service with easy access for the bureaucrats to the political leadership, while the latter combines potentially weaker control of the civil service with poorer access of the bureaucrats to the political leadership (Egeberg, 1989b). This illustrates that any structural solution has both advantages and disadvantages.

A crucial question concerning political control is also whether there is accordance in priorities, norms and values between political and admini-strative leaders. In this respect it seems less politically problematic to separate political and administrative functions at the central level in Norway, for example, where this accordance is rather high (Christensen, 1991; Christensen and Egeberg, 1997).

Separating Administrative Functions by Creating New Units

Another form of structural devolution, found in many countries that have implemented NPM-related reforms, is the differentiation of administrative functions by structural separation. Functions that have traditionally been organised together, such as policy advice, regulative tasks, ownership functions, control functions, and purchaser/provider functions are separated into distinct units. This can be seen as the result of a sharper division between political and administrative functions. New Zealand is the most typical example of this type of structural change, adopting the principle of single-purpose or single-mission organisations (Boston et al., 1996, p. 13, pp. 58–66 and 77–80). Arguments for this solution are that it enhances effectiveness and efficiency by clarifying the administrative functions and avoiding overlap and ambiguous coupling of functions that blur the lines of command and authority.

It is worth noting that Australia chose a more integrated solution in the machinery of government questions than New Zealand, through the creation of mega-departments in the late 1980s. The potential result is the centralisation of decision-making power (Stewart and Kimber, 1996), despite measures to separate political and administrative functions earlier in the same decade. In Norway the tendency in the 1990s has been to separate the surveillance and regulating functions from the production and service functions by establishing independent control authorities.

One possible effect of such strong administrative specialisation of functions is an increase in the need for co-ordination, because there is more fragmentation in the system. Another effect could be that the new specialised units will grow by adding tasks they have lost through specialisation – e.g., purchaser units might add policy advice functions. All this could potentially lead to an increase in the number of civil servants and resources used. But this feature could be changed by politically controlled cutback. New Zealand has, as one of few countries, cut down on the number of civil servants at the central level, even though some resources have been moved down to lower levels and institutions (Gregory, 1998a). Decreasing size may imply less capacity to control and co-ordinate subordinate institutions and enterprises created through devolution.

Vertical Inter-Organisational Specialisation

A third form of structural devolution related to NPM, and coupled to the other two mentioned, is the tendency towards vertical inter-organisational specialisation. Many countries are changing their main organisational political-administrative forms or moving units to organisational forms that are further away from the central political leadership.

Economic arguments for this structural devolution are based on a kind of deterministic logic. Global pressure to co-operate and compete in new ways is pointing in the direction of more market competition and vast change processes that a single country or administrative unit cannot easily cope with. They have to adjust to this development by bringing about more structural devolution of commercial functions to meet the increased competition. This is a reflection also of the axiom that politics and business should be separated, and that private actors are better market actors than public ones. So, the most effective way of doing business for the public sector is either to create organisational forms that attend more systematically to commercial functions or to let private actors take over some of the public commercial functions (Boston et al., 1996).

There are many varieties of this form of devolution. The coupling of economic values and devolution through vertical inter-organisational specialisation is most clearly seen in the reforms in New Zealand, both in the corporatisation and privatisation processes. Early in the reform process it was stated that the government should not be involved in activities that could be performed more efficiently by non-governmental bodies (Boston et al., 1996, p. 4). First, this meant more focus on the economic or commercial aspects of public policies. Second, it implied that these aspects should be differentiated from other aspects, like more general societal and sector-political considerations. Third, it defined the government as an actor not well equipped for handling commercial activities.

Through the reforms Australia came up with the concept of political management that indicated a wish to combine political control with managerialism and centralisation with decentralisation and devolution (Campbell and Halligan, 1992, pp. 39–41 and 203). An analysis of devolution in Australia in an early phase, when it focused on budgetary and financial management reform, indicates that Australia managed to combine enhanced flexibility and devolution with better central control (Keating and Holmes, 1990). The strengthening of the political leadership started in the 1970s, with more resources for the cabinet and the ministers, alternative policy advice, more support from the political parties, a gradual politicisation of the appointment of top civil servants and more emphasis on political priorities and directives. The 1980s brought more corporate identity and collective strategy, more central financial co-ordination through cabinet reforms and the Expenditure Review Committee, more control by the prime minister and his chief ministers over other ministers and civil servants, the creation of mega-departments and more focus on personnel management closer to the political leadership (Halligan, 1996). The management elements were evident in the establishment of a senior executive service, changes in financial management, more emphasis on clear goals and strategies, programme budgeting and efficiency scrutinies. This was combined with more devolution from the core departments to the line departments and further down the hierarchy, exemplified by increased commercialisation of public activities and more privatisation in the 1990s (Guthrie and Parker, 1998). Taken together, this resulted in a move towards management culture. Painter (1997, p. 148) points to the fact that Australia's public sector was transformed by focusing on market efficiency as the ultimate standard. It started out with a focus on 'efficiency in government' in the 1980s, but moved on in the 1990s to 'efficiency of government'. Commercialisation of public enterprises was followed by contracting out and privatisation.

Norway is in the 1990s gradually transferring more decision-making authority and autonomy from ministries and agencies to independent subordinate bodies and within ministries and agencies to lower levels of management (Lægreid and Roness, 1998). Some administrative units have been reorganised as foundations, while others have been changed into state-owned companies. The argument is that this kind of structural devolution will enhance both competitiveness and governance. This development can be seen as a device for a defensive state – i.e., devolution is a necessary instrument for protecting the core of the welfare state (Grønlie, 1998). Some of the agencies whose status has changed are quite large – e.g., the national telephone company, the postal service and the state railways. When asked in a survey about the significance of changing the inter-organisational structure in the direction indicated, only a quarter of Norwegian civil servants in ministries and central agencies said the significance was high in their own field of work, indicating gradual reform and reluctant reactions (Christensen and Lægreid, 1999a).

Counter-arguments to some of the economic arguments behind structural devolution might be that political and commercial functions in many countries for a long time have been integrated without many problems, that the public sector gains a lot of money from commercial activities and that these should be kept there for collective purposes, and that it is important for the public sector to control and regulate economic activities, including by ownership.

Structural Devolution and Political Control

The main idea of structural devolution is that political and commercial activities should be separated organisationally, leading to the establishment of different organisational forms of control. The aim is to devolve functions that don't need to be controlled politically and to keep politically important tasks under central control. Together with greater transparency this is intended to allow 'more steering in big issues and less steering in small issues'. We argue that this is easier in theory than in practice and that the result might easily be less political control, both formally and in reality.

Reforms based on such ideas have taken place primarily in the communications sector. The changes are driven by a combination of actors: political and administrative leaders convinced that increased competition enhances control and efficiency simultaneously; institutional leaders who would like to see both increased discretion and a more commercial profile; and private actors who see new business options.

Devolution is inspired by the slogan 'let the managers manage', meaning discretion for managers and boards and not too much daily interference from the political leaders. The implication of this slogan is that chief executives are better at managing and therefore should be given the discretion and opportunity to do so, thereby reducing the burden on the political leadership and, through a sharp division between politics and administration, increase political control. But one could also argue that the slogan reflects an anti-political trend, potentially undermining political control. 'Let the managers manage' may mean that managers gain more resources, tasks and responsibility, making it less legitimate for the politician to interfere in their business. And structural devolution often means less capacity for central political control.

One obvious effect of increased structural devolution of commercial functions is both a slimmer core and generally a slimmer public sector, due to cuts in the workforce in public enterprises and to privatisation (Gregory, 1998a). Another effect is growing structural complexity or hybrid forms, because there are new combinations of political and commercial interests built into new public units.

But does increased structural devolution undermine political control, regardless of whether it is efficient? One main argument for answering 'yes' is that structural devolution changes the instruments of control and increases the distance between the political leadership and subordinate units and lower levels of management (Egeberg, 1989b). This logic is based on the notion of erecting new structural barriers or limits. Surveys in the Norwegian civil service have shown, for example, that civil servants in central agencies outside the ministries see political signals and considerations as significantly less important for decision-making than bureaucrats in the ministries (Christensen and Egeberg, 1997; Christensen and Lægreid, 1998a). The more structurally separated civil servants are from the political leadership, the greater the importance of other decision signals – like cost-efficiency, professional norms, user and customer interests – probably meaning that actors in public enterprises and comparable units will attend even less to political signals. A report on public ownership in Norway indicates that, even though public companies are formally supposed to take into consideration general or sectoral political signals, in reality they pay increasing attention to commercial interests (Statskonsult, 1998).

The main lesson is therefore that structural devolution potentially means a decrease in the central capacity for control and in the authority to exercise control and less attention to political considerations in subordinate units, especially market-oriented units (Mascarenhas, 1996b, p. 69). There is a tendency to define political involvement in public enterprises as 'inappropriate' interference in business matters.

One elaboration on this line of reasoning is that even commercial activities in the public sector are subject to political control and that it is up to the political leadership to politicise their function and develop active control. This could be done by politically appointed agency leaders, like in the United States, or by using more actively the different control instruments, such as laws and rules, regulatory bodies, boards, the annual general assembly or informal contact. Active public ownership of commercial activities may often depend, however, on the control exercised by top civil servants on behalf of political leaders. This could potentially weaken the political leadership, either by giving top bureaucrats an independent power base or through public corporations' making alliances with the administrative leadership.

New Zealand is a kind of extreme case regarding structural change, because it chose to combine strong horizontal specialisation with strong vertical specialisation. Boston et al. (1996, p. 13, pp. 87–89 and 353–355) argue that in New Zealand devolution has had a certain dual effect. One the one hand, the separation of non-commercial and commercial functions, highlighted in the establishment of public enterprises, is said to be efficient and to secure accountability, even though it is designed to weaken political control (Evans et al., 1996). On the other hand, some Crown entities, in competition with private actors, have made political control and co-ordination more problematic and lines of authority more ambiguous, and this has made it more difficult to secure collective interests. In addition to this there are the costs of change, which in general have been large.

Australia has a similar profile concerning structural devolution, but chose another, much more integrated horizontal solution in the machinery of government. Sixteen core departments were established, so-called mega-departments, and this feature supported Hawkes' policy of strengthening the integrative features of the cabinet (Campbell and Halligan, 1992, pp. 16–20).

Compared with a more fragmented solution this probably strengthened the influence of the political leadership, both with regard to top civil servants in the central agencies and departments and as a counterbalance to the subordinate institutions and commercial entities. On the other hand, megadepartments are complex units to control as policy instruments.

There are different ways to see the effects of these development trends in Australia. One view, based on a political-democratic perspective and focus on the parliamentary chain (Olsen, 1983), is that structural devolution, commercialisation and privatisation, especially in the 1990s, generally weakened the central political leadership, even though its control over the core of the public sector was still rather strong. An alternative view might underline that the Australian reforms meant a strengthening of the central strategic and control capacity overall and that the reform altered, but did not substantially weaken, the role of the central civil service. And indeed, structural devolution, commercialisation and privatisation may change rather than obviously weaken political control. In such a system the control tasks are of a more regulatory nature, attending to social goals, while direct control over service provision is left to the market, a view that perceives democracy as direct and consumer-oriented.

Norway has chosen a structural reform path more similar to Australia than to New Zealand. The emphasis is more on the moderate horizontal specialisation of ministries, although there is nothing like mega-departments. Regarding structural devolution Norway has been more reluctant than both Australia and New Zealand. This has resulted in more emphasis on political control and centralisation than in the other two countries. It is also worth mentioning that there is generally less to devolve in Norway and Australia, because of, respectively, a large local government sector and strong federal features.

There are some interesting parallels between Norway and Australia concerning the devolution of state commercial units. Both countries have a very long tradition of statutory corporations (Australia) and state-owned companies (Norway), forms that historically very much attended to political control of commercial activities (Grønlie, 1998; Wettenhall, 1998b). In the late 1980s and early 1990s these traditional forms were transformed in both countries, so that the commercial aspects received more emphasis and the political ones less. But in Australia the 'new' government-owned company form is different in some respects from the Norwegian: it is more explicit concerning contracts for securing general or sectoral collective interests; ownership is split between the portfolio minister and the minister of finance;

and some companies are more designed for future privatisation. In these respects they fall somewhere between the Norwegian and New Zealand models.

Structural devolution raises questions about the development of control systems. When the political leadership decentralises decision-making authority or the authority to administer and implement, whether through structural devolution or not, how should control systems be designed? One solution is systematically to use regulatory bodies, laws, rules and formal meetings as instruments to control subordinate units and activities. This may modify capacity problems for the political leadership by transferring more of the burden to civil servants, but it may also in itself create extra work because there are more instruments of control to attend to (Christensen and Lægreid, 1998a). A possible disadvantage is that such systems are often in reality more formal than real control instruments – i.e., the political levers do not work. Another is that such systems may be controlled primarily by administrative leaders. This implies that professional control may dominate, a solution that is more reassuring if political and professional norms and values are compatible, but less so if there are conflicts and cleavages. Mutual understanding, trust and shared norms and values between the political leadership, the central administrative leadership and possibly the institutional/commercial leadership in subordinate public organisations may replace formal systems of control with informal ones. Another solution to the control problem is contracting, which we now turn to.

Contracting: A Device for More Political Control?

The price for more devolution, flexibility, autonomy and discretionary power for managers in many countries is a more formal, rigid, hierarchical control system that makes extensive use of contracts. The idea is that detailed control should be relaxed and that the contract system should permit better central capacity for control of more important issues. Through contracts political leaders are supposed to specify targets and objectives more clearly, and performance is to be controlled by use of quantitative indicators for monitoring results and measuring efficiency. The audit explosion has potentially strong elements of centralisation and implies an increased focus on formal and external management by numbers at the expense of more traditional internal and informal forms of control based on trust (Power, 1994).

The integrated concept of the New Zealand model of administrative reform is government by contract (Schick, 1998). Most of the reform elements have been designed to enhance contract-like relationships between the government and ministers, on the one hand, and subordinate entities, including institutions and individual leaders, on the other. New Zealand has gone to extraordinary lengths to create conditions under which formal contracts are negotiated and enforced. Australia also started out in the late 1980s with microeconomic reforms aimed at 'government failure' (Painter, 1997, pp. 149–150). Extensive use of contracting-out was evident, inspired by economic thinking and supported as attacking 'vested interests'.

In contrast, contract systems have very little significance for civil servants in the Norwegian central administration (Christensen and Lægreid, 1998b). In 1996 only 9 percent of civil servants reported that contract systems had great significance in their own field of work. In contrast to New Zealand, the contract element in the Norwegian civil service is more agency specific than individually oriented. One example of this is a soft version of contracting adopted in Norway, which uses management-by-objective-and-result (MBOR). This system is based on the principle that subsidiary bodies should be given more autonomy in selecting appropriate means and more flexibility in the use of financial resources in exchange for more control through performance assessments. The MBOR system was put into practice through budget reforms in the mid-1980s and activity planning in the early 1990s and was followed up partly through reforms of salary systems. One effect of this system, when adapted to financial management, was that it enhanced autonomy to a greater extent than central control (Ørnsrud, 2000).

One type of contract affects functions that traditionally have been removed from competition, such as policy advice (Boston et al., 1996, p. 6). In all three countries studied, a major source of policy advice to political leaders has traditionally been permanent top civil servants, who provide professional expertise. But Australia and New Zealand now allow contracting out some parts of such advice, leading in theory to competition between private consulting firms employing former civil servants and permanent secretaries and other administrative leaders (Martin, 1998, pp. 71–95). Contracting policy advice blurs an increasing use of lobbying and adds complexity to the political interchange between political leaders and interest groups.

One reason for such contracts is obviously to weaken the bureaucracy and strengthen the political leadership, something that can be achieved if private consultants primarily tell political leaders what they want to hear. But another, less cynical reason is actually to increase the quality of advice and the variety of decision premises, so that political leaders receive well-documented alternatives to the advice of administrative leaders. However, it is quite likely that this way of organising policy advice will create ambiguity and undermine the political leadership. Private actors and administrative leaders can establish networks and alliances that work against the political leadership, a tendency seen in the United States (Christensen and Peters, 1999). Private actors can deliver advice that is a poorly disguised solution favouring interest and pressure groups and probably does not increase the quality of decision premises. What is more, trust between political and administrative leaders can diminish through competing policy advice. Contracting out policy advice thus has clear limits. It is not likely to enhance the efficiency or effectiveness with which policy advice is produced. There is a greater risk of opportunistic behaviour by the suppliers of advice and a greater problem with respect to policy co-ordination (Boston, 1994b, p. 1).

The case of contracting out of policy advice in New Zealand and Australia illustrates the limits of contracts in a political-administrative system. The reform is meant to enhance governments' control over their advisers, but may potentially end up diminishing that control. Political uncertainties, such as changes of ministers or governments, will increase the problems of external contracting and there are potentially negative consequences for maintaining trust between ministers and advisers (Boston, 1995a, p. 98).

Another type of contracting, which is important in New Zealand but almost absent in the Norwegian state administration, is the contract between the government as a purchaser of output and the agency as a provider and supplier. The argument is that contracts enhance both efficiency and accountability because they combine market competition with a more rigid performance control system. Dividing politics and business by use of contracts and statements of corporate intent is supposed to make it easier for public enterprises to compete, easier to compare efficiency in the public and private sector and in different public bodies, and easier to attract market expertise. These are arguments often put forward in analysis of the effects of the contract reforms in New Zealand (Boston et al., 1996; Nagel, 1997).

But dividing well-functioning public bodies into organisational units with ownership, provider and purchaser roles might lead to a weakening of public expertise, increased use of resources through the employment of more people than before, a reduction in co-operative relationships, the hiring of expensive private consultants and possible tendencies towards private monopolies or cartels. And the evidence that increased competition and the use of contracts produces better services and lower prices is inconclusive.

A third type of contracting, used in Australia and New Zealand, is competition for auditing, leading to a structural division in the audit organisations between an administrative unit and a unit conducting the practical auditing in competition with private firms (Guthrie and Parker, 1998). This way of organising auditing may lead to questions about the independence and neutrality of the auditing process, even though the public audit capacity is still rather strong. This is especially the case for a new type of auditing which is gaining in importance – namely, performance auditing, which invites more typically political processes, alliance building and discretionary power in the auditing process.

A fourth type of contracting, as an element of NPM, concerns recruitment and employment, whereby increased use of individual, short-time contracts, replaces more permanent employment based on collective agreements. This is a result of a more competitive labour market both inside the civil service and between the public and private sectors, leading to less frequent compensation according to position and seniority and more market-based pay and pay-for-performance systems and to less interest in membership in labour unions and more use of private consultants and lawyers for negotiating wages. This type of contracting is most visible in New Zealand but is also evident in Australia (Yeatman, 1998). NPM has in this way also participated in changing the demography of the civil service, or some parts of it. Examples are the dominance and spread of economists in the civil service, originating in the Treasury in the two countries, advocating more models of economic rationalism (Campbell and Halligan, 1992, p. 105). Even Norway has introduced a light version of the individual contract system for top civil servants, with more devolution, flexibility, market pay and pay-for-performance elements. In practice, however, there has been a reluctance in Norway to make active use of this new pay system, especially when it comes to individual contracts and the pay-for-performance element (Lægreid, 1994, 1997). The system became a test case for the consensus on administrative reforms in Norway.

What are the effects of individual contracts for political control? One view is that these features strengthen political control, because political leaders may politicise the recruitment of administrative leaders and make them more directly responsible, undermining traditional merit principles (Boston et al., 1991). Chief executives appointed on contracts may be more reluctant to give 'frank and fearless' advice to politicians. In addition, the incentive structure, with a widening gap between administrative leaders and civil servants on lower levels, is increasing the political loyalty of the top bureaucrats. Campbell and Halligan (1992, p. 31) conclude that one effect of NPM-related reforms is that politicians and top bureaucrats in Australia live more in a symbiosis, because of the higher salary and status of the administrative leaders, especially those in the core central agencies with economic competence.

An argument against individual contracts for top civil servants is that they imply, but make it difficult to formulate, specific objectives and performance indicators for these kinds of positions, a feature traditionally less emphasised. Another argument is that individual contracts increase competition and conflicts between institutions, groups and individuals. A third argument is that politicised recruitment may turn out to weaken the political leadership, a point put forward to explain why Australia embarked on the reform path it took. The newly recruited administrative elite of economists is said to have convinced political leaders of the new direction of reform.

Moreover, in practice contracts are not normally formulated or controlled by political leaders but by administrative leaders, as exemplified in New Zealand. Individual contracts might also reflect a weakening of political control through the undermining of political responsibility and of the collective identity and public ethos of administrative leaders (Boston et al., 1996, p. 87). While the commitment of top civil servants traditionally has been based on a long-term, institutional and collective sentiment with high political loyalty, now the situation is characterised more by strategic, short-term, individual incentives for executive officers who shop around in search of the agencies which can offer the best contract. This might lead to an undermining of political control, less continuity in public institutions and poorer professional expertise. The new type of administrative leaders are less dependent on the political leadership in many ways.

But one can also argue that these features can be modified in various ways. Top civil servants can have close formal or informal connections to the political leadership and thus execute more control on their behalf. And less ambiguous measures and goals in written contracts may make it easier for political leaders to intervene and use incentives, related to performance-oriented contracts, for example.

Gregory (1998b) emphasises that the reforms in New Zealand are moving the political process in a more technocratic direction. The traditional egalitarian culture, gradually undermined by economic reforms, has been replaced by a more elitist one, furthered by a new class of well-paid top bureaucrats with private sector attitudes, who are generally sceptical about political processes and control. Accountability is more managerial than political (Nagel, 1997). Schwartz (1994), in comparing state reorganisations involving typical NPM features in Australia, Denmark, New Zealand and Sweden, concludes that the politicians have lost influence while the top bureaucrats, among them the fiscal bureaucrats, are the winners. One general lesson is that the new contract regimes adopted for top civil servants do not necessarily follow the intentions of the architects of reform (Hood, 1998b, p. 443).

One lesson from Norway is that introducing the MBOR technique made it difficult for politicians to live up to their obligation to define unambiguous, stable and consistent objectives and to evaluate thoroughly the results. MBOR has been more successful as a technique for administrative control of subordinate agencies than as a tool for improving political governance and control (Christensen and Lægreid, 1998a). This may reflect the fact that contract arrangements complicate the role of civil servants as policy advisers and that increasing emphasis on managerial control reduces the possibilities for political governance (Ingraham, 1996; Mascarenhas, 1990; Peters, 1996a).

One important question of principle about the use of contracts is whether they should be used, in a strictly legal sense, for any kind of task in the core civil service, or whether they should be used in a more differentiated fashion, primarily in selected sectors. The discussion about policy advice highlights this problem. A big issue in New Zealand has been whether contracts should be used in areas like health, social work and conservation. The argument is that reformers in New Zealand have failed to discriminate intelligently, when using contracts, between different types of core public departments with differing functions and tasks (Gregory, 1995a).

The Ambiguity of Accountability and Responsibility

An important aspect of administrative reform is the issue of political control and accountability of senior civil servants. With its principles of accountability based on output, competition, transparency and contractual relations, NPM represents a departure from 'old public administration', where accountability was based upon process, hierarchical control, trust and cultural traditions. There has been a development from simple to complex models of accountability (Day and Klein, 1987). The traditional notion of accountability, namely, top-down authority responsible to the people through elected policymakers, is challenged by the twin emphasis on customers and results, which makes administrators focus downwards, towards citizens, rather than upwards towards elected officials.

In administrative reforms such as NPM, much attention has been paid to managerial accountability with very sparse consideration of political responsibility. By managerial accountability we mean the obligation to provide an account of one's actions *to* those in superordinate positions of authority. Responsibility, on the other hand, is accepted *for* actions performed by oneself or others and is a more subjectively felt sense of obligation (Gregory, 1995a, p. 60). This means that accountability might be a necessary component of responsibility but not the only one. To be responsible connotes the ability to act as well as simply to report and implies concern for the consequences of this action. There is a moral flavour missing from accountability (Martin, 1997a).

March and Olsen (1989) emphasise the same difference by making a distinction between aggregative and integrative processes in public organisations. Civil servants will in integrative processes have a feeling of belonging, a shared history and traditions that make it easier to have a sense of integration, obligations and a common purpose and to act appropriately (March, 1994). In aggregative processes actors are more atomised and do not have a sense of integration; they need incentives to act in certain ways. Instead of being socialised into an administrative culture and a code of ethics, they are disciplined to change their behaviour by use of various kinds of formal motivation (Lægreid and Olsen, 1984).

There are at least two facets to this question. First, how are senior civil servants themselves to be accountable; and second, how can ministers best be provided with political analysis and advice to support their policy-making activities? On the one hand, managerial accountability may have improved in the New Zealand government. On the other hand, the reforms have led to fragmentation of the public sector and the acceptance of political responsibility by ministers has been attenuated. The problem of 'many hands' (Thompson, 1980) has grown. The conceptual distinctions drawn by the reform with regard to the roles of minister and chief executive are amply clear on paper, but they fail in practice. The ambiguity of responsibility becomes especially clear when things go wrong (Gregory, 1998b). This means that the reduction in political responsibility would need to be balanced against possible gains in effectiveness and efficiency (Boston et al., 1996, p. 360).

A preoccupation with efficiency tends to overvalue the need for managerial accountability rather than promote political responsibility. Efficiency is no guarantor of good political and social judgement, which is essential in securing genuine political responsibility and legitimacy (Gregory, 1998b). The pursuit of accountability can exact a price in the decline of a sense of responsibility. Basing accountability on *ex ante* specification of performance can have unanticipated consequences, such as when unspecified matters escape accountability. This problem will not be remedied by more detailed indicators of performance. Rather, the solution may have to come from embracing a responsibility model (Schick, 1996, p. 87).

There is an in-built inconsistency in NPM. The model is supposed to increase the influence of elected politicians over the bureaucracy, while at the same time reducing their responsibility for the bureaucracy's actions. One of the greatest concerns in administrative reforms is the balancing of freedom and accountability (Dunn, 1997, p. 35). The traditional bureaucratic model, with little freedom or accountability for results but much responsibility for following rules, has been an extraordinarily successful and durable model of public administration. Today, public administrators around the world are seeking greater freedom but they are also more anxious to obtain greater accountability. A system that extends freedom to managers without strengthening their accountability undermines the power of politicians and is inferior to the traditional, bureaucratic model of administration. A reform that involves an imbalance between freedom and accountability is dysfunctional. The system will not work well if officials are given freedom without clear expectations about performance (Scott, 1996, p. 89).

At the same time, there is a basic dilemma in all large organisations: Can you have greater accountability (read control) and more proactivity (read freedom) simultaneously? Some say 'yes', because they see a flexible, transparent control system as better than the old bureaucratic one; others definitely say 'no' to this argument and underline the advantages of the traditional system (Gregory, 1997, p. 96). More emphasis on entrepreneurial behaviour by administrative leaders is likely to make central co-ordination and control more difficult.

There might be a 'zone of indifference' (Simon, 1957) in which bureaucrats might operate with great autonomy. If, however, they exceed a certain limit, politicians might tighten up political control. This means that the relationship between politicians and bureaucrats might be more a pattern of ebb-and-flow than a linear development towards less political control. NPM ideas about decentralisation, devolution and consequent fragmentation create a need for greater co-ordination and control in order to ensure policy coherence in government (Hart, 1998, p. 286; Peters and Savoie, 1995, p. 17). Giving public managers more authority to manage programmes might result in ministers' gaining greater capacity for setting central discretion and priorities, so as to resolve problems of loss of control over policy implementation raised by NPM reforms (Maor, 1999). And shrinking the institutional capacity of the central bureaucracy might enhance the power of political leaders. Managerialism may allow executives to exercise greater control over its agencies, but it is greater control over a smaller domain (Davis, 1997).

It is, however, a paradox that, while administrative reform has become more comprehensive, it has also become more problematic for the political leadership to meet the requirements of a rationally planned reform process (Lægreid and Roness, 1999). In order to understand this paradox it is necessary to consider the fact that time, energy and attention are scare resources for political leaders.

In Australia public sector reforms have caused worries over accountability, with a special focus on the distinctive character of public accountability and on the role of the public interest in the world of Australian public administration (Uhr, 1999). There is an underlying tension between the accountability standards of traditional public administration and contemporary public management (Shergold, 1997). Minson (1998, p. 49) states that:

> Today, 'formal external standards' have come to the fore. Around Australia, public sector ethics are undergoing codification. In general, these ethics reforms seem bent on renewing rather than displacing the traditional ethos of office. Why should this reaffirmation be necessary, at this time and on this scale, if new managerialism had not made many of the old safeguards against maladministration ambiguous, irrelevant and questionable?

In Norway and New Zealand there has traditionally been a doctrine of ministerial responsibility, which states that the minister takes the political blame as well as the credit for the actions of the administrators, who must remain anonymous and beyond credit or blame. The administrative reforms have enhanced public knowledge of the identity and policies of many senior civil servants and separated ministers further from the administrative process, and thus challenged this doctrine. In New Zealand the administrative reforms may have altered the doctrine of ministerial responsibility, while a new version of accountability has developed based upon contractual relationships between ministers and their chief executives (McLay, 1995, p. 197 and 205). Accountability by contracts is based on the idea of opportunistic behaviour, whereby people learn to distrust each other. This might make control more visible but it is an open question whether this is a better form of control than the old internal control based on trust.

Transforming the Civil Service through NPM – In Some Countries More than Others

The transformative perspective outlined in Chapter 2 identifies several dimensions for explaining the background of public reform, the reform content and the effects and implications of reform. The latter aspect is especially emphasised in this chapter. The environmental-deterministic dimension in a more technical sense, exemplified by the economic crisis, is important in explaining why New Zealand's leaders set the reform wave in motion and probably also explains partly why they chose a radical reform path. Later, however, the reforms in New Zealand seemed to take on a more ideological character, with economic ideas of dismantling and rolling back the state dominating the institutional environment. New Zealand became a test case for NPM supported by the OECD, a success story that gained a myth status; and New Zealand was able to lean on that myth when designing and implementing its reforms. The reinforcing character of this myth also seems to have been important for the development of reforms in Australia, even though the content of reform in Australia was different to that in New Zealand in many respects.

The environment for reform was less threatening in Norway than in the other two countries (Christensen and Lægreid, 1998b). No obvious economic crisis was looming that could justify a reform wave, and support for the public sector was high in the 1970s and early 1980s, even though more questions than before were being asked about the efficiency of the civil service. This resulted in a slow and late start for the reforms and when they got underway in the late 1980s their content was less extreme.

Moving to the more national or internal dimension, both the structural and cultural variables show a complex and puzzling picture. There are major similarities among the three countries in their advanced welfare states, in the structure of their political-administrative systems, in their political and administrative culture, in their corporatist traditions, and in the strength and ideology of the labour parties – all features that led one to expect gradual reforms. But there are also some differences, which may explain different reform paths, such as the importance of the Westminster model in Australia and New Zealand, the federative features of Australia, and the structural and cultural homogeneity of Norway (Christensen and Peters, 1999). It is especially puzzling that labour governments in Australia and New Zealand started the NPM-related reforms (Castles et al., 1996a), while in Norway the Labour Party was much more reluctant, like labour parties in many other countries at that time.

The economic crisis seems to explain why New Zealand started on a reform path at all, but the internal conditions do not easily explain why this was an extreme path (Goldfinch, 1998). On the contrary, one would have expected the reforms to be more incremental and less influenced by simplistic economic models, because of their lack of compatibility with the political-administrative culture and because none of the major reforms were mandated by the public. But once the radical path had been taken it was understandable, given the Westminster system, a tradition of centralisation and weak counter-vailing forces, that the reforms were forcefully implemented, without too much attention to the sentiments of the general public. A small group among the strategically located institutional elite led by the Treasury was the driving force behind the reform. There was no effective opposition within the bureau-cracy, cabinet and caucus, and the reforms were carried out by two different governing parties (Goldfinch, 1998; Nagel, 1998). It is, however, puzzling that the economists in the Treasury gained so much influence over the strong political leaders who were important for driving the process (Pallot, 1998).

An evaluation of the New Zealand experiment concludes that organi-sational performance has been enhanced but also that there are several problems (Schick, 1996, 1998). Chief executives attribute most of the improvement in government performance to the discretion given to managers through devolution rather than through formal contracts. What is more, enforcing contracts entails high transaction costs. Another side-effect is that contracts sometimes enhance self-interest at the expense of the government's collective interest. Reforms based on a narrow economistic view of human behaviour in organisations may change officials' behaviour in that direction. They may be expected to behave as if they were untrustworthy, self-seeking, opportunistic and morally unscrupulous (Gregory, 1995a, p. 71).

Contractualism may also weaken traditional values of public service, personal responsibility and professionalism. There are fears that the quality of policy advice and of policy services might deteriorate and that the level of policy co-ordination has been reduced (Scott et al., 1990; Verheijen, 1998). It can allow managers to take a checklist approach to accountability– i.e., 'if it is not specified, it is not my responsibility' (Schick, 1998, p. 126). Some empirical research indicates that a more legalistic mentality might be emerging among senior civil servants in New Zealand, owing to the introduction of contractualism (Gregory, 1998b). The reforms may threaten the social capital of public service and render it more difficult to sustain public service as a community of trust over time (Gregory, 1999). The extent to which NPM is likely to induce corrosion of ethical capital in public service remains to be systematically tested (Hood, 1991, p. 16), but there are some indications of increasing ethically problematic behaviour.

Australia's administrative reforms seem mainly to be explained by a variety of internal factors. The Labour Party needed to come to power again, after many years without major political influence, and public reforms were one of the instruments for doing so. It saw the need for redefining political and administrative roles and this influenced heavily the reform path taken, meaning less early emphasis on the economic and commercial aspects of reform than in New Zealand. The heterogeneity of the federal system in Australia was a potential obstacle to reform, in that it made control of implementation difficult, but it could also further reform by building on radical reform elements in the states with parallel political-administrative systems. Potential obstacles to reform were also the corporate traditions and the tension between factions in the Labour Party. But senior officials embraced the main tenets of economic rationalism (Pusey, 1991). In addition, a strong prime minister as a reform entrepreneur created momentum for the reform by fostering a collective leadership feeling and winning over the leaders of the trade unions, who reluctantly accepted reform as necessary for getting the Labour Party back into office (Campbell and Halligan, 1992). The prime minister chose, surprisingly to many who had supported the Labour Party in the election, a reform direction more heavily influenced by economists in the Treasury than was thought possible considering the party's traditions and election programme.

The Australian case is further complicated by the fact that the solutions to issues concerning the machinery of government were partly copied from Britain, while other reform elements, such as some of the commercial elements that came later, imitated some states in Australia and New Zealand. All this complexity makes it difficult to gain a clear impression of the reform effects (Campbell and Halligan, 1992, p. 35; Verheijen, 1998, p. 274).

The cases of Australia and New Zealand show that radical reforms do not necessarily produce better results, even in economic respects. The advantage of the Australian option over the New Zealand option is that co-ordination is less likely to be a problem than in the more fragmented New Zealand system. The gradual introduction of reforms combined with attempts to obtain broad consensus on their introduction seems to have had a positive effect in Australia (Verheijen, 1998). One lesson from Australia is that, paradoxically, increased political control has led to a reduction in control over the system (Halligan, 1997c). The key reform objective of political control was to break the civil service monopoly over political development and advice and to redistribute power within the executive branch in favour of the political executive. The result has probably been a loss of control over public policy due to a loss of confidence in the competence of the state.

Norway scores low on both external and internal factors triggering reform. The absence of an economic crisis together with strong confidence in an active and large public sector makes for relatively low external pressure. This, combined with parliamentary turbulence, minority governments, reforms driven internally by bureaucrats and a traditional administrative culture probably incompatible with many NPM elements, might explain why Norway started late with the NPM-related reforms and chose an incremental path. But the reforms – both the management reforms and structural devolution – gained more momentum in Norway in the 1990s, so far with few of the privatising elements used in Australia and New Zealand. There seem to be both internal and external reasons for this development. It is of importance that the Labour Party has been through a soul-searching period, struggling with its traditional identity, and has now come out more in favour of NPM reforms, which has also lead to some changes in the attitudes of the associated trade unions. Norway's gradual adaptation to the EU through the EEA treaty, pressure from OECD and a more strongly felt globalisation process have also lead to more acceptance of the NPM reform ideas than before.

Studies of NPM in the Norwegian civil service emphasise that reactions are reluctant, clustered and varied (Christensen and Lægreid, 1998b and 1999a). They are reluctant in the sense that few reform elements are seen as significant and having effects, and clustered because management elements are seen as much more significant than structural and market-oriented reforms, even though relatively few see any major fulfilment of the goals attached. They are varied because NPM is generally more favoured by administrative leaders than by executive officers, and more by staff and development personnel than by executive officers having traditional judicial functions. Recent years have brought more emphasis on structural devolution of commercial activities in Norway, and this has clearly led to more confusion about new political and administrative roles and a potential undermining of traditional political control. Political control of such activities is formally strong, but in practice seen as inappropriate, a tendency furthered by international myths connected with NPM (Statskonsult, 1998).

Conclusion – Less Political Control and Less Good Governance?

Our general conclusion is that the dividing line between management and politics has moved further in favour of management in New Zealand and Australia than in Norway (Pollitt and Bouckaert, 2000). NPM-related reforms, especially in the extreme version seen in New Zealand, have created more scepticism towards collective solutions, a de-politicisation of the public sector and increasing conflicts over what is public (Boston et al., 1996, pp. 356–357). The reforms have changed the instruments of control to make them more numerous, economically oriented, elaborate, formal and transparent, but probably also less realistic in facing a complicated public sector characterised by numerous interests, differing considerations and ambiguous goals. Devolution seems to have decreased political control over the most non-core, commercial institutions, like public companies, and this has often been by design, as in New Zealand and Australia in the 1990s. Decreased control over non-core units through devolution might indirectly lead to a decrease in control over the core civil service too, but a variety of factors may modify this tendency. In Australia 'political management' was a way of trying to strengthen the central, collective capacity of the executive, while New Zealand has a small core and emphasis on performance control and transparency, something that might enhance political control in some ways.

These effects seem to be the result of many interweaving factors. First, the global ideological dominance of economic norms and values connected with NPM has substantially changed political-administrative culture, especially in countries like New Zealand with weak countervailing forces. Second, this dominance has been coupled with strong arguments favouring increased horizontal and vertical specialisation of the public apparatus. The combination of these two types of specialisation has paved the way for structural devolution of commercial units and activities, meaning more fragmentation and less political control generally and over commercial activities specifically. Third, NPM has generally increased competition and the use of contracts, thereby changing the relationship between political leaders and subordinate institutions and individual actors.

There are different ways to see the effects of these NPM development trends. Our main view, based on a sovereign rationality-bounded state and the parliamentary chain (Olsen, 1988), is that they are hollowing out political-democratic control in a centralised state (Weller et al., 1997). They are obviously catering more to the ideas of the supermarket state, where the state is a service provider and the public is viewed as sovereign consumers or clients (Christensen, 1999). There is also a possibility that more use of formal, legal contracts may result in a return to a more juridical public service with more use of rules, rights and the use of the law court. This might also constrain the use of political governance through majority rule.

While NPM reforms in New Zealand have followed a radical path enhancing the supermarket state model and those in Australia have taken a more pragmatic path inspired by the same model, Norway has chosen a more moderate reform path, building on the sovereign rationality-bounded state model and traditional political-administrative norms and values and less on international trends. This 'modified modernity' has tried to implement reforms more gradually and in a more balanced way, making some changes in the direction of structural devolution and contracts, while keeping political control at the centre and making moderate changes in the central political and administrative roles.

From these different models of political control of public bureaucracy follow a number of alternative views on the effects and implications of NPM, underscoring the message that new governmental systems and structures seldom have only one type of consequence. One interpretation proceeds from the premise that NPM is a reflection of an international crisis in the public sector, encompassing economic problems, inertia and structural problems, decreasing trust and problems with service quality. This has led to an emphasis on economic values and norms and to devolution of commercial activities, competition or contracts. According to this argument, NPM has helped many countries, like New Zealand and Australia, to regain their economic strength and to be more effective and efficient in many respects (Evans et al., 1996, Scott, 1996). The relationship between reforms and economic parameters is, however, highly debatable. Some will argue that New Zealand, for example, is economically worse off now than it might have been without the reforms, while others will say that it remains economically weak and vulnerable in spite of the reforms.

Another argument sees NPM reforms as a response to a need to clarify and strengthen political control. Political processes are said to have become too complex, political leaders are experiencing capacity problems, administrative leaders are gaining influence and the government is involved in too many activities. In this situation the role of political leaders must be narrowed down and made less ambiguous. This role implies a smaller public sector, more devolution of commercial activities and competition and a clearer definition of the roles of political and administrative leaders through contracts and incentive systems. This is said to result in stronger political control, even though what the political leaders now claim to control has become narrower. The control is also changing qualitatively, because the emphasis is more on general, long-term policy development and guidelines and less on short-term specific political involvement.

One lesson from NPM reforms is that a rigid and comprehensive system of performance indicators with strong efforts to monitor and evaluate output might strengthen superior administrative control. Whether this will also enhance political control and good government is, however, an open question. NPM has replaced a system based on mutual trust among civil servants on different levels and between politicians and administrators with a system that potentially furthers distrust. The main idea of NPM is that, as long as the external incentives are right, good governance is guaranteed whatever the character of individuals. NPM has been characterised as a 'worst-case scenario' of institutional design which makes no assumptions about solidarity, shared collective identity or democratic attitudes among civil servants (Olsen, 1997b, pp. 222–224). In contrast, the 'old public administration' argues that without officials who are civic-minded and self-restrained, good government is impossible. It is difficult to construct workable democratic administrative institutions in a civil service where the bureaucrats are driven solely by external incentives and private benefits. There is, therefore, a need to go beyond the assumption of the worst-case scenario and take more interest in how administrative reform shapes the mentality, character and identity of individuals and collectives. In this respect there is an interesting dualism in NPM. On the one hand, it is based on theoretical models which build on the maximisation of self-interest. On the other hand, it builds on the idea that man's mentality and culture can and ought to be changed.

Notes

1   The focus is on the relation between politicians and top civil servants in ministries and central agencies, and chief executives in state owned enterprises and Crown Entities. This means that the role of parliamentarians and the role of other civil servants is discussed only to a limited degree.

2   We have no intention to analyse the effects of reforms in all the states in Australia, even though there is a lot of interesting variety between them. By Australia we mean here the federal level, the Commonwealth.

6 The Effects of Corporatisation on Political Control

HANS ROBERT ZUNA

Introduction

From around 1980 onwards a large number of government enterprises in the states of the Organisation for Economic Co-operation and Development (OECD) were converted into various forms of company. The status of these enterprises changed from being part of the administrative apparatus of the state to that of autonomous judicial entities owned by the state, with company structures similar to those used in the private sector. The stock company seems to be the main model, so the term *corporatisation* is used to denote this type of public reform (Spicer et al., 1996, p. 1).

Two essential characteristics define government enterprises. First, they are public in the sense that they are either part of or owned by the state through the ministries. Second, they engage in commercial activities – i.e., they produce goods and services for sale. While sometimes a government's main motive for engaging in such activities may be (like that of private entrepreneurs) the maximisation of profits, more often government enterprises are hybrids in the sense that their purpose is to achieve dual political and commercial goals (Farazmand, 1996, p. 1). For instance, one task of the Norwegian government owned forestry enterprise is to cater for the environment, while government owned broadcasting enterprises are widely responsible for programming that promotes the national culture.

The wave of corporatisation that has taken place throughout the OECD was primarily motivated by the wish to improve efficiency and has most often been evaluated on this basis. G.C. Scott (1996, p. 23), for instance, claims that the reforms have produced considerable efficiency gains in New Zealand, and Spicer et al. (1996) support this conclusion. However, the theme of this chapter is the impact of this reform on the political control of government enterprises. Researchers in the area have pinpointed the balance between political control and managerial autonomy as a central problem in government enterprises (Grønlie, 1998; Mascarenhas, 1996b). In order to gain efficiency,

121

increasing managerial autonomy has been deemed necessary and company forms are designed to secure this autonomy. Control is to be secured through deregulated markets, but also through strategic political control. In fact, total political control is to be kept intact or improved at the same time as increasing managerial autonomy (Grønlie, 1998; Spicer et al., 1996). The question is whether political control is really maintained when government enterprises are converted to company forms with increased autonomy.

Corporatisation is intended to change the relationship between the political authorities and government enterprises via the establishment of new formal rules. However important they are, formal rules are not likely to be the only dimension influencing political control of government enterprises. The transformative perspective, which we use here, regards the dynamic reform context as of considerable significance for the effects of the reforms on political control.

By comparing corporatisation in two countries a system dimension is created in addition to the temporal dimension obtained from following developments during the periods before and after corporatisation. The two countries, Norway and New Zealand, have been chosen because of the profound differences in their reform paths. This makes it possible to use a broad range of empirical variations in the discussion. Norway and New Zealand use different corporate forms and started from different initial positions. Before 1984, New Zealand relied heavily on ministerial departments to run government enterprises (Boston et al., 1996, p. 77). The reforms changed the organisation of government enterprises in a fundamental way, mainly by introducing a new form, the State-Owned Enterprise (SOE). The commercial parts of the ministries' functions were separated out and converted into this form. The new SOEs are stock companies and are subject to the SOE-act. In Norway, government enterprises were organised at sub-departmental level as agencies from the 1960s onwards. As in New Zealand there has been a significant degree of corporatisation in Norway over the past two decades, using both existing corporate forms and new ones. In both countries one main justification for corporatisation has been to improve efficiency by increasing managerial autonomy.

A Transformative Perspective

The notion that *formal structures* can influence behaviour is the prima facie of classical organisational and constitutional theory (Egeberg, 1994; Gulick,

1937; Scott, 1998; Simon, 1961; Weber, 1971). Corporatisation implies a change in formal structures and is thus expected to influence control of enterprises. The notion of control is a broad one. It includes setting the enterprises' objectives or giving other forms of directions as well as monitoring enterprise affairs in order to ensure the fulfilment of these directions.

The main feature of the transformative perspective is that the reform's effects on political control also depend on the influence of other external and internal dimensions (see Chapter 2; Christensen and Lægreid, 1998a; and Peters, 1996b). The dimensions included in this perspective are drawn from an institutional research tradition in sociology and political science (March and Olsen, 1989, 1995; Peters, 1999a; Scott, 1995, 1998). This reform context is regarded as dynamic in the sense that the dimensions also have a propensity for change. Constitutional reforms change the polity in which reform takes place, good times turn bad and so on.

For the purpose of analysis, internal dimensions are separated from external dimensions by the organisational boundaries of the political administrative system. The external dimensions are contested by institutional theory in political science, since this tradition has evolved in opposition to contextual approaches (Olsen, 1988b). However, the environment is seen as of vital importance in the neo-institutional approach in sociology (DiMaggio and Powell, 1983; Scott, 1998) and also in institutional economics (North, 1990; Scott, 1998, p. 133), where organisations are regarded as closely embedded in society and the economy (Peters, 1999a, p. 102). Environmental influence has been divided into technical and institutional aspects however, with reciprocal effects likely between these categories (Scott, 1998).[1]

Technical environments are seen as exerting regulative pressure on organisational output – i.e., the goods and services produced (Scott, 1998). In this perspective government enterprises and political authorities are rewarded with resources or input for production that meets the environment's demands or else sanctioned for deviance (Scott, 1995, pp. 35–37; Scott, 1998, pp. 131–133). The political-administrative apparatus faces demands for the output of government services and needs the input of resources to be able to deliver these. Three variables are investigated on the basis of this dimension: national financial pressure, societal pressure and market pressure.

Within neo-institutional theory, this conception of environments has been broadened to encompass *institutional environments*. This means the impact of values, norms and conceptions of reality generated in the environment (Berger and Luckmann, 1966; Meyer and Rowan, 1977; Scott, 1995). Values, ideas and knowledge are generated in a more or less global society and become accepted by governments through normative and cognitive mechanisms (Scott, 1995). In this dimension we first investigate how international trends in political ideology have changed and influenced the two states in question, paying special attention to the transition from economic interventionism to liberalism. Second, but closely linked to this first set of ideas, changes in administrative doctrine are important. Administrative doctrine – i.e., the body of principles stipulating how the civil service is to be organised – are seen as developing and changing in the course of international political and academic discourse. Possible changes in this environment have an impact not only on the reforms but also on civil service practice in the two countries.[2] The emergence of New Public Management (NPM) (Hood, 1991) is of special relevance at this point.

Internal dimensions include the polity within which reforms take place and what can be broadly labelled the political and administrative culture within the elected and administrative apparatus of the state (March and Olsen, 1989, 1995). *Polity* is an important internal dimension, stemming from the same theoretical traditions which emphasise formal structure. The term polity encompasses the formal constitutional and principal political-administrative organisation of the state. Political control is influenced by the polity at large, not only by the form of affiliation between government enterprises and the political authorities. Three principal features of the polity are discussed: the parliamentary system, the affiliation of government enterprises to different types of ministries and the degree of horizontal specialisation. The polity influences political-administrative behaviour by influencing the distribution of political power and focusing organisational attention (Egeberg, 1984; Simon, 1961).

Under the influence of these internal and external pressures a certain *political-administrative culture is likely to emerge* (Selznick, 1957). This culture might be unique to each enterprise or political authority but there may also be common traits within administrative systems, such as the civil service. This dimension enables us to include the significance of already existing or changing beliefs, values and conceptions of reality to the effects of the reforms. Such cultures are to a certain extent institutionalised (Selznick, 1957), making established traditions important determinants of behaviour. The mechanism called 'path dependency' implies that a reform's compatibility with an established culture is important for its effects (Wærness, 1990).

From a transformative perspective the effects of corporatisation are best seen as filtered through a set of institutional frames consisting of environments, polity and culture, as shown in Figure 6.1. Through their interaction with these dimensions the effects of corporatisation may be reinforced, weakened or changed. These dimensions are capable of transforming the effects of a certain reform, which is why the term 'transformative perspective' is used. For instance, traditionally ministerial cultures might be incompatible with the new rules for political control and thus reduce the effects of the reform. These dimensions affect both the scope for strategic action and political and administrative leaders' preferences and perceptions of reality.

Figure 6.1 The logic of a transformative perspective on corporatisation

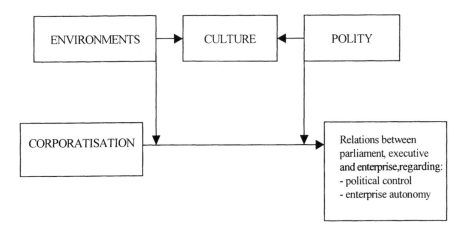

The Reform Context

By combining the dimensions in Figure 6.1 a broad theoretical basis for discussing the effects is obtained. We start out by sketching the various reform contexts and conclude by outlining the features of corporatisation in the two countries. This gives us the premises for a broad discussion of the effects of the reforms.

Environments

Technical environments. First, at a macro level national financial pressure involving income, debt and public expenditure – i.e., the available input – defines the financial constraints within which national politics can be conducted. Over time these financial constraints will probably influence what kind of control government enterprises are subject to. Scarcity enhances financial control, while a large degree of slack is likely to further broader objectives and looser control regimes.

When the reforms started in New Zealand in 1984, the political elite perceived the country to be in severe financial trouble (Easton, 1997, p. 244; Evans et al., 1996). Government trading enterprises accounted for 12 percent of GNP and 20 percent of investment and were also significant in a budgetary and debt context (Duncan, 1996; Spicer et al., 1996). Any improvement in their financial performance was expected to contribute substantially to alleviating the pressure of the deficit, so pruning public expenditure was an important objective of the reforms (Mascarenhas, 1999, p. 10). Later the economy has improved but is still not keeping pace with OECD-trends (Easton, 1997, p. 146; Roper, 1997, pp. 19–20). In Norway the discovery of oil in 1969 started to fuel the economy in the mid-1970s and at the same time the important shipyard industry generated good profits (Furre, 1993). Norway hade the highest growth in Europe from 1974 to 1980. Even if Norway did experience economic problems later on, they seem to have been less severe than in New Zealand and there was a total absence of any profound crisis like the one in New Zealand in 1984 (Hanisch et al., 1999). What is more, government enterprises did not occupy the same dominant position in the Norwegian economy.

Second, citizens are able to put pressure on the political system through organised interests and the election channel. This demand to the political authorities is likely to influence what kinds of control government enterprises are subjected to. Corporatisation in both Norway and New Zealand has had continuous support from the private sector corporate elite (Easton, 1997). Owing to the staff reductions that would obviously follow from corporatisation (Duncan, 1996), the unions were critical of these changes in New Zealand. The Norwegian unions were highly sceptical too, but having reached compromises with the Norwegian Labour Party they supported some of the changes. Unlike in New Zealand, the unions have always exercised control directly through the boards of government enterprises and continue to do so. In New Zealand corporatising government enterprises was among the earlier and more popular reforms, for it promised to improve the performance of units which were seen as highly inefficient by the general public. But as an issue that is low on the political agenda, government enterprises are not particularly subject to popular pressure in either country and do not play a significant role in elections.

Third, citizens are able to put local pressure on government enterprises through the market, and in this way also influence the leeway for control from above. In this last respect the deregulation of markets is highly relevant. In New Zealand substantial efforts have been made to expose the new SOEs to competitive environments in the same way as their private counterparts (Spicer et al., 1996, p. 47). Even though some monopolies are still held (Statskonsult, 1998, p. 18), the conversions in Norway have also been accompanied by increasing exposure to competition. Part of this deregulation is a result of pressure originating from Norway's associate membership of the European Union.

Institutional environments. The two states are both part of the OECD area. Within this area and particularly through the OECD and its Public Management Committee (PUMA), prescriptions for good government are collected and distributed among states (Lerdell and Sahlin-Andersson, 1997). In addition, bilateral communication between states, participation in international organisations and the internationalisation of political parties allows a measure of exchange of political ideologies.

Prior to the evolution of the 'new right' and NPM ideas in the late 1970s and the 1980s, a fundamentally different set of ideas dominated in the OECD area. These ideas had several characteristics, but of particular importance were their commitment to Keynesian interventionism and the notion of the welfare state, implying an academically and politically based belief in state interventionism. Traditional government enterprises are a legitimate child of these ideas, for they are hybrids between the state and the market (Mascarenhas, 1999, pp. 3–4). On the administrative side this meant faith in the machinery of government that emphasised the self-sufficiency of the public sector, direct control through hierarchies, upward accountability and a politically neutral public service (Peters and Wright, 1996).

The dominating trend since the late 1970s has been a critique of the size and the interventionist style of the public sector (Olsen, 1996, p. 186). The NPM movement is characterised by attempts to make the public sector into a modern welfare state functioning more like the private sector, which is perceived as more efficient. Among the academic foundations for this trend are recent economic theories of organisations, like property rights, transaction costs and agency theory (Mascarenhas, 1996a, p. 290). This implies increasing deregulation, privatisation, marketisation and the increasing use of contracts instead of traditional governmental hierarchical controls (Boston et al., 1996; see Chapter 2). One of the major features of NPM in the area of government enterprises is an imitation of their 'prettier sisters'– i.e., private companies competing in markets.

Certain differences between the two countries may have made New Zealand more receptive to these reform traits than Norway. Both NPM and neo-conservatism are of Anglo-American origin, and New Zealand has closer links with this Anglo-American tradition than Norway (Olsen and Peters, 1996b, pp. 17–18). In the first paper published by the New Zealand treasury on state-owned enterprises, twenty-three of the twenty-nine foreign references were American (Easton, 1997, p. 93).

Polity

In the Westminster model, which guides New Zealand constitutional practice, the electoral system, until 1996, was based on single constituencies. This 'first-past-the-post system' (Pollitt and Bouckaert, 2000) mostly generated majority governments in a two-party system. The implementation of a mixed electoral system based on the German model (MMP) in 1996 has changed this pattern, generating more parties and coalition governments. In contrast, Norway has had a proportional electoral system all along, generating a multi-party system mostly with minority governments. These differences are likely to influence the parliament's power relative to the executive and hence patterns of political control.

Norwegian government enterprises were, and still are, owned by or subordinated to the ministry responsible for the sector in which they operate. This sectional specialisation was also dominant in New Zealand before the reforms. However, the reforms concentrated ownership of all SOEs in the hands of the minister of finance and a responsible minister of state-owned enterprises. A unit called the Crown Company Monitoring and Advisory Unit (CCMAU) was established in 1993 to advise the shareholding ministers in setting objectives, appointing directors and monitoring performance (CCMAU, 1996). This unit is an extension of the Treasury (Mascarenhas, 1996a, p. 310). We discuss how these organisational variations might influence the effects of corporatisation.

Both polities are characterised by an increasingly horizontal specialisation of traditional government enterprises. Organisations, including government enterprises, are increasingly divided according to their functions. Government enterprises are increasingly focused on production, while regulation, and in New Zealand policy advice too, has been relocated (Boston et al., 1996; Stats-konsult, 1998). This increasing complexity is also likely to have consequences for the political control of government enterprises, since the scope of their activities may change and political control over them has been resituated.

Political and Administrative Culture

Norway belongs to a group of countries which derive their political culture from statist, public and legalistic traditions found in continental Europe (Olsen and Peters, 1996b). New Zealand, on the other hand, can be said to belong to an Anglo-Saxon tradition of government. In this tradition the government is seen as separate from society, and the civil society is seen as having primacy over the state (*ibid.*).

Among the Anglo-Saxon countries, however, New Zealand has probably had the most interventionist political culture. Geographical isolation and a small population legitimised extensive government involvement in the economy (Easton, 1997). Both the parties alternating in majority positions, the social-democratic New Zealand Labour Party (NZLP) and the conservative National Party (NP), were strongly inclined towards economic interventionism and traditional public sector management (Easton, 1997; Gustafson, 1997). After reforms were initiated in 1984 by the NZLP, both the dominant parties began to favour wide-ranging reforms based on economic liberalism and NPM ideas. A plausible explanation is that the outside pressures created by the technical and institutional environments led to a shift in the culture of the political elite in New Zealand, especially in the NZLP (Easton, 1997).

Agreement on these macro-political questions is far from total in Norway, making reforms a question of negotiation between a large number of political parties. The different positions are illustrated fairly well in their stances on corporatisation. In parliament the socialist parties and the agrarian party constitute an anti-devolutionary alliance, advocating continuous state interventionism (Grønlie, 1998, p. 81). The proponents of corporatisation are the liberal and conservative parties, which see it as a first step towards privatisation. The Labour Party is a more moderate reformer. It favours corporatisation of the most market-oriented enterprises, but more to secure continuous interventionism and a welfare-oriented public sector than to decrease the governmental apparatus. The Labour Party together with the anti-devolutionary alliance held a majority in parliament in the period when commercial devolution became a theme. Norwegian political culture can, therefore, not be said to have experienced a clear swing towards liberalism.

On the ministerial level in New Zealand, financial pressure and NPM-thinking, partly imported through the recruitment of reformist economists, seem to have changed the organisational culture in the Treasury and made the ministry strongly committed to NPM-thinking (Easton, 1997*)*. The CCMAU is characterised by the same profile, strengthening the commercial focus

(CCMAU interview; Spicer et al., 1996, p. 57). The pre-reform spread of ownership probably implied a greater variety of cultural influences on enterprise policies, in particular the effects of belonging to different policy sectors.

The Norwegian practice of continuing to divide ownership between different ministries gives reason to expect variations due to different ministerial cultures. In general, this administrative culture has gone through some modernisation in Norway too, marginally strengthening NPM elements. Christensen and Lægreid (1998a) show that such elements have not changed the culture in any fundamental way, but found their place among traditional elements. In 1996 fewer than 5 percent of civil servants saw privatisation and commercial devolution as reforms which should be given higher priority, although there are differences in orientation between the ministries (Christensen and Lægreid, 1998a, p. 155; Zuna, 1998).

In New Zealand a clear private sector recruitment profile has emerged in the new SOE management (Duncan, 1996). Combined with organisational forms and competitive environments similar to the private sector, this has contributed to the development of a commercial culture in corporate enterprises. In Norway, directors with business experience seem to have been considered a strength even in the pre-reform era (Grønlie, 1995, p. 119), but both members of the boards and CEs still have to a large extent gained their experience in public administration or politics. Adding to this picture is the permanent representation of labour unions on the boards. Even though the environments have created pressure towards changing corporate cultures, the public sector background might preserve the semi-public culture that existed in the old form of enterprise.

The Pattern of Reforms

The conversion to company forms is often presented as a novel reform, unique to the reform ideas that gained currency from approximately 1980 onwards. Such a view of corporatisation is not entirely accurate for New Zealand, but especially not for Norway. Both countries already had traditions of conducting government enterprise in corporate forms, although it was adopted in only relatively few cases in New Zealand (Boston et al., 1996, p. 65; Mascarenhas, 1999). Norway has a strong corporate tradition, which dates back to the 1920s and experienced a peak period in the two decades following World War II

(Grønlie, 1998, pp. 70–73). Bearing in mind these historical roots, we focus on the reforms after 1980.

The New Zealand Reforms

Despite flirting with company forms, New Zealand for the most part relied on ministerial departments for public enterprise. Insurance, postal services, telecommunications and the power supply, for instance, were organised as trading departments (Mascarenhas, 1999, p. 7; Wettenhall, 1995, p. 9). Non-departmental enterprises had a variety of corporate forms, depending on the historical situation (Easton, 1997). Railway and airline services, banking and oil extraction were among the enterprises organised in this way (Boston et al., 1996, pp. 65–66).

The performance of these traditional government enterprises was deemed inadequate and, given their dominant position, seen as a burden to a strained national economy (Mascarenhas, 1999, p. 6). In order to solve this problem the minister of finance launched a programme of seven principles for organising public enterprises in 1985 and 1987 (Wettenhall, 1995). These included removing non-commercial functions from trading organisations, making managers responsible for performance objectives set by ministers, removing competitive advantages, paying tax and shareholder dividends to the government and moving regulatory or policy functions to other organisations.

These policy objectives were mainly implemented through the SOE Act of 1986. The main direction of the reform in New Zealand has been converting commercial parts of existing government enterprises into SOEs on the basis of this act. Subsequently, many of these corporatised assets were privatised, a solution chosen mainly to reduce debts and because of doctrines that consider private ownership better than public (Mascarenhas, 1999). However, further commercialisation has added to the stock of SOE's, making the implications of this form for political control a matter of continuing relevance. As of July 1999, there were a total of nineteen SOEs, including airports, forestry, energy, post and radio and television (CCMAU, 1999).

The Norwegian Reforms

Government enterprises in Norway were traditionally organised at a sub-ministerial level. The principal sub-departmental form used was the directorate or agency. Despite being vertically specialised, this form had relatively tight links to the ministries. These units were judicially speaking government entities and thus subject to ministerial directions. Within this directorate form government enterprises were normally given enhanced budgetary leeway, and for this reason were called Central Administration Enterprises. Until 1980 major public activities organised in this way were railways, telecommunications, postal services, power, forestry, grain sales and public broadcasting.

As in New Zealand, corporate forms were also used for government enterprising even prior to the reforms. Some of these were stock companies, albeit with formal arrangements to secure increased departmental control and non-commercial objectives or functions. Others were companies specially designed by own laws to meet the need for certain kinds of activity. These traditional company forms included iron mills established in the years after World War II, parts of the defence industry, the monopolised part of the alcohol retail sales and the state-owned oil company.

The reform process in Norway has proceeded more incrementally than in New Zealand (Olsen, 1996). Corporatisation of government enterprises did not come about as a result of an isolated initiative but was coupled to changes in sectoral policy. A public committee on governance suggested such a piecemeal reform strategy (NOU 1989:5, pp. 5, 23). As in New Zealand, a new corporate form was launched during the period, called the State Enterprise (NOU 1991:8, p. 8).

There has been significant conversion from directorate forms to corporate forms during the last two decades. The stock company is the dominant form, but the state enterprise and special forms are still used. Railroads, postal services, telecommunications, public broadcasting, electricity production and distribution, grain sales, forestry, public food services and computing are among the directorates that have become various forms of company. Unlike in New Zealand, there are few examples of privatisation, leaving Norway with a considerable number of corporate forms when entering the new millennium.

For simplicity's sake, the following discussion addresses only the dominant patterns of corporatisation. In New Zealand this means the transition from trading departments to SOEs, and in Norway the conversion of Central Administration Enterprises to several almost equally dominant corporate forms. However, the Norwegian corporate forms have strong similarities with regard to political control and enterprise autonomy, enabling us to treat them en bloc for most of the discussion.

The Effects of Corporatisation from a Transformative Perspective

As shown, the reform context is highly dynamic, especially in New Zealand. The reforms are linked to economic crisis, the deregulation of markets, changing political and administrative ideas in an international society, a new electoral system and a renewal in the political and administrative culture. In Norway the changes in the reform context have been more modest. From a transformative perspective the effects of corporatisation are likely to be influenced by these differences in context. By using this perspective in the discussion on the consequences of corporatisation for political control, a broader perspective on the reforms than is normally used can be obtained. Both the opportunities and desire for political control are discussed. We start by looking at the use of government enterprises in order to analyse what happens to the content of political control after conversion to company forms. The next section analyses the means of control and how they are used.

The Use of Government Enterprises: Corporatising Objectives?

There was no formal regulation of the aims and objectives of government enterprises prior to the reforms, either in Norway or in New Zealand. Instead, they were determined on a case-by-case basis. In our view, the other dimensions identified in the transformative perspective will strongly influence how aims and objectives are determined in this absence of formal regulation.

In both countries government enterprises were generally regarded as multi-purpose organisations with a variety of objectives (Boston et al., 1996; NOU 1989:5, p. 5; Spicer et al., 1996). This follows from the strong interventionist and welfare tradition in their political cultures and institutional environments. For instance, public broadcasting companies in both countries had particular obligations concerning minorities and national culture. Government enterprises, especially in New Zealand, were also used to create jobs (Mascarenhas, 1996b). Such objectives might be interpreted as a reaction to societal pressure from the populace and as financially viable from the perspective of Keynesian demand-side economics. National financial pressure is, according to such a perspective, not necessarily an argument for reducing government involvement. Regulated markets often facilitated internal financing of non-commercial objectives through cross-subsidisation.

Administrative doctrine in the pre-reform era seems to have included a favourable view of multi-purpose organisations in both states. Delivery operations, commercial and non-commercial, were run in the same units as policy-making and regulatory functions (Boston et al., 1996; Duncan, 1996), emphasising self-sufficiency and the synergetic effects of integrated solutions. For instance, the Norwegian forestry enterprise was engaged in forestry on a commercial basis at the same time as issuing regulations in the commons and providing services in leisure areas. This multi-purpose organisation was also likely to be reinforced by the ministerial organisation, with sector ministries and specialists using the enterprises as a universal instrument for implementing sectoral policy.

The New Zealand State-Owned Enterprise Act of 1986 narrowed down the range of objectives and functions the government enterprises being converted would be allowed to have after the reform. Section 4 of the act states the principal objectives of the SOEs. They are to operate as successful businesses and to this end be as efficient and profitable as private businesses, they are to be good employers and exhibit social responsibility towards the society in which they operate. However, only the successful business objective is monitored through the formalised system (Spicer et al., 1996). Regulatory functions and policy advice seem to be totally excluded from the objectives of these enterprises after corporatisation. The commercialisation of objectives is stronger than expected from a strictly formal perspective. Being a good employer and undertaking social responsibility seem to be of less importance (Spicer et al., 1996, p. 15).[3] One reason for this may be that the new administrative doctrines, coming from the same pool of ideas, delegitimise multiple objectives and non-commercial objectives within government enterprises. Deregulation of markets reinforces this pressure, for the increased financial strain on the enterprises makes other objectives hard to achieve. Added to this is the fact that the newly established SOEs are linked to the Treasury, which is among the ministries most influenced by NPM doctrine. This doctrine highlights the importance of SOEs being put on an equal footing with private enterprises.

Beyond these commercial objectives, Section 7 of the SOE act states that the SOEs' non-commercial objectives are subject to due payment through contracts (Spicer et al., 1996, p. 16). The use of contracting between government and SOEs to secure production of non-commercial goods and services is thus supposed to be a substitute for the giving the enterprises non-commercial objectives. However, one criticism of the reforms has been that many non-commercial objectives are in reality lost (Duncan, 1996). For instance the Broadcasting Commission, set up to fund public service broadcasting by contracting, has been criticised for not being able to counter commercial pressures (Atkinson, 1997). From our perspective this may be explained by the lack of financial resources combined with increasing economic liberalism. The use of government enterprises for non-commercial purposes is hindered by a lack of resources, and the new ideologies have reduced the legitimate area of state intervention compared to the area of the market. While making provision for contracts is one thing, the material means and willingness include non-commercial objectives is another.

None of the Norwegian company forms have rules regulating objectives in government enterprises. This leads one to expect that corporatisation will not change their objectives and functions, and the general tendency is indeed for the political authorities to keep social or regional policy objectives integrated with commercial ones in government enterprises. For instance, according to the company clauses, the state-owned telecommunications company is still limited by regional considerations, and public broadcasting still has educational and cultural obligations. However, an increasing use of contracts to pay for these objectives may imply a tendency towards commercialisation of policy objectives. Significant change has also been effected by separating delivery and regulatory functions. This has taken place in the telecommunications, postal and railway sectors. The commercial parts of the enterprises have been corporatised, while the regulatory parts have retained the directorate form.

The retention of traditional non-commercial policy objectives within government enterprises may be accounted for by the absence in Norway of national fiscal pressures. This allows room for financing non-commercial objectives and is also likely to reduce the impact of new political ideologies or administrative doctrines, because they seem of limited relevance (Christensen and Lægreid, 1998a). However, some changes indicate a certain commercialisation of objectives once the company form has been chosen. The companies' success is increasingly judged in terms of commercial objectives (Statskonsult, 1998, pp. 21, 57), and contracting and procedures of payment for non-commercial objectives indicate the influence of NPM in Norwegian government enterprises. The deregulation of markets probably reinforces this tendency by making the internal financing of non-commercial objectives harder. There also seems to be some reluctance to combine delivery functions with regulatory functions within company forms. The company form thus seems to be institutionalised in the sense that expectations of a commercial orientation emerge once this form has been chosen. Nevertheless, the continued inclusion of non-commercial objectives within the enterprises suggests that the influence of institutionalised environments is limited compared to New Zealand. Furthermore, Norway has kept its system of linking government enterprises to their respective sector ministries, implying their continuing use as instruments for policy implementation.

The New Zealand reform was thus characterised by a strong commercialisation of objectives as a result of corporatisation. This was only in part a consequence of the SOE act, which was reinforced by fiscal stress and changing environments, polity and culture – i.e., dynamics in the other dimensions identified by the transformative perspective. Social policy objectives are increasingly perceived to be too expensive, and integrated solutions are perceived as a threat to effectiveness. The Norwegian case is more ambiguous. The fact that social policy objectives have continued to exist and provision made for them indicates that corporatisation does not necessarily change objectives. At the same time, the division of functions, increasing contractualisation and a tendency to overestimate the importance of commercial objectives points towards increasing commercialisation. Choosing an organisational form used in the private sector thus seems to have implications for perceptions of government enterprises. This illustrates the influence of institutionalised environments, in particular how NPM ideas tend to reinforce private sector ideals. The Norwegian experience seems to indicate that corporatisation inevitably leads to a strengthening of commercial objectives and delivery functions, despite internal dimensions that point in the opposite direction. Nevertheless this commercial tendency seems weaker than in New Zealand.

Improving or Losing Political Control: Structural Change in a Transformative Context

We have established that corporatisation, at least in New Zealand, but probably also in Norway, changes the content of political control towards more commercial objectives. The second stage is to discuss how the conversion to corporate forms affects the degree of political control, given these objectives.

The idea behind corporatisation is first that increasing autonomy secures improved realisation of given objectives, a form of 'letting the managers manage'. Second, corporatisation is often implemented parallel to the deregulation of markets. Thus, while consumer choice is thought to be an increasingly important control mechanism, the authorities is still to control the enterprise through their ownership position. The discussion here revolves around whether this political control is weakened.

New Zealand. The nature of a government's control over its enterprises is highly influenced by changes in formal structural arrangements. In this sense corporatisation in New Zealand has been far more radical than in Norway. The previous trading departments were strongly integrated in the executive, being formally led by a minister accountable to parliament, and there were no organisational boundaries between the minister and the enterprise. Influence and control were directly executed through the minister's formal position as head of the enterprise, the closest subordinate normally being a director general. In this position the minister formally had something akin to absolute power (Smith, 1997), indicating strong political control and low enterprise autonomy. This formal integration was likely to secure the necessary political control of enterprises and the pre-reform enterprises seem to have been subject to significant political interference (*ibid.*). However, the increasing complexity of the organisations created problems in monitoring production and expenditure, despite the formal integration.

The formal possibilities for political control were reinforced by regulated markets. Being a monopoly increases the scope for control without concern for the enterprise's survival. Given these possibilities for influence and control, a political culture characterised by welfare-interventionism accounted for a high level of political influence, even though the ministers often shared power with powerful unions.

The reforms changed government enterprises' formal affiliation with the political sphere in a fundamental way. The establishment of an SOE with its own responsible board of directors and chief executive creates an organisational boundary between it and the political sphere. This is likely to reduce communication and the sensitivity to political signals of the government enterprise (Egeberg, 1989a; Egeberg, 1989b). The owner – i.e., the state represented by the ministers – is only supposed to manage the companies directly once a year through the stock-holders meeting. The form of direct influence and control thus changes from the ministerial-led department to the annual general assembly, giving reason to expect a sharp decline in contact between the enterprise and the minister.

The nature of this post-reform relationship is specified in the Statement of Corporate Intent system (SCI) in the SOE act. The responsible board of directors is to submit to the minister a draft of the SCI. This document consists of strategic goals and systems for monitoring their achievement and functions as a contract between ministers and the board, which is held accountable for performance. The ministers assisted by the CCMAU, as owners of the company, have the power to change this statement according to certain procedures (Spicer et al., 1996, p. 20), involving consultation with the board and submission of a copy to parliament. This is a change from earlier models based on trust between ministers and enterprise directors (Mascarenhas, 1996a, p. 298). In this new model the minister is only involved in strategic goal-setting and monitoring achievement, while the earlier integrated solution involved the minister more directly in enterprise operations.

As expected, corporatisation seems to have increased the autonomy of government enterprises in New Zealand. Ministers seem more reluctant to intervene in company matters than under the previous regime (Boston et al., 1996, p. 58). The Auditor General has claimed that the increasing autonomy of enterprises stemming from these reforms has led to a decline in the political control of ministers (Mascarenhas, 1996a, p. 298). Moreover, the Auditor General has repeatedly criticised the information framework that has been created on the basis of the SCI system as too vague (Boston et al., 1996, p. 301). The comments from the Auditor General seem to indicate low control in the commercial sphere as well, contrary to the intention of the reforms. At the same time, some researchers have found commercial control of enterprises to be quite good, as might have been expected (Smith, 1997; Spicer et al., 1991, 1996). Thus, the experienced effects seem to be somewhat ambiguous.

The other dimensions in the transformative perspective are likely to reinforce the tendency towards a loss of control inherent in the formal structural arrangements. In this new regime the deregulated market has a central role in controlling the production of SOEs. As owners, the role of ministers has been reduced to securing a proper return on investment in keeping with the enterprises' commercial objectives, although they still retain the possibility of governing through contracts or legislation. This marketisation reduces the room for political intervention without threatening market shares, and the private sector profile of the SOE boards creates resistance towards political influence and control beyond the commercial area. The reallocation of ownership management to the Treasury and eventually also to the CCMAU is of similar importance. This is a change in polity arrangements whereby responsibility for controlling government enterprises is concentrated within units whose organisational culture is highly influenced by the new administrative doctrines. The rules concerning the form and frequency of contact, which imitate the private sector, are thus likely to be viewed as the only appropriate forms. Increasing economic liberalism in the political sphere may have a similar effect. Since commitment to reform ideas has made them part of party ideology, it is unlikely that parliament or ministers will press for tighter political influence and control or re-establish non-commercial objectives.

This loss of ministerial influence also leads to a weakening of parliament's influence. The minister cannot be held accountable in parliament for matters formally beyond his reach. The weakening of parliament is reinforced by the fact that corporatisation means leaving the executive to decide the nature of an enterprise's activities and to determine the resources to be allocated, a problem also emphasised by the Auditor General (Boston et al., 1996, p. 302). Another problem is that SOEs have claimed secrecy on the grounds of competition and refuse to disclose information to parliament (Mascarenhas, 1996a, p. 301). This illustrates the distance created between the political sphere and the SOEs compared to the old system.

The degree of political responsibility for the activities of enterprises thus seems to have been clearly reduced by the reforms. This might be perceived as a problem because ministerial responsibility in matters regarding state property is a fundamental parliamentary principle. Even after receiving corporate status, the enterprises remain government property and as such are subject to parliamentary scrutiny. In consequence, the minister may find himself in the paradoxical situation of being accountable but not to blame (Martin, 1997b, p. 111). In this respect government enterprises continue to generate dilemmas in post-reform New Zealand.

However, the parliamentary situation may also be of significance for parliament's ability to monitor. Ministerial accountability is likely to improve in cases of minority governments, owing to the lack of partisan support in parliament, irrespective of corporatisation. The reforms towards the MMP-system may thus increase the significance of parliament in these matters and counter the effects of the conversion to company forms. On the other hand, the continuing liberal trends in political parties make politicians less inclined to push for strict control of companies that are being compared to private companies and subjected to the pressure of the market-place.

Norway. The Norwegian reform and corresponding changes in the dimensions identified by the transformative perspective have been much less radical than in New Zealand. The pre-reform directorates, the CAEs, were already vertically specialised units beneath the ministerial level. Although they were led not by ministers but by boards and chief executives they were nevertheless directly subordinated to ministerial control (NOU 1989:5, p. 5). The ministerial potential for influence also means that the minister is accountable for the enterprises' operations. However, the fact that these enterprises are vertically specialised from the ministries and have their own boards implies a reduction in political control and increased autonomy, compared with New Zealand's integrated departments (Egeberg, 1989a,b).

As in New Zealand, regulated markets and a traditionally interventionist political culture legitimised frequent political control and intervention. Even though the organisational separation created a formal obstacle to influence and control, the appointment of boards may in fact contribute to a strengthening of political control. The reason is that there is a tendency to appoint representatives from the unions and interest organisations and people with political experience. Given this composition it is likely that they will have a favourable view of the political use of these enterprises. On a more strategic level the appointments themselves reinforce certain values. In the forestry enterprise, for instance, environmental interests are represented to ensure that environmental objectives are taken into account by the board.

The main rule in all three Norwegian company forms is that ministerial influence is conducted on an annual basis, through the general assembly. This is the only form of direct formal binding influence after the reforms. None of the Norwegian enterprise forms has a formalised, unitary monitoring regime like the SCI. Ministerial influence is directly focused in the general assembly, in which the ministers have almost supreme formal powers. The forms are strongly inspired by the stock-company form used in the private sector, but certain rules deviate from this form in order to enhance political influence. For instance, in the State Enterprise form the board is obliged to submit information to the minister in matters of significance for the companies' objectives or which might change the enterprise's character (§ 23 in Law on State Enterprises). In addition, the protocols of the board meetings are to be sent to the ministry in charge. The purpose is to give the ministry information and the opportunity to intervene by calling an extraordinary assembly before the board takes any action on the matter. Similar rules are also often included in the other company forms. By extension these rules also provide for broad ministerial responsibility, owing to the right accorded to ministers to have access and to intervene in all matters.

Combined with the continuing inclusion of non-commercial objectives these rules enhancing political influence in corporate forms should be expected to contribute to political control. Given that the CAE-form was already separated from the ministries, the effects of corporatisation are thus likely to be less dramatic than in New Zealand. Narrowing the forum for influence and control to the general assembly is nevertheless expected to reduce political influence and enhance corporate autonomy.

The other dimensions in the transformative perspective point in diverse directions. Most Norwegian government enterprises have had their market environments deregulated, as in New Zealand. On the other hand, the spread of ownership to sector government departments contributes to political control, since it emphasises the companies' role as instruments for implementing policy. The limited impact of NPM in the ministries as well as of liberal ideas in the political sphere makes more hands-on political control more likely than in New Zealand, with a corresponding reduction in corporate autonomy. In the corporate sphere, continued public sector and interest group representation on the boards is expected to secure that sensitivity towards political signals will continue. However, tension between the demands of the market and the demands of the political sphere is likely to be present in Norwegian companies trying to realise both non-commercial and commercial objectives.

Studies indicate that enterprises' contact with departments drops and is assigned less weight when they are converted from CAEs to company forms and that less weight than before is given to political and typical non-commercial objectives (Assmann, 1997; Christensen and Egeberg, 1997, p. 103). This indicates a reduction in political influence. The stockholders meeting seems to be the most important arena for control (Statskonsult, 1998). This constitutes a major change from the CAE form where there was a frequent exchange of decision-making premises. While the rules providing for more contact between enterprises and ministries contributes to ministerial information, in practice ministers rarely take action on the basis of this information. In general ministers and politicians seem reluctant to make full use of their formal opportunities to control enterprises. One possible interpretation of these findings is that the image of the corporate form goes against the idea of strong political control. However, there is an indication of additional informal interaction between ministers and their companies in Norway. Some ministries arranging quarterly informal meetings that are reminiscent of the traditions of the more integrated CAE solution (Blindheim, 1999; Statskonsult, 1998, p. 18), and historically patterns of contact have tended to be more informal (Grønlie, 1998, p. 93). This may reduce the real autonomy of enterprises, but the flexibility of such an informal system also blurs the lines of political responsibility between minister and enterprise.

The provision of unlimited formal opportunities for ministers to intervene in enterprise operations is probably one reason why the implications for ministerial influence of corporatisation have not become an area of political conflict. Nevertheless, ministerial reluctance to make use of these opportunities seems to be at odds with the traditional Norwegian political and administrative culture. Viewed from the transformative perspective the institutionalisation of the corporate form might be one explanation for this, given that it affects not only the determination of objectives in government enterprises but probably also the political authorities' understanding of their role. In combination with the deregulation of markets, this institutionalisation causes reluctance in the political sphere. Trying to imitate private sector management as a result of insecurity about their new role causes a ministerial 'hands-off' policy. This gives reason to believe that corporatisation has in fact undermined political control and increased enterprise autonomy in Norway too, despite formal rules that seek to secure that control.

There have been few complaints about information not being made available to parliament in the Norwegian post-reform state, but ministerial reluctance to exercise control seems to have been replaced by a more active parliament in this area. The polity that generates minority governments implies a strong parliament, and the parliament has increasingly started to use its almost supreme powers to control government enterprises – possibly as a result of the more 'hands-off' policies of ministers in ownership positions.

The Transformative Dynamics of Control

In New Zealand the dimensions in the transformative perspective seem to constitute a cumulative tendency. Parallel with corporatisation the management of enterprises has become concentrated in the Treasury and the CCMAU, markets have been deregulated and the political and administrative culture has changed in a fundamental way. As a consequence the traditionally close relationship between the political leadership and government enterprises seems to have vanished. Political control has been accused of being too weak, even in priority commercial areas. This is seen as the result not just of the changed rules brought about by corporatisation and marketisation but as an interaction of these developments with the new set of ideas that have entered the political and administrative culture via the new institutional environment, changing politicians' willingness to exercise control.

The Norwegian pattern is more ambiguous. A traditional political and administrative culture and sectoral specialisation of ownership give reason to expect relatively tight control. Nevertheless, corporatisation in itself potentially weakens political control, as does the institutional environment, which is imbued with a particular set of values and beliefs about the governing of companies derived from the private sector. The result of such a confrontation between traditional public values and company forms seems to be a certain reluctance and insecurity on the part of political officials to control companies. On the one hand, control in the formal arenas seems to be very loose and vague, considering the continuing existence of non-commercial objectives in Norway. In this respect corporatisation itself, marketisation and the institutional environment seem to be of importance. On the other hand, there are indications of more informal governance along traditional lines, thus indicating the significance of political and administrative traditions and continuing sectoral ownership. Thus, corporatisation in Norway seems to have created a hybrid, reflecting the different dimensions identified by the transformative perspective, which point in different directions.

On balance, however, corporatisation is likely to have reduced political control, not only because of the lack of formal possibilities for control but also because of political uncertainty and the imitation of private sector norms which follows from using corporate forms.

Reform in a Dynamic Context

The argument behind a transformative perspective is that analysing corporatisation merely as changes in the formal structure is insufficient when effects are to be considered. Corporatisation, like other reorganisations, does not occur in a vacuum, and its effects are influenced by interactions with other dimensions in the theoretical framework. The dynamic context may influence the effects of the reforms.

There are interesting differences in the patterns of change between the two countries. The commercialised and 'hands-off' regime in New Zealand seems to be the product of a cumulative tendency. All dimensions seem to lead in the same direction, probably triggered by the economic crisis and a blanket acceptance of the ideas of what is broadly speaking called 'New Public Management'. The Norwegian regime is also influenced by these ideas, but a better financial situation and perhaps a more firmly embedded statist culture probably act as a buffer against more radical change. The absence of this cumulative tendency makes the regime into a hybrid of different dimensions pulling in different directions.

In sum, corporatisation in both countries is likely to create more autonomous enterprises and reduce political control. One reason is that political influence and control tend to be focused on the commercial sphere, even in Norway. Another reason is that control is expected to be executed on a less frequent basis and in a more strategic manner through the new main arena, the annual general assembly. But just as important is the fact that the changing ideas generated by corporatisation seem to have reduced the willingness to exercise close control of government enterprises. This management at a distance might stem from a perception of reduced political relevance, given the commercialisation of objectives in New Zealand, but it is more problematic in Norway, where government enterprises have retained their non-commercial objectives.

The chapter shows that differences in the national specification of corporatisation and change or lack of change in other dimensions might create substantial differences in how the new regimes for managing government enterprises operate in practice. The effects of corporatisation on autonomy and control are thus highly dependent on the given context, even though they clearly have the potential to reduce political control.

Notes

1   The notions as used here deviates marginally from Scott (1995, 1998) in that it regards technical environments as influence through regulative processes through an input/output perspective and institutional environments as influenced by cognitive and normative aspects explicit to those environments.
2   This implies doubt about the decoupling of ideas and action put forward by Meyer and Rowan, 1977 and Brunsson, 1989.
3   SOEs have also expressed concern about being subject to the Official Information Act and the Ombudsman Act because this involves costs that are not incurred by their private sector counterparts (Spicer et al., 1996, p. 52).

7 Transforming Top Civil Servant Systems

PER LÆGREID

Introduction

Over the past ten years increased interest in managerial thinking and the market mentality has changed personnel policy in the public sector. Previously an autonomous area entrusted to parties in the labour market, wage and employment policy has now moved into the domain of general administrative policy and become an active tool in restructuring the state. This chapter focuses on how this strategy has been adopted to change the position and working practice of top civil servants.

Traditionally, public administration has been based on two main doctrines aimed at ensuring competent, effective and equitable government (Dunleavy and Hood, 1994). The first doctrine emphasises the public sector as a distinctive domain and makes a clear division between it and the private sector. Under this doctrine, civil servants enjoy the status of professionals working within a closed career system isolated from the private labour market, with their own employment practices, salary scales and promotion and retirement schemes. The second doctrine implies that a number of general procedural regulations should restrict the discretionary power of leading civil servants. These regulations are designed to maintain neutral and impartial treatment and to prevent personal or particular interests from finding expression.

Today these two doctrines are being challenged by New Public Management (NPM), which envisages a public sector organised more along the lines of the private sector and a civil service whose leaders have greater flexibility and more opportunity to exercise discretion. The classical role of the civil servant as a Weberian bureaucrat has been challenged by a new role as managing director. In this chapter I will take a closer look at these changes in administrative doctrines by focussing on one particular administrative reform: the introduction of contract systems for top civil servants in New Zealand in 1988 and in Norway in 1990.

The reforms in New Zealand and Norway were important parts of efforts that began in the mid-1980s to launch a more active and comprehensive administrative policy in the two countries. Pursuing an active administrative policy assumes that alternative organisational forms exist or can be created, that different organisational forms have different effects, that there are criteria which may be used to assess the effects and that the administrative forms to be used are open to choice. A study of the contract reform case may illustrate the degree to which these conditions are met in specific cases. A central question in this chapter is how this reform affects the relationship between political leaders and top civil servants under contract.

This chapter challenges the globalisation thesis, which views the introduction of individual contracts for senior civil servants as a worldwide process of diffusion of similar reform ideas and solutions (Hood, 1998b). This convergence hypothesis states that the introduction of NPM reforms has reduced the differences between public administration in OECD countries. This is not the case when we look at New Zealand and Norway. Even though both countries introduced contractual arrangements at roughly the same time, the content of the reforms and their scope, scale and intensity were very different.

NPM reforms can be divided into two overlapping categories: those that seek to enhance managerial discretion and those that seek to introduce contract-like arrangements in government (Kettl, 1997). The former approach assumes that managers want to do the right thing and will do so if given the chance. Once managers have been empowered, they will take initiatives that improve performance. The latter approach assumes that managers are motivated by self-interest, which might take precedence over the interests of the organisation. It questions whether managers will be tough enough to make the required changes if they are not prodded to act. The more distinctive the contract reform, the greater the likelihood that it will fall into the second category (Schick, 1996).

An additional distinction that is important for this investigation is that between relational contracts, on the one hand, and transaction contracts and agency contracts, on the other hand. Relational contracts are implicit understandings which endure not because of legal sanctions but because of the shared needs of the parties involved. In such contracts trust is essential (Martin, 1995). Both transaction contracts and agency contracts, on the other hand, are formal, binding legal arrangements. They are goal-oriented, incentive-based, concrete and specific and have a limited time horizon. A typical form of transaction contract in government would be contracting out, whereas a typical form of agency contract would be the employment of chief executive officers (Lane, 1999, p. 183). Agency contracts are based on the idea that people act in their own self-interest and they extends the study of such behaviour beyond market transactions to situations where other values such as loyalty and duty are important.

NPM employs both transaction and agency contracts. The main argument for using such contracts is the belief that contracting enhances efficiency. In this chapter I will focus on agency contracts and discuss how useful they are with respect to top civil servants. The contractual arrangements for administrative leaders in New Zealand and Norway represent an interconnected system of employment agreements and performance agreements.

Agency contracts are a main element in the market model of administration (Peters, 1994). In such a model, the rank-in-position system is replaced with a merit principle, which states that civil servants should be paid according to the market and that better performance should be rewarded with better pay. Managers are hired under individual contracts that contain specific performance standards. Thus far, the performance element in the contract system has been investigated to a greater extent than the employment elements. In the United States management by contract has been less widespread than in many other OECD countries and the performance contracts being written do not appear to be contracts in any sense of legal enforceability (Peters, 1996b). Several US studies have revealed the   paradox of performance pay. While   performance-based pay reforms have been very popular, they have not been particularly successful. They have yielded no clear improvement in performance and have failed to create a more flexible or more satisfactory evaluation and compensation system (Ingraham, 1993; Kellough and Lu, 1993; Perry, 1992; Rainey, 1998b).[1] Pay-for-performance systems have not increased either motivation or productivity for public managers; nor have they made any difference in these managers' commitment or loyalty to the organisation (Ingraham, 1998; OECD, 1996c). In spite of this lack of success, performance pay is still an important element in NPM reform (OECD, 1997). I will try to arrive at an understanding of this paradox by using a transformative perspective. The transformative perspective focuses on the external, environmental dimension and on the internal dimension, which embraces political-administrative culture and national polity features in order to understand the background to the reform, the reforms paths taken and the effects experienced and achieved (Christensen and Lægreid, 1999a and 2001).

In the context of these dimensions, I will discuss why the content, effects and implications of contract reforms may differ as well as why the links between measures, actual changes and practice may vary. First, the formal changes, their implementation and the experience gained from them in the two countries studied are described and compared along different analytical dimensions. Second, the diverging reforms are interpreted using a transformative perspective. Third, the lessons learned from using agency contracts for top civil servants are discussed.

Formal Changes

Prior to 1988, New Zealand had a unified public service career system based on the principles of merit-based recruitment and promotion. The State Services Commission (SSC) had control over staff numbers in departments and managed a detailed array of occupational classes that governed pay scale and promotions (Boston et al., 1991; Walsh, 1998). Civil servants had permanent positions and were nominally employed by the SSC under a centralised wage fixing system, which included collective determination of pay and conditions. Ten years later, public servants found themselves employed by departmental chief executives on a basis similar to that of their private sector counterparts (SSC, 1998a).

Prior to 1990, the salaries of top civil servants in Norway were determined through joint negotiations between strong civil service unions and the government in a system whose chief features were an egalitarian wage policy, central control, standardisation, permanent positions and salaries determined by rank and seniority (Lægreid, 1995). In combination with the strong egalitarian norms of Norwegian society, this tradition resulted in low salaries for top civil servants compared with other countries. Indeed, the salary table for Norwegian state employees was one of the most contracted of all the OECD countries. A survey of ten OECD countries in 1991 revealed that the salary level for top civil servants was lowest in Norway (Hood and Peters, 1994a).

The contract reform resulted in broad formal changes in the principles of wage determination for top civil servants in both New Zealand and Norway. There were changes with respect to *who* was to determine the salary, *how* the salary was to be determined, *what* was considered to be an equitable salary and *which* criteria were to be used in determining salary levels. In contrast to most countries contractualisation in New Zealand and Norway was supposed to infiltrate high up the chain of minister/administrator command.

In designing the broad system of reforms in New Zealand, the government believed that the quality of the top management team was essential for achieving results. New approaches to manager recruitment, remuneration and training were demanded. The new individualised system of contractual appointment was implemented by the State Sector Act (1988) and the Public Finance Act (1989). The contract system was not limited to top leaders but was part of a wider change in New Zealand's industrial relations brought about by the Employment Contract Act (1991).

In Norway NPM reform ideas constituted the basis in 1990 for a change in the general collective agreement with the government. The new agreement stipulated that all leadership positions, from the rank of director general upwards, were to be excluded from future general agreements and made subject to an individual employment contract system. Under the new system, the minister was responsible for determining the leader's salary. Approximately 450 top state sector management posts were encompassed by the new system, which took effect as of 1991.

Temporary or Permanent Contracts

The new system in New Zealand introduced annual performance agreements between ministers and chief executives, an annual system of performance assessment and a related system of performance-linked remuneration. Furthermore, the minister was made formally responsible for specifying the performance requirements of the departmental chief, who, in turn, was given the authority to decide how to meet these performance requirements. A five-year contract term was established in place of the previous permanent tenure, and departments were to be headed by chief executives in place of their former permanent heads. The reform granted no automatic right of renewal, although those who had performed satisfactorily were typically offered an extension for a further three years or encouraged to apply for a position within another government department.

In Norway, too, a performance contract system was introduced in which clear and precise objectives were to be agreed upon between the secretary general and his minister and between director generals and the secretary general. The achievement of these objectives was to be evaluated once a year and this evaluation was to provide the basis for annual revision of the contract. The leaders would, however, retain a permanent position within the civil service. The idea was that a good result would lead to an increase in salary, while poor performance could lead to a reduction in the personal supplement, or, in the worst case, to a transfer to another position. This part of the system had clear similarities to the principle of performance-related pay. The size of the personal supplement was considered confidential.

In contrast to the strictly formal numerical performance-rating system for federal managers in the United States, the Norwegian performance assessment system is soft, qualitative and is applied with great discretion. The New Zealand system is somewhere in between. The chief executives carry out a self-assessment, which is aligned to a performance matrix of results and behaviour. The views of the minister, central agencies and referees are sought and their performance is also linked to the annual departmental performance assessment.

Large or Small Income Increase

In New Zealand the new contract system was designed and implemented by a Labour government. The new contract of employment for chief executives is a formal legal contract and stipulates how remuneration is to be determined and how performance is to be assessed. The contract also obliges executives to act in accordance with the values and ethics of the civil service and to be concerned with the wider collective interests of the government, in addition to serving the minister of the day. A bonus system for senior executives rewards performance that exceeds expectations and envisages a formal reprimand or dismissal for performance below expectations. The annual lump sum bonus can be up to 15 percent of the base salary. Individual contracts with flexible pay and incentives were intended to attract highly competent private-sector managers (Scott, 1996). Remuneration was determined provisionally by comparison with the salaries of similar jobs in the private sector. New Zealand salaries were supposed to be comparable with the private sector as senior civil servants moved from permanent tenure to five-year terms. This process involved substantial pay increases for those in jobs with considerable responsibility. Officials in smaller departments with less responsibility received only minimal increases to their existing salaries.

In Norway the specifics of the contract system were outlined by a group of leading civil servants, and the result was a compromise between traditional salary policies and new salary doctrines, with a further compromise brought about as a result of a change in government. Before the Conservative/Centre government could implement the contract system, it was replaced by a Labour government, which inherited responsibility for the new system. Both the terms of the final agreement and its implementation in practice were approached cautiously by the new government in order to prevent an indefensible increase in leading civil servants' salaries. This resulted in lower increases than were originally envisaged and also a less decentralised and less flexible system. Four salary categories were introduced, with the option of earning a personal supplement of up to 20 percent of the basic salary in each category. Three-quarters of the positions were placed in the lowest category and the opportunities for earning a personal supplement were very restricted. There was also little differentiation within the same group of positions– all secretary generals were placed in the same category. The same applied for almost 90 percent of director generals, who comprised the largest single group. These decisions resulted in a fairly standardised system with the same regulations pertaining both to positions that were not exposed to market pressure, such as generals and ambassadors, and to those institutions which were particularly exposed, such as financial institutions and public enterprises.

Elitist or Egalitarian Political Administrative Culture

The State Sector Act was driven by managerialist concerns. It sought to import private sector management practice into the New Zealand public sector to improve efficiency and effectiveness (Walsh, 1991, p. 73). The strong uniformity of the old system was replaced by a new system much more subject to discretion and flexibility. There was a shift to a more technocratic style of governance, and the egalitarian public service adopted a more elitist, managerialist ethos (Gregory, 1998a). This new contractualism replaced the implicit or relational contracts that characterised traditional public administration. Performance agreements and performance review displaced the old service ethic of trust and responsibility with accountability for the results from each chief executive (Schick, 1998). The performance of chief executives is now evaluated on the basis of three fundamental accountability principles. First, the chief executive should be personally responsible for the department's performance. Second, performance expectations should be specified in advance. Third, actual performance should be compared to ex ante targets.

In Norway the egalitarian norms were strong and the new contract system became a part of the government's moderate income policy called the 'solidarity alternative'. In addition to the incentive function, the new system allowed for the granting of personal supplements to reflect labour market conditions or the position held, but a main objective was to keep the wage increments as low as possible. The level of a salary was thus a combination of a basic salary linked to the position held and an individual supplement based on market conditions or performance. Even though the relationship between supplementary salary and performance was presented as a mainstay of the new system, the reform was still not a clear-cut pay-for-performance system. It was a combination system designed to increase the competitiveness of government agencies on the labour market, to improve leader mobility through more flexible salary arrangements and to create a more active leadership policy with more precise and more objective requirements and systematic follow-up, but within the confines of very narrow wage supplements. The overall aim was to contribute to a more effective administration.

In sum, the general ideas behind the reforms focusing on efficiency were rather similar in the two countries, but the New Zealand approach was more radical than the Norwegian and it was also more internally consistent. The performance management system in New Zealand was more formalised, comprehensive and exacting. The new legislation had drastic implications for state employment. The traditional centralised employment structure and the collective award, tenure and grievance procedures of the public service gave way to decentralised employment, enterprise bargaining and individual, temporary contracts. Contracting for performance replaced the rules and regulations that characterised the old system. In contrast, the Norwegian system remained more centralised, allowed for smaller income increases, had permanent contracts and was embedded in a stronger egalitarian political administrative culture.

Implementation and Experience

In New Zealand the new model was implemented aggressively and thoroughly. In contrast, the Norwegian contract system was implemented cautiously and reluctantly. In practice, the labour government introduced a more detailed, restricted and centralised system than had been intended by the architects of the reform.

Remuneration

In New Zealand early assessments of the new regime indicated more flexible conditions of employment and a marked increase in the range of salaries paid to chief executives (Boston, 1991, p. 83). Even so, in the period from 1988 to 1998, the salaries of chief executives drifted steadily away from their private sector benchmarks set in 1988. In 1996 they were as much as 30–50 percent below them. This resulted in a new remuneration policy for public service chief executives in 1997, the aims of which were to end the direct link with the private sector, and to strengthen the link between professional performance and remuneration (SSC, 1998a). In practice, political and fiscal constraints have limited the state's capacity for giving chief executives an enhanced level of remuneration. The bonus system represents only a relatively small proportion of chief executives' salaries. Nevertheless, when compared with the average New Zealand wage, current public service chief executives are now far better off than were permanent heads under the pre-1988 regime (Gregory, 1998a). There is a growing disparity within the leaders' group and also between this group and other employees. Under the previous fixed-pay arrangements, departmental heads in the top bracket earned about 50 percent more than those in the bottom bracket. By the mid-1990s, the basic salary for those at the top of the range had become double that of those at the bottom (Boston et al., 1996, p. 105).

In Norway the original idea was that top civil servants would not automatically go over to the new contract system but that a specific evaluation would be made for each individual. In practice, however, a collective transfer to the new system took place. Upon entering into a contract, top civil servants received, on average, a wage increase of 14 percent, while other state salary increases were set at 4 percent that year. However, subsequent salary increases for top civil servants were generally lower than those for other groups. In 1995 a secretary general earned 70 percent of what his counterpart in the private sector earned, and this was also the approximate differential at the time the reform was introduced (St.prp. nr. 1, 1996–97).

By the end of 1995, individual supplements or changes in salary category had been implemented for about half of all leaders covered by the system, but in most cases the level of the supplement was very low (Lægreid and Savland, 1996a). There were, however, major differences between the ministries in the use of personal supplements, partly due to different market exposure and focus on economic values. The Ministry of Finance and agencies under the Ministry of Transport and Communications were notable for having the largest number and highest level of individual supplements.

Recruitment and Mobility

The new appointments procedure in New Zealand was intended to create as wide a recruitment pool as possible for senior civil servants. Even with market-based remuneration and the high visibility of the reforms, however, it has not been easy to recruit better candidates from outside the government than from within it. Appointments from the private sector in the senior civil service in New Zealand have been few and far between. In the period from 1989 to 1998, just 7 percent of the appointments of public service chiefs were made from the private sector (Gregory, 1998a).

One central aspect of the reforms was the desire to achieve results through effective decentralised management in other words, to make it easier to remove poorly-performing staff. There is, however, little senior management development taking place in the new zealand public service (SSC, 1998a). Up to 1996 only one chief executive had chosen not to have his contract renewed and only one had failed to have his contract renewed. Boston et al. (1996, p. 106) conclude that the desirability of fixed-term contracts remains debatable.

The majority of Norwegian top civil servants in the contract system have made their careers within the state labour market and worked their way to the top through internal promotion within their own sphere. They have long records of service in the government administration and in their own institution, and few had thoughts of resigning. Even among those who did intend to resign, the majority were planning to move to another position in the civil service. At the same time, there was very little recruitment from the private sector.

One reason for these developments may be that the restrictive practice of the contract system has not resulted in a narrowing of the gap between public and private sector salaries. There is no doubt that the sizeable gap between salaries in the two sectors has made it difficult to recruit highly skilled– and highly paid – leaders from the private sector.

The Norwegian contract model does not appear to have had a significant effect on the pattern of mobility (Lægreid and Savland, 1996b). Neither recruitment from the private sector nor the resignation of leaders to join private institutions appears to have changed particularly. Where the reform has had an influence on mobility is in apparently encouraging transfers between state institutions. In general the internal labour market within the civil service as a whole appears stable. Sixty percent of top leaders considered that the reform had had little or no effect upon the problems of recruiting and retaining qualified top and middle levels of management. There was particularly little effect upon mobility within the defence and foreign services, but quite a number of respondents in public enterprises thought there had been a positive effect on the mobility pattern.

Performance Agreements

In New Zealand the introduction of annual performance reviews in 1989 has been a mixed blessing. On the one hand, the reviews have brought significant benefits. Chief executives take their performance agreements seriously and use them as a device for monitoring departments' work and for measuring progress. The use of performance agreements had the potential to improve the accountability of chief executives and to enhance the political direction of the bureaucracy. Experience suggests that chief executive performance agreements can provide a valuable management tool (Boston et al., 1996, pp. 113, 115).

On the other hand, few were happy with the SSC's effort to operate the review system, and many ministers were ambivalent about the merits of both performance agreements and performance reviews. A clear distinction between political and managerial aspects has been difficult to achieve in practice. Criticism has been directed at the difficulty of specifying performance standards, the amount of time involved and the increased danger of inflexibility and rigidity (Boston, 1991, pp. 103–4; Whitecombe, 1990). The performance agreements may also be a bit narrow, for they give chief executives a strong incentive to go by the book. Management by agreement and checklist behaviour can be problematic for accountability, since basing accountability on ex ante specification of performance according to contractual duties and information flows may mean that unanticipated– and therefore unspecified – matters escape accountability (Schick, 1996, pp. 48, 87). Another problem of specifying all work in advance is that this does not leave sufficient leeway for dealing with shocks and surprises that occur during the year. This problem is particularly relevant when it comes to policy advice. There is also an ongoing problem of determining what constitutes a successful chief executive, and the application of rewards and sanctions under the new performance management system has been a constant bone of contention (Boston et al., 1996, p. 116).

In Norway the performance-related element of the reform turned out to be even more difficult to operate in practice (Lægreid, 1997). A survey conducted of the top civil servants under contract two years after the introduction of the reform revealed that it was hard to determine precise and operational objectives and performance indicators. Fewer than one-third believed that the defined objectives were, in fact, measurable. The language of the first generation of contracts was quite vague when it came to defining the personal objectives of the individual concerned (Lægreid, 1994). The formulation of objectives and results was for the most part ambiguous and used loose phrasing and terminology, which was open to a wide range of interpretations. The leaders were also uncertain about whether the salary system had, in fact, contributed to increased efficiency. A larger number disagreed than agreed with the statement that the reform had contributed to increased cost efficiency.

In contrast to the New Zealand system, which is closer to a strict pay-for-performance system, the Norwegian one might be described as a mutation, based on the principle of pay-for-contribution, which implies a softer and broader value-added system balancing different criteria (Kanter, 1987; Wise, 1994; Wise and Sjöström, 2000). The combination of limited resources, central control, standardisation, a lack of specific objectives and demands for results which could scarcely be measured has dealt a severe blow to what was supposed to be the mainstay of the reform – namely, a direct link between salary supplements and achieved results. This part of the contract system has, in practice, been very limited. The contracts provide for only a minimal association between formal performance assessment and salary adjustment. Fewer than 10 percent of the personal supplements granted were based on performance assessments. In our data no supplements were reduced or cancelled because of poor achievement.

In practice the main argument used for granting an individual supplement was the importance of the position, responsibility and the range of tasks carried out. This can be interpreted as a form of institutional lag, for traditionally the importance of a position has been reflected in the salary level. The second most frequently used argument was the market one. In more than one-third of cases supplements were justified with reference to this argument. The goal of a closer consideration of the market in the determination of personal supplements has thus been reached to a certain extent. But evidence of the pay-for-performance argument is virtually non-existent, and the new salary system has first and foremost functioned as a position assessment system with a significant element of market evaluation.

The problems of performance measurement for top civil servants in Norway and New Zealand raised in this study are consistent with other research on performance appraisals in the public sector.[2]

Accountability and Responsibility

Taking accountability seriously is an important aspect of the rhetoric of the New Zealand model, and some aspects of managerial accountability have probably been improved. But the acceptance of political responsibility by ministers has been further attenuated. There are problems with a managerialist approach in public administration in that it de-couples management from political processes and undermines cross-sectoral co-ordination. The introduction of 'strategic result areas' and 'key result areas' in 1994 was supposed to address these problems (Boston and Pallot, 1997), but whether this new approach will be successful in the long run remains uncertain.

Something may be lost of professional ethics and a commitment to do one's best when responsibility is reduced to a set of contract-like documents and auditable statements (Schick, 1996, p. 85). Under the corporate model qualities such as loyalty, innovation, integrity and commitment to public well-being are subordinated to the goals of efficiency and managerialism (Kelsey, 1997, p. 142) and the accountability system may have a demotivating effect on chief executives (SSC, 1999a). In New Zealand there has been no widespread breakdown in the standards of behaviour of public officials, but loss of job security has created uncertainty and resulted in lower morale among many civil servants, especially at lower levels. There is a need to 'reinvent' ethical standards and behaviour in the public service (Boston et al., 1996, p. 332; Gregory, 1995e).

One effect of the new system is that it places considerable policy discretion in the hands of chief executives. The question is whether the contractual relationship between a few chief executives and their ministers is sufficient to restore public accountability to this process. One effect of the transition from the role of a traditional departmental head to a new decentralised management role was that some of the traditional functions of policy advice and representation received less attention than previously.

Schick (1996) criticised the rigidity and cost to the chief executive system generated by the elaborate processes for annual renegotiation and review. Annual agreements tend to put undue focus on short-term priorities and problems at the expense of potentially more significant, though less imme-diate, concerns. Moreover, such agreements encourage excessive specification of activities and results in order to ease later assessment of performance with respect to performance pay. This is at odds with the fact that the job of a chief executive is beset by unpredictability and the leadership task is one of exercising judgement as circumstances unfold and of choosing between priorities and options. Excessive specification tends to alter democratic values and reduce risk-taking, and with it innovation and discovery (SSC, 1998a).

In Norway individual evaluation and measurement of results on the basis of contracts has been problematic. Two years after the introduction of the reform, more than a third of the civil servants had neither renegotiated their contracts nor were in the process of re-evaluation, even though the contract had been in force for more than a year (Lægreid and Mjør, 1993). Of those who had renegotiated their contract, only a minority expressed the opinion that a basic evaluation of their achievements had taken place. There was considerable doubt among top civil servants about whether the reform had made it easier for weaker leaders to be reappointed to other posts. Thus, there are strong indications that the contract system has had little direct effect on how leaders in top positions actually function. Very few of those who had gone into the contract system believed that it had resulted in any significant change in the manner in which they carried out their own daily work. At the same time, there were many who felt that their immediate superior had increased his or her control over their work situation, which indicates that the contract system is one step in the direction of a control system.

Satisfaction

The effects of the new system in New Zealand show a mixed picture, and views concerning the effectiveness of contracts are quite divided (Stace and Norman, 1997). The new appointments procedure and the system of contract employment have worked reasonably well and have won the support of most chief executives. On the other hand, ensuring uniformity with respect to performance management and operating the new performance assessment regime has presented difficulties. If the new model of managerial accountability rests primarily on a contractual bond, then there is little scope for loyalty to the broader value of the public sector.

Some managers within departments are complaining that their contracts have become rather like the old rules that the 1988 reforms were supposed to have swept away. The answer is more trust and more 'relational contracting' – looser arrangements which rely on a high degree of understanding between purchaser and provider and between minister and chief executive (James, 1998).

The SSC has expressed concern about the present standard and future supply of management skills in departments, particularly at senior levels (SSC, 1997). The departments continue to struggle with performance management. There has been widespread scepticism about performance appraisal schemes based on perceived inequities in operation, on the complex and time-consuming requirements the schemes entail and on outcomes which have seemed to bear little relationship to individual performance and merit (SSC, 1998a). It takes more to hold managers accountable than to negotiate contracts and report on performance. The conceptual distinctions drawn by the reform with regard to the roles of minister and chief executive are amply clear on paper, but they fail in practice. The ambiguity of responsibility becomes especially clear when things go wrong (Gregory, 1998d).

A good working relationship between ministers and their chief executives requires trust and mutual respect, and these ingredients cannot be manu-factured via performance agreements. In addition, the political environment needs to be relatively stable and ministers must be willing to specify their strategic objectives. However, the nature of politics under a parliamentarian system of government does not normally live up to these expectations. The introduction of proportional representation in New Zealand in 1996 will probably diminish the effectiveness of performance agreements as a manage-ment tool (Boston et al., 1996, p. 114).

In Norway process aspects of the contract reform may have had cognitive effects in the form of improved communication, more clearly defined leadership roles and a more highly developed objectives culture. Even though leaders did not observe significant changes in their own work situation in 1993, many still considered that the reform had contributed to better leadership and goal achievement and had increased leaders' motivation and contribution. This suggests that the leaders had a more positive view of the reforms when asked in general terms or when asked about potential, rather than actual effects. Over time, however, scepticism regarding the contract system has grown. A survey in 1996 revealed that more than 70 percent of leaders had put work with the performance contract aside or else regarded it as a dead ritual (Administrasjonsdepartementet, 1996).

Evaluation

There is a paradox between the emphasis on evaluation and performance assessments in the reform model on the one hand and the lack of real evaluation of the reform models themselves on the other (Lægreid and Roness, 2001; Olsen, 1997a; Pollitt et al., 1997). For the contract model this is of special significance because its legitimacy is based on results. While much has been written about the New Zealand Public Management Model, there have been few systematic and empirical evaluations of its effectiveness. The SSC states that New Zealand's public sector management is not in the habit of carrying out evaluations and does not have the skills to do so (SSC, 1998b, p. 6). Many of the reports of the effects of the reforms have relied heavily on the opinions of senior managers and key players in the reform process. There has been a failure to evaluate the reforms in a detailed, rigorous and systematic fashion (Boston, 1999). Moreover, there are serious methodological problems involved in assessing the costs and benefits of the reforms. Both quantitative and qualitative analyses and assessments are difficult for many of the changes. For example, how might we assess the effect of the new model of performance-related pay and fixed-term contracts on the culture of the public sector, or on staff morale, productivity, innovation and team work?

The absence of any effective, ongoing monitoring and evaluation in a programme whose *raison d'être* was to improve accountability shows the extent to which state sector restructuring was ideologically driven (Kelsey, 1997, p. 145). In other words the contractual model was chosen more for its ideological appeal than for its practical implications, which seem to have been insufficiently explored (Mascharenas, 1996). No specific consideration was given to the problems of measuring performance in the public service. The adoption of performance agreements and performance contracts based on corporate plans suggests that governments are denying the realities of the political process, which involve muddling through and responding to pressure.

Although the contract reforms may have been relatively successful from an efficiency perspective, they have been less effective in ensuring the achievement of government policy objectives (SSC, 1998a). Since the early 1990s there has been a continuous process of adjustment and refinement of the performance agreement system. The aim has been to make performance agreements more specific and exacting, to give them a sharper and more strategic focus. New Zealand officials, having invested more than a decade in trying to improve their government's performance through ever preciser specification of contract goals and better measurement of output, have found themselves drawn into the far fuzzier world of outcomes. The elegant construction of the reforms has been strained by the pressure of coping with the broader links between policy and management, between contract goals and results (Kettl, 1997, p. 457).

During the early years of the Norwegian reform the assessment was that, despite widespread criticism and dissatisfaction with the new system, it was best to go ahead, making minor changes. The contract model was structured first and foremost to meet the problems encountered in the competitive, market-oriented and industry-like agencies; but it was, nevertheless, applied to all administrative bodies, including agencies that operated within a closed internal career system, such as the foreign service and the defence. The paradox is that the public enterprises for which the reform is relatively well suited are partly excluded from the system in Norway as a result of structural devolution.

Since 1997 there has been a certain amount of delegation to individual ministries regarding questions of salary supplements and performance contracts. Flexibility was also increased through the introduction of a new fifth salary categories. At the same time, 91 positions were transferred back to the ordinary collective pay negotiation system in the public sector, and about 280 positions were left in the contract system. It was also intended to revitalise the performance element, but so far this wish has not yielded any significant results. The evaluation concluded that there was nothing wrong with the principles behind the system and that the difficulties in making it function as intended were simply due to unfortunate political and economic conditions or practical administrative problems. Failure was attributed to mis-management and a lack of political skills, management capacity or financial resources; and the suggestions from the evaluators were simply to be patient, persevere and wait for better times.

One lesson that might be learned from the Norwegian experience is that the reform has probably had a greater effect on expectations and aspirations among senior civil servants than on salary conditions and performance – a lesson which has also been learned in other administrative reform processes (March and Olsen, 1995). When the present reform was introduced, it created expectations regarding salary increases which were not met. The result was disillusionment, and presumably the differential between expected salary and actual salary has become greater following the reform than it was before. The changes promised more on paper than they yielded in practice.

Discussion: Diverging Reforms

Whereas in Norway the connection between reform measures and the changes which have actually occurred is relatively loose, in New Zealand there seems to be a tight link between reform ideas, the solution selected and the actual changes made (see Table 7.1).

Table 7.1 Similarities and differences in contract reforms for top civil servants in New Zealand and Norway

	NEW ZEALAND	NORWAY
IDEAS, VISIONS, GOALS (Similarities)	Efficiency Devolution/management *and* market/contract ideas	Efficiency Devolution/management *more than* market/contract ideas
MEANS AND MEASURES, FORMAL CHANGES (Differences)	Contracts and performance assessment. Measures internally consistent, exacting formalized, comprehensive	Management Devolution Flexibility Balancing different values
ACTUAL CHANGES, IMPLEMENTATION (Differences)	Drastic change Aggressive implementation Tight connection between reform measures and actual change Radical, tough, hard-line	Tidying up Caution, reluctance Loose connection between reform measures and actual changes Moderate, soft, light
EXPERIENCES, EFFECTS, RESULTS (Similarities)	The evaluation paradox Possible increased performance but a number of problems Change in relationship between political and administrative leaders Ambiguous, uncertain effects	Low salary increases Reduction in pay-for-performance element Stable mobility patterns. Stable relationship between political and administrative leaders Ambiguous, uncertain effects
LEARNING (Differences)	Extension of the reform	Partly reversed reform

However, in both countries the contract reform for top civil servants has thus far had a mixed reception when it comes to experiences and effects. It is puzzling that reforms with significant differences in formal and actual changes are more similar when it comes to effects and experiences while the learning effect has nevertheless been quite different in the two countries. People have experienced the reforms in similar ways in both countries but have drawn different conclusions from them. This might indicate that the underlying theory behind the reform is uncertain (Egeberg, 1995; Perry, 1986) and that there might be some ambiguity when it comes to the construction of the reform.

The formal transfer to the contract system has essentially been completed in both countries, but in Norway there has been a certain amount of caution about making active use of it. While the Norwegian system has been partly reversed, the New Zealand model has been extended. The recent reforms represent a paradigmatic shift in the instruments of governance, in sharp constant to the incremental and more limited policy changes that had previously characterised public administration reforms in New Zealand. Annual performance agreements and fixed-term appointments for senior executives are some of the more novel and unusual elements of the reforms in New Zealand. In Norway the contract system and the freedom which it was to permit have been only partly realised. Norway has seen more standardisation, collective arrangements, central control and position-related salaries and less flexibility, individualisation, market orientation, local autonomy and result-based salaries than the reform provided the opportunity for. The upshot has been more a collective salary adjustment with a flexible salary-by-results element than an individual contract system. Top civil servants in Norway seem to regard performance and results as their personal responsibility to a lesser extent than in New Zealand. Norwegian contract reform is also less integrated in a broad package of reforms.

The result is a moderate and gentle reform in Norway, as opposed to a radical, tough hard-line reform in New Zealand. The differences between Norway and New Zealand are probably greater under the new contract system in 1999 than under the previous system of ten years earlier, and this goes against the ideas of homogenisation, isomorphism and convergence which a globalisation thesis assumes.

The effects of the reform are ambiguous and uncertain both in New Zealand and Norway, and there is a need for better empirical information about how the contract model really works. We are considering a reform which has been in effect for 8–10 years, so it is not too early to evaluate it and look at the results. If reforms are evaluated too soon after their introduction, one will primarily be measuring the effects of the readjustment that occurs while the reform is becoming established. Such effects may change once the situation has stabilised (Olsen, 1996; Sabatier, 1991). It is important to emphasise that it is mainly the adjustment effects of the reforms which have been revealed so far. Conversely, waiting too long to investigate the effects makes it difficult to isolate the effects of the reform from other factors which influence change and development. This identification problem is especially relevant in New Zealand, where the contract system is part of a much broader package of reforms.

A second issue is the counterfactual problem, or what would have happened if the contract system had not been introduced (Pollitt, 1995). The previous general pay system may not be an appropriate standard of reference, because that system has also changed. In Norway, changes in the general collective agreement have resulted in greater autonomy and flexibility in local negotiations. Thus, it is not valid to compare the contract system today with the situation pertaining in 1990 when leaders were excluded from the general collective agreement.

A third question concerns the criteria to be used in the evaluation. The potential gains in efficiency arising from the reform may, for example, have a negative effect on equity and equality; they may weaken senior civil service ethics and motivation, a senior civil servant's role as political advisor, political responsibility or a government's public legitimacy. It appears that certain unintentional effects, such as considerations of equality, responsibility and the signal effect towards public opinion, have determined the extent to which the original targets may be achieved. In Norway, for example, the demand for equal treatment by each ministry made it difficult to decentralise the system, and a strong egalitarian attitude among the public set a limit on the level of supplements that could be granted to leaders. The contract system did not do anything, either, to rectify inequalities in the pay of male and female leaders (Mjør, 1994).

An evaluation of the contract reform is also problematic because its objectives are ambiguous and partly contradictory. There is an absence of clear benchmarks against which to assess the pay reform (Boston et al., 1996, p. 353).

The result of these evaluation problems is that it is impossible to say clearly or conclusively whether the contract system is really working as promised (Boston, 1999). The contract reform has a weak empirical foundation. Nevertheless, it has survived.

Transforming Contract Systems

To understand the design, practice and evaluation of the contract system the influence of ideas, interests and established norms must be considered. The contract reforms in Norway and New Zealand might be seen as the product of a complex interaction between external and internal dimensions. While the external dimension comprises primarily the environmental characteristics of the economy and international ideas about administrative reform, the internal dimension refers to both national cultural traditions and structural/polity features that each country has at its disposal.

With regard to *environmental characteristics*, the perception in New Zealand in the early 1980s was that the country was in economic crisis and this made it easier to press for comprehensive civil service reforms (Evans et al., 1996). The pressure from the environment was defined as deterministic. In addition, being a member of the Anglo-American family may have made it easier to imitate or build on certain reform elements from the United States and the United Kingdom (Castles, 1989; Halligan, 1998; Hood, 1996a).

In Norway there was no obvious economic crisis that could legitimate comprehensive administrative reform, and the distance to Anglo-American reform was greater. The neo-liberal flavour of the Anglo-American reforms challenged the traditional core concept of a good public sector, as it had become institutionalised in Norway over decades. There was a cultural incompatibility between international criticism of the public sector and the Norwegian model of an interventionist, planning state. The Norwegian model embodied the belief in a large public sector under tight political control as a suitable means for promoting the common good (Olsen, 1996). In contrast to the confrontational style of the Anglo-American reform movement with respect to civil service unions, the Norwegian policy style has traditionally been one of co-operation and mutual understanding.

One internal dimension which could potentially explain reform processes and effects is the *national cultural tradition* – i.e. norms and values that characterise the political-administrative system. In Norway these are a strong statist tradition, complex systems of governance that balance different tasks, mutual trust between political and administrative leaders, equality, incremental changes, and a policy style of peaceful co-operation, pragmatism and revolution in slow motion. All these factors suggest that a contract system will be implemented slowly, reluctantly and in a modified form (Christensen and Lægreid, 1998b; Christensen and Peters, 1999; Olsen, Roness and Sætren, 1982). The institutional bond and contextual constraints have certainly imposed clear limits on the realisation of the reformers' intentions as regards adjustments to market and management.

Those parts of the pay system which did not coincide with the Norwegian bureaucratic culture, such as performance contracts, were considered less relevant. In the course of the implementation process, the new contract system, which was initially planned as a radical change, became more incremental. The main trend has been readjustment and supplementation rather than fundamental transformation and replacement.

New Zealand is also a relatively small country, and it has been built on some of the same values as Norway, with the state as a collective vehicle for popular action. Even so, New Zealand is probably more polarised and culturally heterogeneous and its statist tradition has been in decline since the 1980s (Boston et al., 1996, pp. 10–11; Castles, 1993, p. 17). In contrast to Norway, the relationship between the Labour government and civil servants in New Zealand was one of mistrust for certain periods of the 1970s, even though traditionally there had been relatively close ties between the two groups (Mascarenhas, 1996a). For a long time traditional co-operative, corporatist arrangements played an important political role in Norway and to a lesser degree in New Zealand, as did the close ties between their Labour parties and the trade unions, but this feature began to weaken in New Zealand in the early 1980s.

Two normative questions, linked to different administrative cultures, can be raised in connection with the contract reform (Hood and Peters, 1994a). The first is how much a top civil servant should earn. One relevant criterion here is that of representation – i.e., the principle that civil service leaders are representative of the people and should therefore have incomes similar to the majority. This egalitarian principle has strong roots in Norway. The second criterion is the market, whereby top civil service salaries should reflect the salaries paid to people in corresponding positions elsewhere in society. This is an individualistic principle that has a firmer footing in New Zealand.

The second normative question is how salaries shall be determined. One principle, which is strong in Norway, is that of public access or visibility, which means that the salaries of top civil servants should be transparent, specified and acceptable to the public. Another criterion, which is stronger in New Zealand, is performance, i.e., civil service leaders' salaries should be dependent upon the results they show, giving them an incentive to perform well.

The contract reform was basically an experiment in strengthening the market and performance criteria, while giving less weight to the considerations of representation and public access. But in practice the new system revealed that traditional criteria were not easily set aside in Norway, and the new scheme has become a composite one in which the weight accorded to the two sets of criteria is rather different from what was originally intended.

The second internal dimension, the *political instruments* dimension, is somewhat different in the two countries. New Zealand used to have a first-

past-the-post electoral system, until a mixed member proportional representation system was introduced in 1996, which made a forceful implementation
of reforms more likely than in Norway, where a multi-party system and
minority governments tend to lead to negotiations and parliamentary
turbulence (Campbell and Halligan, 1992, pp. 5–6; Christensen and Peters,
1999). Those responsible for the Norwegian reform made adjustments in
accordance with what was politically possible. In contrast to New Zealand,
Norwegian civil service unions influenced the speed and scope of the reform
process. In New Zealand, the control potential was highly influenced by the
existence of a unitary form of government, a unicameral parliament, a strong
executive and tight party discipline in parliament (Boston et al., 1996, pp.
43–50). In addition, the Westminster system probably also allowed more
scope for strong political leaders to act as reform entrepreneurs than did the
multi-party system in Norway, with a formally weaker prime minister. In
Norway top civil servants were more important agents of change than
ministers (Lægreid and Roness, 2001). The Norwegian model of governance
has a weak central government and delegates more authority for policy and
administrative reform to departments, agencies and civil service unions
(Lindquist, 1999).

The Norwegian government's intention to conduct a restrictive practice
with low supplements has largely been achieved. Although the original
objective of the reform was to reduce the differential between leaders in the
public and private sectors, leaders within the new system have experienced
less growth in pay than other leaders, both in the state and private sectors, and
incremental increases are still made in accordance with earlier traditions. This,
in turn, indicates that the more wages are controlled by politicians, the lower
the wage increase. These moderate changes reflect a Norwegian reform
tradition which avoids confrontation and prefers political negotiation
involving discussions back and forth until a consensus is reached that
everyone can live with (Olsen, 1996). The contract reform illustrates that
administrative reforms are not just a non-political struggle to achieve greater
efficiency but also an experiment to see how far this consensus can be
stretched. In many cases the contracts in practice became pseudo-contracts
reinforcing traditional patterns of work (Bennett and Ferlie, 1996) and the
intention to 'make the managers manage' through formal agency contracts
was hardly fulfilled. The process became more one of political co-operation
than of managerial planning. Even in New Zealand chief executives' general
agreements with their ministers were in practice more quasi-contracts than
strict legal contracts (Pollitt and Bouckaert, 2000). When confronted with

political logic, legally binding contracts between ministers and administrative top leaders became difficult to enforce.

Conclusion

The reform process in New Zealand and Norway ran parallel in the sense that contract models were taken up in each country at about the same time. The models were, however, used to very different degrees and with considerable adaptation to fit the specifics of national administrative culture and administrative policy. Administrative reform processes, such as those related to contractualism, do not simply entail adopting current international administrative doctrines but must be understood from a transformative perspective.

As practice shows, reform concepts are revised, filtered, interpreted and modified through the prism of a two nationally based processes. One such process is the development of a unique national political-adminsitrative history, culture and tradition. Another such process involves the development of a set of institutional arrangements, formal structures and polity features. Within these constraints and opportunities the initiatives of political leaders and their instrumental actions are undertaken through administrative design and active national administrative policy in co-operation with top civil servants and civil service unions to reflect their interests (Olsen, 1992; Olsen and Peters, 1996a). This means that we need to study the connections between ideas, institutions and interests in order to understand the contract arrangements in the two countries (Peters and Hood, 1995).

At one extreme, there might be a de-conceptualization process, which emphasises where environmental reform concepts and internal needs mesh. Ideas from the international environmental may create pressure to adopt contract reforms which have profound effects on national systems, and such pressure may be enhanced by a political-administrative leadership and also by compatibility with historical-cultural traditions. At the other extreme, there might be a contextualisation process, stressing the uniqueness of national systems and the lack of compatibility with externally produced reform ideas (Røvik, 1996). Environmental pressure for reform may produce few changes and effects because political and administrative leaders may consciously try to stop or avoid reforms owing to their lack of compatibility with traditional norms and values (Brunsson and Olsen, 1993). This chapter shows that when externally generated reform concepts and processes are transferred to national political-administrative systems they are more complex and have more varied and ambiguous effects and implications than the extremes outlined above.

Past experience of administrative reform has distinguished between an 'incubated' mode and an 'acute' mode (Dunleavy and Hood, 1994; Polsby, 1984). In the first case, reform ideas do not come into full effect until long after their introduction; in the second case there is a Hawthorne effect, in which the reform programmes peak early and then break up quickly (Hesse, Hood and Peters, 2001). Our case seems to be more in accordance with a third interpretation of administrative reforms – namely, reforms as a recurring triumph of hope over experience (Downs and Larkey, 1986). In this interpretation, contract reforms are transformed to fit the national administrative context, the government's administrative policy and external pressures, and in this way the contract concept keeps running, in spite of repeated disappointments and ambiguous effects. This is not necessarily a bad strategy. It might be wise to slow the learning rate in situations involving noisy experiments and ambiguous feedback. Fast learners tend to track noisy signals too closely and to confuse their own learning by making changes before the effects of previous actions are clear (Lounamaa and March, 1987; March, 1995; Olsen, 1996). The slow learning argument does not, however, reduce the need to query the underlying theory of the reform, particularly as regards what might be achieved through pay-for-performance and individual contracts for senior civil servants who are to function as policy advisors to the political leadership. If managers were self-serving opportunists, it would be naive to expect that contract and accountability reports would compel them to mend their ways. Even a contractual regime is dependent on the good behaviour of public managers. Without a strong ethical commitment and a high level of trust, contractual remedies would be inadequate.

One lesson that might be learned is the instrumental weakness of the contract reform concept. Performance contracts for these kinds of positions look better *ex ante* than *ex post*. They promise more than they can deliver. Another lesson related to this is that the outcome of the new contract regimes adopted for top civil servants does not necessarily follow the intentions of the architects of reform (Hood, 1998b). It is difficult for ministers to live up to the demands of the contract system. The Achilles' heel of this kind of contractualism is the relationship between ministers and top civil servants. Contracts may not always make it easier in practice to dismiss or move public servants and they have a potentially perverse effect on the responsibility and accountability of top civil servants. There is a risk that the cost which is imposed on politicians in the form of more formal restrictions on their ability to reach down into departments and agencies may come without corresponding benefits (Hood, 1998b, p. 458). Hood argues that 'political reengineering' and path dependency are important in understanding the reform processes in New Zealand and the United Kingdom, and this is probably even more true when comparing New Zealand and Norway, countries in which the reform processes produced even less convergent outcomes. The argument is that national differences and path dependency are based on differences between the two countries' economy, polity, national administrative policy and political-administrative culture.

The employment relationship, particularly at senior levels, may not be best served by too specific a listing of responsibilities and expectations. Flexibility and duty have priority over precise job specification. In contrast to a relational contract, which facilitates an easy flow of information and enhances flexibility, an agency contract aims to limit flexibility and flow of information. In New Zealand chief executives and senior managers attribute most of the improvement in government performance to the discretion given to managers rather than to formal contracts, and this is even more true in Norway. Few think contracts have been the main contributor to higher operational efficiency (Schick, 1998). There are thus a number of problems with agency contracts for top civil servants. A hard-edged contractualist approach also has a number of disadvantages (Gregory and Hicks, 1999; Martin, 1995, pp. 40–41; Schick, 1998, p. 126).

First, there is the problem of specifying objectives. It is often difficult to specify contractual obligations in terms that bear a sensible relationship to the nature of the task to be fulfilled. The New Zealand model focuses on matters that can be specified in contracts, such as the purchase of outputs, but gives inadequate attention to outcomes and the government's ownership interests. Second, negotiating and enforcing contracts entails high transaction costs. Provision of information which enables the principal to clearly ensure that the agent has performed as required can be a complex exercise, both because of the difficulty and cost of developing adequate information systems and because of the problem of being 'free and frank' when exposed to sanctions. In a context with many conflicting and changing tasks, where only a few aspects of performance are measurable, a fixed salary system might function better than a pay-for-performance one (Milgrom and Roberts, 1992). Third, a separation of functions does not solve the accountability issue. A shift from implicit, relational contracts based on mutual trust to explicit legalistic agency contracts specified in documentation may undermine the quality of sound judgement and the complex accountability and responsibility obligations of public officials. Robust contracting depends on voluntary, self-interested action. Sometimes, however, self-interest defeats the government's collective interest. Contractualism assumes that performance review can be carried out 'objectively', whereas in practice it might be negotiated in a highly subjective manner. Fourth, the question of values arises. To what extent can agency contracts ensure fairness, justice, due process and administrative behaviour which is honourable and just? A 'mechanical' approach to contractualism might not be sensitive to issues of ethics and ethos and might weaken traditional values of public service, such as personal responsibility and professionalism and other such cultural enhancements of good performance. Fifth, there is the question of flexibility. Much of government is concerned with reacting to uncertainty and the unexpected and with learning from experience, and these aspects of the political process might not be handled properly through government by contract.

Notes

1   In contrast to the US performance pay system, where people are rated according to uniform performance standards, the Norwegian and New Zealand systems are based on written individual performance contracts, which are negotiated in each case. This could make the contract system less vulnerable to performance assessments than the US performance pay system.
2   See Ingraham (1993) for an overview.

8   Transforming State Employees' Unions

PAUL G. RONESS

Introduction

This chapter focuses on state employees' unions and New Public Management (NPM) reforms in Australia, New Zealand, Norway and Sweden during the 1980s and the 1990s. Two themes are discussed: the extent to which the unions responded to and had an impact on NPM reforms, and the extent to which these administrative reforms affected the unions themselves. Particular emphasis is put on the institutional characteristics of the unions: how these characteristics constrained and furthered the participation of the unions in the reform process, and what effect the reforms had on the unions.

State employees' unions are trade unions whose membership includes state employees.[1] Like other trade unions, they attend to their members' interests concerning wages and working conditions. Some of the unions are also professional associations, – i.e., organisations that attend to more wide-ranging interests of a specific profession.

Like many organisations, state employees' unions have not only individuals but also other organisations as members – i.e., they may consist of, or themselves be a part of, other unions. In addition, the state employees belong to organisations at various levels of the state administration. The highest organisational level among the unions is the union confederation. Union confederations often cover the state sector as well as the provincial and municipal sector and the private sector throughout a country. Their members are mostly national organisations, or unions, and the membership of some national unions is cross-sectoral. Some union confederations have a specific bargaining cartel for state employees. In this case, national unions that have state employees among their members are affiliated with the bargaining cartel as well as with the union confederation. The national unions often have several branches, mostly at the local level.

In all four countries state employees' unions have existed for more than 100 years. Of the unions existing in the early 1980s, some of them had been in operation for quite some time, while others had been founded relatively recently. Has the unions' historical legacy affected how they responded to NPM reforms? Did the links that many unions have traditionally maintained with Social Democratic parties affect how they responded to and had an impact on NPM reforms? State employees' unions still exist in all four countries, but their overall strength as well as the relationships between the unions have changed to a varying degree. Are these changes related to the NPM reforms? These are some of the questions discussed in this chapter.

The discussion is based on a broad institutional perspective. Like other organisations, state employees' unions may, to a different degree and in different ways, have institutional characteristics, including specific identities and capabilities (March and Olsen, 1995). Some of the identities and capabilities are expressed through elements of specialisation and hierarchy within and between organisations. At any given time, the historical legacy is ingrained in structural features that will delimit or open up for specific actions and outcomes. Whether these actions take the form of problem-solving, bargaining or rule-following, they are constrained and enabled by the existing structure. In turn, both the results of these actions, and the individual and collective actors' interpretations of what happened, have an impact on the structures that frame future behaviour in organisations. In using this perspective, it is important to clarify, first, what the historical legacy of the state employees' unions is; second, how this legacy and other institutional characteristics affect union response to and impact on NPM reforms; and, third, how this response and the reforms themselves affect the institutional characteristics of the unions.

This broad institutional perspective is compatible with the transformative perspective used in this book (see Chapter 2). The historical legacy and structural features of the unions are among the factors that help to explain the transformation of NPM reforms. The extent to which the unions responded to and had an impact on the reforms also constrains the degree of political control over the reform processes. Likewise, the ways in which the NPM reforms affect the institutional characteristics of the unions is one of the relevant external effects of the reforms. In addition, the participation of the unions in the NPM reform processes implies a dynamic relationship, whereby the NPM reforms as well as the institutional characteristics of the unions, over time are both dependent and independent variables. Finally, NPM reforms may transform perceptions of the role of state employees' unions in democratic systems.

In the next section, I will explain how the institutional characteristics of state employees' unions may affect how the unions respond to NPM reforms and how these characteristics, in turn, are changed by the reforms. The participation of the unions in the reforms and the effects of the reforms on the unions in the four countries is then discussed in separate sections for each country. Since the empirical material available on how the unions responded to, had an impact on, and were affected by the NPM reforms varies from one country to another, the discussions are intended more as illustrations of this way of reasoning than as definitive accounts of what happened and why it happened.[2] In the last section, I will make some comparisons between countries based on the theoretical perspective.

Institutional Characteristics

How are identities and capabilities expressed through elements of specialisation and hierarchy in state employees' unions?[3] With regard to identities, specialisation generally implies the evolution of particular identities, often associated with the dominant professions or work functions, within an organisation or within parts of the organisation. The actors defend diverse interests and values, and their views and behaviour are formed by the tasks for which they are responsible and by the organisation or part of the organisation to which they belong. Hierarchy implies that actors may have several identities at the same time, linked to different organisational levels. With regard to capabilities, specialisation implies that it is easier to strengthen those aspects applicable to competencies and knowledge, simultaneous to the development of organisation-specific types of competencies and knowledge. Hierarchy will particularly be associated with those aspects of capabilities that apply to rights and authorities. The hierarchy gives actors at the superior level the right and obligation to direct actors at subordinate levels by means of instructions and commands, while actors at the subordinate levels are obliged to follow the orders from above.

Identities are related to the basis for the dividing lines between state employees' unions. These lines may be quite complex. Thus, in Norway, at least six different criteria have been used either separately or in combination for creating state employees' unions: workplace (e.g., state agency), occupation, profession, position, hierarchical level of the state administration, and gender.

For national unions, the question of whether they should be based on workplace or on qualifications (occupation or profession) has been a matter of particular discussion. Here, there may be some variation between the union confederations. Thus, national unions in confederations consisting of professional associations represent people with specific qualifications, but when a profession is confined to a particular part of the state administration (e.g., a state agency) and dominates that part, qualifications and workplace coincide.

The extent to which the state employees' unions are restricted to a specific type of workplace and/or qualification may influence what kind of identities are most prominent. When a national union's membership consists almost exclusively of employees within a certain part of the state administration – e.g., an agency – the identities pertaining to the union and to the state organisation may coincide, and these identities may be quite distinctive. These tendencies are reinforced when most employees have a specific type of qualification, such as in the police and customs services. For employees having qualifications that are more widespread throughout the state administration, or that also cover the provincial/municipal and private sectors, the identity pertaining to the part of the state administration to which they belong may be weaker than their occupational or professional identity.

The identities of state employees' unions may also be influenced by the composition of their secretariats (head offices) and boards. When the people working in the secretariat are recruited from among union members or representatives, their links with the union are stronger than when they are recruited from outside. When board members represent affiliated unions, they have several, potentially conflicting identities.

Even for national unions that are affiliated with a union confederation, the importance of hierarchy for identity may vary. Thus, professional associations tend to be more independent of their superior organisation than other national unions. There may be historical reasons for this, since professional associations were often founded to attend to the interests of a specific profession.

The importance of historical legacy for identity is also evident in the strong and lasting connections between unions and political parties, especially Social Democratic parties. Thus, some national unions and union confederations may identify themselves as part of the labour movement, while others are independent of political parties.

The extent to which a state employees' union has developed a specific identity may vary considerably depending on how old the union is. In all four countries some of the first national unions for particular groups of state employees were established in the last decades of the nineteenth century, and some of the professional associations whose members include state employees are even older. Even if some of the union confederations existing in the early 1980s were founded only a few years earlier, they were often based on confederations that may be traced back several decades.

For state employees' unions, the basis for assessing NPM reforms varies according to who their members are and how the unions are linked to other unions and to interest organisations in general. Thus, reforms directed at the whole state administration may be particularly relevant for union confederations and their bargaining cartels, while reforms directed at specific parts of the administration – e.g., state agencies – are most important for the national unions and the branches that include these employees among their members.

Capabilities are related to the resources state employees' unions have for responding to and having an impact on NPM reforms. Both the existence of a secretariat and its composition are crucial. In some unions the secretariat may include specific positions or units for handling administrative reforms, and some of the people working in the secretariat may have acquired relevant expertise through their education or previous experience. The unions may also develop and utilise competencies by having permanent or ad hoc commissions for handling administrative reforms. In addition, state employees' unions may draw upon competencies in unions they are members of or have as members themselves. Thus, when unions form part of a hierarchy, they not only direct, or are directed by, other unions, but may also expand their knowledge base. Unions' opportunities for having an impact on reforms may also depend on their connections with other types of organisations. For example, links with Social Democratic parties may be decisive, especially when these parties form the government. Finally, unions may utilise formal arrangements of co-determination or other types of participatory rights.

The importance of state employees' unions may also depend on the size and composition of their membership and on union density. A large membership provides economic resources through subscriptions and forms a basis for mobilisation through strikes and other kinds of action. The dispersal of union members among the state, provincial/municipal and private sectors affects the strength of state employees within their national unions and union confederations. Likewise, the relative strength of the national unions and union confederations depends on their share of the employees in various parts of the state administration or the state sector as a whole. Union density also expresses the extent to which state employees' unions may claim to represent all state employees.

The outcomes of NPM reforms may, in turn, affect the state employees' unions. Specialised and hierarchical elements may be reinforced or weakened as a consequence of reforms in the state administration. At the same time, however, changes in the state administration are not necessarily the result of reforms. Moreover, other factors may also affect the development of institutional characteristics in state employees' unions. Thus, one must determine the extent to which changes in state employees' unions can be ascribed to NPM reforms or to changes in the state administration. Here, as elsewhere, researchers need to do a certain amount of interpretation.

In the following sections I will try to show how the relationship between NPM reforms and state employees' unions in the four countries may be interpreted on the basis of a broad institutional perspective where historical legacies are central. Since the empirical material is most comprehensive on Sweden and Norway, I will start by discussing what has happened in the two Nordic countries. The discussions on Australia and New Zealand are less complete.[4]

Sweden

Historical Legacy

In the early 1980s, there were three major union confederations in Sweden, generally recruiting different types of people. While the Swedish Trade Union Confederation ('Landsorganisationen', LO) mainly organised blue-collar employees, the Swedish Confederation of Professional Employees ('Tjänstemännens Centralorganisation', TCO) consisted mainly of white-collar employees and the Swedish Confederation of Professional Associations ('Sveriges Akademiska Centralorganisation', SACO) represented people with higher education. All of them covered the state sector as well as the provincial/municipal sector and the private sector. But while most national unions affiliated with SACO spanned the sectoral boundaries, the LO and the TCO generally had specific unions for state employees. Only a small number of national unions did not belong to any of the three union confederations. In addition, almost all local unions belonged to a national union.

Founded in 1898, the LO is the oldest union confederation in Sweden. The LO has always regarded itself as part of the labour movement, having close ties with the Social Democratic Party ('Sosialdemokratiska arbetarepartiet', SAP). Traditionally, most of the national unions affiliated with the LO had members from specific types of workplace. In 1970, nine unions for different parts of the state administration merged to form the Swedish National Union of State Employees ('Statsanställdas Förbund', SF). In 1980, the SF had almost 200,000 members and was the third largest of the 25 unions in the LO (Fredriksson and Gunnmo, 1981, p. 229). Most of the state employees in the LO belonged to the SF, and the union did not as a rule compete for members with other unions in the LO or unions in the two other confederations.

The TCO was founded in 1944 through the merger of two union confederations founded in the 1930s, one primarily for private-sector unions and the other primarily for public-sector unions. From the start, the TCO declared itself independent of political parties and it soon entered into an agreement with the LO on abstaining from competing in the recruitment of members. Like the LO, most of the national unions affiliated with the TCO have represented employees in specific types of workplace. Some unions for public employees, however, are based on specific types of qualifications (e.g., teachers and nurses), which mainly coincide with particular parts of the public sector. The Union of Civil Servants ('Statstjänstemannaförbundet', ST) was founded in 1969 through the merger of several state employees' unions affiliated with the TCO. In 1980, the ST had approximately 120,000 members and was the third largest of the 22 unions in the TCO (Fredriksson and Gunnmo, 1981, p. 230). In contrast to the LO, however, there were still several unions for state employees in the TCO.

SACO was founded in 1975 through the merger of two union confederations founded in the mid-1940s. Like the TCO, SACO have been independent of political parties. Since they were normally based on specific professions, most of the 26 unions affiliated with SACO in 1980 spanned sectoral boundaries and were only in exceptional cases confined to state employees.

In 1980, the LO was by far the largest union confederation, having more than 2 million members, compared to almost 1 million TCO members and approximately 200,000 SACO members. However, only about 10 percent of the members of the LO belonged to the state sector, while this share was about 25 percent for the TCO and 45 percent for SACO (Elvander, 1988, pp. 68–69). Thus, the LO and the TCO had approximately equal shares of the state sector, while SACO's state-sector membership was about half that of the other confederations. The LO (i.e. the SF) was particularly strong in central administration enterprises and state-owned joint-stock companies, while the TCO (particularly the ST) was the largest union in most civil service agencies. Union density was quite high: 78 percent for all Swedish employees and 91 percent among white-collar employees in the public sector (Kjellberg, 1997, pp. 59, 223).[5] This high level was not due to any formal closed-shop arrangements, however, and the unions did not need governmental approval to exist. Nevertheless, particularly since the mid-1960s, there have been specific requirements for having negotiating rights for state employees. In the early 1980s, three unions were allowed to negotiate at the central level: a specific national union (the SF) in the LO, a specific bargaining cartel (the TCO-S) in the TCO and a looser cartel (SACO-S) in SACO. While the SF and the TCO-S had separate secretariats and boards, SACO-S was a more integrated part of the union confederation. Thus, in the cases of the LO and the TCO the identities and capabilities of state employees were built into a separate national union or a separate bargaining cartel, while SACO to a lesser extent had specialised entities for state employees.

NPM Reforms and Union Response

As mentioned in Chapter 11, the incoming Social Democratic government created a new ministry ('Civildepartementet') for public-sector reform in 1982, and service orientation and decentralisation formed the basis of the modernisation programme launched by its minister. In general, the state employees' unions supported the programme, and they signed a service agreement with the minister on the means and goals of reform (Engeset, 1994, p. 110; Mellbourn, 1986, p. 80). There were, however, some differences between the unions, based on the typical hierarchical position of their members. Thus, while the TCO-S was somewhat sceptical towards the emphasis on service orientation, SACO was quite positive (Mellbourn, 1986, p. 82).

The modernisation programme of 1985 also included plans for making the fixation of wages more flexible and decentralised. Until then, wages had been mostly related to positions, and pay scales and wage levels had been determined through negotiations with the unions.[6] These mainly took the form of collective agreements at the national level between the state as employer, through the Swedish Agency for Government Employers ('Statens Arbetsgivarverk', SAV), and the three state-sector unions (the SF, the TCO-S and SACO-S), but since 1977 they have been supplemented by agreements at agency or enterprise level. The wage negotiations in 1986 resulted in several changes. Wages were no longer related to positions, but individuals were still allocated grades on pay scales. Framework agreements for the whole state sector were supplemented by separate agreements for four different areas (the military, civil service agencies, central administration enterprises and schools). In addition, a larger portion of the total wage increases was distributed through local agreements. However, the unions retained bargaining rights at all levels.

SACO had for a long time argued for increased flexibility in wage determination, while the TCO-S and the SF preferred uniformity and thus were doubtful about these kind of changes. However, in 1986 TCO-S accepted the changes in exchange for a major wage increase. The wage negotiations in 1989 resulted in the abolition of pay scales, and the amount paid to each individual was to be based more on performance and market demands than on seniority. This time, too, the unions seemed to have been bought out by a favourable wage increase. In addition, the TCO-S found it difficult to go against the widespread public beliefs in the benefits of using economic incentives (Sjölund, 1996a, pp. 118–119). For the SF, accepting a separate agreement for central administration enterprises was considered a way of reducing the chances of public utilities being converted into state-owned joint-stock companies (Johansson, 1995, p. 153).

In the second half of the 1980s, budget and financial management reforms based on management by objectives and results became more prominent, while service orientation and decentralisation was de-emphasised (see Chapter 11). According to Premfors (1991, pp. 92–93, 1998, pp. 150–151) this was due to a struggle among three loose factions within the labour movement. The group he calls the 'decentralists', headed by the minister of public sector reform, lost out when the two other factions banded together. These were the 'traditionalists', led by some cabinet members running 'spending ministries' as well as public sector union officials, and the 'economisers' with the minister of finance in charge. Although he initially only had scattered support among Social Democrats outside his own ministry, the minister of finance eventually gained the upper hand in public-sector reform discussions.

The 'economisers' also took a more pragmatic view of structural devolution and marketisation of state organisations. Thus, as part of a general strategy for economic recovery in 1990–91, the Social Democratic government put forth specific proposals for converting, amongst others, some public utilities into state-owned joint-stock companies. This was met by protests from the LO and the SF, but even if the traditional union-party co-operation was tested several changes in form of association occurred (Johansson, 1995, p. 39). The more wide-ranging proposals for privatisation and marketisation from the non-socialist government that took over in 1991 implied an even greater challenge for the state employees' unions. SF tried to counteract the negative consequences for its members through hearings and public appeals, but mostly to no avail (Johansson, 1995, p. 64). When the Social Democrats returned to power in 1994 they continued their pragmatic approach towards structural devolution and marketisation, and the size of many state organisations was still reduced whether they had changed their form of association or not.

Even though they were sceptical towards specific proposals for structural devolution in the 1990s, unions like the SF, the TCO-S and the ST have reluctantly accepted most of the changes. Thus, they have been more concerned with securing jobs and working conditions for their members within the new form of association than with actively opposing the conversions. As a part of the central negotiations in 1989, the existing Job Security Agreement for Government Employees was expanded, and a joint union-employer Job Security Foundation was established in 1990. The aim of the agreement and the foundation was to prevent state employees from being dismissed and becoming unemployed when state organisations downsized.

During the 1990s, wage determination became even more flexible and decentralised. Thus, the wage negotiations between the SAV and the three state-sector unions in 1993 set the total level of wage increases, consisting of a relatively small minimum fixed amount for all employees and a relative large pay kitty to be distributed through local agreements. In 1994, the ties between the SAV and the Ministry of Finance were loosened, and the agencies and enterprises now had to cover all wage increases from their annual appropriation. In the mid-1990s, individual pay was a non-issue among state employees' unions and state employers' organisations, and there was a general acceptance that the fixation of wages was to be primarily based on agency or enterprise concerns (Sjølund, 1996a, p. 119). However, state employees' unions at the local level still negotiate wages on behalf of their members.

In general, state employees' unions have not been central in the formulation and implementation of NPM reforms. This conclusion even applies to the LO and the SF under SAP governments, particularly since the late 1980s, when other forces within the party carried more weight, and economic recovery and marketisation were emphasised. NPM reforms on flexibility and decentralisation, whether they applied to wage determination, budget and financial management or structural devolution, coincided for the most part with the views of the members and unions in SACO. Thus, this union confederation and its national unions did not have to do much to achieve their goals. In addition, since most of them spanned sectoral boundaries, plans for maintaining old distinctions between the state and the private sector were unlikely to receive their backing. On the other hand, the TCO-S and the SF were confined to the state sector and had supported the use of uniform arrangements for wage determination and specific forms of organisation in this sector. Even if they were sceptical towards flexibility in the fixation of wages in the second half of the 1980s, they accepted the changes in exchange for preserving the interests of state employees concerning wage increases and job security. During the 1990s, bargaining cartels and national unions for state employees in the TCO and the LO were in a more defensive position, but they were not necessarily less active with regard to the wages and working conditions of their members.

The Transformation of Union Characteristics

Measured by union density, the overall strength of the unions did not diminish during the 1980s and the 1990s. Thus, even if there were some fluctuations, union density was higher in 1995 than in 1980: 88 percent for all employees and 94 percent of white-collar employees in the public sector (Kjellberg, 1997, pp. 59, 223). The number of members in the three union confederations has also increased, particularly in SACO and in the TCO: recent figures show that the LO still has slightly over 2 million members, while the TCO has approximately 1,200 000 and SACO almost 500,000 members.[7] However, the reduced size of the state sector also means that state employees now comprise a much smaller proportion of the membership of the union confederations: approximately 25 percent in SACO, 10 percent in the TCO and less than 5 percent in the LO.[8]

NPM reforms have also affected national unions and bargaining cartels within the union confederations. In 1995, the Swedish National Union of State Employees (SF) changed its name to the Union of Service and Communication Employees ('Facket för service och kommunikation', SEKO), reflecting the fact that most of its members no longer belong to civil service agencies or central administration enterprises. With its almost 200,000 members, SEKO is still the third largest of the 18 national unions in the LO. In 1991, the TCO-S and the corresponding cartel for employees in the provincial/municipal sector merged to form the Negotiating Council of TCO for Public Employees (TCO-OF). Reflecting the new arrangements of separate agreements for different areas of the state sector, the TCO-OF had sections (with negotiating rights) for the military, civil service agencies and central administration enterprises. In 1995, it changed its name to the Public

Employees' Negotiating Council (OFR), following the inclusion of some national unions not affiliated with the TCO. The Union of Civil Servants (ST) lost many members during the 1990s, mostly due to the transfer of members to other unions in the TCO when central administration enterprises were converted into state-owned joint-stock companies. Having slightly fewer than 100,000 members, the ST is now only the sixth largest of the 18 unions affiliated with the TCO. In SACO, most of the 26 unions still span sectoral boundaries, and the bargaining cartel in the state sector (SACO-S) is even less distinct from the union confederation than before.

To sum up: specific identities and capabilities for state employees are less marked in the Swedish unions than before. SEKO and the OFS are no longer confined to the state sector, and the position of the ST within the TCO has weakened. SACO has increased its share of state employees, but the union confederation, as well as its member unions, is still based on profession rather than workplace. In addition, local branches of state employees' unions have been strengthened at the expense of union confederations, bargaining cartels and, to some extent, national unions. This has mainly been due to the more flexible and decentralised arrangements for the fixation of wages.

Norway

Historical Legacy[9]

Like Sweden, Norway also had three major union confederations in the early 1980s: the Norwegian Confederation of Trade Unions ('Landsorganisasjonen i Norge', LO) mainly organising blue-collar employees; the Confederation of Vocational Unions ('Yrkesorganisasjonenes Sentralforbund', YS), consisting mainly of white-collar employees; and the Confederation of Academic and Professional Unions in Norway ('Akademikernes Fellesorganisasjon', AF), representing people with higher education. Compared to Sweden, the demarcation between the confederations was less clear and the competition for members stronger. Here, too, however, all three confederations covered the state sector as well as the provincial/municipal sector and the private sector. Likewise, while the LO and the YS to a large extent had specific unions for state employees, unions affiliated with the AF spanned the sectoral boundaries. The number of national unions not belonging to any union confederation as well as the number of local unions not belonging to any national union was limited but somewhat higher than in Sweden.

Of the three union confederations, the LO is by far the oldest. Since its foundation in 1899, the LO has constituted a central part of the labour movement, having even closer ties with the Norwegian Labour Party ('Det Norske Arbeiderparti', DNA) than its Swedish counterpart has with the SAP. These ties are expressed through formal union-party co-operation. Most of the national unions affiliated with the LO represent employees in specific types of workplace. In 1939, several national unions for specific parts of the state administration formed a bargaining cartel– the Norwegian Federation of State Employees' Unions ('Statstjenestemannskartellet', LO Stat)– exclusively for unions affiliated with the LO. In 1980, somewhat more than 100,000 state employees and 20 of the 32 unions in the LO also belonged to the LO Stat. Several of these unions also had some members in the provincial/municipal sector or the private sector. Others recruited members exclusively from specific parts of the state sector (e.g., telecommunications, postal services and railways), while the largest one – the Norwegian Civil Service Union ('Norsk Tjenestemannslag', NTL), founded in 1947 – spanned many parts of the state administration. Thus, compared with Sweden, state employees in the LO were concentrated to a lesser extent in a specific union and they had negotiation rights at the central level through a bargaining cartel instead of through a national union.

The YS was founded in 1977, based on two former union confederations and some independent national unions. It had a specific bargaining cartel for state employees (the YS-S). In 1980, six of the fifteen national unions in the YS also belonged to the YS-S, and all of these six unions were exclusively for specific groups of state employees.

The AF was founded in 1975, replacing two partly overlapping confederations of national unions/professional associations. Like the YS and its predecessors, the AF and its predecessors were independent of political parties and included state employees. In contrast to the YS, however, the state sector did not constitute a separate part in AF. In 1980, 53 unions belonged to the AF, and most of them drew some, but not all of their membership from the state sector.

Like in Sweden, in 1980, the LO was by far the largest union confederation, having approximately 700,000 members, compared to just under 100,000 in the YS and the AF. Thus, while the size of the LO and the AF was comparable to its Swedish counterparts (the LO and SACO), the YS was much smaller than the TCO. While just over one in three members of the YS and the AF worked in the state sector, this applied only to every sixth member of the LO. Nevertheless, the LO had more members among state employees than the YS and the AF taken together. Union density for all employees was about 60 percent (Kjellberg, 1983, p. 36). Among state employees, however, it was about 90 percent. Like in Sweden, this high level was not due to any formal closed-shop arrangement, and union existence was not contingent on governmental approval. Since the late 1950s, there have been specific requirements for having negotiating rights for state employees. In the early 1980s, three unions were allowed to negotiate at the central level: the LO Stat, the YS-S, and the AF. While the LO Stat and the YS-S had separate secretariats and boards, the AF did not have specialised entities for state employees. This implies that in the cases of LO and YS the identities and capabilities of state employee were built into a bargaining cartel as well as into several national unions, while in the case of the AF neither the union confederation nor most of its affiliated national unions were restricted to the state sector.

NPM Reforms and Union Response[10]

In the second half of the 1980s, administrative reforms gained a more prominent position on the agenda of the LO Stat, the YS-S and several of their affiliated unions. This increased attention reflected the presentation of the comprehensive reform programmes of the non-socialist government in 1986 and the Labour government in 1987. The reform programmes included some NPM elements, particularly regarding service orientation and budget and financial management. However, in the programmes and in later reform efforts, the extent of structural devolution and of decentralisation and flexibility in wage determination was less marked than in Sweden. Does the participation of state employees' unions in the reform processes account for the fact that the changes that have taken place since the late 1980s have been relatively modest?

With regard to structural devolution, since the early 1980s the form of association of a number of state agencies and central administration enterprises (see Chapter 6) has been under discussion. A couple of agencies and enterprises were reorganised as foundations, while others were converted into state-owned joint-stock companies. Only a few companies were privatised, however. In general, the LO Stat and the YS-S were sceptical about structural devolution and privatisation, while the AF was more positive. All three union confederations (or their bargaining cartels) were represented in the public commission appointed in 1987 to discuss improving the organisation of the state. In its report, presented in 1989, the commission considered the wide range of tasks, objectives and management regulations in the public sector and concluded that the existing forms of association were satisfactory. The establishment of new foundations was not considered advisable, and the report focused on the criteria to be used for choosing the state agency, central administration enterprise or state-owned joint-stock company as a form of association. However, the commission did not make many specific recommendations for reorganisation.

For the state employees' unions, this issue was most relevant with regard to telecommunications, postal services and railways (see also Jensen, 1998; Sørlie, 1997 and Vathne, 1998). The non-socialist government that took over in 1989 soon signalled that it was considering converting the three central administration enterprises into some sort of state-owned or private companies. The LO Stat, the YS-S and their affiliated unions in the enterprises mobilised broadly against the plans. However, before the government had had time to present specific proposals to the Storting, it resigned in late 1990. The new Labour government quite soon decided to keep these central administration enterprises the way they were, with the option of reconsidering the form of association three years later. Union-party co-operation between the LO and the DNA seem to have been quite crucial for this decision. However, for the telecommunications service the proposal to convert it into a state-owned joint-stock company was raised again before the three years were up. This time the proposal went through the cabinet and the Storting, despite major protests from some state employees' unions. The strikes, lobbying, and negotiations through formal union-party co-operation channels undertaken by the LO Stat and its affiliated union in the enterprise failed to prevent the reorganisation taking place in 1994. Later the form of association of postal services and railways was also discussed in a separate union-party ad hoc commission. Here, a compromise was reached, and in 1996 the commission proposed converting the postal services and major parts of the railways into independent state companies through special legislation. The proposal was later presented to the Storting by the Labour government and approved by the majority of parliamentarians.

With regard to wage determination arrangements in the 1980s were even more standardised and centralised than in Sweden. Wages were mostly tied to positions, and pay scales and wage levels were determined through negotiations with the unions. Collective agreements at the national level between the state as employer, through what is now the Ministry of Labour and Government Administration ('Arbeids- og administrasjonsdepartementet', AAD), and the three state-sector unions (the LO Stat, the YS-S and the AF) constituted the main element in wage determination, but they were supplemented by some limited reform experiments during the 1980s. Around 1990 an attempt was made to bring about a comprehensive revision of the wage system in the state sector in accordance with the NPM idea of results-oriented management. The main purpose of the reforms was better recruitment and increased efficiency within individual state agencies and enterprises. This was to be brought about through less standardisation, less centralised control and fewer collective agreements. The plans were discussed in a public commission including representatives of the three union confederations/bargaining cartels and state employers. While the AF and most of the state employers argued for extensive flexibility and decentralisation, the LO Stat, in particular, wanted to make only minor changes. The report presented by the commission in 1990 contained few radical proposals and was largely seen as providing a balance between, on the one hand, the desire for greater productivity orientation, and, on the other hand, realistic ends, given the historical legacy and established power structures and wage policy norms. The same generally applied to the new wage system for some 450 top civil servants who were removed from the collective wage negotiations and general pay scales (see Chapter 7).

Even if wages were still determined mainly through collective agreements, central negotiations and state-wide pay scales during the 1990s, the revisions of the early 1990s provided opportunities for a certain degree of decentralisation and greater flexibility through local negotiations and individual placement on extended scales. While the AF and employers in state agencies and central administration enterprises continued to argue that these opportunities should be exploited, the LO Stat and the YS-S were more cautious. In general, the wage agreements between the three state-sector unions and the AAD were characterised by central authority control. The increase in the number of places where wages are negotiated locally, and in the size of the pay kitty to be distributed locally, has been moderate. Thus, so far state employees' unions like the LO Stat have had a major impact on reforms concerning wage determination under both Labour governments and non-socialist governments, while the AF and its affiliated unions have played a less prominent role.

Like in Sweden, the state employees unions' have been concerned with securing jobs and working conditions for their members when state organisations are restructured. Thus, as part of the central wage negotiations in 1992, the Labour government pledged to guarantee job security for state employees. The pledge was initiated by the LO Stat and the YS-S, and the unions (including the AF) subsequently also participated in formulating guidelines for handling the restructuring of the state by the AAD (see Jacobsen, 1998).

The state employees' unions were also involved in the process leading to the establishment of the Norwegian Association of Public-Owned Enterprises ('Arbeidsgiverforeningen NAVO') in 1993 (see Halvorsen, 1996). The AF saw no need for a new association, pointing out that the enterprises could join some of the existing private-sector employers' associations. The LO Stat and the YS-S, however, wanted a separate employers' association for devolved state organisations, setting this as a precondition for supporting further devolution. Here, too, the negotiations through formal union-party co-operation channels seem to have been quite crucial for the outcome. For employees in state organisations that have joined NAVO, wages are determined through agreements with the unions, but with more flexible pay scales and more emphasis on local negotiations than in the rest of the state sector. In addition, working conditions are based on private-sector practices rather than those applying specifically to the public sector.

In general, since the mid-1980s administrative reforms have occurred through dialogue with the state employees' unions. The tempo and extent of the changes have largely reflected what was acceptable to the unions and, with the exception of the AF, the state-sector unions have been sceptical towards many NPM reforms. The LO Stat, in particular, has played a central role in many reform processes. Through formal union-party co-operation, this particular union has had direct access to the (Labour) government throughout most of the last 15 years. Particularly within the area of wage policy and regarding specific proposals on structural devolution, the union has also had considerable influence on the extent of the changes. However, some changes in the form of association (e.g. the conversion of the telecommunications enterprise into a state-owned joint-stock company) have been implemented despite union protests.

The Transformation of Union Characteristics

Measured by union density, the overall strength of the unions did not change much during the 1980s and 1990s. Thus, in 1998, 57 percent of all employees and 84 percent of state employees were union members.[11] The LO is still the largest union confederation, having more than 800,000 members. However, the YS has increased its membership, and now has approximately 230,000 members. The AF and the new Federation of Norwegian Professional Associations ('Akademikerne') each have approximately 115,000 members, more than the AF had in 1980.[12] Thus, the position of the LO is not as dominant as it was 20 years ago. Partly as a result of the expansion of the provincial/municipal sector, public employees now constitute a larger share of union membership than before: more than 50 percent of all active union members work in the public sector, and even in the LO almost every second member is a public employee (Nergaard, 1999, p. 9).

NPM reforms, or rather the relatively modest extent of actual changes, have affected some of the state employees' unions. Thus, some of the professional associations in the AF who were dissatisfied with what their union confederation had achieved in the preceding public-sector wage negotiations founded Akademikerne in 1997. Now, most of the 14 unions affiliated with Akademikerne and the 18 unions affiliated with the AF embrace more than one sector, but the AF has a much more marked public-sector emphasis than before the split. However, neither of the two union confederations has specialised entities for state employees.

In the LO, 110,000 members and 19 out of 27 unions also belong to the LO Stat.[13] While some unions still recruit members from a specific part of the state sector, more unions than before draw some of their members from the provincial/municipal sector or the private sector. In addition to the central negotiations with the AAD, the LO Stat now also negotiates with NAVO. The creation of NAVO did not mean that union members had to be transferred to other unions in the LO. Thus, structural devolution has not weakened the position of the LO Stat and its affiliated unions to any great extent. In the YS, 14 of the 19 unions have some form of affiliation with the YS-S, while 9 are almost exclusively for specific groups of state employees.[14] Like the LO Stat, the YS-S now also negotiates with NAVO and still constitutes a separate entity within the union confederation. However, the relationships with NAVO imply that the bargaining cartels have to handle a broader set of arrangements on wages and working conditions than when they were confined to the traditional state sector.

It may thus be concluded that specific identities and capabilities for state employees have not been weakened in Norway to the same extent as in Sweden. The LO Stat and the YS-S still cover only the state sector, but this sector has become more complex. The AF is now primarily a union confederation for public employees, and in its national unions profession often coincides with a specific type of workplace. Even if the extent of decentralisation in the fixation of wages has been much less than in Sweden, here too local branches of state employees' unions became somewhat stronger during the 1990s.

Australia

Historical Legacy

In the early 1980s there was only one union confederation: the Australian Council of Trade Unions (ACTU). It had recently merged with two other union confederations: the Australian Council of Salaried and Professional Associations (ACSPA) in 1978, and the Council of Australian Government Employee Organisations (CAGEO) in 1981. While ACTU's membership had previously been mainly blue-collar, ACSPA consisted mainly of white-collar employees and CAGEO of federal employees. Thus, ACTU now included unions for federal employees as well as unions for employees in the provinces (i.e., states and territories), municipalities and the private sector. More than 90 percent of union members belonged to unions affiliated with ACTU.

ACTU was founded in 1927 and has since then had close ties with the Australian Labor Party (ALP). The elements of hierarchy are weaker in ACTU than in the LO in Sweden and Norway. The federal state structure is reflected in ACTU, where state trade and labor councils are formally branches of ACTU but generally have a much longer history than the union confederation and display some independence and considerable power in their localities (Bamber and Davis, 1992, p. 16). In contrast to most of their Nordic counterparts, the affiliated unions were traditionally based on specific qualifications (occupations or crafts). The extent of specialisation was also much higher, with a total of approximately 2.5 million members and 150 affiliated unions in the early 1980s (Rawson and Wrightson, 1980, p. 16).

ACSPA (founded in 1956) and CAGEO (founded in 1921) did not have the same traditional connections with the ALP. However, by maintaining close and cordial contacts with ACTU since the mid-1960s, they also had a special relationship with the ALP which had no counterpart in their relations with other parties (Rawson, 1978, p. 15). While affiliated unions in ACSPA covered specific groups of professionals and other white-collar employees, affilation with CAGEO was confined to unions recruiting federal employees. Before the merger with ACTU, CAGEO had slightly over 200,000 members in 25 affiliated unions, mainly covering specific positions, occupations or parts of the federal sector. Around 1980, the largest unions for federal employees had approximately 50,000 members (Spann, 1979, p. 375; Rawson and Wrightson, 1980, pp. 9, 16). For public employees in general, some unions were confined to a specific state or territory. Thus, in the public sector specialisation based on workplace or qualification was supplemented by specialisation based on geographical location.

Overall union density was 50 percent in 1982, and the difference between the public sector (73 percent) and the private sector (39 percent) was even higher than in the Nordic countries. Among the union members there were almost as many working in the public sector as in the private sector.[15] However, even if most public-sector employees belonged to the same union confederation, elements of hierarchy were quite weak and the extent of specialisation quite high and rather complex. In contrast to the private sector, closed-shop arrangements were quite uncommon in the public sector. Unions that were registered under the arbitration system had the exclusive rights to represent workers who fell under the jurisdiction of their membership clause (Bray and Walsh, 1998, p. 362). Combined with the existence of only one union confederation this meant there was no inter-union competition. On the other hand, specific identities and capabilities for federal employees were less marked than for state employees in the Nordic countries.

NPM Reforms and Union Response

The administrative reforms launched by the incoming ALP federal government in 1983 were mainly based on managerial ideas and were not intended to be construed as hostile or confrontational towards the administration (Zifcak, 1994, p. 20). The incremental and cautious approach also rested on formalised co-operation between the ALP government and ACTU (Castles, Gerritsen and Vowles, 1996b, p. 11). The Australian unions had begun to co-operate more effectively with the ALP in the late 1970s and early 1980s. The party became receptive to the possibility of a corporatist relationship, whereas the unions demonstrated both a similar interest and an organisational capacity to participate in such arrangements (Bray and Walsh, 1998, p. 366). Just before the ALP entered office, the party and the union confederation had negotiated an agreement on incomes policy. The subsequent agreement (Accord) between the ALP government and ACTU was the first in a series of eight agreements in the 1983–1996 period. In addition to incomes policy, the Accords also covered elements of economic, social and industrial relations policy (see Bray and Walsh, 1998, p. 358; Peetz, 1998, pp. 3, 157).

Many of the administrative reforms of the ALP governments in the 1983–1996 period seem to have been cleared through these party-union relationships. Compared to its Swedish counterpart, the faction system was more explicit in the ALP. ALP party and government policy formulation have also to some extent been characterised by a divison of labour and 'inner accord' among the three factions (Boston and Uhr, 1996, p. 51; Castles, Gerritsen and Vowles, 1996b, p. 14). Thus, various reform efforts seem to have been handled by specialised networks, including specific union leaders and ministers.

A vital part of the first Accord was an even stricter regulation and centralisation of the wages and arbitration system. Wages were directly linked to prices through a form of wage indexation determined in a series of national wage cases (Peetz, 1998, p. 157). In the federal sector, standard pay, classifications and employment conditions had for many years been determined centrally for all agencies and employees in the Australian Public Service (APS). A Public Service Board performed the employer role on behalf of the Australian government, and awards and agreements were settled with unions and/or arbitrated by a separate Public Service Arbitrator (Yates, 1998, pp. 82–83). However, as a part of the creation of mega-departments in 1987, the Public Service Board was abolished, with most of its former functions being transferred to the Department of Industrial Relations, the Department of Finance and a new and more limited Public Service Commission (Halligan, 1996, pp. 94–95; Zifcak, 1994, p. 25). The specialist public service arbitrator was also abolished in the mid-1980s, and in general public servants were now incorporated into the industrial relations systems applying to private sector employees (Thornthwaite and Hollander, 1998, p. 99).

The information available on federal employees' union participation in NPM reforms during the 1980s is quite limited. The general impression is that the unions, through consultations at various levels, approved most reforms. Thus, one of the major unions (the Public Sector and Broadcasting Union) supported the reform agenda because the ALP government modernised the public service while recognising essentially public sector features and incorporating changes relevant to its members, like job satisfaction, skill development, career paths, industrial democracy and participation in agency decision-making. Nevertheless, the union expressed concern about a number of issues, including contracting out (Halligan, 1996, p. 93).

For federal employees and their unions, agreements on the fixation of wages and working conditions were most important. As part of the new Accords and the law on industrial relations, some decentralisation of wage determination to industry and workplace level occurred between 1987 and 1990. However, this was closely managed within a national framework by the arbitration tribunals (Bray and Walsh, 1998, p. 368). Enterprise bargaining was adopted by the Accord partners as their wages policy in 1990. The federal national wage case decision the following year focused almost exclusively on wage increases being negotiated at enterprise or workplace level. Subsequent national wage systems and legislative change continued this emphasis on enterprise bargaining, with the support of almost all the major industrial relations players (Bray and Walsh, 1998, p. 373; Dabscheck, 1995, p. 80). In the federal sector the Labor government strongly supported enterprise bargaining linked to productivity improvements in the APS. After more than 18 months of negotiations, the Department of Industrial Relations and the unions in December 1992 reached a service-wide APS agreement establishing a two-tier system, involving some funded wage increases linked to several APS-wide productivity initiatives (tier 1) and pay negotiations over workplace reforms at agency level (tier 2) on a self-funding basis (Yates, 1998, p. 83). The elements of agency-based pay negotiations were regulated by the terms of service-wide framework agreements. However, these elements were reduced by the Labor government in 1995, reflecting both a preference for pursuing a range of service-wide productivity initiatives and opposition from unions and some agencies to their continuation (Yates, 1998, p. 86).

While service-wide or enterprise negotiations and agreements until 1996 involved unions and employers at various levels, the new federal law on workplace relations initiated by the incoming coalition government made it possible for agencies to exclude unions and to conclude individual agreements (Australian Workplace Agreements, AWA) with employees at all levels of their organisation (Thornthwaite and Hollander, 1998, p. 105). The new government also implemented many budgetary and other economic reforms affecting the federal sector, including downsizing the APS. During 1996–97, the federal employees' unions staged several protests against the government's budget and workplace relations legislation, which were seen as weakening the unions, undermining collective bargaining and eroding award conditions and job security more generally. Attempts to negotiate a new service-wide agreement failed. Instead, based on consultations with agencies and unions, the government in 1997 issued a set of policy parameters providing a framework for agency agreements in the APS. In devolving the authority to conclude agreements to agencies, these broad parameters recognised the government's interest, as the ultimate employer, in introducing greater flexibility while maintaining a coherent approach to its workforce as a whole. Unions like the Community and Public Sector Union (CPSU) refused to accept a role for the AWAs, but reluctantly recognised the growing inevitability of agency-level negotiations if they were to secure an active role in negotiating agreements (Yates, 1998, pp. 85–88).

Most public-sector unions had joined ACTU just before the ALP came into office in 1983. During the following years their influence on NPM reforms depended on their status within the union confederation, the union-party relationships and the party faction system. Approval of the incremental and cautious reforms of the ALP government also seemed to be regarded as important to increase the chances of keeping the party in office. The major opposition parties had signalled their intention to carry out more radical NPM reforms and to adopt a more anti-union stance, which made a change of government a worse alternative for the unions (Dabscheck, 1995, p. 51). The new laws on public-sector and workplace relations issued by the coalition government in 1996–97 also met with protests from the unions. The largest union for public employees (the CPSU) launched a comprehensive public opinion and lobbying campaign. Even if some of the more far-reaching proposals were set aside, in general the unions did not succeed in stopping reform.

The Transformation of Union Characteristics

Measured by union density, the overall strength of the unions diminished during the 1980s and the 1990s, and in 1997 it was 30 percent for all employees and 55 percent for public employees. The reduction in the number of union members was less marked, from 2.57 million in 1982 to 2.11 million in 1997. The decline in the relative share of public-sector employment also contributed to a decline in the relative share of public-sector union members among all union members, from 47 percent in 1982 to 40 percent in 1997 (Peetz, 1998, p. 6).

ACTU is still the only union confederation, covering the public as well as the private sector, and including most of the union members. It has 52 affiliated unions and branches (labor councils) in all states and territories. The CPSU is the principal public-sector union (see O'Brien and Hort, 1998, p. 48) and one of the largest unions affiliated with ACTU. The CPSU also has branches in all states and territories and sections for government departments or agencies. It represents 250,000 public-sector employees – i.e., approximately 12 percent of all Australian union members.[16]

NPM and industrial relations reforms have had extensive effects on union structure. In return for union approval of enterprise bargaining provided for by the law on industrial relations in 1988, the government also passed legislation facilitating the reorganisation of the union movement in accordance with the plans of the leadership of ACTU to drastically reduce the number of unions (Svensen and Teicher, 1999, p. 338). Unlike its predecessor, the new law stipulated that unions seeking registration must have a minimum of 1,000 members and be industry-based. This amendment was an attempt to reduce the proliferation of small, occupationally-based unions. In 1991, the federal government amended the law to facilitate union mergers and further increase the minimum size of federal unions to 10,000 members (Bamber and Davis, 1992, pp. 105–106). The number of unions also fell, though not to the extent planned by the ACTU leadership (Peetz, 1998, p. 133).

The CPSU was founded through one of these union mergers in the early 1990s. Following the prevalence of enterprise bargaining in the public sector, the CPSU was reorganised in 1997. The workplace is now the basic unit of the new structure. All workplaces must be single agency under the new structure. All members are allocated to a section – i.e., a single government department or agency or a group of employers with some common interest. In addition, they are also a member of a geographically-based branch.[17]

Thus, in Australia union identities and capabilities related to the whole federal sector have been somewhat weakened. The CPSU and other public-sector unions constitute a smaller part of the union movement than before. However, the emphasis on enterprise bargaining and the workplace as the basic unit in unions means that union identities and capabilities related to the various government departments and agencies may be strengthened.

New Zealand

Historical Legacy

In the early 1980s, there were two union confederations: the Federation of Labour (FOL), mainly consisting of unions for blue-collar employees in the private sector; and the Combined State Unions (CSU), consisting of unions for state employees. Thus, in contrast to the three other countries, private- and public-sector employees in New Zealand belonged to different union confederations. The FOL was the key player, but it did not represent either the public sector or many white-collar employees (Bray and Neilson, 1996, p. 71).

The CSU was the oldest union confederation, founded in 1932. It did not have any formal affiliation with political parties. The FOL was founded in 1937. As part of the labour movement it had ties with the New Zealand

Labour Party (NZLP), but they were not as close as those between its Australian counterpart, ACTU, and the ALP. The elements of hierarchy in the CSU and the FOL were even weaker than in ACTU. Like in Australia, the unions were traditionally based on specific qualifications (Bray and Walsh, 1998, p. 363; Roth, 1973, pp. 113–115). Here too, the extent of specialisation was quite high, with a total of approximately 250 unions and 700,000 members in 1981.[18]

With its approximately 50,000 members in the early 1980s, the Public Service Association (PSA) was the largest union in the CSU and also one of the largest unions in the country. It comprised various groups of state employees, while most of the other unions in the CSU were smaller and more specialised according to workplace or qualification. The PSA was founded in 1913, but there had been unions specifically for state employees before that as well. State employees' unions were quite centralised, reflecting the character of the system in which they operated (Walsh, Harbridge and Crawford, 1997, p. 2).

In 1981, overall union density was 48 percent. Public employees accounted for approximately 27 percent of all union members, indicating that union density was higher in the public than in the private sector. Thus, although membership in state employees' unions like the PSA was voluntary, unlike in (parts of) the private sector, membership levels were quite high. Like in Australia, unions that were registered under the arbitration system had the exclusive right to represent workers who fell under the jurisdiction of their membership clause (Bray and Walsh, 1998, p. 362). Even if this exclusivity did not apply to state employees' unions (Boston et al., 1996, p. 227), inter-union competition was not prevalent in the state sector. In contrast to Australia, the existence of a separate union confederation (the CSU) and a large union (the PSA) for public-sector employees indicates that specific identities and capabilities for state employees were built into the union structure. At the same time, ties between state employees' unions and the Labour Party were weaker than in the other countries.

NPM Reforms and Union Response

Unlike its Australian counterpart, the NZLP launched its major economic reforms after it was elected in 1984. Moreover, unlike the ALP, the NZLP government did not pursue a corporatist strategy, despite this having been a central feature of its election manifesto (Easton and Gerritsen, 1996, p. 45). In contrast to the ALP, the NZLP has never had a formal system of factions.

Hence, the composition of the cabinets in the 1980s was not strongly influenced by the need to ensure a politically acceptable balance among the main groupings within the party (Boston and Uhr, 1996, p. 52). In the early years of the Labour government the union movement lacked unity and vision and it found itself always one step behind as Labour policy moved off at a terrific pace. Reforms bringing about deregulation and liberalisation drew a degree of union opposition, but this opposition was diverse and unco-ordinated. The opposition of public-sector employees to staff cuts and to corporatisation was scattered, and there were no deep links between private- and public-sector unions (Bray and Neilson, 1996, p. 76).

The first major state-sector reform was launched through the State-Owned Enterprises Act 1986 (SOEA) and converted trading departments and government enterprises into more devolved state-owned enterprises (see Chapter 6). Unions like the PSA were effectively excluded during the early phases of the process (Kelsey, 1995). When the bill was introduced, the unions tried to use their links to the NZLP to oppose it, but mostly to no avail. Meetings arranged with the minister of finance took the form of briefings about a policy that had already been decided (Gregory, 1987, p. 117; Slotnes, 1994, p. 117; M. Wilson, 1989, pp. 80–83). Nevertheless, the PSA was able to negotiate a deployment agreement, which set out a number of options in the event of redundancies, with voluntary severance being the last option (Walsh, Harbridge and Crawford, 1997, p. 16).

In state-sector industrial relations, however, elements of deregulation and liberalisation were for some time quite scarce. Standardised and centralised arrangements for service-wide occupational classifications, in which the State Services Commission (SSC) represented the New Zealand government as em-ployer, were maintained for the first three-year Labour period in office. Legislation required pay and conditions in the public sector to be fairly comparable with those in the private sector. Most state employees received their pay increases through a general wage adjustment, based upon a survey of private-sector pay rates. The average private-sector pay increase was uniformly applied to all state employees. Occupational pay claims, which supplemented general wage adjustments, were used as a mechanism to remedy any anomalies this created for particular occupational groups or to resolve exceptional recruitment or retention difficulties (Walsh, Harbridge and Crawford, 1997, p. 1; see also Walsh, 1991, p. 56). The emphasis on occu-pational class bargaining made it possible to mobilise particular groups with a strong sense of occupational identity. However, by lodging more than 150 occupational pay claims annually in the mid-1980s, the PSA was in danger of coming to operate as a federation of occupational or craft unions (Walsh, Harbridge and Crawford, 1997, p. 5).

In its 1987 election manifesto, the NZLP government made an explicit commitment to consult with the unions over any changes on the fixation of wages and working conditions in the state sector. Following the re-election of the government, the SSC and the PSA in December 1987 agreed to move from the service-wide occupationally-based bargaining system to a system of departemental agreements (Walsh, 1991, p. 61). However, without any prior warning, the government the following morning introduced a State Sector Bill containing more radical administrative and industrial relations reforms. State employees and their unions mobilised against the bill, but their protests made no difference. Their arguments and concerns were treated as the special pleadings of a protected workforce who were afraid of being held to account for their performance (Kelsey, 1995). The chances of mobilising the union movement on a broader basis were reduced by the recent replacement of the separate private- and public-sector union confederations (FOL and CSU) with the more inclusive New Zealand Council of Trade Unions (CTU) in 1987. The CTU was keen to show that it could resolve disputes rather than escalate them and it discouraged open resistance towards the bill (Bray and Neilson, 1996, p. 77).

Through the State Sector Act 1988 (SSA), state employees and their unions were now subject to the provisions of the Labour Relations Act, which previously had applied only to the private sector (Boston et al., 1996, p. 211). The new accountability arrangements for chief executives made departmental negotiations necessary. The SSC and the PSA negotiated national departemental collective agreements for each department, which then were separate organisations in every respect. The PSA recognised that many senior staff were in favour of being on individual employment contracts and traded it for industrial democracy and union facilities clauses in most departmental agreements negotiated in 1988 (Walsh, Harbridge and Crawford, 1997, pp. 5–6). Thus, even if the fixation of wages and working conditions no longer had to be standardised, negotiations were still quite centralised, with the SSC and the PSA as the main parties.

Like the reforms on state-sector industrial relations, the sale of state-owned enterprises was not mentioned by the NZLP government before the 1987 election. Despite extensive conflict within the Labour Party, many enterprises were privatised during the following three years. Even if mostly unsuccessful, the CTU and its affiliated state employees' unions for the most part argued against economic, social and administrative reforms through the party: like in Australia, a change of government was seen as a worse alternative.

After the election in 1990, the new National government also introduced more far-reaching NPM reforms, characterised by deregulation and liberalisation. For the state employees and their unions, the Employment Contracts Act 1991 (ECA) was the most important. According to Kelsey (1995), the ECA had two goals: to force wages down and to break the unions. Under this act, unions had no special privileges. No employment contract could require workers to join, or not to join, a union. Instead, unions were compelled to compete with one another and with outside consultants who were selling their services, sometimes with employer support, to potential employee clients. Collective contracts were still allowed but not encouraged. Even when an individual employee had authorised such negotiation, employers could not by law be compelled to negotiate a collective contract (Kelsey, 1995). The bill went through parliament, despite being widely opposed through a comprehensive public opinion campaign by the CTU, marches and rallies in many cities and strikes by some unions and at some workplaces. While there was strong evidence of rank-and-file support for a general strike, the CTU leadership discouraged this kind of action, and at a special conference the majority of officials voted against it (Bramble and Heal, 1997, pp. 137–138; Kelsey, 1995).

Starting in 1991, the SSC delegated negotiating authority to chief executives in government departments and state agencies. In the mid-1990s, the PSA negotiated more than 300 collective contracts, although the great majority of government departments still negotiated a single national collective contract (Boston et al., 1996, p. 236). In addition, when downsizing of the state administration continued in the 1990s, the PSA and the SSC negotiated an enforceable redundancy agreement covering all public servants. By contrast with existing private-sector agreements, the PSA/SSC agreement on restructuring and redundancy provided a specific process of consultation and review and generous compensation in the event of an employee accepting redundancy (Walsh, Harbridge and Crawford, 1997, pp. 16–17).

Recent activities by state employees' unions on administrative reforms have focused on workplace relations. Thus, through what it calls the 'Partnership for quality strategy' the PSA aims to strengthen employee participation and workplace democracy. The PSA does not believe that the role of state employees' unions should be narrowly confined to pay and conditions. It argues that people who are expected to commit themselves fully to their work should be involved in decisions bringing about changes at their workplace.

The Employment Relations Bill launched in 2000 by the incoming Labour government is also regarded by the PSA as an important step for developing a real partnership between workers and employers and for rebuilding the capacity of the public service.[19]

The role of state employees' unions in the formulation and implementation of NPM reforms in New Zealand was even more minor than in Sweden. This applies to reforms introduced by Labour as well as by national governments. The impact of the unions has been mainly restricted to repairing some of the major damage done to the wages and working conditions of their members by the reforms. The NPM reforms, such as those introduced through the ECA were also adversarial towards the unions themselves. The extent to which they affected state employees' unions will be discussed next.

The Transformation of Union Characteristics

Measured by union density, the overall strength of the unions diminished even more than in Australia. While it was quite stable during the 1980s, it declined markedly in the 1990s: from 45 percent in 1989 to 20 percent in 1996 (Bramble and Heal, 1997, p. 128; Bray and Walsh, 1998, p. 363). Thus, the ECA seems to have had a major impact on union support (see Walsh and Brosnan, 1999, p. 107). In 1995, there were about 360,000 union members, of which public employees accounted for approximately 46 percent.[20] This indicates that union density was much higher in the public sector than in the private sector and that public-sector unions lost fewer members than private-sector unions after the introduction of the ECA.

The CTU was established as a new union confederation in 1987 rather than as a merger of the FOL and the CSU. In an attempt to consolidate their resources, the majority of unions affiliated with the FOL and the CSU, along with some independent unions, agreed, after long discussions, to join together (Kelsey, 1995). However, this confederation of private- and public-sector unions and of blue- and white-collar unions did not clearly bind unions to the corporatist approach of its leadership (Bray and Neilson 1996, 78). In the early 1990s, the CTU had 57 affiliated unions and 420,000 members, making up 83 percent of all union members (Vowles, 1992, p. 346). Later on, the CTU lost many unions and individual members and it now has 19 affiliated unions representing approximately 200,000 employees.[21] This reduction was partly due to the creation of a rival union confederation in 1993, when 12, mainly small blue-collar unions joined together to form the New Zealand Trade Union Federation (NZTUF). These unions were highly critical of the

CTU's passive response to the introduction of the ECA and its support for trade liberalisation (Kelsey, 1995). However, the CTU still accounts for approximately 80 percent of all union members.[22]

With its 45,000 members, the PSA is still the largest state employees' union and one of the largest unions affiliated with the CTU.[23] The handling of the ECA also affected the PSA, as some member groups critical of the PSA's passive response in 1992 defected to form the National Union of Public Employees. The following year, however, two unions for local government employees merged with the PSA (Walsh, Harbridge and Crawford, 1997, p. 10). This helped the PSA to maintain a stable membership from the mid-1980s to the mid-1990s (Boston et al., 1996, p. 234).

NPM and industrial relations reforms affected state employees' unions like the PSA in many ways. The ECA broke the automatic link between trade-union membership and representation and created the potential for state employees' unions to be challenged as the dominant bargaining parties in the state sector. Until the mid-1990s, this did not happen as the PSA still negotiated the contracts of most employees. However, many of the PSA's collective contracts covered only a small number of employees, thus stretching its resources to negotiate and service these contracts (Boston et al., 1996, pp. 233–236). Management efforts to develop a collective sense of organisational identity and commitment and to build a common culture in the organisation have the potential to jeopardise the loyalty of members to their unions. State employees' unions thus face the problem of remaining relevant in the workplace, and their main threat may come less from a direct manage-ment assault than from its standing with its members through its inability to be seen as delivering improved working conditions (Boston et al., 1996, p. 244). The recent reorganisation of the internal structure of the PSA may also reflect an attempt to confront this challenge. While the PSA previously had 24 geographical branches, in 1999 it was divided into six sections (called sectors) covering specific parts of the public sector. Within each section (or sector), workplaces and enterprises comprise the basic units.[24]

To sum up, even if state employees' unions were affected by NPM reforms, they have been less weakened than other unions. Partly as a result of having specific public-sector unions like the PSA, identities and capabilities for public-sector employees have become more marked in the New Zealand unions than they were before. Unions like the PSA have also become less dependent upon their union confederation, indicating that elements of hierarchy within the union movement are even weaker than they were in the early 1980s. As workplaces and enterprises have replaced occupations as the point of departure for the fixation of wages, the basis for developing specific identities within the state sector has also changed.

Conclusion

As shown in the previous sections, the extent to which state employees' unions have responded to, had an impact on, or been affected by NPM reforms varies. In Norway, for example, the LO Stat was more involved and influential in the reform processes than the AF, while in Sweden the TCO-S was changed more by the reforms than its affiliated national unions. Unions also responded differently to, and were affected differently by, different types of reforms in different countries and at different times. In general, state employees' unions were most interested in reforms related to wage determination, personnel policy, structural devolution and privatisation, while reforms related to budget and financial management mostly went unnoticed. Radical changes in wage determination and in the form and scope of the state administration also had the most direct effects on the unions. In Norway and Sweden, many unions have paid much attention to administrative reforms since the second half of the 1980s, but the Norwegian unions, particularly the LO Stat, had more impact on the reforms than the Swedish unions. While ACTU in Australia was involved in many of the reform processes from the early 1980s on, the union confederations in New Zealand were often excluded. Measured by union density, the strength of state employees' unions in Sweden and Norway has not changed much since 1980, while the unions in Australia, and even more so in New Zealand, have been markedly weakened since 1990. While union confederations or bargaining cartels still play a major role in wage determination in Norway, local branches related to specific workplaces assumed a more prominent role in the other countries during the 1990s.

With regard to response to and impact on NPM reforms of the state employees' unions, the importance of their historical legacy and their links to Social Democratic parties have been emphasised. Historical legacy and union-party relationships constitute relevant institutional characteristics, like specific identities and capabilities. The institutional characteristics are also expressed through elements of specialisation and hierarchy, delimiting or opening the way for specific actions by the unions in the reform processes, thus contributing to the transformation of NPM reforms.

The importance of historical legacy, union-party relationships, institutional characteristics and structural features for union response to NPM reforms was quite marked in Norway. While the LO Stat, the YS-S and several of their affiliated unions increased their attention on administrative reforms in the late 1980s, the AF and its affiliated unions continued to be quite passive. This difference is partly due to the ways in which institutional characteristics are built into the union confederations and their affiliated unions. Thus, the LO Stat, the YS-S and many of their national unions were confined to the state sector, often to specific parts of it, while the AF and most of its professional associations spanned sectoral boundaries. For the LO Stat and its affiliated unions, the long-standing relationship between the LO and the DNA also gave these unions specific identities and capabilities, and the formal union-party cooperation proved to be quite decisive in many reforms concerning wage policy and structural devolution.

Like the LO and its affiliated unions in Norway, the LO in Sweden, ACTU in Australia, the FOL in New Zealand and most of their affiliated unions have for a long time regarded themselves as part of the labour movement and have maintained various types of links with Social Democratic parties. Many of the NPM reforms launched by Social Democratic governments in Sweden and Australia were also cleared through the party and party-union relationships, but the unions in these countries were less successful than in Norway. At the other extreme, in New Zealand major reforms were formulated and implemented by a Labour government without any significant union involvement. In addition to country-specific union-party co-operation, differences in union response to and impact on reforms may also be related to the extent to which state employees' were organised through unions that had links with Social Democratic parties. In Norway, the LO was for a long time by far the largest union confederation, and the LO Stat was also the largest bargaining cartel for state employees. Thus, a majority of state employees were represented by a union with a state-sector identity through specialisation, and capabilities including regular access to Labour governments through the union hierarchy. While the LO in Sweden was also the largest union confederation and the state-sector union SF was one of the largest unions affiliated with the LO, union confederations, bargaining cartels and national unions that were independent of political parties represented a larger share of state employees. Here, the acceptance by the TCO-S of reforms launched by the Social Democratic government related to increased flexibility in wage determination was as crucial as the response of the LO and the SF. In New Zealand and Australia the unions for state or federal employees joined the union confederation that had links with the Labour parties in the 1980s, just before the major NPM reforms were formulated and implemented by Labour governments. Thus, even if some unions specifically for state employees were quite old, strong union-party co-operation was not part of their historical legacy.

With regard to the effects of NPM reforms on the state employees' unions, the importance for institutional characteristics and structural features has been emphasised. NPM reforms related to wage determination and the form and scope of the state administration are some of the factors that have contributed to the transformation of state employees' unions. More flexible and decentralised arrangements for wage determination sometimes, but not always, imply a reduction in union membership. Thus, union density for state employees has remained at a consistently fairly high level in Sweden, while it has decreased markedly in Australia and New Zealand. In Sweden, the downsizing of the state administration has implied that state employees now account for a much smaller proportion of union membership as a whole. For the three other countries, the numbers are less accurate. However, in New Zealand, employees in a reduced state sector seem to make up a larger part of an even more reduced union membership, while in Australia, the relative share of public-sector union members among all union members has declined.

The institutional characteristics of state employees' unions also depend on whether they cover specific parts of the state administration, the state sector only or other sectors as well. In Sweden, structural devolution and more flexible and decentralised arrangements for wage determination have contributed to the transformation of major state-specific unions (the SF and the TCO-S) into more wide-ranging unions (SEKO and the OFS). In Norway, on the other hand, structural devolution and modest changes in wage determination have not affected the structural features of bargaining cartels like the LO Stat and the YS-S to any great extent, while the split in the AF was partly due to its failure to obtain more flexible and decentralised wage determination. In Australia, NPM and industrial relations reforms, combined with plans of the ACTU leadership, have led to mergers and transformed unions from being mainly occupationally-based to being workplace-based. The major public-sector unions in Australia and New Zealand (the CPSU and the PSA, respectively) now have local banches at workplace or enterprise level as their basic unit. Local branches of state employees' unions have also been strengthened in Sweden and to some extent in Norway. While in Sweden this has happened at the expense of the national-level unions, in Norway bargaining cartels like the LO Stat and the YS-S and their affiliated unions for state employees have not been markedly weakened.

Thus, in Sweden, Australia and New Zealand, NPM reforms have implied a strengthening of identities and capabilities related to specific parts of the state administration, while identities and capabilities related to the state sector as a whole have somewhat weakened. These changes in the institutional characteristics of the state employees' unions may, in turn, affect how the unions will respond to administrative reforms in the future. Even if many state employees' unions were sceptical towards NPM reforms, particularly those introducing more flexible and decentralised wage determination, they have adapted to the new conditions, making a return to the old arrangements quite unlikely. Nevertheless, the role of union confederations and bargaining cartels, and even national unions, may change as a result of recent NPM reforms. Unions at the higher levels of the hierarchy are now increasingly expected to provide services to unions at the lower levels, rather than regarding them as subordinates in a more or less centralised organisation. In addition, the relationship between the different union confederations as well as between unions covering specific groups of state employees may change. Thus, in Sweden as well as in Norway, mergers of union confederations and closer co-operation between national unions belonging to different union confederations are being discussed. Even if potential changes in union structure are only partially and indirectly related to NPM reforms, they illustrate how the institutional characteristics of the state employees' unions may be affected by their responses to reforms and to changes in the state administration. Recent and potential future changes in the institutional characteristics and structural features of state employees' unions also illustrate how NPM reforms may transform the role of state employees' unions in democratic systems. If they were previously the bearers of collective values related to the state sector, the unions may now increasingly come to be regarded as representing the more narrow interests of specific groups of employees and specific parts of the state administration. This may also contribute to changing the balance between collectivist and individualist notions of democracy in general (see Chapter 12).

Notes

1   I use the term state employees' unions to indicate that I am focusing on trade unions for
     people employed by the central state apparatus and not by provinces or municipalities.
     In unitary states like New Zealand, Norway and Sweden this means that unions for people

related to central government are included, while unions whose members work in local (provincial and municipal) government are excluded. In federal states, like Australia, I am primarily interested in unions for people employed by the federal government.

2   The material is mainly based on previous studies and the web-pages of the unions. With the exception of Norway, few studies have focused primarily on the relationships between state employees' unions and NPM reforms. However, even in the other countries, some relevant information is available in studies of unions or of reforms.

3   This section develops ideas from Lægreid and Roness (1999) and Roness (1997, 1999, 2000).

4   The amount of information available on the relevant institutional characteristics varies. I do not have very much information, for example, about the composition of the secretariats and boards of state employees' unions other than in Norway and, to some extent, Sweden. Thus, in the discussions I will not be able to consider all the impacts of, and on, the institutional characteristics mentioned in this section.

5   Comparing union density over time and across countries is no easy task, since different criteria are used for calculating the number of employees and the number of union members (Kjellberg, 1983, pp. 33–53, 1997, pp. 58–99). However, even if the percentages are somewhat inaccurate, the main trends are evident.

6   The presentation of wage determination is based on Engeset (1994), Petersson and Søderlind (1992) and Sjølund (1996a, 1996b).

7   All figures on union membership are taken from their web-pages. They are mostly for 1999 and include passive members (cf. http://www.lo.se/, http://www.tco.se/ and http://www.saco.se/).

8   These figures are also based on information from the web-pages of the unions, where the state sector seems to include agencies and enterprises in the Swedish Agency of Government Employers ('Arbetsgivarverket').

9   Most of the information in this section is based on Roness (1996, pp. 60–75), where more specific references can be found.

10 This presentation is primarily based on Jacobsen (1996), Lægreid (1995), Lægreid and Roness (1998, 2001) and Roness (1993, 1994, 1996). More specific references can be found in these studies.

11 The figures on union density are based on surveys of the workforce (see Nergaard, 1999, pp. 7–9).

12 The figures on union membership are taken from their web-pages and mostly apply to late 1999 or early 2000 and include passive members (http://www.lo.no/, http://www.ys.no/, http://www.af.no/ and http://www.akademikerne.no/).

13 The information is based on the web-pages of the LO Stat (http://www.lostat.no/).

14 The information is based on the web-pages of the YS-S (http://www.ys-stat.no/).

15 The figures on union density and union membership are based on surveys of the labour force (see Peetz, 1998, p. 6).

16 The information is based on the web-pages of ACTU and the CPSU (http://www.actu.asn.au/ and http://www.cpsu.org/).

17 The information is based on the web-pages of the CPSU.

18 The information on the number of unions, union members and employees is somewhat incomplete and does not always give separate figures for the public and private sectors. The figures are primarily based on Bramble and Heal (1997, p. 128) and Bray and Walsh (1998, p. 363).

19 The information is based on the web-pages of PSA (http://www.psa.org.nz/).

20   These figures are calculated from Walsh and Brosnan (1999, p. 108) and are based on a workplace survey in 1995.
21   The information is based on the web-pages of the CTU (http:// www.union.org.nz/).
22   The information is based on the web-pages of the CTU.
23   The information is based on the web-pages of the PSA.
24   The information is based on web-pages of PSA.

9 Policy Capacity and the Effects of New Public Management

MARTIN PAINTER

Introduction

The principal question addressed in this chapter is what effects do New Public Management (NPM) reforms have on policy capacity? The main focus is on Australia, and the approach involves the analysis of a case study of housing policy development. A number of general questions are addressed first, in particular some conceptual, theoretical and methodological issues. The conclusions drawn are that the effects of NPM on policy processes are mixed and ambiguous. More fundamental political, administrative and other contextual factors shape and moderate NPM effects in ways that are sometimes contradictory or paradoxical. The concluding section of the chapter reflects on these lessons for the understanding of the impact of NPM reforms both in Australia and in Scandinavia.

Policy Capacity

NPM reforms seek to enhance the responsiveness of government, to make scarce public resources go further, to borrow the best from private sector successes, and to refocus the powers and capacities of government on achievable, targeted outcomes. Ironically, however, some critics of the impacts of this wave of reform identify the loss of state problem-solving capacity by the 'core executive' as one of the outcomes (Dunleavy, 1995). In the United Kingdom, the phrase 'the hollow crown' (Weller, Bakvis and Rhodes, 1997) has been used to capture a set of concerns about the loss of policy capacity and declining policy competencies (Foster and Plowden, 1996; Rhodes, 1994), and similar concerns have been expressed for Australia (Davis, 1997). Four major trends are claimed to have contributed to 'hollowing out': privatization, loss of functions by government departments to alternative service delivery systems, loss of functions to supra-national institutions, and limitations on the discretionary roles and functions of senior public servants through NPM (Rhodes, 1994, pp. 138–139). The outcome, it is argued, is in some cases serious 'policy disasters' and, more generally, an inability to produce 'logically and consistently related policies' (Rhodes, 1997b, p. 222).

In these discussions, what constitutes 'hollowing out' is given a variety of meanings, including transfer of functions, loss of expertise, and the breakdown of traditional role relationships. Implicit in the idea is a set of propositions linking structural changes with the content and quality of outputs and outcomes. If the diagnosis is to go beyond analysis from hindsight, it is important to specify clearly what sorts of things contribute to as well as constitute 'capacity'. For example, there is a need to distinguish between control and coordination, or between different types or scopes of executive capacity. Conceivably, NPM could improve the ability of elected governments to control their public services and budgets – that is, enhance the responsiveness of public officials to the political executive – but at the same time reduce their collective problem solving capacities when faced with issues requiring complex, negotiated solutions.

Terms like 'loss of capacity' carry an evaluative and normative load, but they are principally about effectiveness, a means-end criterion concerning the attributes of a process that contribute to objectives. As used here, policy capacity is a measure of the effectiveness of a range of processes within government that are essential and continuing parts of the policy making process. This includes the policy advising process (Halligan, 1995) as well as policy implementation. The focus of the analysis in this chapter is not so much on policy implementation as on the process of policy formulation. Recent work in Australia on evaluating the quality of policy advising has had a similar focus (Weller, 1998; Uhr & Mackay, 1996). For example, the following elements of the process of 'good policy advice' have been identified (Weller and Stevens, 1998, p. 582):

- Taking a difficult and sometimes poorly understood problem or issue and structuring it so that it can be thought about in a systematic way,
- Gathering the minimum necessary information and applying the appropriate analytical framework,
- Formulating effective options addressing, where necessary, mechanisms for implementation and evaluation; and

• Communicating the results of the work to the government in a timely and understandable way.

In the present context, the question is whether NPM reforms enhance or diminish the conditions under which such attributes of effective process can be realised.

Does NPM Undermine Policy Capacity?

What characterizes NPM, and what aspects of it might impact on policy capacity in the sense just discussed? The characterization adopted here follows that outlined in chapter 2. First, in the realm of ideas and doctrine, economic norms and values are dominant, lending a 'one-dimensionality' to reform and practice. Associated with the primacy of economy and efficiency is the origin of much reform doctrine in economic theory. This theory embodies various critiques of public bureaucracy, including the tendency to waste and inefficiency in the absence of market forces or clear, transparent mechanisms of accountability. Second, NPM is a 'shopping basket' of management ideas and techniques. They include managerial devolution and discretion, explicit performance standards focused on outputs, 'hands-off' strategic control and accountability mechanisms based on clear objectives and measurable outputs and outcomes (for example, the contract), and performance incentives based on greater autonomy and self-regulation (for example through competition) (see Hood, 1991).

John Halligan (1998) nominates only three countries – the United Kingdom, New Zealand and Australia – where NPM has been effective as a comprehensive reform movement. Even then, differences exist between NPM in these countries. Australia in the 1980s started its reforms with a 'political management agenda' – reforms to budgets and financial management and the machinery of government – which aimed to place ministers more firmly in charge of management and policy processes, as well as make public servants more effective and accountable as managers. This agenda grew out of concerns about the power of the public service that pre-dated the hey-day of NPM, and it gave the Australian reform process a distinctive content and impact. The effects of the political management agenda is of particular significance for the discussion of policy capacity. Although economic liberalism dominated Labor Government economic policy as it entered the 1990s (Painter, 1996), only later did such doctrines prompt public sector 'marketisation'. When reformers turned their attention to intergovernmental relations in the 1990s, NPM models of clean boundaries, performance agreements, and purchaser-provider splits were applied (Painter, 1998b).

Most of the promise of NPM is captured by talk of 'better management', while less mention is made of 'better policy' and mostly lip service is paid to the distinctiveness of public policy and political management, as against generic qualities of management. Perhaps, as Owen Hughes (1994, p. 166) suggests '...policy analysis...was absorbed into public management ... (I)t has become less relevant as governments...found analysis being replaced by economics, allied with modern management, as applied to the public sector.'

Where NPM reforms were meant to impact directly on policy work, various reports suggested less than helpful effects. For example, Zifcak (1994, p. 106) argues that in Australia '...for policy personnel, the corporate planning process was perceived as being of distant relevance', and it was 'not regarded as particularly helpful by ministers.' In Britain, the Financial Management Initiative was regarded 'sceptically' in the policy divisions, where 'it was the form rather than the substance...that was adhered to' (Zifcak, 1994, p. 41). The systems were 'designed without a clear appreciation of the fundamental questions which they would be required to answer. These were not primarily managerial in nature. They were political' (Zifcak, 1994, p. 44). In Australia, the one-dimensional emphasis of NPM on management values such as efficiency led to arguments that good policy would suffer due to the neglect of other values (Harris, 1990; Painter, 1990). A powerful critique of the one-dimensionality of NPM doctrine characterized it as a component of a wider phenomenon labelled 'economic rationalism' (Pusey, 1991). The range of options considered appropriate and legitimate for solving policy problems narrowed to a small sub-set, namely a preference for market solutions and smaller government. In this view, NPM systematically imposed limits and biases on the process of selecting and considering possible policy instruments.

Many of the potential impacts of NPM on policy capacity are likely to be indirect. For example, the use of short-term contracts and performance reviews might undermine the capacity of senior managers to give 'frank and fearless advice' to ministers. Also, devolution to managers may weaken the integrative, coordinating capacity of the centre (Rhodes, 1994, p. 149). The push to separate politics and administration exhibited by 'agencification' drives a wedge between those who know and understand the intricacies of implementation, and those who advise the minister. As the latter lose touch, ministers lose confidence in them and seek advice elsewhere (Foster and Plowden, 1996, p. 178). The higher reaches of the public service are downgraded in preference for private management consultants, political staffers and think tank gurus, who tend to provide one-dimensional advice (Bakvis, 1997).

Figure 9.1 provides a starting point for analyzing possible NPM effects in the policy process. It assumes NPM reforms are actually implemented (see below). It borrows Bridgman and Davis's (1998) depiction of the policy cycle, which is particularly well adapted to an executive-centred view of policy-making in a Westminster system such as Australia's. The cycle includes additional phases to those in Figure 9.1 – namely, implementation and post-implementation evaluation – but the focus of this discussion is on policy formulation, not implementation. The examples of the types of effects are hypothetical and illustrative rather than exhaustive. They are categorized as 'type 1' or 'type 2'. Type 1 effects reflect the intended outcomes of reforms. Type 2 effects – the 'other face of NPM' – are of several different kinds. First, we can divide them between sins of omission and commission. NPM focuses on some things but finds others unimportant, or is blind to them. NPM may 'solve the wrong problems'.

Figure 9.1   Potential effects of NPM on the policy process

Phase in the Policy Cycle	Type 1 Effect	Type 2 Effect
1. Issue Identi-fication	Attention is strategically targeted on economy and efficiency	Produces one-dimensional views of inherently complex issues
2. Analysis	Analysis is results-oriented	Analysis is process-blind
3. Instruments	Expands range and effectiveness of available instruments by using the market in the public interest	Diminishes range and effectiveness of available instruments by under-valuing the public sector
4. Consultation	Improves quality of advice through information gathering outside the public service as a 'contestable' process	Encourages 'yes-men', discourages debate, threatens 'institutional memory'
5. Coordination	Uses performance management contracts to achieve better strategic coordination and control	Empowers agency managers and drives horizontal, network-based, accommodation underground
6. Decision	Benefits from clear, unequivocal advice based on strategic, corporate goals	Encourages 'group-think' and 'macho-politics'

Second, we can distinguish between type 2 effects according to the way in which they are caused. Some effects arise from a neglect of an essential pre-existing characteristic of a situation in the models lying behind an implemented NPM reform. For example, the Type 2 effect in row 1 arises from a false understanding that policy problems can be simplified to the extent of focusing only on one set of values or ends (or thinking that government is just like any other business). Others are side effects, or 'third party damage' due to chains of unintended consequences beyond the immediate context. For example, the Type 2 effect in row 2 suggests that an over-emphasis on results and outcomes produces behaviour that interferes with other goals that may be equally important, such as accountability or meeting the requirements for consensus-building. Then there are perverse or reverse effects, where the very opposite of what is intended is actually achieved because those subject to reforms react to the new incentive structures in ways that defeat their object (Hood, 1998a, pp. 213–215). For example, in row 5, a perverse effect of arm's length contracting to agents might be to encourage them to 'go native' and set up their own self-serving coordination mechanisms, by-passing and undermining the principals.

As already mentioned, the framework as it stands assumes that NPM reforms were actually implemented. It identifies collateral and indirect paths of cause and effect triggered by the implementation of reform, resulting in possible unintended consequences and paradoxes (Hood and Peters, 2000). Empirical analysis may also lead one to conclude that the reforms were not implemented as intended, or even were not intended to be implemented. For example, displacement activity might have dominated over behaviour designed to achieve stated reform purposes, or political leaders could have been more concerned with rhetorical rather than substantive pay-offs. In other words, NPM could be symbolic and rhetorical, rather than substantive and purposive (Premfors, 1998). Because institutional tradition and culture stimulate resistance to externally derived reform ideas, outcomes are a mix of overarching intentional design and localised adaptation, with more or less decentralised implementation systems allowing the expression in some degree of 'institutional identities and capabilities' (Lægreid and Roness, 1999).

In the present analysis, we adopt the strategy of looking backwards from the effects (Scharpf, 1997, pp. 25–27), and asking whether or not there is a strong connection with NPM as a set of causal factors. Methodological problems lie in being certain that the independent variable– an NPM initiative – is the cause. We must be wary of reading back from an outcome to only one set of causes. NPM may be only one factor among a more entrenched or pervasive set of forces and influences that shape outcomes in a particular political and administrative system or culture, as the historical-institutionalist perspective would lead us to expect (Premfors, 1998). It is at this point also that we must be on the lookout for the possibility that the NPM reforms we have identified as possible causes were rhetorical rather than real, symbolic in character and intent, or so significantly adapted in their implementation that they emerged in other forms.

The case study that follows provides one, admittedly imperfect, empirical method to pursue this kind of analysis. It seeks to tell a story of policy failure with a view to identifying the reasons that made it unravel. Case studies are good instruments for exploring possible causes and linkages in their context, and for suggesting the significance of one as against another. What does this case tell us about policy capacities in the modern, 'reformed', Australian state? To what extent can we identify some of the effects of NPM as a significant element in the processes that led to the failure of social housing policy in the 1990s?

Australian Social Housing Policy in the 1990s

The Policy Context

Housing policy has been a shared responsibility of state and federal governments in Australia. State governments have focused primarily on provision of public housing, albeit with significant inter-state differences in priorities. Some states used public housing as a means of reducing the costs of labour to employers, and as an instrument of regional policy, although by the 1980s the priorities in most states had shifted largely to providing housing to those fully dependent on social security payments for their income. About 6 percent of Australians rented public housing, approximately 20 percent rented in the private market and 70 percent were owner-occupiers. The Commonwealth through the Commonwealth State Housing Agreement (CSHA) has provided most of the funds for capital investment in public housing – in 1995/6, $1billion out of $1.5 billion. In addition, the Commonwealth paid $1.6 billion in rent assistance to social security·clients in privately owned rental accommodation. About 45 percent of private renters were social security beneficiaries. Rent assistance rates had been increased significantly by the Commonwealth Labor Government in the 1980s. Coupled with the growth in social security beneficiaries, expenditure on rent assistance in constant dollars grew fourfold in ten years. Over the same period, CSHA funds declined by about one third, part of a broader budgetary squeeze on commonwealth-state finances. Until 1996, different Commonwealth departments administered the CSHA and rental assistance (respectively Housing and Social Security).

Defining the Problem

Between 1990 and 1996, the Commonwealth Labor Housing Minister, Brian Howe, who was a senior figure from the left of the Party, drove a radical strategy to re-focus social housing policy away from public provision to an emphasis on market-based solutions. Howe had long been critical of the quality of state public housing provision and saw a need to focus more attention on the private rental sector. But how the reform strategy emerged as a set of demand-side market instruments, that at the same time dismantled core aspects of the public housing system in Australia, is a more complex story, in which the prevailing climate of NPM and wider market-liberal doctrines played their role.

In the reformed Australian public service as it existed in 1990, some Ministers relied as much on their private offices as on their departmental advisors for policy work. Managerial reforms in the 1980s had been less concerned with developing departmental policy skills than with economy and efficiency measures. The Housing Department was preoccupied in large part with overseeing the Commonwealth State Housing Agreement and was viewed by the minister as too close to public housing to take a balanced view. Howe and his advisors looked to outside advice for re-shaping the policy agenda, setting up a special inquiry that produced a National Housing Strategy (NHS) report in 1992. The NHS relied heavily on commissioned external research and consultations. It drew particular attention to the importance of the private rental market for social housing policy. It called for increases in rent assistance, the establishment of 'housing affordability benchmarks', and new measures on the supply side, including housing bonds (effectively, government subsidies for private capital devoted to the construction of housing for the poor). Housing affordability benchmarks sought to establish a floor beneath which no family or individual would fall with respect to the amount of their income devoted to direct housing costs.

The influence of neo-liberal doctrine on the housing reform strategy was strengthened when in 1993 the Government asked the Industry Commission (IC) for a report on housing assistance, with a view particularly to evaluating the performance of public housing. The Industry Commission was a well-established expert body, dominated by economists, and well-known for espousing market solutions drawing on neo-classical economic models. The Industry Commission report was heavily critical of the manner in which public housing was funded, provided and managed, albeit agreeing that it had a role to play. The Commonwealth State Housing Agreement was criticised for blurring accountability and for not providing incentives for effective performance by state housing authorities (SHAs). The Industry Commission recommended that the states take over full responsibility for purchase and construction of public housing, with the Commonwealth assuming responsibility for all rental assistance. The SHAs should charge market rents and commercialize their housing operations, while rent assistance should be based only on income and need.

Identifying the Solutions

Both the NHS and the IC Reports highlighted a key flaw in the current system, namely the much lower levels of support afforded private renters through rent assistance than went to public tenants through rental subsidies. Equally, they were critical of aspects of current public housing – it hindered flexibility in supply and discouraged mobility, and it often produced dysfunctional neighbourhoods. Brian Howe and his advisers accepted these points. They recommended seeking alternative community and private sector methods of supply. However, supply side strategies were blocked by Commonwealth Treasury, which was implacably opposed both to market-distorting interventions in capital markets, and to tax expenditures aimed at encouraging large-scale private investment in social housing provision. The solution had to be found in private rental assistance, and the recasting of the CSHA.

A key issue for this strategy was how to fund it. Part of the solution lay in the abolition of capital grants through the CSHA, made possible by the full commercialization of the states' public housing stock. SHAs would be required to fund their additions to or replacement of stock from commercial returns on their housing assets. In other words, the rent assistance payments passing to the public landlord at market rents would flow in part into servicing capital expenditure. As well, commercialization of operations would generate additional opportunities for efficiencies and profits. But for the Commonwealth, the financial implications remained a problem, in particular the prospect of a major expansion to entitlements and uncertainties over the level of future commitment, compared with the existing situation of a cap on capital funding to the states.

Consulting and Coordinating: The Intergovernmental Arena

The reform package was radical and comprehensive. It was at one and the same time conceptually elegant, intellectually challenging and ideologically confronting. In each of these respects, cynics and sceptics might argue it contained the seeds of its own destruction. Both state housing ministers and treasurers saw an uncertain future. Inter-state relativities would be disrupted, for example. CSHA grants to the states were distributed on a per capita basis. If distributed through rent assistance payments on the basis of relative need and the affordability benchmarks, these funds would be redistributed to cities and states with higher levels of rent, in particular to Sydney. In New South Wales, this was a plus for the proposal. But it was feared that the required level of subsidy to match the very high Sydney market rents would not be forthcoming, and that this would either make the SHA insolvent (without state government subsidy) or require rent increases.

These objections and fears came to light in a process of discussion and negotiation that proved, in the long run, to be fruitless. In February 1994, Howe took the issue to the peak coordinating body for intergovernmental relations, the Council of Australian Governments (COAG), which comprised all state premiers and the prime minister. COAG asked Housing Ministers to address the proposals and report back. Past experience would have suggested that progress would be slow. Housing Ministers and their advisers in their intergovernmental meetings were not noted for innovative thinking. Mostly, they were concerned with preserving the status quo and ensuring the Commonwealth met its commitments through the CSHA. The consensus norms and veto powers of federal politics could be expected to have been a severe brake on reform.

But in this case, such was not the main problem. One reason was the involvement in the deliberations of central agency officials through the Council of Australian Governments. These central agency officials were all trusted personal appointees of the premiers and prime minister, while the chief executives of state housing agencies enjoyed similar relations with their ministers. The new breed of officials shared common experiences of selection, recruitment and appointment, and had a vision of their role that was more proactive and entrepreneurial than those of previous generations. The common experience of setting up COAG in the early 1990s brought together what came to be dubbed the 'central agencies club', a group of like-minded officials with a mission to reform intergovernmental relations along more business-like lines (Weller, 1996). They developed both a strategic focus and a sense of political mission. Their sense of common purpose was invaluable in facilitating negotiation and bargaining. The political and personal commitment to the project shown by key senior officials and ministerial advisers was an important element.

By the 1990s, all governments in Australia had adopted more overtly politicized senior personnel systems as part of the wave of NPM reforms, along with various forms of contracting and corporatisation aiming to mould senior officials and ministers into more coherent units and executive teams (e.g. Laffin, 1995; Zifcak, 1997). Not only were central agency officials more politically attuned and focussed on core strategic objectives, so too were departmental chief executives. Several of the latter, in particular those from the larger states, decided to cooperate with the housing reform process with a view to co-opting it to their own reform purposes. They were pursuing their own NPM reforms in housing, including commercialization of SHAs and the introduction of purchaser-provider models within the housing portfolio. Equally significant in shaping the policy development process in the intergovernmental arena was the existence of effective coordinating capacities within each jurisdiction. During the 1970s and 1980s, as part of the first wave of 'political management reforms', governments had built up new central policy and coordination machinery, had put in place policy and planning instruments that facilitated prioritizing and policy review, and had reformed cabinet procedures and instituted powerful cabinet office clearance mechanisms (Davis, 1995; Halligan and Power, 1992; Painter, 1987). The offices thereby created were peopled by policy activists and managers with a sensitivity to political strategy and to broader, long-term policy priorities in the context of the electoral cycle.

Discussions over the housing reform agenda took place in this context. The agenda was driven by Commonwealth officials and Brian Howe, with state housing ministers largely looking on. Progress of discussions among housing officials, channelled through the forum of the Housing Ministers Conference, was reported at intervals to a steering committee of COAG senior officials. The discussions on housing reform were part of a wider COAG agenda to reform intergovernmental relations along 'quasi-market' lines, using divisions of role such as 'purchaser and provider', rather than those that had evolved from the inherited federal division of powers (COAG Task Force 1995; Edwards and Henderson, 1995; Painter, 1998a). The Housing Ministers presented a report to the April 1995 COAG meeting, and COAG endorsed the in-principle agreement that the role of the Commonwealth was housing subsidies and affordability, and the role of the states was management and delivery of public housing services. State housing ministers were again asked to report back on a more detailed agreement, including a transitional CSHA. At this point, however, in spite of the careful marshalling of the process through officials' committees and the Housing Ministers Conference, the housing reform strategy lost some of its momentum. The COAG agenda was always crowded, and political issues of the day (of which housing reform was not one) tended to dominate. Despite being endorsed by COAG, the proposals were never fully discussed in that forum. For example, the lingering reservations of states such as Queensland were never confronted by their colleagues, with the result that some key issues of principle and politics were left unresolved.

A common problem in all intergovernmental negotiations is their secretiveness. They do not take place in public arenas, and there are no formal, continuing mechanisms for public consultation and participation. Deep scepticism existed within the social housing lobby– for example organizations such as National Shelter – about the viability of the proposals. The lack of government commitment to a supply side strategy, and the withdrawal of the Commonwealth from capital grants to public housing were primary concerns. Scepticism existed about the willingness of Government to fund rental assistance at the level required to meet the affordability benchmarks in high rent cities. Public housing groups lobbied fiercely against the commercialization of state housing and the removal of direct rental subsidies. Throughout, the social housing lobby adopted a critical, although not always hostile, stand.

Critical Decisions and Regime Change

The broad outlines of the housing reform plans were launched publicly by the Prime Minister in December 1995, as the centre-piece of a pre-election statement called 'Community and Nation'. The March 1996 election resulted in defeat for Labor, but shortly after the election the new Government under John Howard affirmed its support for the reform process, and work continued. A further in-principle agreement on long-term reform was announced at the June 1996 COAG meeting, and re-affirmed at a meeting in September 1996 of Housing Ministers, with a new task force to pursue the issue. But as it turned out, that was the end of it. Coincidentally, COAG as a significant forum for driving intergovernmental reform was also disbanded, tainted as it was by its inheritance from the previous government. Sweeping personnel changes in the Prime Minister's Department resulted in a lack of awareness of and interest in the significance of the COAG intergovernmental reform agenda, of which housing reform was an important part.

At first, the new Government was attracted to the housing reform model for doctrinal reasons, and because they believed it might be able to deliver budget savings, but backed off from it when the true financial implications became clear. By the end of 1996, whatever support existed in the states for the housing reform program had turned into supreme scepticism if not hostility, because the Commonwealth would not commit itself to finding the funds necessary to make the model work. The Prime Minister was committed to three incompatible aims. First, no existing public housing tenants would be disadvantaged, and no new ones would pay more than 25 percent of their income in rent. Second, no state government would be disadvantaged in budgetary terms. And third, the Commonwealth would not be required to provide more recurrent funds than currently expended in rent assistance and the Commonwealth State Housing Agreement. The sums did not add up, and the scheme sank from sight. The Prime Minister placated the states by quarantining the CSHA from the worst of the Commonwealth budget cuts. The Agreement was renegotiated as a transitional arrangement, with a primary focus on business reforms to State Housing Authorities. When, in 1999, a further four-year CSHA was signed, it maintained the funding status quo but required the signing of detailed agreements with each state on the implementation of efficiency measures.

Re-Evaluation and Problem Redefinition

In the first few months of office, the new Commonwealth Government elected in March 1996 devoted itself single-mindedly to expenditure cuts, and the exercise was repeated in succeeding years. In achieving such quick and effective control over the budget, it was putting to use inherited instruments of NPM political management, such as cabinet's Expenditure Review Committee and the tightly-managed expenditure review process. When these instruments of NPM were aligned with a single-minded focus on economy, they proved remarkably effective. At the same time, the effects on policy capacity was in other respects more damaging. Within the Commonwealth social security and housing portfolios (which in 1996 were brought together in the one Department) rent assistance was a prime target for the economizers. As an entitlement program it seemed to 'grow like topsy'. While it was closely targeted and of immediate benefit to a clear category of need, it was also difficult to administer and open to abuse. All sorts of anomalies were visible to a Government intent on 'stamping out fraud' and 'targeting the most in need'. To give two examples, the rent declared by many sub-tenants was suspected in many cases to be fictitious, and no reliable methods of verification were in place; and single couples sharing rental accommodation were eligible for individual assistance, while a married couple was treated as a single unit and was paid a lower rate. In the first three budgets of the Howard Government, the rent assistance scheme was a repeated target for savings, and various measures to limit eligibility, reduce rates or stamp out fraud were introduced.

If the failure of the earlier housing reform agenda was a case of over-ambitious strategic thinking, some minor policy disasters during this process of eking out savings were examples of a virtual lack of strategic thinking. Short-term issues were more important. The new Minister, Jocelyn Newman, was driven by the imperative of finding quick savings. She ran policy from a tightly managed private office of political appointees, which was suspicious of some sections of the Department for being too close to the welfare lobby. Her portfolio was a prime target for cuts, and she had to battle hard in Cabinet to minimize the damage. She drove the Department hard to deliver cuts so as to maintain credibility with her cabinet colleagues. But the Department was going through a difficult period. First, housing was amalgamated with social security after the 1996 election; and second, in 1997 the service delivery units of the Department were hived off and amalgamated with employment services in a new business agency, Centrelink. The relocation of housing in 1996 was disruptive, not only for the staff losses that accompanied it but also because housing policy staff found themselves adjusting to new policy settings and a new culture. Equally, hiving off Centrelink brought considerable upheavals, diverting resources and skills to managing the transition. In policy discussions over matters of implementation planning in this period, uncertainty and friction were evident between the department and the agency.

There were signs that all these factors diminished the effectiveness of the policy process. For example, the measure in the 1996/7 budget to pay a lower level of assistance to single persons sharing accommodation appeared hastily put together in order to meet the budget savings target. In the passage of the initial legislation through the Senate, where the Government was in a minority, several amendments had to be made 'on the run' as minor anomalies and grievances surfaced. In the following year, in the face of strong opposition from community groups such as the Salvation Army, the measure had to be amended by new legislation in order to exclude a category of 'sharers' whose rent assistance had been reduced, but who were clearly not benefiting from sharing, namely single people in rooming or boarding houses. Ad hoc savings measures continued to nibble away at rent assistance until a major review of the administration of the program was undertaken in 1998. The review produced a promise of savings through tightening up on verification and administrative procedures.

In sum, after nearly a decade of effort, only a very small part of the agenda of policy reform identified in the early 1990s, and accepted as part of a cooperative reform process by the states, had been acted upon. The principal issues raised in the longer term housing reform strategy concerning affordability and supply in the private rental sector had not been tackled, while the issue of the division of roles between Commonwealth and state governments dropped out of sight. The legacy was a set of efficiency improvements in state housing provision, a movement towards more realistic levels of public housing rental subsidy through increasing rents, tighter targeting of public housing to the needy, and tougher eligibility rules for Commonwealth rental assistance, and (for some groups) lower rates.

The Effects of NPM

Figure 9.2 summarises some of the findings of the case study, using the categories of effects identified in Figure 9.1, and distinguishing between period 1 (pre-1996) and period 2 (post-1996). The change to a conservative government marks the divide.

During the period of attempted reform under Labor in the first period, the pervasive influence of NPM doctrines may be argued to have limited the definition of the problem and the search for solutions, with a bias towards market instruments. But other reasons were also evident for this preference, including the perception of Minister Howe that public housing had 'failed', and the bias on the part of the Commonwealth for using its own policy instrument – rent assistance – in preference to public housing provision by the states. However, in turning away from the Commonwealth Housing Department and the inter-state housing policy community as the source of advice and intelligence, on the grounds that they were blinkered by their public housing connections, the policy process came under the influence of the 'economic rationalists', whose faith in the market was accompanied by prejudice against the public housing sector. This one-dimensionality in framing the issues was also evident in the false expectation that redesigning the industry along quasi-market lines would dissolve the jurisdictional and political problems of federalism (Painter, 1998a).

Figure 9.2   Some direct and indirect effects of NPM on housing policy processes 1990–1996

Phase in the Policy Cycle	Type 1 Effect	Type 2 Effect
1. Issue identification	Attention strategically targeted on economy in line with Government's priorities (period 2)	Narrow targeting of economy produced inattention to other issues and need for subsequent error correction (period 2)
2. Analysis		Outcomes-focused analysis of market solutions led to neglect of feasibility analysis (period 1)
3. Instruments	Incorporation of full range of market instruments in the analysis of models of social housing policy (period 1)	Bias in favour of market instruments and against public provision, generating unrealistic options (period 1)
4. Consultation	New sources of outside intelligence and advice, introduced new perspectives into social housing policy formulation (period 1)	Discrediting of housing policy community officials stifled dissent and devalued 'practical knowledge' and institutional memory (period 1) Loss of institutional memory due to changing personnel and departmental restructures, contributed to error (period 2)
5. Coordination	'New breed' NPM managers and advisors facilitated 'positive coordination' across jurisdictions through strategic focus on process and outcomes within COAG (period 1)	
6. Decision	NPM-style political management and budget process reforms enabled speedy, effective cost-cutting strategies by a new Government (period 2)	Central agencies club, imbued with economic rationalism, were victims of groupthink (period 1) Short-term time horizons in cost-cutting decisions, contributed to errors (period 2)

Dunleavy (1995) has identified the dangers of groupthink in the British core executive, arising from its internal dynamics and lack of external connectedness. Perhaps the closed world of intergovernmental high politics within the central agencies club in this period was equally prone? So long as planning remained at an Olympian height in COAG's closed circles, important reality tests could be avoided. The grand plan was elegant and challenging, and the negotiated outcomes were a fine balance of competing interests, but the detail was messy, threatening to stir up a hornet's nest of vested interests and ideologues. The deep scepticism of the social housing lobby towards the reform package turned to outright hostility once they lost faith in the Howard Government's capacity to deliver all of its elements. Such might well have been the fate of the scheme had the Labor Government remained in office, once the detailed implementation of the proposal was grappled with in the context of real world fiscal restraints.

At the same time, the kinds of roles, relationships and structures constructed in the process of dealing with analysis, consultation, coordination and joint decision-making in some respects benefited from the effects of NPM. The most challenging aspects of the process of policy formation involved negotiation and consensus-building across levels of government. Effective management of a process across these arenas requires the kinds of resources and skills encapsulated in Rhodes's (1997a) concept of 'governance'. The machinery and processes constructed to make COAG work were put together by an enthusiastic, committed band of central policy managers and advisors from all jurisdictions. COAG was a product of the success of the Australian style of NPM political management reforms (Painter, 1998b). It helped fill a void that is Australia's version of the hollow state – a void in the intergovernmental sphere, where issues and problems drop from sight, and blame is shifted and avoided. COAG was designed not just for 'minding the shop' of inter-jursidictional coordination but as a vehicle for strategic policy-making, (that is, for effecting 'positive' as well as 'negative' coordination (Scharpf, 1997)). Effective management of the process required tightly managed and strategically focused coordination and control processes in each of the participating governments, which is what the NPM reforms helped to deliver.

Both type 1 and type 2 effects of NPM were more clearly revealed after the change of government. The new government's success in asserting control over the budget and the public service was plain to see. NPM in Australia has delivered a set of instruments for tight and effective control by the political executive over the instruments of state power. Once the new government had set itself publicly on a course of ruthless economy, the system delivered the goods. Housing policy reform was one victim. The personnel, institutions and processes that had been instrumental in policy development to that point were disbanded in the name of downsizing and restructuring. In effect, the new political executive used its instruments of control to dismantle policy capacity. We can also identify a number of indirect effects that contributed to diminished policy capacity. Major restructuring (including agencification) and personnel changes undertaken for political reasons caused disruption in the Commonwealth Government's policy advising processes, while a doctrine of 'efficiency and economy at all costs' within a tight, centrally dictated time-frame contributed to policy errors. Thus, policy capacities were both indirectly undermined and deliberately sidelined under the influences of NPM, not only within the Commonwealth Government itself but also in the intergovern-mental sphere.

Lessons and Conclusions

Two sorts of lessons and conclusions are drawn from this analysis. The first concerns the broad political implications of a comprehensively implemented set of NPM reforms. The second contextualises these findings by considering the implications of national institutional and political styles and traditions.

NPM's effects are not necessarily one-dimensional in the ideological sense, but the probabilities are strongly in favour of such an alignment. NPM is ideologically more at home on the right of the political spectrum, and it may well be that the default condition, in the absence of strong political leadership to energise the public sector for the purposes of 'progressive' social reform, is capacity-diminishing. As we noted in concluding the case study, what was left after a decade of reform ideas and activity was a set of cost-cutting, efficiency-driven changes that diminished the role of public housing and targeted housing assistance more narrowly on a small residue of welfare-dependent poor. Left to its own devices, NPM's managerialist biases mostly support and reinforce the diminution of the scope and reach of the state. Aligned with anti-statist political ideology, it may result in deliberately dismantling some important elements of policy capacity, not to mention a number of unintended and counter-productive effects. Where NPM fails by design, it may succeed by default in diminishing capacity.

The case study draws our attention to a particular aspect of the Australian NPM reform variant, that is its emphasis on political management. A number of political management reforms, such as larger and more effective ministerial staffs and more coherent and powerful policy coordinating instruments in first ministers' department, also belong in frames of reference other than those provided by NPM doctrines. In some respects, they were an indigenous, Australian invention prompted by a drive by governments in the 1970s and 1980s to assert more political control over established bureaucratic structures. But coupled with NPM reforms to budgets, corporate planning and program management and review, they provided the political and bureaucratic elites in the 1990s with a set of instruments and structures capable of a considerable degree of strategic control over policy development and innovation. The development of Howe's social housing reform strategy was one example. The direct and indirect effects on policy capacity of these aspects of NPM reforms were, on balance, enhancing rather than diminishing, given the direction and drive provided by strong political managers intent on reform.

If the emphasis on political management distinguished Australia's style of NPM reforms, a number of accounts of the implementation of administrative reform under the NPM banner in Norway and Sweden also stress how NPM design principles and objectives are modified and reshaped by national institutional traditions, resulting in an identifiable 'Nordic trajectory' (Bergstrom, 1999; Lægreid and Roness, 1999; Premfors, 1998). Premfors (1998) gives an account of Swedish administrative reform in the past twenty years that stresses the importance of factors such as continuity and tradition; an agenda of problems peculiar to the Swedish welfare state; and political shifts of fortune that produced swings in priorities and issue definitions. Imported NPM models, and local versions of them, were one factor, but they did not exert a continuous or uniform influence.

Indeed, the strongest conclusions and points of comparison to be drawn from the case study concern the importance of a range of contextual and institutional factors for understanding policy capacity, aside from the intent or impact of NPM. In Australia, critical variables in understanding the prospects for success or failure of housing reform were first, the effects of federalism and second, the impact of strategic choices by political executives at the national level. Australia exhibits a peculiar federal mix, in which the states express strong identities and have significant blocking and inertial power, while the Commonwealth has most of the financial power, the greatest capacity to innovate and reshape policy, and a persistent habit of unilateralism. This contrasts sharply with a highly decentralised polity such as Denmark or Sweden (Premfors, 1998), where devolution in critical areas of policy and administration seems to place greater limits on the capacity of the centre to dictate policy terms, and (coupled with a more consensual tradition) discourages unilateralism.

The housing policy case is but one example of the dramatic impact across a wide range of policy fields of the change of government in 1996. Unilaterally, the new government shelved, reversed and terminated a wide range of policies and programs, many of which had been subject to extensive discussions and agreements with the states. The central driving force of the elected government of the day in Canberra is a distinguishing feature of the policy style of the Australian state. The Commonwealth's assertiveness in its relations with the states is a regular pattern of Australian federal politics, with continuous swings between cooperative and confrontationist styles. One reason is that the Westminster traditions of strong, majoritarian party government institutionalise adversarialism and legitimise assertive executives with a 'mandate to rule'. In such a polity, NPM as a comprehensive doctrine of governance, particularly when combined with political management reforms, and in the hands of a right-wing government, is likely to be a much more potent force than it is in the Nordic systems, where power is more dispersed and politics more consensual. Moreover, NPM doctrine is nicely aligned culturally with the Westminster tradition's view of the unity and instrumentality of the executive, in which all organs of the state exist at the behest of the sovereign, and none is indispensable or endowed with other than pragmatic status. For these reasons, NPM's effects on policy capacity are likely to be much more pervasive in Australia than in Norway and Sweden. However, the first order variables in understanding the chains of causality are to be found not in universalising models of administrative reform, but in national political traditions and policy styles.

10 Transforming Governmental Culture: A Sceptical View of New Public Management

ROBERT GREGORY

Introduction

In 1986 the New Zealand government embarked on a radical programme of public sector restructuring which has been acknowledged by many academic commentators as the most comprehensive and theoretically coherent application of New Public Management (NPM) ideas. The changes were a component of wider socio-economic reforms, based on neo-classical economic theory. Against the background of what was perceived to be an under-performing economy, they largely deregulated the New Zealand economy, with the aim of increasing allocative efficiency and productivity. New Zealand, a small parliamentary democracy of some 3.8 million people, came to be widely viewed as a social laboratory of neo-liberal social and economic deregulation and transformation.

The initial element of the reforms was the corporatisation of government trading organisations, bringing New Zealand into line with practices followed in other parts of the world. That process was followed in 1988 by parliament's passing of the State Sector Act, which, together with the Public Finance Act of 1989, established a *sui generic* NPM model of public management in New Zealand central government. The changes struck deeply at the administrative systems, processes and culture that had been developed in New Zealand since the introduction in 1912 of a unified and centralised state services career system within a parliamentary democracy fashioned quite closely along Westminster lines.[1]

The architects of the changes argued that any efforts to improve the efficiency and productivity of the New Zealand economy as a whole had to encompass the public sector. Government expenditure, including transfers, accounted for about 39 percent of Gross Domestic Product (Scott, Bushnell and Sallee, 1990). The state sector, particularly the Public Service, was seen to be inefficient, inflexible, cumbersome and far too bureaucratic in its preoccupation with process rather than results. According to one of the principal architects, departmental objectives were not clearly specified, the respective responsibilities of politicians and public servants were confused, control systems administered by central agencies inhibited effective management, generally destroying incentives to perform. In addition, there were few sanctions for poor performance, and ministers were making 'inappropriate' decisions about the internal management of departments (Scott, 1996, pp. 30–31).

In the meantime, the public's perception of how their central government operated had been influenced by the popular television series 'Yes Minister' (Borins, 1988), which caricatured senior civil servants as cunningly and conspiratorially reactive. A locally produced comedy series, 'Glide Time' (later, 'Gliding On'), portrayed public servants as shirking time-servers. A more objective perspective has been offered by a well respected and long-time academic commentator on New Zealand politics and government. It is sympathetic if not entirely flattering:

> The Public Service since 1912 has offered modestly attractive careers to men of modest background and ambitions. They were recruited to positions which offered no certain hope of advancement. Their whole life represented a socialisation into a culture which valued order and regularity in the performance of a given task...Ambition, the desire to shine or to be different or to innovate, was narrowly confined by the rules governing advancement. A few remarkable men could break through these constraints and attain some independent authority based upon their advocacy of reform, their articulate analysis of policy needs or their great professional accomplishment. They were rare exceptions...[T]he system was so well established and kept so low a profile in public life, that the politicians were largely disposed to take the Public Service for granted when in office. (Roberts, 1987, p. 28)

Although Roberts was writing mainly of the public service from the 1930s to the 1960s, a period when its upper reaches were the almost exclusive preserve of men, the picture he paints is entirely consistent with the image that helped to energise the state sector reforms in the late 1980s. It was believed that no matter how stable, reliable and generally competent government officials were, as a collectivity they lacked the sort of dynamism and drive that could only be ensured by the inculcation of a much more 'business-like' approach to public sector management. Managers (rather than administrators) had to be free to manage, and be made to manage.

The Main Thrust of the Reforms

The components of the New Zealand reforms have been well detailed elsewhere (Boston, Martin, Pallot and Walsh, 1996). In general terms they constituted a shift from a traditional 'rationality-bounded' model of governmental institutions to one much more in keeping with the model of the 'supermarket state' (Christensen, 1999). More specifically, they comprised the organisational separation of commercial and non-commercial functions; the single-purpose restructuring of advisory, delivery and regulatory functions ('one purpose, one organisation'); the separation of policy-making from operations; the abolition of the unified career service and the decentralisation of personnel management to the chief executives of individual government agencies; the use of incentives to enhance performance, through short-term contractual appointments as distinct from the permanent tenure which had characterised the previous regime, performance agreements and performance-based pay; contracts specifying the obligations of principals and agents, in particular between ministers and chief executives; the decentralisation, as much as possible, of managerial decision-making; the implementation of an accrual accounting system of financial management in the state sector; the increasing use of competitive tendering for and contracting out of goods and services; and the much greater use of cost-recovery, 'user pays', or commercialised public services. The reforms, however, hardly affected the long-standing dominance of central over local government in the fulfilment and provision of public functions and services.

The changes were implemented suddenly and forcefully, with little genuine attempt to consult with those affected by them, including the state sector unions (see Kelsey, 1995). They were designed by economic analysts located in the Treasury, the most powerful central agency; and were impelled by the concentration of power in the hands of a small group of bureaucrats and politicians (Goldfinch, 1998). At one critical juncture, one of the main architects of the changes was appointed State Services Commissioner, to provide reformist impetus to what had been a rather sceptical agency.

Theoretical and Ideological Bases of the Reforms

The reforms' theoretical coherency contrasted with the more piecemeal collection of ideas, conventions and convenient fictions that had guided the development of New Zealand public administration through the earlier decades of the century. As Roberts has observed, the 'only virtue' of the Westminster system, as adopted in New Zealand, was that it worked 'largely because everyone has learnt not to push for precise definitions of role and power' (Clark, 1999, p. 200). The apparent rigour of public choice theory, agency theory and transactions-costs analysis – what Hood and Peters (1994b) have called 'economics-of-politics' theories – promised much more precision than that afforded by a longer, more eclectic, tradition of public administration scholarship.

The reforms introduced to the language of New Zealand governance a novel set of conceptual dualities. The government is now an 'owner' and 'purchaser' – an owner of institutional capacity in all its various forms, as well as a purchaser of the vast range of 'outputs' produced by executive agencies. In turn, outputs are distinguished from 'outcomes', which are the consequences for the community of public policy interventions and initiatives. And the government is both a provider and funder of services, especially in the area of public health (see Ashton, 1999).

The simultaneous quest for greater efficiency and accountability saw a reassertion of the difference between policy and management (formerly called administration) and a consequent 'decoupling' of policy formulation from service delivery; the granting of more operational autonomy to the chief executives of public organisations and their managers in the production of 'outputs'; the need to match this greater freedom to manage with appropriate accountability requirements (that is, the imperatives of letting managers manage, and making them manage); and a general thrust towards a much more decentralised system of public management, including the delegation of personnel policy to individual organisational chief executives. Public choice theory's underlying assumption of self-interested utility maximisation on the part of public officials who had allegedly 'captured' policy processes informed the need to separate policy formulation from service delivery. Its espousal of the perception of 'government failure' impelled the move to much greater 'out-sourcing' of public goods and services and the creation of quasi-markets in the delivery of some such services. Agency theory and transactions-costs analysis justified the introduction of a contractual regime of senior executive appointments to ensure greater accountability of public officials.

Mechanistic and Organic Paradigms

The New Zealand state sector reforms were impelled by an essentially *mechanistic*, as opposed to an *organic*, interpretation of governmental institutions (Gregory and Hicks, 1999).[2] As the name suggests, the former approach tends to focus on such things as physical structures, deploying metaphors like 'the machinery of government', 'levers of control' and 'policy settings'. It stresses the formal and quantifiable dimensions of governance arrangements, matters of efficiency and economy, control, and lines of accountability. By contrast, the organic perspective focuses on the less tangible and measurable aspects: on informal interactions and on values such as democracy, equity, community and responsibility. It uses metaphors such as 'the spirit of administration', 'departmental mindset' and 'the human face of bureaucracy'.

The two paradigms are equally important in raising questions about and suggesting answers to a broad range of issues surrounding the structures, processes, aims and culture of democratic governance. While they are conceptually separable, with each focusing on different dimensions of the total governmental sphere, any intellectual preoccupation with one or the other is likely to generate less understanding and insight than that afforded by a fuller realisation of the on-going dialectical relationship that exists between them. For example, organic public opinion in the form of widespread popular concern over abuses of political power, in both the pre-reform (under Prime Minister Robert Muldoon) and post-reform periods, led to the introduction in 1996 of the Mixed Member Proportional electoral system, replacing the 'first-past-the-post' method – a change in constitutional mechanisms.

Public choice theory's quest for clarity and certainty in the roles and functions of politicians and officials, based on an over-reliance on a mechanistic perspective, is gained at the cost of insights generated by a more organic perspective. The view of a smoothly working machine, with all parts logically interconnected and integrated, is an elegant one with much intrinsic appeal. But when used as a rigorous blueprint for organisational reform it is most unlikely to take adequate account of the *deus ex machina* – those more ephemeral, organic qualities of human interaction that in the final analysis will be at least as decisive in shaping governmental practice. Its aspirations are founded upon a strong belief in its own scientific integrity, at the heart of which is the model of the individual rational egoist, whether politician or bureaucrat. Public choice theory has little regard for the idea of the public interest, since it cannot easily accommodate the prospect of a collective interest that transcends the sum of individual interests. Individuals can be understood mechanistically; the idea of the public interest only organically.

This strongly positivist approach is immensely uncomfortable with (organic) uncertainty and ambiguity, and relentlessly seeks greater levels of predictability and certainty in governmental behaviour. It assumes 'the one best way' to organise governmental (or other) institutions. In New Zealand, this assumption is apparent in the reformers' commitment to the viability of generic management (Easton, 1995), and particularly in the implicit (sometimes explicit) denial of any essential differences not only between the private and the public sectors, but also in regard to the diversity of tasks undertaken across the wide panoply of public organisations.[3] Thus, the mechanistic paradigm is much less comfortable than the organic with the *paradoxical* dimensions of public organisations and of governance generally.

Evaluating the Reforms

There can be no objectively true and accurate evaluation of the reforms. Causal relations, counterfactual situations and unintended consequences are far too complex and ambiguous to be gauged in any definitive way. Just as NPM theory itself is heavily ideological (Pollitt, 1998), so too is any attempt to provide an assessment of the reforms' efficacy, no matter how well balanced the attempt. In the years since the reforms were implemented there have been two main, officially commissioned assessments, one in 1991 and the other in 1996.[4] Both were largely favourable in their judgements. There have also been innumerable academic pieces written, embodying a wide range of perspectives and judgements.

Academic and other commentators generally agree that the quality of financial management in New Zealand government is much better than it was before. However, there remains considerable room for debate about many other aspects of the reforms. For example, it is virtually impossible to gauge conclusively whether overall 'efficiency' has been enhanced or diminished. At the macro-level assessments of 'efficiency' have more rhetorical than scientific substance. The point is well put by Pollitt (1998, p. 67):

> There is a sense in which we know we have made a whole series of specific efficiency gains in specific agencies and departments but that we do not yet have a very clear or reliable picture of what we have 'paid' for these achievements...in a variety of incommensurable currencies such as increasing inequalities and

inequities, failing morale among certain groups of public servants, lessening trust, increasing stress and uncertainty, and so on.

In the knowledge that any assessment of the impact of the state sector reforms on governmental administration in New Zealand (as elsewhere) must be ineluctably speculative and impressionistic, and in large part rhetorical and ideological, this discussion will focus on some of the possible costs alluded to by Pollitt, with particular reference to questions of public trust and governmental legitimacy.

Notwithstanding the insights of NPM, the task of understanding the changing culture of governmental activity remains an art or craft rather than a science. Perceptive observation, drawing on a keen appreciation of historical background, is at least as effective in this endeavour as any amount of survey research or opinion polling.

'Fate in Modern Times...' Making it Better or Making it Worse?

Reverse Effects

Theoretical coherence in governmental reform is not necessarily a virtue if the cost of that coherence is unnecessarily limited understanding. The New Zealand state sector reforms, founded upon the theoretical base of institutional economics, have placed huge weight on an individualist approach rather than on the former hierarchist idea of a public service (although not necessarily an elitist one) dedicated to the collective public good.[5] This is readily apparent in the shift to a network of contractualised relationships in the public sector, the adoption of quasi-markets in the provision of public goods and services (including the institutionalisation of government as a purchaser of agency outputs) and in the quest for 'contestability' in policy advice, through the decoupling of policy ministries from operational agencies.

Because of this overriding emphasis on the individualist approach, based on the view of politicians and officials as rational egoists and embodying a mechanistic preoccupation with reified structures and roles, the New Zealand reforms offer some 'lessons' both in reverse effects and in the need to be more sensitive to paradox in institutional redesign. Reverse effects, or 'fatal remedies' (Sieber, 1981), are created when 'social interventions achieve the very opposite of the desired effect for some reason' (Hood, 1998a, p. 211). In his discussion Hood draws on Sieber's seven 'conversion mechanisms' which produce reverse effects, the most well-known of which is probably that of 'goal displacement', derived from the writing of scholars like Merton (1952) and Blau (1963). Hood argues not that public management reforms are uniquely vulnerable to reverse-effect problems but rather that *any* approach to public management is likely to produce negative effects, *and that those effects 'can be expected to be more severe, the more weight is put on any one approach...'* (Hood, 1998a, p. 217).

Although a 'hierarchist' rather than a 'fatalist' himself, it was Max Weber who resignedly observed that, 'Fate in modern times is the consequence of man's actions contrary to his intentions'. The following interpretations of some aspects of the New Zealand state sector reforms might have appealed to his unerring instinct for the unintended, not to say reverse effects, of the never-ending quest for organisational perfection.

Bureaucratisation: More or Less?

The reforms promised 'debureaucratisation'. Managers were to be granted real freedom to manage, to get on with the job without being too hedged about by inflexible bureaucratic procedure and red tape. NPM would create a new 'results-oriented' regime, much more purpose-focused than 'constraint-driven' (Wilson, 1989).

It is not at all clear that this has been the outcome. On the contrary, because NPM is by definition a *managerial* initiative, it is unsurprisingly impelled by management imperatives, the most central of which is that of *control*. The task of managers is to control subordinates to ensure that the organisation as a rational system is best able to achieve its objectives, to produce the outputs expected of it. Management therefore tends to breed management, not necessarily in terms of numbers but in terms of the search for more certain and effective means of control. Something of a 'Catch-22' emerges. The increasing need for clearer and more specific agency outputs and the accompanying preoccupation with measurement as a means of facilitating managerial control transmutes the outputs themselves, and in the pursuit of further control (usually called 'accountability') there emerge increasing pressures to specify and measure outcomes as well as outputs.[6] The tail of managerial necessity comes to wag the dog of effective governance. Management thus becomes more bureaucratic, rather than less, since there develops a rational need to ensure that as much organisational activity as possible is accounted for in ways that are readily visible and quantifiable – that is, more controllable. As a former minister of state services has observed:

'I fear that compliance has become the measure of success rather than the quality of the outcomes being attained' (Upton, 1999, p. 14).

NPM in New Zealand addressed the intractable bureaucratic paradox of means becoming ends in themselves, but in so doing it has managed to transform rather than resolve it. Now, a new form of 'goal displacement' has increasingly emerged from a managerialist impatience with any form of operational activity that is not readily amenable to sensible quantification. The main casualties of this fixation are likely to be common sense, sound judgement, experienced insight and wise decision-making.

If a valid measure of bureaucratisation is the degree of control imposed on governmental organisations by other – say, central – agencies, then it is undoubtedly true that in New Zealand the demise of the central personnel function constitutes a bureaucratic 'roll-back'. Agency heads now exercise far more independent authority over the 'hiring and firing' of their own staff, uninhibited by the formerly cumbersome system of centralised classification, grading and appeals. There is much less evidence to suggest, however, that in other important respects agencies enjoy more autonomy. They are no less constrained by the powerful Treasury department; scrutiny of departmental activities by parliamentary select committees has been enhanced; the Controller and Auditor-General breathes down their necks in ever more vigilant ways; and the demands of the Official Information Act have to be constantly negotiated.

Moreover, it can be argued that while the decentralisation of personnel management has reduced bureaucratic transactions in one way, it has enhanced them in another. The contractualist regime that now prevails (about which more later) generates a huge amount of procedural specification, negotiation and codification, in the form of employment and performance contracts, statements of corporate intent, purchasing agreements between ministers and their agencies, tendering and the like. It is highly probable that the levels of managerial time and energy expended on formalistic transactions is at least as great, quite possibly greater, than that demanded of officials under the preceding, more traditional, bureaucratic regime. There is no question, at least, that the new environment is hugely more litigious than the old, notably in the realm of employment contracting. There is also evidence that an increasingly legalistic culture is associated with a generally more 'reactive' orientation at the upper levels of the public service, possibly running counter to the reformers' aim of enhancing results-centredness or 'programmatic commitment'. It is just possible that the reforms may have helped foster the sort of public servants they were intended to replace, but who probably did not exist as a dominant type in the first place.[7]

By 1999 the State Services Commission had identified 'three specific areas of concern' that needed to be addressed. First, there was too much complexity and duplication in the new accountability system, 'as a result of incremental accretions over time'; second, this accretion had not captured important information on capability, strategic alignment was weak, core business was under-emphasised and performance indicators for non-financial information were lacking; and third, the accountability system was demotivating chief executives (SSC, 1999a). The last factor, in particular, indicates that the intention to 'make managers manage' has dominated the concomitant desire to 'let managers manage', with reverse effects. According to the Commission (1999a, p. 23), 'The use of small output classes, tight specification and activity measures [have] forced managers to move into a narrow compliance and conformance mode that can discourage innovation and responsiveness'.

Clarifying Political and Managerial Accountability?

Managerialism's promise to reduce greatly the degree of 'bureaucratisation' in New Zealand government seems unfulfilled. Constitutionally the situation is also highly problematic. This has particularly been the case in regard to the array of crown entities, which exist in an 'arms-length' relationship with the political executive and which give collective expression to the desire to reduce the number of government departments and create quasi-independent bodies which are better able to run themselves along 'business' lines.[8] But NPM in New Zealand has been insufficiently sensitive to the peculiar realities, especially the political context, of public administration. As Pollitt (1998, p. 70) argues, '...there are problems at the heart of government that have no real parallel in the world of corporate affairs'.

Especially in the past couple of years a number of public controversies have centred on the ways in which government executives have chosen, and been able, to exercise their enhanced discretionary authority. All of them involved adverse news media reaction, often initiated by members of parliamentary opposition parties, to what was perceived to be inappropriate spending of the taxpayer's money on apparently inordinately large salary packages for some public executives, on severance payments for other governmental appointees and on departmental activities (like costly training courses and exercises and associated travel) and overly expensive furnishings, as well as huge spending overruns on unsuccessful computer technology. The then prime minister, Jenny Shipley, publicly admitted to being 'infuriated' about the damage done to the image of the Public Service; the leader of the parliamentary opposition, Helen Clark,[9] called for a 'cultural change' in the Public Service 'in which senior managers will learn how to spell the words 'Public Service' again'; and a top public servant, the secretary for justice, made a public call for government officials to earn back the public's trust: 'It is critical that leaders in the public sector demonstrate that they have a real grip on the basics. That means going back to the basic values and ethics of public service'.

The political heat generated by these events resulted in the State Services Commissioner – the official responsible for the appointment of departmental chief executives and the monitoring of their performance – being given greater oversight over the remuneration paid to board members and chief executives of crown entities, formerly not within the commissioner's purview. The government also strengthened ministerial powers over a group of crown entities, which it categorised as 'agents of the crown', as distinct from independent decision-making bodies, trusts, crown companies and other bodies such as schools.[10] The episodes demonstrated again that political necessity is its own virtue: freedom to manage can only be sustained so long as the costs are deemed to be politically acceptable.

The internal contradiction embodied in the reforms has been well remarked upon by Aucoin (1990), among others. On the one hand, chief executives were to exist in an 'arms-length' relationship with the political executive in exercising their new-found freedom to manage their agencies. On the other hand, the reforms were intended to ensure that chief executives, especially of government departments, were more directly under the control of their ministers than had previously been the case with permanent heads. Before the reforms the Westminster doctrine of ministerial responsibility, considered by constitutionalists to be the cornerstone of the New Zealand government system, had been open to quite a wide range of practical interpretations (see Palmer and Palmer, 1997; Roberts, 1987), all of which depended upon the ebb and flow of political circumstance and opportunism. The doctrine has remained as flexible as ever after the reforms, despite (or probably because of) the innovative notion that ministers of the crown are responsible for policy outcomes, while departmental chief executives are responsible, *inter alia*, for producing the specific outputs that are intended to generate those outcomes. Two highly publicised cases have underscored this flexibility: the resignation of a chief executive after his minister had decided that a departmental appointment was not in the public interest (see Boston, 1994a); and the tragedy of Cave Creek, where a wilderness viewing platform built by the Department of Conservation collapsed, killing 14 people (see Gregory, 1998d, 1998b). In the former case a minister sought to exercise control over a personnel matter that had been legally delegated to his chief executive. In the latter instance – a virtual worst-case scenario of departmental failure in which causality was clearly identified by a commission of inquiry – fine distinctions between 'outcomes' and 'outputs' did nothing to ensure that political and managerial responsibility for the tragedy was satisfactorily brought home either to the minister or to the chief executive.

These and other incidents have shown once again, if any further evidence were needed, that attempts to specify role relations according to categories like 'outcomes' and 'outputs' are politically naïve and offer a poor guide to understanding the ambiguities and uncertainties in the lived reality of governmental relationships. As the State Services Commission itself has observed, 'Ministers have not necessarily acted in the manner envisaged by the New Zealand public management model, either in terms of specifying outcomes or results, or in terms of operating as discerning purchasers of outputs' (SSC, 1999a, pp. 21–22).

Politicisation?

There is also some irony in the fact that although there is widespread agreement among commentators that the reforms have greatly improved financial management in the New Zealand public sector, the past few years have been marked by the sorts of controversies referred to above. This may be partly because there is now greater 'transparency' in the spending of public money; but most of the public disquiet has focused on the instances of apparent profligacy in departments and agencies, which under the former regime would have been subjected to closer, centralised, spending controls.

Nor has the statutory delineation of the respective responsibilities of ministers and officials in New Zealand served to limit partisan attacks on public servants. The reforms certainly gave many public sector chief executives a much higher public profile than had generally (but not exclusively) been the case before. On a number of occasions they have been at the centre of major public controversies, sometimes without the political support of the government and often subject to intense criticism from the government's political opponents. Such instances demonstrate a major weakening in the doctrine of ministerial responsibility, in the case of departmental chief executives, particularly in view of the failure of the new 'arms-length' arrangement to provide satisfactory reference points by which political responsibility might fairly be judged. These sorts of reasons lend support to arguments that the New Zealand public service has become more 'politicised', rather than less, if 'politicisation' means the blurring of political and managerial responsibility.

Some commentators argued that the reforms would 'politicise' the public service, by inviting political patronage in senior appointments at the expense of the long-standing values of a professional, non-partisan, service. However, there has been no return to the older, cruder, forms of political patronage which prevailed in New Zealand before the introduction of a unified career service in 1912. It would serve no government's best interests to appoint chief executives on the basis of their political or ideological views, at the expense of job competence, notwithstanding the legitimate need to ensure a compatible working relationship between ministers and their chief executives. Yet the issue has not been fully tested in practice, as National Party governments have effectively held office since 1990. In the lead-up to the general election of November 1999 the leader of the parliamentary opposition expressed concern about the ideological leanings of some government departments and doubted whether the Ministry of Commerce had the 'capacity or will' to drive the Labour Party's industry policy.

Contractualism: What Price Trust?

'Contractualism' here refers to the appointment of senior public servants on renewable term contracts – in New Zealand these can be of up to five years' duration. This contrasts with the 'relational contracts' which characterised the pre-reform era when, barring exceptional circumstances, officials enjoyed permanent tenure (hence the former 'permanent heads' of government departments). By 1999 over 40 percent of Public Service staff were employed on individual contracts, compared with 17 percent in 1994. Thirty-eight percent of employees of crown entities were on individual contracts in 1999, up from 2 percent five years earlier.

Lane (1999) has argued that there are some major theoretical problems with contractualism, which is based on the application of agency theory (principal-agent relationships) to governmental systems. He suggests that a sort of 'prisoner's dilemma' operates, in which both principals and agents will tend to behave opportunistically to maximise their respective advantages. In doing so, both parties focus upon 'the formal terms of the contract [rather] than upon what the [work] situation requires' (1999, p. 188). According to Lane, governments behave opportunistically by blaming chief executives when outcomes are not met, regardless of whether or not the contractee is performing well. This creates an impression of firmness and control, especially *'pour encourager les autres'*. Executives, on the other hand, shirk for similar reasons, since they stand to be punished regardless of their efforts, or because governments cannot conclusively demonstrate their shirking, especially in the so-called 'soft sector' agencies, where the nature of the organisational task makes it very difficult to relate executive performance to unambiguous outcomes and where organisational 'technologies' are tenuous.

In New Zealand there is substantial evidence to support Lane's suggestion that, 'Agents seem to have been very successful in avoiding signing 'boiling-in-oil' contracts, as seen from the frequent occurrence of very lucrative compensation schemes when agents are in fact fired'. Some of the public controversies mentioned above related to just such instances, which focused on government appointees who appeared to be in a win-win situation, when the only way they could be removed from their jobs was by paying them large 'golden handshakes'. However, there is little apparent evidence of governments harshly treating chief executives in order to 'set an example'. Notwithstanding that, the New Zealand experience would seem to confirm that contractualism can become something of an end in itself, consuming huge amounts of time and effort and creating perverse behavioural incentives which do little to guarantee more competent and effective management. An ethos of mutual trust and fairness can be supplanted by one of self-seeking opportunism, rationalised on the grounds that, 'everyone's doing it so I'd be a mug not to join in'.

Under these circumstances the chief casualty is trust, not only the trust which underpins an effective relationship between (in, say, the case of government departments) ministers and their chief executives, but also the public's trust in its governmental institutions, especially when it appears that the only way for the government to get rid of top executives is to pay them off exorbitantly. In the former case, a core value in the relationship is the 'full, frank, and fearless' advice that a chief executive/permanent head is expected to provide for his or her minister. It cannot be asserted categorically that under New Zealand's contractualist regime, chief executives are now disposed to tender advice which is less full, less frank and more fearful. The State Services Commissioner, rather than the minister, is formally responsible for the renewal of chief executives' contracts, and to date none has been terminated before its expiry for poor performance, though one was not renewed, and several chief executives have chosen to resign before the termination of their contracts. But if contracts are intended to be a means of ensuring stronger control by ministers over their top officials, then it is difficult to envisage ministers being content with chief executives who persist in tendering advice which is contrary to ministerial preferences. Those chief executives who resign early may tend to be those who experience compatibility problems with their ministers.

The main problem with contractualism, as with other aspects of the New Zealand state sector reforms, is the narrow theoretical base on which it is founded. Essentially, all means of generating organisational control, whether they be the rules-based compliance fostered through hierarchical bureaucracy or the individual contracts derived from agency theory, are ultimately based on the belief that people cannot be trusted. But those applying any of these means need to remain alert to the paradox that, in government as elsewhere, trust may best be fostered by trust. The converse – that mistrust fosters more mistrust – also seems true, for agency theory's founding assumption that all individuals are self-interested utility maximers becomes something of a self-fulfilling prophecy. In the light of the New Zealand experience it is hard not to agree with Lane's main conclusion that governments need to add to NPM contractualism management approaches based on trust, as well as traditional bureaucratic mechanisms. The organic generation of relational trust in and within governmental arrangements remains as essential today as it ever was.

The problems of contractualism in senior appointments reflect the mechanistic artificiality not only of the principal/agent dichotomy, but also of the purchaser/provider split. The latter, for example, is central to the New Zealand health service reforms. But the government is both purchaser and provider simultaneously and must reconcile the competing demands of health care in a way that transcends both roles. This transcendent function of public trusteeship embodies the time-honoured governmental process of balancing conflicting and multiple objectives and values. It cannot be wished away by bifurcated structural re-engineering.

Remuneration and the Culture of Distrust

New Zealand has not been an 'egalitarian' political community in the democratic sense described by Hood (1998a, p. 120): 'radically decentralized self-governing units rather than conventional large-scale state structures...' Unlike Sweden, for example, New Zealand does not have a strong tradition of local government based on principles of decentralisation and/or devolution.

Imperatives of centralised hierarchical authority and responsibility, rather than collegial communality, have always been at the heart of the New Zealand brand of representative democracy (even though voting turnout at general elections has traditionally been around the 90 percent mark). This was, in fact, clearly demonstrated in the way the state sector (and other) reforms were implemented, with virtually no consultation with the public sector unions or the public at large, and with no popular mandate derived from an electoral platform.

However, for most of the twentieth century New Zealand society was egalitarian in socio-economic terms (Boston, Dalziel, St John, 1999; Lipson, 1948; Rudd, 1997). The state sector itself, including the Public Service, reflected this egalitarian spirit in various ways, one of which was the fact that top public servants' lifestyle (and that of politicians) was not markedly different from that of the rest of the community. Entrance to the Public Service was not restricted to an academic elite, though those who gravitated to the upper echelons usually had more formal education than those who did not, and advancement could generally be secured by conscientious effort over a working career of several decades within the unified career structure. Roberts (1987, p. 96) has summarised this well:

> What we have is a picture of dedicated long service employees with ordinary social backgrounds... If there is a case for ending the career service in New Zealand, it must rest upon attacking inertia and the preference for the status quo rather than reducing the power of an elite mandarin class.

Since the reforms there has been no emergence of an elite policy-making mandarinate in the classical sense. In fact, informal policy elites may have been more apparent under the old system. Emphasis on the management of output delivery sits uneasily with the statutory requirement that chief executives should also tender policy advice to the government. And by fragmenting the unified service into a collection of individual fiefdoms, the reforms attenuated the sort of policy coherence that emerges from a core of privileged advisers.[11] In any case, a great deal of policy advice is itself 'outsourced' in the same manner as other goods and services, with variable results (see Boston, 1994b).

Nevertheless, the abolition of the career service and the decentralisation of personnel management to individual agencies, the universal use of contractual appointments and the introduction of pay for performance have all challenged the egalitarian spirit, as indeed they were intended to do. This has been perhaps the most transformative element of the whole reform process.

The mimicking of the private sector was expected to create a managerialist public enterprise that was far more dynamic, innovative and efficient than the administrative hierarchy that preceded it.

The neo-liberal social and economic policy reforms in New Zealand since 1984 have arguably created a growing gap between the top and bottom strata of society (Podder and Chatterjee, 1998; Stephens, 2000), an outcome which is reflected in the emergence of a corporate managerial elite enjoying highly privileged rates of remuneration (including, in some cases, massive severance payments), which have been increasing much more quickly than those of the rank and file. Many state sector top executives have shared this privilege. For most of the twentieth century the pay rates for New Zealand's top government officials were justified, though mainly implicitly, by a mix of what Peters and Hood (1994, p. 222) call the *representativeness* and *alimentation* criteria. The former, harking back to classical democracy, is based on the belief that high public officials should be generally representative in their life-style of 'ordinary citizens'. The latter notion says they should be rewarded with a comfortable, upper middle-class living, in order to shield them from corrupting temptations and to help ensure that they are not distracted from the onerous burdens of statecraft. Probably the representativeness criterion was stronger, being consistent with the country's dominant egalitarian norms. However, the reforms have been based overwhelmingly on the third criterion presented by Peters and Hood, the *market* criterion, which is reflected in the 'developing ideology... that top civil servants should be paid at rates similar to those of top business executives'.

The remuneration packages paid to chief executives of state-owned enterprises and many other crown entities are not subject to centralised control by the State Services Commissioner, and many of them are in line with the top rates paid in the private sector. Such high remuneration rates are now being paid at a time when large numbers of general government employees are having to fight for annual wage increases of a maximum of 2 or 3 percent. The huge salary packages may be justified on the grounds that state-owned enterprises must be able to compete effectively with large private corporations in the market place of executive talent. However, it is doubtful whether large sections of the New Zealand public, who themselves struggle to attain minimal wage and salary increases, have easily come to terms with the transformation.[12]

Moreover, the expectation that higher rewards will necessarily reduce the likelihood of corruption bears closer scrutiny. Two points can be made here. First, what actually constitutes corruption in this context is largely a matter of public definition. Corruption may not just be the incidence of individual mal-feasance, such as fraud or bribe-taking, but may also be interpreted as profli-gate, though technically legitimate, spending by and remuneration of govern-ment officials, particularly in the form of large contractual 'buy-outs'. Second, it is also possible that a culture of higher and less visible rewards for top government executives can create a climate of greed, in which much more is never quite enough, and in which competition for rewards and perks becomes a central component of the culture of an emergent managerial elite. If such behaviour is *perceived* to be corrupt, unethical, or inequitable, it will under-mine public trust and confidence in the integrity of public executives.

Viewed in another light the higher remuneration packages that have accompanied the state sector reforms in New Zealand reflect an implicit bargain between the state and its top employees. Higher remuneration and a wider range of salary package components and performance pay constitute a sort of *quid pro quo* for the permanent tenure that was lost when the unified career service was abolished. Enhanced remuneration can also be seen as a form of insurance against the possibility that job security could be threatened by changing and unpredictable political circumstances, not to mention the exercise of political whim, and notwithstanding the legal redress that could be sought against this eventuality. It can be argued abstractly that failure on the part of the state, for whatever reason, to keep its side of this implicit bargain can leave top public officials resentful and prone to cynical and opportunistic, if not corrupt, behaviour.[13]

While this might not necessarily occur in New Zealand, other factors have reinforced public distrust and cynicism. Since the reforms there has been a huge increase in the amount of policy advice contracted out to private consul-tants, many of whom had formerly been in-house public service employees. During the 1990s largely piecemeal, and by no means complete, information on the multi-million dollar sums of money paid for this advice was generated by news media investigations under the Official Information Act and by searching parliamentary questions. No readily accessible ledger is available. Consequently, the public impression is of a largely secretive consultancy 'gravy train' fuelled by taxpayers' money, producing highly priced policy advice which could probably be provided more cheaply by in-house analysts performing to at least the same, if not better, standards. The fact that the information is not publicly available as a matter of course and often has to be extracted from reluctant providers citing its 'commercial sensitivity' casts further doubt on the claim that the reforms have enhanced 'transparency'.

Elements of the news media have also been assiduous in publicising examples of apparently profligate spending of taxpayers' money on travel and on highly priced office furnishings and refurbishments in a number of public sector domains. There have also been some high profile court cases involving allegations of fraud on the part of top level public officials, cases which were virtually unprecedented in the history of New Zealand government administration. The most spectacular of these was the conviction and jail-sentencing in 1997 of no less a personage than a former Controller and Auditor-General, on 10 counts of fraud involving $NZ54,500 of public funds.

Service Delivery: Customers or Citizens?

In addition, question marks hang over the attempt to create a new 'customer-driven', quasi-marketised model of public service delivery. Many New Zealanders might consider that the transformation of the bureaucracy charged with providing welfare benefits has resulted in more efficiently run departments, more responsive to their personal requirements (McDonald and Sharma, 1994; Petrie, 1998). However, the rhetoric of running the agency as if it were a 'business' rather than a government service undoubtedly makes many others feel bemused, even cynical. In 1999 the Inland Revenue Department (IRD) was investigated by a parliamentary committee, set up after a series of public allegations of undue and inhumane harassment of some taxpayers. The committee recommended a series of changes to ensure more fairness in IRD transactions and to overcome what it called 'the department's culture of fear and punishment'.[14] To many New Zealanders, their rhetorical transformation from citizens of the political community into 'customers' or 'clients' of various agencies, most of which have been keen to adopt the trappings and ambience of private business corporations, does not ring true. The language of private management has proven to be inappropriate to most dimensions of public service, where the provision of service is not and cannot be disciplined by market forces, whether real or quasi, where public organisations do not and cannot have full authorship of the policies they implement, and where their financial resources are authorised by parliamentary appropriations and not provided by private patronage.

Nevertheless, the use of contracts between public service providers and users – for example, in the job-seeker contract used by the Department of Work and Income – at least implicitly transforms citizens into consumers, customers or clients. As such, their rights are focused mainly on the consumption of services, rather than on the design, production or delivery of them (Shaw, 1999).

Whether or not it is dressed up in the language of 'freedom to manage', 'empowering' operators and managers in public organisations implies a consequential 'disempowerment' of the political executive. Political executives in New Zealand are invariably held responsible by the public when things go awry, and do not readily welcome 'disempowerment'. The number of political controversies that beset the public sector in the late 1990s indicated that the 'arms-length' principle promoted by the governmental reforms had in no way diminished public expectations of political responsibility.

A New Quest for Legitimacy

During the past 15 years or so New Zealanders have become increasingly cynical and distrusting towards politicians and political institutions generally, not just government agencies, a situation confirmed late in 1998 by a nation-wide survey of attitudes and values regarding politics and government (Perry and Webster, 1999). In response to the question, 'Would you say that this country is run by a few big interests looking out for themselves or that it is run for the benefit of all the people?' 70 percent of respondents agreed with the former proposition, a result that is 16 percent higher than that produced by a 1989 survey (Perry and Webster, 1999, p. 44).[15] Much of the disaffection may reflect the fact that from the 1970s onwards, when stagflation took hold, politics and policy-making became more disputatious and conflictual than had been the case during the post-war years of relative prosperity. However, a great deal also stems from abuses of power by the political executive, particularly during the period of radical social and economic reform of the mid- to late 1980s ('crashing through' policy change over the top of political opposition), from manifest political untrustworthiness, and from perceived inequities in social policy-making.[16]

These attitudes have been reflected in a changing relationship between citizens and the state in New Zealand. Virtually since the mid-nineteenth-century beginnings of representative government in New Zealand, the state has been perceived by citizens as an institutional embodiment of their own collective aspirations, rather than as a dominating, external force. This perception was eloquently described by Lipson (1948, p. 482):

The [New Zealand] people, or at any rate most of them, look upon the state quite healthily as being themselves under another form. When it acts, they feel that they are acting. What it owns, they own.... To them it is simply a utilitarian instrument for effecting their will.

In a similar vein, the New Zealand state was described by the wife of the 1940s prime minister, Peter Fraser, as 'the home enlarged' (Stace 1998, p. 64).

The 1980s and 1990s saw the privatisation of a wide range of former state assets (Duncan and Bollard, 1992). In addition, the welfare state, built progressively since the advent of the first Labour government in 1935 and continued by successive National (conservative) governments, was increasingly depicted as too costly a burden on the country's productive capacity, giving rise to the targeting and cutting of state benefits in the 1991 budget (Boston and Dalziel, 1992; Kelsey, 1995). The state has taken on a harder face towards its citizens. By the end of the 1990s it was being viewed – especially in light of the Cave Creek tragedy and allegations against the IRD – as an increasingly dehumanised, 'external' and unsympathetic force, rather than as an instrument central to the pursuit of the common good.[17] According to a former office solicitor with the State Services Commission (more recently a departmental chief executive), public servants are 'being asked to do more work with fewer resources, their personal accountability has been increased, the security of their positions removed, and the distance between the public and the Public Service widened' (Bradshaw, 1993). The state is now less inclusive and much more divisive; economic and social reforms driven by a commitment to a deregulated marketplace have tended to replace norms of collective co-operation with those of atomised individual competitiveness, in such a short space of time that there exists something of a societal 'culture shock'. As a result, the revamped state sector in New Zealand is having to struggle with real problems of legitimacy.

These are by no means peculiar to New Zealand. Savoie (1998, p. 401) has noted that the message given to career officials by the political leadership in Anglo-American democracies in the past fifteen years has been 'clear and hardly positive'. In New Zealand, rhetoric acclaiming the virtues of the private sector over the vices of the public sector has produced a legitimacy paradox, a sort of vicious circle. Ideologically driven criticism of the public sector's alleged inadequacies has helped transform governmental agencies along private sector lines, in turn undermining the culture of public trusteeship that lay at the heart of the New Zealand public sector. There is a growing danger that this outcome will worsen rather than ameliorate problems of public sector legitimacy.

While 'the public service as traditionally constituted' was certainly in need of change to enhance any number of salient values – be they efficiency, effectiveness, responsiveness, equity or democracy (depending on how any of these were to be operationalised) – the ideological drive to borrow and impose models of private management as the only legitimate mode of reform has created new legitimacy problems, of a sort that were not previously conceivable. The former system of New Zealand government administration was noteworthy, among other things, for its almost total incorruptibility. In this respect the service enjoyed high levels of public trust. The reforms, which at no stage had to address any major problems of ethical probity, much less corruption in the form of opportunistic malfeasance on the part of public officials, were partly facilitated by this trust, since– even if they had had a say – New Zealand citizens would not have balked at the prospect of granting more managerial autonomy to public officials. Peters (1996b) has argued that the relative absence of such trust in the United States has slowed the adoption of NPM reforms in that country (perhaps for the better). But, in keeping with the syndrome of reverse effects, the irony is that public trust in government officialdom is now being undermined partly as a *result* of the reforms.

In New Zealand it is now conceivable, although not certain, that the state services will face increasing problems in maintaining traditional standards of ethical probity, largely because under NPM government officials who are expected to behave in an increasingly 'business-like' manner, in a largely fragmented system of individual agencies, will be less acculturated by any integrating ethos of public trusteeship. Such an ethos is essential in sustaining the legitimacy of state sector institutions, because it is founded on the understanding that they are owned ultimately by the *public* rather than by any particular government, whose ministers, rather than being 'owners' or 'purchasers', are actually relatively short-term trustees on behalf of that public.[18] Such an ethos does not rest easily with 'economics-of-politics' denials of the validity of the concept of the public interest as any sort of normative guide for official behaviour (Gregory, 1999; Gregory and Hicks, 1999). This may be expected to worsen over time, as more and more people come into a service in which the values of public trusteeship have become increasingly weaker, and who are motivated more by the pursuit of careers in an individualised (and increasingly lucrative) 'job market' rather than in a collective 'calling'.

However, remedial action may be taken to curtail such developments. After the general election in late 1999 the State Services Commissioner advised the new government of 'a loss of public confidence in the institutions of government, politicians and public servants'. He observed that, 'the emphasis on good management and efficiency, and on tightly specified contractualism, may have resulted in a loss of the spirit of service and standards of integrity' (SSC, 1999b, p. 1). For his part, the new minister of state services urged public servants to revitalise the notion of public service and refresh its values. 'The public administration model needs to shift away from the narrow business values and recast the full hierarchy of values and ethics that need to guide government operations'.[19]

Conclusion: Learning from the New Zealand Experience

The New Zealand version of NPM is certainly one of the most radically transformative approaches to public sector reform to be found among the Western democracies. The assessment offered here is based on the belief that the process of this transformation informs both its content and its effects. The process by which the New Zealand state sector and most other major components of the economic and social policy landscape was reformed was strongly technocratic.[20] The changes were driven not by political bargaining and negotiation among interested stakeholders, but by reference to a body of economic theory. The intellectual authority of this body of theory was accepted almost unquestioningly by a cohesive policy-making elite that was able to use the concentration of power afforded by the New Zealand political system to impose reform from the centre, in the face of any effective opposition.

Unlike the more pragmatic and piecemeal public sector reforms that occurred in countries like Australia, Sweden and Norway, those that were imposed in New Zealand were not only theoretically comprehensive and coherent, but their implementation was aggressively pursued. Elements of an 'old guard', found in agencies like the State Services Commission, were not permitted to counsel caution in the face of the theoretically based certitude and commitment displayed by the new policy elite grounded upon the analytical firepower and political clout of the Treasury and the executive authority of the inner Cabinet. Impelling this reformist drive was the belief that the country's future could only be secured by a drastic shift away from an over-regulated economy. Facilitating it was a widespread relief at the end

254 New Public Management

of the nine-year period of political authoritarianism and economic control of former Prime Minister Muldoon.

The New Zealand state sector reforms represented a sudden and drastic change to the public administration regime that had prevailed during the previous seven or eight decades. In this they differed markedly from those pursued in most other countries, including Norway, Sweden, and Australia, which have shared with New Zealand some similar statist and egalitarian traditions. And it is doubtful whether in any other country the reformist mindset was so rigidly committed as it was in New Zealand to the view that the key to improving all important dimensions of public service lay in transforming governmental organisations in the image of private business. In no other country, certainly not in Sweden and Norway, and not to the same degree in Australia, were the reforms based on such a narrow theoretical paradigm, in which economic interpretations of political and bureaucratic behaviour were assumed to be superior in all respects to those afforded by other scholarly traditions. In none of the other countries, including Australia, was there so strong an ideological commitment to the tenets of NPM and so strong a disdain for any theoretically or pragmatically generated perspective that might have balanced these ideological views with a keener sense of the historical evolution of the key values and norms of the 'traditional' system. In none of the other countries under discussion in this volume were the perceived virtues of contractualism, both in personnel management and in the outsourcing of goods and services, embraced so quickly and enthusiastically as in New Zealand – certainly not in Norway, where change has proceeded much more incrementally (Lægreid, 1999b). In New Zealand the doctrinaire application of public choice theory seems to have been something of a self-fulfilling prophecy: the assumption that governmental officials are primarily self-interested opportunists has impelled the establishment of a contractualist regime that may have encouraged them to become so. And it is becoming apparent that only by having 'The Crown' run a much more centralised regime to manage the contracting out of governmental goods and services, in place of the plethora of negotiations entered into by individual agencies, will any benefits of contractualism be maximised. In none of the other countries was such a radical and massive process of organisational fragmentation undertaken, based on the perceived malignancies of 'provider capture' and on such a predominantly mechanistic view of the state sector (Christensen, 1999; Christensen and Lægreid, 1999b).

The argument that the state sector reforms in New Zealand were compelled by a degree of economic necessity unmatched in any of the other three countries may partly account for most of the above excesses. But, a decade on, they can be seen to have created a troublesome disjunction between the democratic dimensions of good governance on the one hand and the corporate imperatives of effective management on the other. They have 'politicised' the public sector in ways that threaten to undermine the trust and respect of citizens. In the narrowly focused pursuit of managerial efficiency and accountability, the reforms have tended to overlook the sort of concerns that relate to the democratic institutional backdrop to those managerialist endeavours.[21]

A much more felicitous balance now needs to be struck among a wider range of values than those promoted by NPM. The value of pragmatic common sense needs to be rediscovered in New Zealand, as well as a much more eclectic approach to theoretical insight. Consideration needs to be given to ways in which the broadest possible democratic accountability of government agencies can be secured and enhanced, especially in light of the negative impacts of contractualism in top appointments and an emergent culture of opportunistic managerial elitism. Core competencies of top executives must be defined in ways that are sensitive both to technical demands and to the values of good governance. The practical implications of creating institutions founded upon unrealistic, artificially compartmentalised bifurcations need intelligent re-evaluation to establish a more integrated dialectical relationship between the components. This is probably most essential in the case of the distinctions drawn between the government as 'owner' and the government as 'purchaser', between 'outputs' and 'outcomes', and between 'policy' and 'management' (Gregory, 1999).

The 'owner/purchaser' dichotomy has probably generated most anxiety. In his major report, Schick (1996, p. 43), for example, observed that,

> ...Ministers must also be mindful of the organizational strength of their department; they should be institution builders, and they should forbear from demanding so much by way of outputs and from pushing the purchase price down so far as to jeopardize the department's long-term capacity to perform.

The retiring secretary of the Ministry of Foreign Affairs and Trade commented publicly that, '...the ownership interest in the core capability of the public service is under pressure that cannot be sustained. All too often, policy and capability issues have been seen only through a short-term fiscal prism' (*The Dominion*, 10 August 1999). 'Decoupling', the taking apart of components of an integrated whole, now needs to be replaced by a process of sensible 'recoupling', in order to recover, or prevent the further loss of, those essential qualities of public service that can only be secured by a genuine appreciation of the value of public trusteeship. In his brief to the newly elected government late in 1999 the State Services Commissioner advised that it should direct state sector organisations 'to work together as virtual organisations on cross-sectoral issues, complementing whatever arrangements it adopts for ensuring ministerial leadership on those issues' (SSC, 1999b, p. 9). This would be much more in tune with the ineluctable challenge for governmental endeavours to seek judicious balance among disparate, conflicting and often paradoxical imperatives.

It would be the supreme irony of the New Zealand reforms if they have contributed to the emergence of a culture of self-seeking opportunism among public officials rather than reinforcing commitment to the values of public service. To what extent this will occur remains to be seen; but there have been some worrying signs. A decade after the implementation of the New Zealand state sector reforms it is not only opportune but urgently essential to ask the same sort of questions that Savoie (1998, p. 413) would ask of the Canadian jurisdiction, which has been much less subject to the strictures of NPM: 'We need to redefine the 'core competencies' required from individual public servants and the public service. We need to define what it is that a national public service can do better than any other group in society'.

The complex and paradoxical nature of government administration guarantees the absence of perfect systems, but the quest for technical perfectibility and the play of political power render change inevitable. Transformation of governmental systems is an iterative rather than a terminal process, proceeding over time with varying impetus and emphasis. The moment never arrives when conflicting and diverse values like efficiency, effectiveness, equity, responsiveness, due process, fairness, creativity and the like are ever reconciled in some optimal achievement of reformist design. Rhetoric surrounding the New Zealand state sector reforms, and the international attention they have attracted, suggest that a reformist nirvana has indeed been attained. The reality is otherwise, and the quest continues for a new balance between the imperatives of bureaucratic control on the one hand and the demand for purposive policy outcomes on the other.

Notes

1   In New Zealand, the state sector encompasses all agencies, including but not limited to ministerial government departments, that are owned and operated by the state. The Public Service is defined under the State Sector Act 1988 and incorporates 36 departments under

direct ministerial control, together with the Audit Office and the Crown Law Office.

2   The two terms are derived from Burns and Stalker (1961).

3   The author has argued elsewehre that the New Zealand state sector reforms have effectively treated all public organisations as if they were, or could be, transformed into what Wilson (1989) in his typology calls 'production organisations' (Gregory 1995a, 1995b).

4   Logan (1991) and Schick (1996).

5   The *hierarchist* type has 'a faith in professional expertise dedicated to the collective good of society through an ethos of elite public service'. The *individualist* approach starts from the assumption that 'the world is populated by rational egoists who are bent on out-smarting one another to get something for nothing. Rivalry and competition are central to the individualist view of what the world of public management is and should be like'. (Hood, 1998a, pp. 97–98)

6   In a 1999 report New Zealand's Controller and Auditor-General invited parliament to consider whether it was satisfied with the information it received regarding 'outcomes', suggesting that members of parliament could be provided with 'brief but explicit statements of the nature of the causal links being asserted between each class of outputs and its associated outcome(s)', and that there could perhaps be 'measurement and annual reporting of the extent to which the Government's outcomes have been achieved or advanced' (Controller and Auditor-General, 1999, p. 56).

7   An attitudinal survey provides evidence that since the reforms, New Zealand's top public servants have become less, rather than more proactive, when proactivity is a function of programmatic commitment to policy implementation and a high tolerance of the political dimensions of their work (see Gregory, 1995c).

8   Crown entities usually comprise a board of directors appointed by the government, a chief executive appointed by the board, and staff appointed under the authority of the chief executive. Many of them were created to take over specific functions formerly administe-red within a government department.

9   The general election in November 1999 saw Clark become prime minister, leading a centre-left coalition. The impact of the public sector controversies on the election outcome is unclear, but they would have done nothing to enhance the incumbent government's prospect of winning.

10   These moves addressed New Zealand's verison of the 'democratic deficit' that Jervis and Richards (1997) attribute to Britain's public sector reforms.

11   During the reforms attempts were made to try to develop a senior executive service to act as a unifying force in policy development and management, but this aspiration could not withstand the centrifugal forces of the restructuring. Fragmentation was partly off-set in the mid-1990s by strategic planning and co-ordinated budgetary innovations (see Boston, Martin, Pallot and Walsh, 1996).

12   A parliamentary committee reported that sales of tickets in the state-owned lottery, Lotto, had fallen off significantly after public revelations over the level of remuneration paid to the Lotteries Commission chief executive and the fact that three board members had taken their wives on a trip to Norway. The committee did not accept the Commisision's claims that it had to offer such generous salary packages to attract top-quality staff (*The Evening Post*, 4 April 2000).

13   The State Services Commission has estimated that private sector chief executive base salaries, for positions broadly comparable with the average-sized public service position, rose by about 130 percent in the nine years to 1997, whereas in 1988 the rates had been

almost equal (SSC, 1998a, p. 16).

14   The allegations against the department included charges that the IRD's ruthless approach had driven some taxpayers to suicide. The chairman of the parliamentary inquiry, which ran for six months, was 'extremely concerned that the IRD is seen by many taxpayers as having a culture of fear and punishmen' and believed that 'the pendulum has swung too far towards the use of sanctions and threats to enforce taxpayer compliance' (*The Dominion*, 14 October 1999).

15   The survey also showed, *inter alia*, 'a picture of a high degree of cynicism about the functioning of democracy', with relatively few people believing that central government is responsive to the public (Perry and Webster, 1999, p. 92). Significantly, the coalition agreement between the two parties forming the government after the 1999 general election pledged, *inter alia*, to 'implement a policy platform which reduces inequality, is environmentally sustainable, and improves the social and economic well-being of all New Zealanders'. It also undertook to 'restore public confidence in the political integrity of Parliament and the electoral process'.

16   One of the main authors of the reforms, the then Minister of Finance, Roger Douglas, later spelled out his strategic advice: 'Do not try and advance a step at a time. Define your objectives clearly and move towards them in quantum leaps. Otherwise the interest groups will have time to mobilise and drag you down' (Douglas, 1993, pp. 220–221).

17   Many commentators believe the social and economic reforms have made New Zealand society much less trusting and socially cohesive. For example, Hazledine (1998, p. 173) wrote: 'Perhaps the most fundamentally worrying trend of the past decade or so is the extent to which New Zealanders have become strangers to each other in their own country. This is a *deliberate* result of the more-market revolution, which has relentlessly promoted attitudinal as well as institutional changes in the direction of self-seeking and opportunistic economic behaviour (commercialisation), telling people and businesses that they should just look after their own narrow self-interest on whatever side of the market they happen to be and not worry about anyone else' (emphasis in original).

18   These imporant distinctions are well drawn by Campbell (2000). Jervis and Richards (1997, p. 15) make a similar point, that Britain needs 'a cadre of committed public managers who value the public service ethos and invest, or encourage investment in, appropriate new forms of development that will maintain the ability of this cadre to provide the 'glue that binds' an increasingly fragmented and diverse public policy and management system'.

19   Speech to public service senior managers, Wellington. Reported in *The Dominion*, 9 March 2000.

20   For a discussion of the technocratisation of New Zealand policy-making in the post-1984 period, see Gregory (1998c),

21   Peter Self's observation seems particularly relevant to the New Zealand situation: 'Democracy requires a balance of powers throughout the system, with appropriate roles for the electorate, parliament, political leaders and the bureaucracy. These relationships cannot be captured by so crude a theory as principal-agent and will deteriorate if too much irresponsible power accrues to political leaders' (Self, 2000, p. 108).

THE TRANSFORMATION
OF REFORM THEORY AND
DEMOCRATIC IDEAS

11 Reform Theory Meets New Public Management

ANDERS FORSSELL

Introduction

The phenomenon of New Public Management (NPM) is the central theme of this book. However, as the theoretical perspective of the book – the transformative perspective – indicates, NPM is not a clear-cut concept, and throughout this book the contributing authors have repeatedly pointed to the ambiguity of NPM and the difficulties that confronts anyone trying to caputre, define and fix the phenomenon of NPM once and for all. Nevertheless, in order to be able to discuss NPM at all, some sort of provisional definition must be made. In this chapter NPM is mostly referred to as 'NPM-type reforms' and some examples of these reforms are presented. However, the main subject of study in this chapter is not NPM but reform theory. More precisely, the purpose of this chapter is to examine reform theory in the light of the experience of NPM-type reforms during the last few decades and to suggest some alterations to it in view of this experience.

The reform theory I have in mind here has a particularly Scandinavian flavour, but some of the most important ingredients are American. Early on, Scandinavian reform theory was strongly influenced by the organisational theories of Herbert Simon and James G. March (Christensen and Lægreid, 1998c). In 1976 the collaboration between March and a group of Scandinavian scholars resulted in the publication of *Ambiguity and Choice in Organizations* (March and Olsen, 1976). The importance of this work for Scandinavian research probably cannot be underestimated, as it made a deep impact on a generation of young Scandinavian scholars. Since then, this influence has been both explicit and implicit in much of the work of Scandinavian students of politics, administration and management – the Scandinavian authors of this book included. Since the mid-1980s, another theoretical school has also influenced many Scandinavian scholars. This is the so-called neo-institutionalism in organisational analysis (see, for example, Meyer and Scott, 1983, and Powell and DiMaggio, 1991).

In Scandinavia these two schools of thought – the first of which was basically micro-social and the second basically macro-social – have been combined into a particular body of open system organisational theory (Scott, 1998). Among the leading scholars involved in this mixing of theoretical traditions, Johan P. Olsen and Nils Brunsson must be mentioned. Separately and together they have been involved in elaborating this breed of Scandinavian organisational theory. In 1993 they published a book applying this theory to administrative reform called *The Reforming Organization* (Brunsson and Olsen, 1993).

For this chapter *The Reforming Organization* serves both as a point of departure and as a major source of theoretical ideas. The first part of the chapter attempts to summarise the central ideas presented in the book. The second part tells the story of the Swedish road to NPM. This story is based mainly on studies conducted by Forssell and Jansson (2000). In addition, an attempt is made to trace the impact of NPM-type reforms in the Swedish public administration. In the third part of the chapter the history of NPM in Sweden is examined in the light of two central themes of Scandinavian reform theory.

The first theme concerns the nature of the reforms and is, first and foremost, a legacy of the tradition of decision theory. The question asked is: Are the reforms the effects of decision-making processes of the 'garbage-can' type (March and Olsen, 1976) – processes that can be neither controlled nor predicted and where chance plays an important role – or do they represent strategic intention and direction? In other words, do reforms – to paraphrase March (1991, 1994) – 'happen' or can they – as Brunsson and Olsen (1993, p. 1) asked – be chosen?

The second theme concerns the results of reforms and the connection between talk and change. This theme is also related to the idea of 'garbage-can' decision-making, but in this version it is related even more closely to neo-institutional theory. The question asked is: Are administrative reforms mainly confined to rhetoric or do they also result in actual change? In other words, to what extent is reform rhetoric coupled to actual change? In the final part of the chapter, I will return to reform theory with the intention of proposing some alterations to it that would make it more consistent with the Swedish experience of NPM.

Reform Theory à la Brunsson and Olsen

The theory of Brunsson and Olsen is very much a critique of a *rationalistic* perspective on reforms. This perspective is summarised by Brunsson and Olsen in the following manner:

> In a reform perspective administrative change is assumed to be the result of deliberate goal-directed choices between organizational forms. The structures, processes and ideologies of organizations are shaped and altered to help the organizations to operate more functionally and efficiently. (Re)organization is a tool used by the reformer or reformers. There is a continuous chain of cause and effect starting from the intentions of the reformers and proceeding through decisions, new structures, processes and ideologies to changes in behaviour and improved results.

According to a common view

> two qualities are seen to distinguish formal organizations from other types of social arrangements: they are set up to accomplish specific tasks and to advance quite precise objectives, and they have a formalized structure which determines the distribution of authority and the division of labour (Brunsson and Olsen, 1993, p. 2).

The rationalistic and instrumental view of organisations is questioned by Brunsson and Olsen, thereby also casting doubt on this view of administrative reforms. A key concept often used is *loose coupling* or *decoupling*. What does this mean? An organisation can be described – as it is in the quotation above – in terms of products, structure, processes and ideology. When Brunsson and Olsen talk about organisations often these elements of organisations are referred to. And here loose couplings bcome important – instead of presupposing tight couplings between these elements Brunsson and Olsen often do the opposite, they presuppose loose couplings.

Here Brunsson and Olsen build on March and Olsen (1976), who frequently talk about decoupling, but chiefly from Meyer and colleagues (e.g., Meyer and Rowan, 1977; Meyer and Scott, 1983), who argue that most organisations find themselves in an *institutional environment* where they are expected to respond to many different, sometimes conflicting demands . One way to do this is to create two versions of an organisation: one that is externally oriented and used to present the organisation to the outside world, and one that is internally oriented and used to co-ordinate internal actions. While the latter produces goods and provides services, the former produces mainly words – i.e., written and spoken presentations and accounts – for external consumption. Often these two versions of an organisation are kept separate from each other and are thus only *loosely coupled* or even totally *decoupled*. (Brunsson and Olsen, 1993, pp. 8–9). A few examples may serve to illustrate this idea. Complex calculations are often made and presented before a large investment is made, but when it comes to actually deciding on an investment these calculations are ignored. In another example, budgets may be drawn up and announced in public but be completely neglected in day-to-day operations. Organisations can also be hypocritical (Brunsson, 1989), hailing one set of ideas in public while using another in their internal dealings. In short, the external organisation operates according to a generally accepted rule-book, while the internal organisation operates according to what is most feasible.

So, proceeding from the notion of organisations as loosely coupled entities which keep public presentations and accounts separate from actual practice, how do administrative reforms fit in?

One way to answer this question is to start with organisational problems. The reason for choosing this starting point is that the reform theory of Brunsson and Olsen asserts that reforms are often driven by problems. Since problems are a perceptional category (Brunsson and Olsen, 1993, p. 35) it is very important for potential reformers to be able to influence and preferably to control the agenda of problems. In most administrative contexts there is an on-going political and organisational discourse in which problems and solutions are presented, argued about, rejected or agreed upon – a process very similar to the garbage-can decision process of March and Olsen (1976). Often certain problems are coupled to certain solutions. Therefore, not only do certain problems imply certain solutions, but the logic also works the other way round: popular solutions can be used to drive reforms by identifying problems that they will solve.

Reforms that are most often presented as solutions are attractive because they promise to replace an existing reality perceived as complex, problem-ridden, over-burdened and even chaotic with a brighter future, where organisations are simple to grasp, well-ordered, efficient and run smoothly in accordance with management's intentions. Since most organisations can be shown to have at least one or several major problems at any given time, the potential for reform is ever-present. New solutions are easily more attractive than any present practice.

Attempts to reform are plentiful and reforms are easy to initiate. Although reforms represent attempts to bring about change, these attempts are not necessarily successful and there are many instances of reforms failing to be implemented (Brunsson and Olsen, 1993, p. 33). There are many reasons for this. One form of explanation – concerned with external relations – can be derived from the neo-institutional ideas of Meyer et al; while a second one – more concerned with intra-organisational processes – is more strongly linked to the ideas of March et al.

According to the first line of reasoning, reforms are often primarily responses to external demands on an organisation, so that what it is important to reform are those aspects of the organisation that are *visible* to external observers. In other words, it may be important to present goals, strategies etc that appear to dovetail with those demands; or it may be important to show a new and better structure or to introduce processes that are perceived as being more efficient and effective. But since it is the organisational façade that counts in these cases, nothing else needs to be changed. If, for instance, there is a demand for a gender equality programme, then such a programme may be elaborated and presented in the form of a written document without anything else being done. Hence, a publicly presented administrative reform may have little effect on the internal organisation – i.e., on how the work is actually organised and carried out. Loose coupling between presentation and practice is likely to occur. In cases like these, when reforms are externally driven, little or no efforts may be made to affect the actual operations of the reformed organisation.

According to the second line of reasoning, reformers may be genuinely interested in implementing reforms, but the reforms become eroded during the process of implementation, making actual change negligible. One reason for this may be that reformers lack the power to push through reform against internal resistance. Sometimes this resistance is simply a reluctance to give up old habits and routines. In other cases it may be due to the fact that, particularly in older organisations, organisational identity has evolved over time. Selznick (1957) speaks of these organisations having become *institutionalised*. Organisations of this type cannot easily be cast aside once they are no longer needed, and they tend to resist any change that does not match their own institutional values (Brunsson and Olsen, 1993, p. 22).[1] Other kinds of resistance are political in nature and based on conflicts of interests among different groups and persons within the organisation in question, leading to one group directly opposing an attempt from another group to introduce a reform. In other cases the costs of gaining support for a reform may be too high.

Reformers often promise more than any reform is capable of achieving (see Baier, March and Sætren, 1986), leading to disappointment and frustration later on in the implementation process.

Another common reason for reform failure is that the solutions offered are often too simplistic, so that when they are implemented in a complex organisational context they often prove to be inadequate, leaving the original problems unsolved and in some cases creating new ones. In cases like this the same kind of reform may be repeated over and over again. A reform may continue to be regarded as the logical solution to a given problem, while failed reforms in the past are blamed on poor implementation or poor management rather than on the reform itself. To give one example: SJ – the Swedish national railways – tried for decades to implement a reform designed to transfer certain routine tasks from the general director to lower levels in the hierarchy, but each time with little and never lasting success (Brunsson and Olsen, 1993, p. 41). Other reform attempts in SJ tended to oscillate between two opposing solutions – e.g., between centralisation and decentralisation, or between functionally and geographically based organisational structures. In cases like this, typically one reform tries to decentralise. If it has any success the disadvantages of decentralisation soon become evident, paving the way for the next reform, which will prescribe centralisation. If that reform has any success the disadvantages of centralisation then become apparent...and so on. In these cases it is not the failure of the reform but its success that evokes the need for further reform.

In this way reforms depend on the availability of problems and solutions. Problems are available most of the time, particularly since many of them arise from the inherently complex nature of organisations and their environments, which defy everlasting solutions: many problems can only be handled in an ad hoc manner. Likewise, there is seldom a lack of solutions: attractively packaged new reforms seem to be available all the time, even if they often consist of old wine in new bottles. In fact the number of fundamental problems and ways for organisations to solve them are quite limited.

In cases where one or two solutions are tried over and over again, reforms are very much furthered by organisational *forgetfulness* (Brunsson and Olsen, 1993, p. 41). Two preconditions for the initiation and implementation of any reform are enthusiasm and a belief that they will bring the desired solution. Memories of former failed reforms attempts tend to lower morale and create a general mood of hesitance.

Organisational forgetfulness is promoted by several 'mechanisms' (Brunsson and Olsen, 1993, p. 42). One is high personnel turnover, for employees who have joined an organisation recently will have no memory of previous failed attempts at reform. Another is frequent changes in the top management, enabling fresh and uncynical managers to attempt to do what their predecessors have failed at. A third mechanism is the frequent use of management consultants, who seldom stay long enough in a client organisation to take part in the actual implementation of a reform – they are too expensive – and therefore never have a chance to learn from their mistakes.

In a later elaboration of reform theory, Brunsson (1998) suggested that organisations run through reform cycles, consisting of 1) a phase when problems are experienced and solutions sought; 2) a phase of finding and choosing a reform; 3) an implementation phase, where new problems tend to arise; and 4) a final phase, when disappointment and frustration erode this reform and stop it, opening the way for a new search for solutions and thus for a new reform cycle. When running through this reform cycle organisations are receptive to new reforms only in those phases when disappointment with one reform is starting to grow, thus triggering a search for new reforms. But not only do organisations run through reform cycles, the reforms themselves – as models for organising – vary with time, often being subject to the logics of fashion. In this way, the reform models available will differ from one period to another, thus offering one version of a reform to organisations reaching their search phase at one time and a different version to organisations reaching their search phase at another time.

Brunsson's arguments were supported by Røvik (1996) when he presumed that an organisation would pick up those organisational elements reforms that were most popular at a particular time, because these would confer the most legitimacy on an organisation. Here Brunsson and Røvik elaborate on a line of thinking from a much-cited paper by Meyer and Rowan (1977) where they wrote:

> After all, the building blocks for organizations come to be littered around the societal landscape; it takes only a little entrepreneurial energy to assemble them into a structure. And because these building blocks are considered proper, adequate, rational, and necessary, organizations must incorporate them to avoid illegitimacy (Meyer and Rowan, 1977, p. 45).

What Brunsson and Røvik added to this argument was time: just as the organisational reform cycle takes a certain amount of time to be completed, so the popularity of particular kinds of reform varies over time.

Reforms are common, but they seldom achieve what they set out to do. So what do they achieve? In the reform theory perspective offered by Brunsson and Olsen the most important gain that reforms will bring to a reforming organisation is increased legitimacy. The reason for this is that the adoption of reforms signals to the world that an organisation wants to do better. Another function of the reform show is to let the world know that the organisation has a leadership that is both willing and capable of running and changing it. Since change is held to equal improvement in the modern world (see von Wright, 1993), reform as a sign of intended change signifies improvement, which in turn leads to increased legitimacy. The logic can be expressed thus:*reforms* evoke *changes* which mean *improvement* which, in its turn, increases the *legitimacy* of the reforming organisation.

In summary, according to the reform theory of Brunsson and Olsen, reforms are utopian in character and therefore attractive, but they are seldom able to bridge the gap between simplistic solutions and complex organisational reality. Given that organising is an inherently complex process, they often produce only part of the changes that were intended and/or unintended changes. However, this lack of success opens the way for new reforms: since the present state is always far from ideal, new opportunities for proponents of reform tend to arise all the time. Thus, reforms are a common 'standard, recurring activity...in large modern organisations. Reforms are routines rather than interruptions in organisational life' (Brunsson and Olsen, 1993, p. 33).

Critics of Brunsson and Olsen's reform theory tend to attack it as excessively radical or one-sided (see, for example, Löwstedt, 1991). The claim that one reform after another is implemented with little or no effect on practice is provocative and contradicts much common-sense organisational thinking.

This becomes all the more evident when one compares the theories of Brunsson and Olsen with an instrumental and mainstream view among practitioners that regards organisations as machines and reforms as repairs or reconstruction. Adherents of this point of view blame failed reforms primarily on poor management in the implementation process and/or a wrong choice of tools – i.e., the reforms.

Brunsson and Olsen believe this is a naive way of thinking, since they hold that many, perhaps even most problems with reforms do not arise from poor implementation but from inherent features of the reform process. While this version of Scandinavian reform theory may appear speculative, it should be emphasised that it is based on a wealth of empirical evidence from many spheres of social life.[2]

When I later will discuss the reform theory of Brunsson and Olsen in the light of the experience of NPM, I will be addressing not its alleged cynicism but rather some of its more substantial claims. Two themes of particular interest here were mentioned in the introduction.

The first raised the question of whether reforms 'happen' as a consequence of 'garbage-can' processes or whether they are deliberately chosen. Brunsson and Olsen put themselves somewhere in between these two extremes: reforms are often chosen, they claim, but the choices are restricted by the logic of reform processes. Two options were presented: 'more of the same' reforms and 'oscillating between extremes' reforms. Here I will ask to what extent NPM-type reforms are examples of 'more of the same' or of 'oscillating between extremes'.

The second theme addressed in the introduction concerned the coupling (loose or not) between reform rhetoric and actual change. Here I will therefore ask: How tightly or loosely coupled are NPM-type reforms?

These questions will be discussed in relation to one particular reform story, namely, the Swedish road to NPM. In other words, the reform theory of Brunsson and Olsen will be discussed using data from the same context used by Brunsson and Olsen themselves in formulating their theory.

The Swedish Road to NPM

The story told here tries to explain why NPM-type reforms came to be seen as appropriate, even self-evident, organisational solutions for the public sector from the late 1980s onwards. But the story does not start here. Sweden's approach to NPM was conditioned not least by earlier political processes – i.e., what happened later was dependent on what happened before. Thus, this is a story of path-dependence (see David, 1985 and Chapter 1).

The following is a summary of the story told by myself and Jansson (Forssell and Jansson, 2000). That story is based on an empirical investigation in which government documents and interviews with some of those involved in reform provided most of the first-hand information. For background information Mellbourn (1986) and Elmbrant (1993) were important sources. Other sources and references are mentioned in the text.

When the Social Democrats returned to government in 1982 after having played the uncomfortable role of the political opposition for six years, they were faced with a situation where the public administration, which was a symbol of social democracy, had come to be seen as too slow, too rigid, too centralised, too large[3] and too bureaucratic by large segments of the public.

With the formation of a new ministry – the Civildepartementet – the Social Democrats tried to counteract their image as a technocratic party committed to the rational engineering of society and closely associated with large-scale almost everything. To head the new ministry, Prime Minister Olof Palme appointed a young Social Democrat, Bo Holmberg, who had made a name for himself as a reformer in a northern region. As minister of the new Civildepartementet, his assignment was to tackle the above mentioned 'diseases' of bureaucracy.

Holmberg was put in charge of the Civildepartementet in order to reform and renew the public administration. He identified two different but linked sets of problems. First, the administration was too bureaucratic: it did not respond to citizens in a service-oriented way. Second, there was a democratic problem: the public or the users, as they were often called, had too little influence on public services that were of great importance to them – e.g., schools and day-care centres. Civildepartementet's way of reasoning may be illustrated by the following quotation from a policy document issued in the early 1980s:

> The task of the public sector is not only to be an organisation providing services for citizens. It is equally important for it to be an instrument for realising the demands of the citizens and for making citizens assume a share of responsibility for its services.[4]

The organisational solutions that were suggested were almost the same for both types of problems. The three Ds – decentralisation, deregulation and delegation/devolution – were repeated over and over again like a mantra during Holmberg's period in office. The goal was to permeate the public administration with a spirit of service-mindedness; the idea was that officials should perceive themselves as providers of services to the public – i.e., as (civil) servants.

In practice decentralisation for example meant experiments with 'free communes',[5] where a few local governments were granted the right to decide for themselves in matters normally under central regulation; or experiments that involved organising local government along geographical rather than functional lines. A districts structure was created within larger local administrative entities, where district boards became responsible for most district affairs. This district reform, which was the major reform of local government in the 1980s, was encouraged by the Civildepartementet and chiefly justified with democratic arguments. The local governments were seen as having become too large and the distance between ordinary citizens and local government was regarded as too great. In an attempt to bring them closer together, district boards were formed with elected members, and the functionally organised central administration was replaced by district offices.[6]

Local government has for a long time been an important element in the Swedish public sector, since most of the social services provided by the public sector are provided by local and regional governments. Constitutionally they have a semi-autonomous status: local and regional parliaments are directly elected by the people, and they are authorised to impose income taxes on the inhabitants.[7]

Deregulation is often associated with economic reform, and indeed in Sweden and in many other Western countries the whole of the finance sector, including the banks, was deregulated during the 1980s. But when the Civil-departementet talked about 'deregulation' it meant replacing the slow and rigid bureaucratic ways of working with a more service-oriented approach. To do this, individual officials needed to be given more autonomy, and decision-making authority had to be delegated as much as possible from the upper level of the administrative hierarchy to the lower level – i.e., to those actually engaged in operational work: clerks in the post office, headmasters and teachers, social workers, engineers in technical departments etc.

With regard to privatisation, an issue that was raised particularly by neo-liberals, Holmberg drew a distinction between 'commercial private operations – i.e., operations intended to make a profit – and idealistic private operations – i.e. operations that had other purposes than to make a profit for the entrepreneur'.[8] Non-profit organisations were considered as valuable complements to the public sector, whereas commercial operations were seen as presenting large risks from an egalitarian perspective, since commercial operations would only be started where purchasing power existed. And since equality was at the heart of social democratic ideology, this was a powerful argument that had, and still has, strong support within the party and among its traditional voters.

From the start, Holmberg encountered some resistance. First of all, the reorganisation of the government created problems. Most government work is sectoral – e.g., defence, communications and education – but the Civil-departementet had to work horizontally. Thus, a matrix organisation was formed: sector ministries operated vertically, while the Civildepartementet tried to stretch its purview horizontally across the entire public administration. In practice most power remained within the sector ministries, and the success of Holmberg's programme depended to a great extent on the sympathy and approval of other ministers.

Initially the support of Prime Minister Palme was important, as was the support of the Treasury. The Treasury and the minister of finance, Kjell-Olof Feldt, also wanted to reform the administration, and at the beginning the Treasury and the Civildepartementet looked like a team working for reform and renewal. In this endeavour they both met with resistance from traditionalists within the party who wanted to change the forms of administration as little as possible (see Premfors, 1991). But after a while it became clear that the Treasury and the Civildepartementet actually had different ideas about what the problems, goals and solutions of the public administration were.

In the Treasury's view the main problem with the public administration was its use of resources. The administration needed to be more efficient, and traditional bureaucracies were not very efficient. In this respect, the Treasury and the Civildepartementet concurred. But since their goals were different, the proposed solutions also differed.

The reforms suggested – decentralisation, deregulation and delegation/devolution – were accepted by the Treasury, but in order to achieve a more efficient provision of services these measures were accompanied by suggestions to introduce more economic incentives, more price mechanisms, more market relations, and more separation of politics and administration – i.e., mainly internal reform measures. The Treasury also suggested that more services should be contracted out to commercial or non-profit providers and that the mechanisms of competition should be more widely used.

At first, this did not imply large-scale or far-reaching reforms; the Treasury knew that ideas like these were regarded with much scepticism or even hostility by large parts of the party, so it had to be careful. But later on the Treasury pressed harder for its solutions and succeeded, at least partially. One of its successes was the replacement, after the general election of 1988, of Holmberg as the head of the Civildepartementet with Bengt Johansson, who previously had been an adviser to the head of the Treasury, Minister of Finance Feldt. This change may have been facilitated by the fact that, after the assassination of Palme in 1986 and his replacement by Ingvar Carlsson, Holmberg lost support. However, a more important factor is probably that Holmberg and the Civildepartementet after six years had earned a reputation of producing '... too much talk and too little action'.[9] Second, the Treasury succeeded in getting many of its ideas accepted by the party executive and later on by the congress. This was manifested in several important documents, such as the 'Programme for the 90s' and the 'Guidelines for the 90s'.[10]

In the general election of 1991 the Social Democrats lost to a right-centre coalition led by the Conservative Party, which was much influenced by neo-liberal thought (Boréus, 1994). The conservative prime minister, Carl Bildt, appointed Inger Davidson of the Christian Democrats as the new minister of the Civildepartementet. With regard to the public administration reforms she not only adhered to the policies of her Social Democratic predecessor but intensified them. During Davidson's period in office the Civildepartementet focused particularly on the importance of competition and contracting-out of services, even more than the Treasury had done before.

This right-centre coalition managed to stay in power for only one term, and by the end of 1994 the Social Democrats, now headed by their new chairman, Göran Persson, had returned to government. In the meantime, an economic recession that had begun in 1991 had turned into the most severe economic crisis since the early 1930s. The economic crisis hit the internal market and the public sector the hardest. Unemployment, which had been practically non-existent, exploded in a few years and reached levels that had been unprecedented since the 1930s; the state budget deficit grew completely out of control for a while; and the Swedish crown fell to its lowest value in modern times. In this situation the new government focused on regaining control over expenditure. Thus, most of its efforts were directed at intensive cost-cutting, which hit almost every part of the public sector. After several difficult years, the government proved to be quite successful in this endeavour. The crisis reached its peak during the first half of the 1990s. But from then on things improved, first slowly then faster, so that by the late 1990s the depressive mood that had haunted Swedish society, particularly the public sector, for most of the decade was starting to give way to a new feeling of optimism.

During this period the government was reorganised several times and the Civildepartementet was abolished in 1994. But this does not mean that the reform debate stopped. Throughout this period efforts were made to reduce the cost and increase the efficiency of the public administration. For this purpose reforms like deregulation of the economy, corporatisation of state-owned companies and contracting-out of services[11] continued to be seen as appropriate organisational solutions by the Social Democratic government.

As outlined here, the Swedish road to NPM started with the Civildepartementet's preoccupation with improving public services and introducing more service orientation into the public administration. The public administration was supposed to serve the public and that meant less bureaucratic attitudes and faster, easier and user-adjusted delivery. The public debate about these matters was much influenced by a debate in the private sector, in which the crucial role of human resources and the corporate culture, particularly in the service industries, was emphasised. The 'role model' often mentioned was Scandinavian Airlines and its CEO, Jan Carlzon.[12] In addition, there was an emphasis on democratic openness and participation.

By the end of the 1980s this programme for a democratic, service-oriented public administration that was less bureaucratic and more sensitive to the needs of the public was being challenged by another programme – that of a more efficient public administration put forward by the Treasury. To avoid misunderstanding: both these programmes had supporters in many places. They were not confined to these two ministries. The Civildepartementet and the Treasury represented important political currents in Swedish society, but not in a passive way, as mirrors. Instead, they were among the foremost proponents of these lines of political thought.

At this point, the reform movement reached a *crossroads*. The question was whether Sweden should continue along the road on which Holmberg had launched it or take a different direction. How important the differences between these two roads were was not clear at the time. The efficiency program did not exclude the concept of service-orientation, but it placed the emphasis elsewhere. It saw increased efficiency as the main goal of the reforms, from which certain administrative solutions followed – all of which could be found in the NPM 'recipe book' presented inter alia by the OECD.[13]

The programme for a more efficient public sector advocated by the Treasury was, of course, heavily influenced by contemporary economic thought. Several key officials in the Treasury were economists by training and their networks of contacts included academic economists. In particular the ESO (Expert Group for Studies of Public Economy) constituted an important link between the Treasury and the academic economists, producing a number of reports on the Swedish economy, particularly the public-sector economy (Hugemark, 1994). According to Hugemark, the economic doctrine prevailing in the ESO and in the Treasury and generally informing the debate on economic issues was neo-classical micro-theory. It was preoccupied with issues of allocational efficiency and it advocated standard solutions, such as effective price-setting and the use of competition mechanisms (Hugemark, 1994). Keynesian ideas that had been almost hegemonic a few decades earlier now seemed obsolete and the influence of institutional economics on the Treasury programme was negligible.

'More of the Same' or 'Oscillating between Extremes'?

The story told above started by identifying a strong and wide-spread feeling of dissatisfaction with the public sector in the early 1980s, a dissatisfaction that made the public administration vulnerable to reform attempts. In terms of Brunsson's reform cycle mentioned above, Sweden seemed to have reached a 'search phase', when it was frustrated with the status quo and political actors were looking for something better. But whereas in Australia and New Zealand managerialism was advocated quite early on, emulating the path followed by Britain under Margaret Thatcher, Sweden chose a different road.

During the Holmberg period there was little talk of managerialism, arm's-length relations, relations between principals and agents or other important themes of the NPM-debate 'down under' (see, for example, Considine and Painter, 1997). One reason for this, of course, was that the semi-autonomous status of the Swedish public administration, both at the national and the local level, meant that managers were already authorised to manage. The NPM slogan 'let the managers manage' perhaps made a little more sense in relation to local government than to the central state, since there was more political interference at this level, but it was not an important issue at the time.[14] Instead, the public debate was heavily influenced by a private-sector debate on service-orientation. This debate opened the way for broader comparisons to be made between public-sector and private-sector service-provision. And since the models were companies like Scandinavian Airlines, it was only natural to make comparisons of other aspects as well. How were private companies organised? What were the typical features of their production process? What kind of corporate culture was prevalent within them? How were they administered and controlled? Thus, models and ideas from the market and business world came into the public sector, but apparently from another direction and through a different door than in the NPM-prototype New Zealand, for example.[15] In other words, once the logic of the market and the business sector had been acknowledged as a legitimate frame of reference, new issues and ideas were allowed into the public debate that had formerly been ignored or considered irrelevant.

What was also emphasised during the Holmberg period were openness and democratic participation. This led to new ways of thinking about administrative means and solutions. Privatisation, for instance, was on the whole considered incompatible with the values and goals of democracy, open-ness and participation. These goals were thought to be better served by non-profit organisations, which were considered to be possibly valuable complements to the service-provision of the public administration by the Holm-bergians. Co-operatives and non-profit organisations rather than private companies were the models espoused by this line of thinking. But Holmberg and the Civildepartementet never succeeded in making their vision of a participatory democratic administration concrete, even though they were quite successful at the service-orientation part of the programme. In this sense, the Holmberg programme was ambiguous and contradictory and opened the way for different and contradictory administrative solutions. This made it more vulnerable to attack by the Treasury, whose main goal was a more efficient administration. The Treasury's arguments, based as they were upon a seemingly coherent and consistent doctrine of economic thought, were difficult to contradict. Arguments about the economy seemed more real than the Holmberg rhetoric, which always seemed rather woolly and idealistic.

During the efficiency programme managerial ideas came further to the fore than they had done during the previous phase. For instance, when management by objectives and results and provider-purchaser models were introduced, the importance of arms-length relations and clearer roles were emphasised. And throughout these two decades there was an interest in leadership, control and steering. Yet, management on the whole never became as big an issue in the Swedish debate as it seems to have been in Australia, for example (Considine and Painter, 1997).

This interest in management issues, which almost became an obsession in both the Australian and New Zealand debates, corresponds with the economic theories that seem to have prevailed in those countries – namely, institutional economics, which to a large degree focuses on the relationship between principals (politicians) and agents (managers) and on the risk of opportunistic behaviour (see, for example, Boston et al., 1996). In Sweden, on the other hand, institutional economics is rarely mentioned (Hugemark, 1994).

So it was the market and the private company that became the models for the administrative reforms in Sweden after the triumph of the efficiency programme in the late 1980s. Up till then another development had seemed possible, one that leaned more heavily on the ideas and principles of the non-profit-sector and in that sense would have resembled the German welfare system (Lundström and Wijkström, 1997). But from then on the reform path became one of many cumulative steps leading in the same direction, infusing the public sector with more business-like attitudes, ideas and practices.

In conclusion: the pattern that I have revealed is neither one of oscillating reforms – the swing between two extremes – nor one of the same reforms being repeated over and over again. During the 1980s the Swedish road of public administrative reform took a particular national route, but as Sweden entered the 1990s it reached a crossroads and opted for a turning that clearly led in the direction of NPM.

From 1990 onwards the pattern was not one of the same reform being repeated, but rather one of a number of interconnected reforms. All are offshoots of certain ideas of economic theory; all can be derived from the abstract idea of the market; and the overriding motive for all of them is the need for increased efficiency. In that sense they are market reforms. But since this is a highly abstract and vague concept it needs to be expressed in more concrete reforms, such as corporatisation or contracting-out in order to materialise in practice. Reforms like these are more detailed manifestations of the market reform idea; they are edited versions – as Sahlin-Andersson calls them[16] – of the institutionalised, general idea of market reform.[17]

As NPM is closely connected to general ideas of the market and the business sector as a superior system of resource allocation and transformation – ideas represented in their purest form by neo-classical micro-economic theory – NPM-type reforms represent attempts to move or push public administration organisations closer to this ideal. One can therefore talk about the direction of reforms using NPM as a metaphor for a utopia, a 'New-public-management-land' where NPM reforms are played out in full.

Loosely Coupled Reforms?

So far the story of NPM reforms in Sweden has revealed what the main themes of the reform debate were. In other words, what has been presented so far has been *talk* about reforms, but little has been said about actual changes. What do we mean by change when talking about reforms? Is it valid to talk about change as soon as the implementation of a reform starts to alter structures or processes? Or should we conclude that change has taken place only when some of the intended results materialise – e. g., when efficiency or service-orientation increases? In other words, does change relate only to the goals of reform, or does it also embrace the organisational means of reform?

If a reforming organisation were a machine or had machine-like pro-perties this question would not arise. The machinery could, after some adjust-ment, be constructed or reconstructed to produce the desired effects. But as soon as we start to view organisations not simply as machines but as organisms, systems, political arenas, cultures or any other common metaphor (Morgan, 1986), this tight coupling between means and outcomes becomes more problematic. Thus, the idea of loose coupling seems to be inherent in most perspectives on organisations (albeit for different reasons in each case). The question then becomes not whether reforms are loosely coupled but rather to what extent and in what ways.

If, in trying to answer this question, we were to choose the first of the two definitions of change mentioned above, there would be very little to say about most reforms. This is due to one typical feature of reform processes: namely, that proponents of reforms almost invariably promise that the reforms will be evaluated at a later stage. In practice, however, this evaluation often fails to take place (Brunsson and Olsen, 1993). What we are then left with is an abundance of subjective impressions and perceptions of those participating in reform but very little impartial or undisputed data on what the effects of the reforms have really been (Brunsson, Forssell and Winberg, 1989).

The NPM-type reforms were no exception in this respect. Studies of the effects of NPM-type reforms are relatively few and far between – partly because of the difficulties involved in conducting such studies, such as finding valid kinds of measurement, isolating causal links etc. Some of the studies that have been done report some intended effects (e.g. Hansson and Lind, 1998), others reported unintended effects (Rombach, 1997), while others still have not been able to detect any significant effects at all (Statskontoret, 1996). However, the studies are too few and too ambiguous to allow any definite conclusions about the effects of NPM-type reforms to be drawn.

We know more about the means of reforms – i. e., about changes in structures and processes (Brunsson and Olsen, 1993, 1–2). If we classify the reforms in the Swedish public sector during the 1990s according to NPM-type reforms we can discern three main types (Forssell, 1994, 1999).

First there are internal reforms, aimed at increasing the internal efficiency (or productivity) of the public administration. This is to be achieved by introducing more economic incentives. For this to work, administrative units must first be held accountable and responsible for their results, not only for their budgets – i.e., they should be responsible not only for costs but to a larger degree for revenues as well. So the reforms here are about internal price-setting, about buyer-seller relations between units and of management by objectives and results. This type of reform has been extended to individual employees working in the public sector, replacing a system of fixed and uniform pay with a system of individual and variable pay, a reform inspired at least partly by the same ideas of efficiency as those guiding the structural reforms – i.e., using economic incentives to increase performance.

Second, there are reforms that aim to give citizens (or 'customers', as they are frequently called) greater freedom in choosing service-providers. In theory citizens are to be provided with 'vouchers' or 'cheques' that can be exchanged for specific services – e.g., at schools, day-care centres or old people's homes. In practice, no citizen has ever seen such a voucher. Nevertheless, citizens do now have more freedom of choice in certain fields, such as education and health care. Moreover, service-providers attracting a large number or customers also receive more money, so competition among them – whether they are public or private contractors – has certainly increased. Until recently, schools did not use to compete, but nowadays it is not uncommon for any young person moving to the senior level of the nine-year compulsory school system to receive marketing material from different schools trying to convince him/her to choose their school. It is important for schools to stay popular among students and parents, since large numbers of students mean more resources for the school.

A third type of reform is aimed to increase allocational efficiency by introducing competition mechanisms among service-providers, whether public or private. Traditionally, contracting-out has always been important in certain areas of operation, particularly in technical spheres like construction work or public transport. During the 1990s contracting-out has become common in a large number of other services as well, in particular the so-called 'soft' ones, like education, health care, day-care and care of the elderly. Moreover, EU regulations have made bidding for contracts mandatory in many more areas than it was before. Still, it seems to be more problematic to contract out operations that contain large elements of what is usually called the 'exercise of authority' – i.e., operations that imply the use of compulsion, such as certain types of social work and, of course, the law courts and the police.

The idea of strengthening competition is also the main motive for another version of the third type of reforms, namely the corporatisations and privatisations of operations that were previously organised as public agencies. These include the so-called natural national monopolies, such as postal services and telecommunications or public utilities provided by local governments, such as energy or refuse collection. During the 1990s, about 100,000 of a total of 300,000 national state employees were affected by corporatisation (Statskontoret, 1997). Among privatised operations, the national telecom company Telia has been the most important so far.

Of these various kinds of reform only corporatisation, management by objectives and results and individual pay have been introduced on a large-scale at the national state level, whereas all types of reform, except privatisation, have become common at the regional and local levels, though there is considerable variation (Henning, 1996; Johansson and Johnsson, 1994 and 1995). Nevertheless, services that are contracted out still account for only a small part of public-sector services as a whole. For instance, among local governments, who provide most welfare services, less than 8 percent of all services were contracted out in 1998. Still, the proportion is rising, and the costs of services contracted out rose by 49 percent between 1996 and 1998 (Erixon, 2000).

An evaluation of the distribution and frequency of the reform elements described here is summarised in Table 11.1. One conclusion that can be drawn from this summary is that local and regional administrations have reformed more than the state administration. In addition, the pattern (not shown in the table) seems to be that more peripheral state agencies, like the National Road Administration, tend to introduce more NPM-type reforms or reform elements than agencies that are closer to the government, like the Swedish Agency for Administrative Development, or, for that matter, than the government itself.

Table 11.1 Evaluation of NPM-type reforms in the Swedish Public Sector in the 1990s

	Frequency* of NPM-type reforms	
	Central state government	*Local/regional governments*
Internal efficiency reforms		
Individual pay	W	W
Management by objectives and results	W	C
Internal price-setting	R	C
Provider-purchaser models	R	C/W
Internal profit centres	R	W/C
Extended freedom of choice reforms		
Voucher systems	R	C
External competition reforms		
Contracting-out	R	C
Corporatisation	C	C
Privatisation	R	R

* Frequency is classified as rare (R) = occasional examples, common (C) = frequent examples, or widespread (W) = standard forms.[18]

There is some disagreement among observers about the frequency of reforms introduced. For instance, Brorström and Rombach (1996) claimed that the reform wave among local governments, where reforms like management by objectives, provider-purchaser models and voucher-systems were debated and in many cases introduced quite quickly, had run out of steam by the mid-1990s. While Håkansson agreed that the reforms had come to a halt, he added: 'During this period (the early 1990s) steps were taken that will enable an extensive programme of systemic change in the future'(Håkansson, 1997, p. 43).

However, the disagreement is about the extent of reforms introduced. Neither Brorström and Rombach nor Håkansson claim that there was only talk and no organisational change. In other words, they all agree that NPM-type reforms have been implemented and have affected Swedish public-sector organisations to *some* extent. Thus, claims of zero coupling between talk and actual change must be rejected. On the basis of our evaluation, I conclude that there has been some coupling between talk and actual change but that it is loose rather than tight.

Does the introduction of NPM-type reforms mean that traditional forms of organisation have been abandoned? This would be the logical conclusion if the organisations in question were like machines: repairing machines often means that you replace an older part with a new one. But since I do not accept the machine metaphor, at least not in this simplified version, the answer is no. Instead, as both Bergström (1999) and Forssell and Jansson (2000) assert, they are added to the organisational repertoire already in place, creating what Røvik (1992) calls a *multi-standard organisation*, whereby old and new forms exists side by side in the same organisational body. Assuming that this is so, do any set of organisational forms predominate? Yes, Bergström (1999) says, the older, basically bureaucratic, forms still predominate and the new forms, associated with NPM, have had only marginal effects on the operations of the public administration. So what Bergström claims is that there has been a lot of talk but very little change – in other words, reforms really are loosely coupled. Forssell and Jansson (2000) argue, on the other hand, that while this may be the case for the central state administration, things are different at regional and local level. Moreover, they discern a definite trend towards NPM-type reforms, which they say are gaining ground all the time in all parts of the public administration, including the central state.

This debate highlights the difficulty of trying to interpret a historical process that is still in progress. The outcome is ambiguous, and therefore different observers discern different patterns and tendencies. Only after more time has elapsed will we be able to judge who was more right and who was more wrong.

What is obvious and probably undisputed, though, is that there is a considerable time-lag between talk and the introduction of new structures and processes, whether or not these lead to significant change. NPM-type reforms first began to be debated in the late 1980s, but their implementation is still going on more than ten years later.

Reform Theory in the Light of NPM-Reforms

The claim that the components of administrative reform – talk, structure, processes, outcome – are loosely coupled is not a particularly controversial one. Only the most mechanistic sorts of theories would reject an assertion of this sort. But there are different perspectives on what the reasons are for loose coupling. Mostly it is attributed to the implementation process and to organisational inertia. A distinguishing feature of the reform theory of Brunsson and Olsen – which follows on from the work of Meyer and colleagues (Meyer and Rowan, 1977; Meyer and Scott, 1983) – is the idea that the separation of talk/presentation and actual operations has a function: the presentation is aimed at increasing legitimacy, while the actual operations are aimed at increasing the efficiency of production; and since the actions taken to achieve these two goals are not always in accordance with one other it makes sense to separate them.[19]

This strategical use of loose coupling is hard either to negate or to verify using the accounts of NPM-type reforms in Sweden presented in this chapter. The data are simply too inadequate to draw any firm conclusions. What can be said, though, is that reformers who try to bring about change via reforms experience varying degrees of success. Whether they are successful and how long it takes for a reform to bear fruit depends on a number of different factors: sometimes reform ideas need to ripen in the minds of reformers before they can be transformed into practice (Forssell and Jansson, 2000; Røvik, 1998), in others cases, reformers encounter resistance from parts of an organisation as ingrained habits and routines hamper the implementation of reforms. In other words, most of the internal organisation reasons for loose coupling (see part one above) remain relevant in the era of NPM. In addition, organisations will continue to be beset with problems and look for solutions, and reforms may continue to fail. Therefore, the idea of reform cycles (Brunsson, 1998) may also still be relevant.

Let us now return to the two Scandinavian reform theses outlined at the beginning of this chapter and 'test' them against the experience of NPM-type reforms in the Swedish context. With the regard to the thesis of loose coupling, the Swedish experience would seem to indicate that talk about reform and actual change are not completely decoupled but loosely coupled and that this is mainly due to internal organisational characteristics, which produce a time-lag between talk and change.

More definite conclusions can be drawn regarding the other thesis, concerning the (in)coherence and sequence of reforms. The NPM reforms introduced in Sweden neither oscillate between two extremes nor do they represent 'more of the same'. This would seem to contradict Brunsson and Olsen's theory, which sees the reform process either as a constant repetition (and failure) of one kind of reform or else as an oscillation between opposing reforms, thus implying that organisations are basically unchangeable. While I believe that this may hold true in some cases, it certainly do not hold true in all cases. Otherwise it would not be possible to explain why many organisations – and not only those that have been subject to NPM-type reforms – have changed significantly following reform.[20]

When Brunsson and, before him, Røvik (1996) attributed the supply of reforms available to any organisation at any given time to fashion, they at least admitting the possibility of change. But since fashion is a chance phenomenon – anything might be fashionable at any time – this would seem to contradict the idea of reform as a routine and repetitious exercise.

Our conclusion, after having studied NPM-type reforms in Sweden, is that they contain, or are manifestations of, one general and abstract idea: the idea of market reform. I suggest that this general idea works as a *selection mechanism*: reforms that comply, or at least do not compete, with this idea will be selected, while those that are not compatible with it will be rejected. For instance, Holmberg's idea of democratic participation was abandoned after the idea of market reform triumphed in the late 1990s. In addition, it would have been absolutely impossible to advocate reinforced bureaucratisation during this period, since this was incompatible with NPM-type reforms. On the other hand, reforms aiming at improving quality, such as the introduction of ISO 9000 standards, were possible because they did not compete with the market idea. In other words, during this period the market reform idea functioned as a guideline or compass charting the general direction of reform. Czarniawska and Joerges (1996) proposed the concept of *master idea* to denote ideas of this kind which function as social compasses and selection mechanisms. As was noted in the first section of this chapter, the idea of a selection mechanism is not altogether foreign to the reform theory of Brunsson and Olsen (1993, pp. 22–23). It ties in with their idea of a need for compatibility between the values of a reform and the values of the organisation to be reformed as well as between the values of a reform and long-term trends in society, though their idea is more that of a *rejection* than a *selection mechanism*.

Master ideas do not necessarily always prevail, however. For instance, the account of the reform debates during the 1980s shows that the master idea of market reform was beginning to crystallise at that time. In Sweden the market reform idea was competing with the Holmberg programme, which proposed more democratic participation, but neither of these political programmes became dominant during this period.

If we add the concept of master idea to the reform theory of Brunsson and Olsen objections to the relevance of applying their theories to systemic reforms like NPM can also be met. The master ideas described here are abstract guidelines for systemic change, but systemic change can only be accomplished by applying similar kind of organisational reforms in many parts of the system simultaneously.

The use of the term 'system' indicates that systems are different and larger than organisations. In the context of this book I regard systems as comprising organisations and the relations and connections between them. The system considered here is the public sector, which consists of numerous organisations of many sorts, from the local public agency to the central government, all of which are connected in some way. Some public sectors are very hierarchical and are controlled from the top. The New Zealand public sector might be cited as an example of this sort of system.[21] Other public sectors are more decentralised or even fragmented. Australia, as a federation of states, or Sweden, with its semi-autonomous central authorities and regional and local governments, are examples of this sort. Here the central government cannot directly control the whole public sector. But independently of how hierarchical or how centralised a system is, a strong prevailing master idea will permeate it and thus affect reforms throughout the system. This is clearly the case with NPM in Sweden. All levels of the public sector have been affected by NPM-type reforms, regardless of whether the government has actually proclaimed them or not. However, the reforms are not evenly distributed throughout the public sector. Some units have tried almost every reform in the book, while others have not tried any reforms at all.

My final point is a speculative one. One of the metaphors used in the above account of the Swedish road to reform was that of a crossroads – i.e., a point at which the direction taken by reform may change. This is not to say that reforms may be completely reversed, but that reforms may take another direction whenever a new master idea will take over from an older one.

In the case of NPM reforms, the master idea that prevailed before this cross-roads was reached was that of the welfare state. The welfare state started to evolve in many developed countries in the early-to-mid 20th century. In Sweden the welfare state was founded in the 1930s when programme for combatting unemployment were introduced together with general social security benefits and pensions, but it was not until after the Second World War that the public sector and the public administration started to expand more significantly, a process that has been called the 'public revolution' (Tarschys, 1979).

Altogether these reforms constitute a 60-year period of the welfare state, a period that, in turn, succeeded a long period of the liberal state.[22] As the ideas of NPM have come to the fore in New Zealand and elsewhere in the 1980s and in Sweden and elsewhere in the 1990s, one might ask whether this represents the beginning of a new era that will last long into this new century. While it is impossible to tell at this point whether NPM will become the same kind of master idea that the welfare state was, it cannot be denied that some remarkable changes have taken place over the past 10–20 years, changes that would be very difficult to reverse in all the public administrations that during this period set out on the road to 'New-public-management-land'.

Notes

1   This point in fact contradicts many other arguments of Brunsson and Olsen that emphasise the randomness element in the selection of reforms. In this chapter most attention is given to that line of reasoning. In the final part of this chapter I will return to the idea of selection mechanisms.

2   That is, spheres of Scandinavian social life. The question then is to what extent this experience is applicable to other geographical, political or cultural contexts. But this question applies to any theory, whether it is based on Scandinavian, British, North American or any other experience.

3   Too large, rather than too big. It was the scale of the administration that seemed too large, not its total size.

4   Government declaration on the renewal of the public sector, 1984–85, p. 202. The Civil-departementet's texts often had this abstract and vague quality.

5   Local governments in Sweden are called 'kommuner'.

6   Although much discussed at the time, only a minority of local governments actually introduced the district reform; most stayed with the old functional organisation.

7   Varies around 30 percent.

8   Government letter on the renewal of the public sector, 1984–85, p. 202. The word 'idea-
    listic' is the Swedish term translated literally. In English the term corresponds to terms
    like 'voluntary' or 'non-profit'.
9   Mellbourn, 1986. Whether this judgement was justified or not has been much disputed
    since. For instance, both Mellbourn, 1986 and Elmbrant, 1993, defended Holmberg.
10 'Nittiotalsprogrammet' and 'Riktlinjer för 90-talet', respectively. The latter was accepted
    by the party congress in 1990.
11 A longer list of NPM-type reforms in the Swedish public sector will be presented later on
    in this chapter.
12 During this period Scandinavian Airlines and Jan Carlzon were regarded world-wide as
    a success story.
13 See Chapter 3.
14 If devolved management was already in place in the Swedish public sector and therefore
    never a big issue, the same goes for accrual accounting, a NPM-reform element that
    gained much attention in Australia and New Zealand during the late 1990s. In Swedish
    local government, accrual accounting was in practice decades before anyone had ever
    heard of NPM (Olson and Sahlin-Andersson, 1998).
15 On the emergence of this prototype or model, see Chapter 3.
16 See Chapter 3.
17 Institutionalised ideas and knowledge in general, based upon the theories of Schutz, is
    dealt with more thoroughly in Forssell and Jansson, 2000.
18 This rough evaluation is based on Johansson and Johnsson, 1994 and 1995; Montin,
    1997; Håkansson, 1997; Statskontoret, 1997; Mattsson and Forssell, 1998; Forssell, 1999
    and Svedberg Nilsson, 2000.
19 This idea of separating the external image of an organisation from the demands of pro-
    duction seems to be borrowed from Thompson (1967).
20 See, for example, Brunsson and Olsen, 1993, Chapter 4.
21 This may be an explanation for the seemingly rapid and radical changes introduced during
    the 1980s. See other chapters in this book for accounts of the New Zealand story.
22 Meaning mainly two things: Deregulation of the economy and the introduction of demo-
    cratic reforms.

12 Transforming Politics: Towards New or Lesser Roles for Democratic Institutions?

SYNNØVE JENSSEN

Introduction

The conditions of representative democracy are changing. During the past few decades the public sector has come under increasing pressure, as both politicians and civil servants have found themselves having to deal with changing conditions. Distributive issues are becoming urgent, the allocation of welfare goods is being questioned and citizens' trust in politicians is being put to the test. Lack of trust in politicians is not necessarily an established fact, but there are indications that public policy decisions are increasingly being questioned. We need to reflect on why, for so many people, the fact that something is a recognisably 'political' statement is almost enough to bring it instantly into disrepute (Held, 1987, p. 267).

Traditionally, the main task of government was to regulate the market. Today, both central and local government are called upon to solve a wide range of problems concerning individuals, groups and social institutions. Public activities are increasing in *quantity,* creating pressure on public budgets. This has created a demand for reform and rationalisation of government. Increased public engagement also involves government in *qualitative* new ways. The public agenda is more than ever dominated by *moral* and *ethical* questions. Pollution, inadequate health care and unemployment are all problems which need collective and public solutions (Eriksen, 1993, p. 9). Politicians also have to decide what constitutes a good old age and what should be defined as a good adolescence.

Some people have suggested that everything would be better if all these questions were removed from politics, but as long as we are talking about democratic states, we do not have the option of 'no politics' (Held, 1987, p.

289

196). On the contrary, the democratic decision-making process will be important to make *legitimate* decisions and to set the right priorities in a situation where public resources are scarce. The question is how the ideas of modernisation and the renewal of government pertain to the challenge of maintaining the *democratic* aspect of politics.

The main task for the reformers has been to undertake fundamental changes in the structure, role and management of the public sector (Boston, 1995b, p. x). Principles and practices from private management have served as a model (Pollitt, 1990). The main objective is to draw a clear(er) distinction between political and administrative matters (both responsibilities and functions) so that the managers can manage (Boston, 1995b, p. xi). The relationship between political governance and administrative autonomy has been at the core of efforts to reform the public sector (Chapter 5). Important objectives have been to increase political control, effectiveness and efficiency, and to make public administration more sensitive to public demands and citizens' needs. In general, an important measure taken towards this end has been decentralisation and delegation, thereby increasing administrative autonomy (Boston, 1995b; Hagen and Sørensen, 1997; Pollitt, 1990).

Another important aspect of the 'new' relationship between politics and administration is that politicians are now expected to delegate minor decisions and concentrate on the major ones pertaining to goals, principles and policies (see Chapter 2). Taken together, these are the basic and general ideas of New Public Management (NPM).

The question I want to discuss in this chapter is whether, and in what way, the concept of NPM can influence the *democratic* aspects of public governance. Are the management ideas behind this concept adequate to cope with the challenges that political-administrative institutions will face in the future?

I will argue that we need more than management ideas to improve public policy: what we need is an *extended* concept of modernisation.

Standards of Evaluation

The normative perspective here is that the main goal of the modernisation process should be to strengthen *political* co-ordination and *democratic* *influence* on public policy. To what extent do the new political instruments take this into consideration?

I want to present two different views of politics generally, and of the democratic system specifically. The first view sees a) the political process as an instrument rather than an end in itself and b) the decisive political act as private rather than public. The goal of politics is to achieve an optimal compromise between given, and irreducibly opposed, private interests (Elster, 1997, p. 2).

The other view denies the private character of political behaviour. This view sees a) the goal of politics as rational agreement rather than compromise and b) the decisive political act as engaging in public debate with a view to the creation of consensus (Elster, 1997, p. 2). According to the theory of Jürgen Habermas (1992) rational political discussion has an object in terms of which it makes sense. This represents a deliberative perspective on politics; it is concerned with substantive decision-making and is to that extend instrumental.

Theorists put different labels on these views of politics and democratic systems. Lijphart (1984) distinguished between the 'Westminster' or 'majoritarian' model of democracy and the 'consensus' model of democracy. March and Olsen (1989) identified 'aggregate' versus 'integral' political processes and institutions. Another distinction along the same dimension is to define politics as a pure 'struggle of interests' or as a 'problem of governance' (Dahl and Tufte, 1973; Sejersted, 1983).

Theorists subscribing to the former view have their roots in liberalism and its concept of society as individualised and autonomous (Bentham, 1830; Hobbs, 1651; Locke, 1690; Mill, 1859).

The latter view is founded on a tradition stemming from Aristoteles and a deliberative concept of democracy: 'Deliberation occurs in cases which fall under a general rule, if it is uncertain what the issue will be, and in cases which do not admit of an absolute decision' (Aristoteles, 1987, p. 77). Deliberation is needed when we do not know for sure what constitutes a rational decision, and when the issues are ambiguous and in need of clarification. In a civilized society decisions which affect all of us must be based on knowledge about the common good (Eriksen, 1995, p. 17). To attain this knowledge requires deliberation, where *arguments* are decisive for political outcomes. This view was especially revitalised by Hannah Arendt (1958), who was a representative of the communicative theoretical concept of politics.

Today, the idea of a transformation of preferences through public and rational discussions is especially associated with the works of Jürgen Habermas (1981, 1992). He introduces a discourse model of politics.

These two views of politics and democracy are also represented by different metaphors of the relationship between economics and politics: *the market* and *the forum* (Elster, 1997, p. 25). I will go on to describe these metaphors in more detail and discuss the concept of modernisation that follows from each.

The Market

The economic theory of democracy is a market theory of politics. The act of voting is seen as a private act similar to that of buying and selling. The theory also rests on the idea that the forum should be like the market, both in its purpose and in its mode of functioning. 'The purpose is defined in economic terms, and the mode of functioning is that of aggregating individual decisions' (Elster, 1997, p. 26).

According to this view, reforms and modernisation of the public sector should focus on improving the aggregating mechanisms so that the political system is able to reach a better balance between the expectations of citizens and the decisions of government.

The economic theories of democracy, elitism and pluralism are all indifferent to concepts of a good life and to moral questions in general (Eriksen, 1994, p. 4). Advanced industrial societies are understood as 'inherently pluralistic and diverse' (Crick, 1962, p. 62). The participants only have to agree on *the procedures*. In politics legitimacy stems from the aggregation of preferences in ways that are considered fair and neutral (Eriksen, 1994). The political system is seen as a supermarket driven by the sovereign consumer. The government becomes a byproduct of the customers' preferences and their demands for service. The political leadership becomes shopkeepers (Olsen, 1988c).

The economic approach represents a rigorous theory, deductive and completely free from romantic illusions (Dryzek, 1992). The theory of public choice is a wholly positive and scientific theory without values (Buchanan, 1991). Legitimacy is achieved through elections that are free, fair and secret, and majority rule may be seen as a response to the problem of finding *the* right answer (Mansbridge, 1992, p. 33). Today, this problem is solved by letting the consumers decide.

The strength of this perspective is that it has improved the analytical precision of hypotheses and also the empirical foundation of political studies. But, at the same time, its concepts represent only one particular way of understanding politics and the democratic aspects of government (Almond, 1990).

The Forum

The deliberative perspective conceptualises politics as the art of solving common problems and at the same time shaping a collective identity (Eriksen, 1995). Rather than aggregating or filtering preferences, the political system should be set up with a view to changing them through public debate and confrontation. The political process is both *public* and *instrumental* (Habermas, 1992).

In the process of forming goals and opinions, different kinds of procedures are needed to solve different kinds of problems. Habermas (1992) distinguishes between three different forms of rational discourse: the *pragmatic*, the *ethical* and the *moral*. In pragmatic discourse the answer to what ought to be done is found in the free choices of actors, and rational decisions are made on the basis of given ends and interests. Only empirical knowledge and technical expertise are needed to give rational answers, as long as the questions pertain solely to utilitarian norms of action (Eriksen, 1994, p. 12). Pragmatic questions assume that the political-administrative system is able to reflect people's preferences and to translate them effectively into public policy. Pragmatic discourse harmonises with the market concept of public politics and is best taken care of through the principles and practices of managerialism.

Ethical-political discourse is oriented towards collective self-interpretation and authentic identity formation. Many questions involve the *value* aspects of politics. What are our values and norms? Who are we and what makes us different from other groups? What is happiness for our community and what is a good life for us? These are more than pragmatic questions. Our conduct and our ideas of a good life cannot be chosen on a pragmatic or scientific basis (Walzer, 1983). Solutions to these kinds of questions require social interaction and the contribution of other people.

Moral discourse comes about when interests are affected and values are conflicting. How can we validly answer the question of what to do when there are different cultures, different concepts of a good life and conflicts of interests? Such moral questions require *democratic* institutions, where the participants are forced to take a neutral and disinterested stand and ask what is in the common interest of all. When political decisions will have consequences for different kinds of interests and concepts of what is a good life, the decision-makers have to discuss what it is *legitimate* to do. Moral discourse in politics is needed to decide what is in the common interest of all, *in spite* of disagreements on values and notions of the common good. In other words, a basic part of politicians' work is to discuss what is right and wrong, good or bad. These are questions which can only be solved by *arguing* (Habermas, 1981). The procedures of decision-making have to be rooted in a deliberative idea of politics, where the purpose is to reach agreement on moral and political questions. The deliberative theory of democracy rests on the idea of the decision-making process as a forum, where procedures are inclusive, enlightened, innovative and facilitate symmetric co-ordination (Kettner, 1993). Such a procedure is very idealistic and intensive. For practical reasons, the discourse will often be interrupted by voting and hierarchical intervention (Knight & Johnson, 1994).

When we talk about modernisation of public policy and the democratic system, I think it is, nevertheless, important not only to look for ways of improving the aggregating mechanisms, but also to question the system's capacity as a forum for argumentative rationality and the ability of political leaders to further the common purpose (Jenssen, 1995). In this view political dialogue and the political engagement of citizens are crucial. Citizenship is seen as a quality that can only be realised in public. The forum should there-fore be more than, and also something qualitatively different from, the distri-butive totality of individuals queuing up at the election booth (Elster, 1997, p. 26) or acting like consumers and shopping around (Olsen, 1988c, p. 106). The essence of the discourse model is that it ties legitimacy to a *free* and *open* debate in public forums. It focuses on the public sphere and the channels of communication as crucial in determining democratic legitimacy and auto-nomy:

> It is the free debate in public, the possibility of cleaning base preferences, the scrutiny of social power, the channeling of communicative power into the parlia-mentary system and the design of deliberative processes in decision making bodies that makes for the achievement of democratic legitimacy (Eriksen, 1994, p.16).

Do the new ideas of reforming public policy and democratic institutions take into consideration *both* the pragmatic and the moral aspects of rationality?

Modernisation of the Public Sector – Politics and Administration

Since the mid-1970s, social democracies have been increasingly challenged by free market philosophies, in particular by the rise of Thatcherism and Reaganism. More generally this philosophy has been described as neo-liberalism (Giddens, 1998). Since the 1980s, social-democratic regimes have started to break with their past. Although social-democratic regimes have varied substantially, as have the welfare systems they have nourished, they have shared a broadly similar perspective. This is what Giddens refers to as 'old-style' or classical social democracy. Some of the key elements in the old Left policy were: pervasive state involvement in social and economic life, state dominance over civil society, collectivism, a confined role for markets, the mixed or social economy, full employment and a strong egalitarianism (1998, p. 7).

The break-away process seems to have taken the same direction everywhere, although the countries in question have chosen different paths and started modernisation at different points in time. Its ideas include: minimal government, an autonomous civil society, market fundamentalism, the welfare state as a safety net and strong economic individualism (Giddens, 1998, p. 8). How have the governmental renewal, reinvention and restructuring processes handled the democratic aspects, or more specifically, the relationship between politics, administration and citizens?

The welfare state, seen by most as the core of social-democratic politics, today creates almost as many problems as it solves. Australia, New Zealand, Sweden and Norway have in different ways and to different degrees actively responded to this idea of governmental renewal. Of these states, Norway is by far the most reluctant. Not because it is a slow learner, but rather due to a privileged economic situation. The most radical and comprehensive programme of public sector reforms has been pursued in New Zealand, but Australia has also attracted international attention for its governmental reforms (Boston, 1995b; Halligan, forthcoming). The reforms started in 1983 in Australia and in 1984 in New Zealand. The old system was replaced by a package of reforms based on management and market incentives (ibid). Despite these similarities between the two countries, they diverged in their handling of the relationship between politicians and bureaucrats. Australia chose a political approach and New Zealand a managerial model (Halligan, forthcoming).

NPM is called different things in different countries, but the basic philosophy is still the same – namely, that private-sector principles should be applied much more comprehensively and rigorously to the public sector. Government should play a catalytic role in establishing policy priorities, but at the same time this role should be sharply distinguished from the role of delivering goods or services according to these priorities. The prevailing ethos is substantial devolution or decentralisation of government functions to community organisations, more competitive government to be achieved by introducing competition into service delivery, and mission-driven and result-oriented government to be achieved by rewarding outcomes. (Hood, 1991; Pollitt, 1990; Trebilcock, 1995).

Regulation

The main purpose of the modernisation of government so far has been to enable it to *regulate* conflicting interests more efficiently and keep public spending under control. This has been done by reducing the number of internal monopolies and encouraging strategies such as contracting out and emphasising market incentives in order to improve bureaucratic performance (Trebilcock, 1995, p. 2). The idea is that by decentralising decision-making authority and flattening managerial hierarchies, bureaucratic performance will be improved; and by streamlining the budget process, better public services will be provided at less cost. Altogether, private-sector organisational analogues should be applied more comprehensively and rigorously to the public sector. Government should play a catalytic role in the delivery of goods and services but not be directly involved (op cit). This approach calls for 'steering rather than rowing' (Osborne and Gaebler, 1992, cited in Trebilcock, 1995, p. 2)

In Sweden local governmental reforms have been dominated by three basic ideas (Jacobsson, 1994, p. 231f). First, the idea that the functions of policy advice, regulation and policy implementation should be separated in order to increase political control and make public administration more effective. Second, the idea of the market as a fair judge. The assumption is that supply and demand are able to decide the profile of public spending relatively independently of politicians. Again, the confidence in the logic of the market as an effective regulator and, as a way of relieving the political system of difficult choices, is striking. The third idea is the great belief in organisation as a solution to all problems. To improve the administration's ability to attend to the achievement of considerable efficiency gains, governmental activities should be divided into result units. The argument is that, whatever the policy objective, it ought to be achieved at the lowest possible cost.

There are several problems in applying these ideas to public policy and government. Inspired by public choice theory, they assume that public policy and the political administrative system are instruments for the satisfaction of wants and the provision of goods. The modernisation scheme seems to assume that actors tend to be motivated purely by self-interest and that they pursue this either through market activity or through political action, depending on where the net gains are likely to be greater (Trebilcock, 1994). The standard of evaluation is the institution's ability to satisfy individual preferences (Buchanan 1991, p. 88). The role of politicians is also affected by this. When they have to retreat from 'minor' issues and particular cases, they also withdraw from politics and the process of mediating interest-group conflicts over distributive claims as well as from the process of creating common solutions.

Political issues become purely pragmatic questions to be solved by the administration, or preferably by the users themselves. Is it possible to define the proper boundary between politics and administration? A dichotomy between means and ends is in many cases non-existent. The so-called objectives or ends, such things as increasing economic growth, the level of education or the health status of the population, are themselves means to more overriding objectives: 'For example, reducing inflation or increasing levels of educational attainment are not ends in themselves, but means to achieving some more ultimate ends' (Trebilcock, 1995, p. 25).

Even if the political issues are specified, it is not possible to choose the best policy instrument in an ethically or morally neutral manner (ibid). In the NPM concept, democratic institutions become providers of *services,* which also has consequences for the role of politicians and bureaucrats and for the relationship between citizens and public institutions.

For the politicians it is a question of finding economic and technical solutions. For the political system it is a question of improving governance so that it will be able to more effectively reflect and fulfill the needs and demands of citizens. By delegating authority and giving the administrative units more autonomy, politicians reduce the pressure on themselves in difficult matters of ethical and moral judgements (Eriksen, 1994). It seems as if the mechanisms for 'hiving off' responsibility become increasingly sophisticated as the pressure on public budgets increases. When the allocation of goods and duties becomes too difficult to handle, political influence seems to become more indirect. Politicians are supposed to disassociate themselves from hard choices and make the customers themselves decide about such difficult questions (Baldersheim, 1993, p. 167).

This strategy of modernisation is inspired by economic concepts of rationality. The public sector is perceived as an instrument for keeping the customers satisfied. The standard of evaluation is the ability of public institutions to meet the expectations of citizens (Buchanan, 1991, p. 88). The new management tools are assumed to be politically neutral, and they are intended to make the political debate less complicated. They are not supposed to have any influence at all on the allocation process. In reality, however, these management tools challenge the logic, norms and values on which public decisions should rest. These values are not only relevant in the process of deciding the government's objectives; they may be equally important when it comes to defining how these can be achieved in a legitimate way.

The New Individualism

Collectivism has been a distinguishing feature of social democracy. However, the development of the welfare state has led to growing *individualism*. The citizen has acquired new individual rights, which have weakened the political obligations of citizenship (Eriksen and Weigård, 1993). Most of the rights and entitlements of the welfare state are designed for individuals, and they invite people to perceive themselves as individuals pursuing private interests and rights. Citizens have become users and consumers, and the relationship between the government and citizens is referred to as customer-driven. The aim of modernisation is to meet the needs of citizens as customers and consumers, and the best way to do so is by forcing the logic of the market onto government. This growing individualism goes hand in hand with pressure towards greater democratisation (Giddens, 1998), but it is the *autonomous consumer* who is being offered increased influence.

The glorification of consumer choice in the market represents a version of individual freedom, but it is a thin, one-sided version (Self, 2000, p. 44), for it represents a narrow, essentially economistic view of human behaviour (Gregory, 1995d, p. 71). An important question is whether the new roles are able to replace the traditional political obligations of citizenship.

From a deliberative perspective one of the main critiques of NPM ideas is that democratic procedures are supposed to be replaced by non-political forms of decision-making (Bobbio, 1987). The consumer perspective is closely related to the *service* aspect of governmental activity. It does not, however, give any guidelines for how to establish *priorities* when there is a plurality of consumer needs and interests. If the allocation process does not involve or reduce the possibilities for deliberation and balancing the different preferences, it also means that the arena for the active pursuit of political rights is reduced.

If public policy is evaluated by market criteria, ethical and moral questions become pragmatic questions.

Political Integration

Why do we need to stress the importance of political rights and political discussion when we talk about improvements in the political-administrative system? Is it not sufficient to focus on the management part?

Politicians are thought to play an *indirect* role in the new concepts of government. The *substance* of politics is ignored. What matters is functional efficiency, which does not give us a tool to understand the political discussion or to improve it (Dryzek, 1990). It is a paradox that at the same time that politicians are supposed to be more influential, they are also alleviated of the task of making difficult and substantial choices. In the NPM concept, political institutions are no longer required to address difficult matters of judgement or make unpleasant choices, even though this will continue to be a significant feature of public policy in the future (Jenssen, 1995).

From a deliberative point of view, the political process is necessary in order to discuss the *quality* of individual preferences and interests. Are some needs more legitimate than others? Do individual preferences break with common interests and a common concept of legitimacy? Such questions can only be answered if the political aspect of citizenship is activated and citizens participate in public deliberations.

> By replacing democratic procedures of consensus building by such other methods of conflict resolutions, government elites avoid the 'official' institutions of politics in a constant search for non-political forms of decision-making (Offe, 1984, p. 168).

Politics is not only about tackling disagreement, it is also about deciding what is the right thing to do. In addition, decisions have to be made within budgetary constraints. In other words, there has to be a debate about priorities in all cases where the standard of welfare must be balanced against other important tasks and economic considerations. These are moral and ethical questions and can never be redefined as pragmatic calculations if we want to sustain the democratic aspects of government.

Political Autonomy

The new ideas about improving the political-administrative system do not include the normative dimension of politics. Political decision-making is more than, and also something significantly different from, the aggregation of preferences. Moral and ethical questions need 'democratic autonomy' (Held,

1987, p. 289) to enable us to define legitimate solutions where the strength of the arguments is decisive (Habermas, 1981, p. I). From this point of view, the biggest challenge today is to extend political activity in the forum and increase the opportunities 'for citizens to act as citizens, as participants in public life' (Held, 1987, p. 289). This entails deliberative procedures that enable the participants to define common identities and to engage in joint concerns (Dahl, 1989). Society is nevertheless both value-pluralistic and consists of heterogeneous interests. The possibilities for consensus are not too overwhelming. Still, the most important challenge for government will be to bring about understanding and acceptance of public policy: 'The challenge to democratic rationality is to arrive at acceptable formulations of the common good despite this inevitable value-pluralism' (Benhabib, 1994, p. 34).

This requires that politicians do not primarily act as regulators in a market. For this purpose politicians need a forum where they can fulfill their role as integrators. This means that they have to involve themselves in normative discussions about what is legitimate and 'right'.

Conclusions

A basic tenet in organisation theory is that structure affects decisions. From this point of view, it is important to look for decision-making procedures that will not only improve the market mechanism but facilitate deliberations as well. In other words, we should look for procedures that will strengthen the 'forum-aspect' of the public decision-making process. There are at least two reasons for directing attention to the conditions for deliberation. First, it will be possible to identify common interests and the best way to fulfill the objectives that follow from these. Second, deliberation is necessary for defining the *legitimate standards* for the allocation of public resources and tasks (Miller, 1989, p. 265). These two aspects cannot be defined only through pragmatic calculations. As long as we have a public sector, such considerations presuppose ethical and moral deliberations and autonomy for the political debate. This means a forum or an arena where the main purpose is to facilitate rational discussion so that arguments can be scrutinized and 'tested'.

13 Transforming Governance in the New Millennium

TOM CHRISTENSEN AND PER LÆGREID

The Complex and Dynamic Transformation of NPM

Modern public reforms like NPM consist both of reform ideas and of more specific reform programmes and elements. The globalisation thesis emphasises that the ideas of NPM are spreading fast around the world, generating specific, efficiency-oriented reforms and producing isomorphic effects, so that countries that were previously quite different from one another now appear to be much more similar (Peters, 1996a, p. 16). This argument stems chiefly from a belief in the impact of deterministic processes (Olsen, 1992) on a global level and from the one-dimensional economic-normative dominance that is a feature of NPM (Boston et al., 1996).

This book does not deny the universal features of NPM, features that constrain national reform processes and influence reform effects in the same way everywhere; but its main emphasis is on diversity, on the transformation of NPM in national contexts. The sources of reform ideas are not just global but also emerge out of particular national circumstances and combinations of circumstances. While the pursuit of efficiency may be a *leitmotif* running through reform ideas, both the aims and means of reform are multiple and often inconsistent. They include such apparently contradictory goals as increasing political control and increasing management autonomy or increasing effectiveness and quality as well as other features that are chiefly symbolic or concerned with maintaining legitimacy (Pollitt and Bouckaert, 2000). Reform ideas engendered on a global level, through the dominance of certain countries or international organisations, are transformed when they spread, meaning that reform ideas with similar labels may acquire a different content (see Chapter 3). Some reform ideas are never implemented, while others are implemented partially, pragmatically and through editing processes (Røvik, 1998). All this results in country-specific reform elements which may nonetheless belong to certain 'families' of NPM-related reforms (devolution,

301

contracts, privatisation, market- and consumer-oriented reforms, etc.). The aim of this book, therefore, is to give an insight into the problems and variety produced by a 'one size fits all' reform wave like NPM (Peters, 1996a, p. 18).

To understand the diversity of reform processes, effects and implications, we have used a transformative perspective that focuses on the complex and dynamic interplay between environmental – i.e., external – pressure and national structural and cultural contexts (Olsen, 1992). Environmental conditions, whether national, international or transnational, are important for furthering reforms. Some countries have had to cope with severe economic or legitimacy crises, while others have experienced strong pressure from international organisations, similar countries or national public authorities. The historical and cultural traditions of a country, and thereby its 'path-dependency' (Krasner, 1988), also contribute to explaining how reforms like NPM are received and handled. A crucial question is how and to what extent reforms are compatible with traditional norms and values (Brunsson and Olsen, 1993). The structure of the political-administrative system is also important for assessing the capacity of political and administrative leaders to further, resist or control reforms. Taken together, environmental, cultural and structural contexts define in a complex way the leeway leaders have in responding to global reform ideas and to specific reform programmes.

This book has focused on different empirical areas in the four countries studied and tried to show how they are scoring in terms of different reform parameters and thus how complex the transformative mechanism is that produces diversity in reform processes and effects. New Zealand had the most severe economic crisis background for reforms. This led to reforms being defined chiefly in economic terms, supported by political entrepreneurs and furthered by a Westminster-type political system that allowed the government to make radical changes without paying heed to cultural obstacles (Aberbach and Christensen, 2000; Pollitt and Bouckaert, 2000, pp. 183–184). Australia had a less severe crisis and initially chose a more collaborative reform style, reflecting important cultural features. It embarked on a more collectively oriented and less extreme reform path. The choice of this path was determined largely by the federal structure of the country, whose intergovernmental and multi-level negotiation features impede rapid change but also offer the possibility of experimenting with more radical reform at state level (see Chapter 9). Norway and Sweden chose more reluctant and incremental reform paths in the 1980s, reflecting their historical and cultural roots and more turbulent multi-party systems. However, Sweden eventually became the more radical of the two, reflecting both an economic crisis around 1990 and a more centralised and action-oriented system.

Three forms of transformation have been studied in this book. The first was the transformation of NPM reforms. The reform processes in the four countries led in different ways to the transformation of NPM ideas, solutions, content and implementation. Under the NPM umbrella we have revealed different mixtures of ideas, solutions and contents in the four countries studied and over time. NPM is a loose collection of means and measures that allow for flexible adaptation. Generally speaking, the reform ideas are imbued with a common vision of a 'new' orthodoxy, with a strong market and management orientation (Olsen, 1997a). But beyond that, the mixture of market, management and privatisation components in the reform ideas, solutions and content in the four countries studied varies considerably. Each country develops its own variant of NPM and this country-specific recipe also changes over time.

The second form of transformation we looked at was that of administrative systems. We asked what the results and effects of NPM reforms implemented in different public administrations were. The national administrative systems were transformed by the NPM reforms, but not in a simple and straight-forward manner. Moreover, the experience, practice and implications of NPM reforms are not easy to measure. It is hard to distinguish between, on the one hand, potential, assumed and promised effects and, on the other hand, actual and well-documented effects. One lesson from this book is that one should not infer too easily from intentions, plans and processes to effects. Radical and aggressive NPM reforms do not necessarily lead to greater efficiency, effectiveness, economy and good government than moderate NPM reforms. Another lesson is that it is important to expand the concept of effect from a narrow focus on economy and efficiency to a broader concept that includes effects on political-administrative control, organised interests, policy capacity and governmental culture.

Third, we discussed the transformation of theory and asked what the implications of NPM are for reform theory and democratic ideas. The reform theory focussing on an oscillation between extremes, 'more of the same' and loose coupling between talk and action needs to be revised in the light of NPM, for NPM is not only talk: there is a connection between talk and action, even if it is ambiguous. The countries studied are all travelling towards 'NPM-land', albeit at different speeds and towards different regions. Some, like New Zealand, are heading rapidly towards the centre; while others, like Norway, are moving more slowly towards the periphery. In addition, the normative implications of NPM reforms for democracy need to be taken more seriously. There is a need for a more explicit debate about the normative standards for evaluating reforms and this is done by contrasting the NPM model with the forum model.

The Democratic Aspects of NPM – Political Control and Accountability

The main ideas of NPM focus on economy and efficiency, and the organisational changes made are efficiency-motivated. This conflicts with the principles of political-administrative systems traditionally characterised by multiple goals and means, where economic aspects have been only one of many considerations (Egeberg, 1997). Unlike many other studies of NPM, this book is primarily preoccupied with the effects and implications of NPM for political democracy. More specifically, we have analysed the consequences of NPM for political control at the central level, for the roles and relationships of political and administrative leaders and for the relationships between different levels and institutions of governance.

One main theme is that central political control is undermined by NPM, but in different ways and to different extents – more in the non-core than in the core civil service, for example (Boston et al., 1996). Increased devolution, managerialism, contractualism and market orientation has resulted in many different transformative features, but the capacity of the political leadership for control is generally undermined. The distance between political leaders, on the one hand, and the actors, institutions and levels to be controlled, on the other, is increasing, and autonomy from political leaders is more evident. The new administrative and institutional actors are less loyal than in the traditional system, more instrumental and individually oriented, and less preoccupied with collective interests, public accountability and ethos. Commercial aspects of public activities have come to the fore while traditional political considerations have tended to be pushed aside. Administrative leaders often both initiate and benefit from reforms, as do directors of state-owned companies and comparable units.

The countries studied differ concerning this undermining of political control. New Zealand has for nearly two decades followed the most radical reform path in marketising and minimising the state (Pollitt and Bouckaert, 2000, p. 178) and has even managed to shrink the central civil service substantially. At the same time, however, the country has tried to introduce more control over less by, for example, co-ordinating the ownership function in the Ministry of Finance. Australia started out in a less radical way, trying to retain some of the traditional negotiation system and to develop a collective 'political management' profile that would maintain a fair degree of political control. The 1990s, however, have lead Australia down a similar path of minimisation and marketisation to New Zealand. Norway and Sweden have been more cautious reformers and more reluctant to undermine political control. These two countries have sought to preserve the tradition of trust in the civil service while introducing gradual modernisation, participatory elements and moderate deregulation and marketisation. The 1990s brought more devolution and market orientation in both countries, especially in Sweden, but also more problems in adjusting to the transformed roles of politicians and administrative leaders.

If we broaden the democratic focus of NPM and base the discussion on the main findings of our comparative study, we can ask whether NPM is changing the role of people in a democracy (Christensen and Lægreid, 2000). To answer this question it is important to underline that people have a number of different channels for articulating and aggregating their interests in a democracy and that they can act in several different capacities i.e., as citizens and voters, but also as consumers, clients or as members of interest groups. Is NPM changing the way these channels work or the balance between them?

Our theoretical point of departure for answering these questions is 'the sovereign, rationality-bounded state' and 'the supermarket state' models (Olsen, 1988a). The first is based on the election channel and the 'parliamentary chain', meaning a centralised, hierarchical state with a large public sector, emphasising standardisation and equality. In this model the public are first and foremost voters. The people are supposed to participate in political parties and elections, choose between party lists and programmes and give political signals and decision-making premises to the politicians (Olsen, 1988a, p. 237). But it is then up to the elected representatives and parties to handle this mandate. In this respect politicians are supposed to be responsive and reflect the attitudes of the voters, channelling these attitudes into public decisions, while also trying to influence public opinion.

In this book we have discussed one important mechanism for furthering the will of the people via the election channel: namely, the control of the executive over the civil service. But what about the input function in this model: the systematic participation of citizens and the expression of their opinions, the mandate they give their political representatives as a basis for public decisions? Traditionally, the input from citizens could be handled in two ways: either through an unambiguous mandate and tight party discipline or through giving the representatives more autonomy to use their best judgement (Pitkin, 1972, pp. 144–167). Olsen (1984) emphasises that this mandate is becoming more ambiguous, because party programmes consist of broadly defined issues, policies are complicated and subject to change and it is difficult to understand the logic of conflicts and consensus-building that inform the decision-making processes. Moreover, people do not formulate specific demands when voting. This makes it more difficult for representatives to handle their popular mandates but also more problematic for voters to follow the 'fate' of their opinions, even though they are now better educated and more knowledgeable than some decades ago. This could also be one reason why the role of consumer or user promoted by NPM might seem more attractive to people than the role of voter, because the issues and the channels for action may appear simpler.

The supermarket state model presumes that the government and the state in general have a service-providing role, with an emphasis on efficiency and good quality, and conceives the people as consumers, users or clients (Hood, 1998a, p. 98). In this model the hierarchy is in a way turned upside down: instead of the state controlling society on the basis of a democratic mandate from the people, society more directly controls the state through market mechanisms. The public are viewed as sovereign consumers or clients. What is lacking is a perspective on the relationship between the influence of voters or citizens on politicians through the election channel and through their role as consumers. Nor is this model particularly preoccupied with the importance of resources in providing public services and products.

But some elements of the supermarket state model do potentially present an alternative view of democracy, a democracy that is directly oriented to the individual, with economic overtones. However, it does not answer the question of how atomised actors making choices in a market can contribute to creating a stable and responsible democratic system.

The supermarket state model is a central feature of NPM. This model of the state should be used where the task is to provide public services with the highest possible degree of productivity and flexibility (Olsen, 1988a, p. 246). It could be argued that, from the point of view of popular sovereignty, the most important part of this state model is not concerned with democracy but with efficiency, quality and direct consumer influence on public services. This might be labelled an 'empowering the people' aspect. But how can people actually influence the provision of public services? Indirectly through the election channel and the political constraints and frames or more directly as consumers choosing providers? Aberbach and Rockman (1999, p. 19) are sceptical about the consumer thesis. They point out that service providers often think more about profit than about consumers. There might also be several problems with using service to clients as the primary standard for determining the appropriateness of government activity (Peters, 1998b).

In conclusion, NPM implies that the channels for popular participation and influence, as represented by the two state models, are changing in favour of the supermarket state. It is certainly true that popular attention has shifted from the role of the citizen to the role of the consumer. While this might be seen as undermining democracy and the election channel, it may also give people more channels for influence, albeit of a different kind, and ones that are not easily co-ordinated.

There are three main problems of accountability in modern representative democracies (Day and Klein, 1987, p. 28). First, the institutional and organisational links between political responsibility and managerial accountability are often loose; second, political processes often do not generate the kind of precise, clear-cut objectives and criteria that are necessary for managerial accountability to be a neutral and value-free exercise; and third, the organisational structure is often such that the managers accountable to politicians cannot answer for the direct action and performance of the service providers.

Our argument is that NPM does not necessarily reduce these problems. The role of political leaders is ambiguous under NPM: elected officials have a role as strategists in defining the long-term goals of the public sector and assessing the results, but at the same time they are expected to give considerable discretion to operative agencies (Peters and Pierre, 1998, p. 228). Public services are to respond directly to the demands of the market and not to political decisions, and providers should ideally receive information about their performance directly from customers without having to go through elected representatives.

Under NPM the political power derived from elected office is replaced by a remote and indirect model of political leadership. If elected political leaders have limited control over the public administration, is it then reasonable to hold them accountable for the actions of the public bureaucracy? And if elected officials should not be held accountable, then who should? The emergence of NPM reforms thus seems to have made accountability a more ambiguous and complex issue (Thomas, 1998). To what extent is consumer choice a good instrument of accountability in situations of shared responsibility, where different officials contribute in many ways to the decisions and policies of government (Bovens, 1998)? There is also the question of whether executive politicians are willing or able to adopt the role of strategic managers envisaged for them by NPM (Pollitt and Bouckaert, 2000).

In NPM there is a shift in accountability from the political to the managerial sphere and from input and processes to output and outcomes. NPM reforms have led to a fragmentation of the public sector, and the acceptance of political responsibility by ministers has been attenuated. De-emphasising input and process and emphasising outcomes and output does not necessarily mean that government administrators are more or less accountable (Romzek, 1998). There is also a certain ambiguity in much of the rhetoric about strengthening accountability through NPM, in so far as some executive politicians have used the new politics/administration split to define weaknesses of political programmes as managerial failures (Pollitt and Bouckaert, 2000).

There is a built-in inconsistency in NPM. The reformers' claim to empower customers, free managers and strengthen political control, but these three things are difficult to achieve simultaneously (Pollitt and Bouckaert, 2000). The traditional bureaucratic model, with little freedom and accountability for results but much responsibility for following rules, has been a successful and durable model of public administration. Today, public administrators around the world are seeking greater freedom, but they are also anxious to obtain greater accountability. A system that extends freedom to managers without strengthening their accountability undermines the power of politicians and is thus inferior to the traditional, bureaucratic model of administration. NPM has exposed the gap between the doctrine and the reality of accountability and highlighted the need to reconstruct the traditional doctrine of ministerial responsibility (Barberis, 1998).

The new role of the populace is to confront politicians and civil servants directly and demand better services rather than to trust politicians to fulfil the mandate they have received through general elections. Ministerial responsibility is challenged by contract-based accountability, which is rooted in the idea of opportunistic behaviour, whereby people learn to distrust each other (Christensen and Lægreid, 2000). This might make control more visible, but whether this is really a better form of control than the old internal control based on trust is an open question.

NPM is built on the idea that public goals should be unambiguous. However, in a multi-functional public sector, goals can in fact often be imprecise or not clear-cut, without having negative implications for other goals and with clear causality. Accountability in such a system means being answerable for the achievement of multiple and often ambiguous objectives.

Another aspect of NPM replacing the sovereign state model is the actual structural changes taking place, especially devolution and privatisation. Again, these are not clear-cut. While very few advocates of NPM argue that the state should be shrunk, they believe it is relatively easy to do two things at the same time: namely, to give managers and their subordinates more autonomy and to strengthen political control through contracts, monitoring and incentive systems. Our conclusion is that these changes may in fact undermine political control. Managerialism may allow executives to exercise greater control over state agencies, but it is greater control over less (Davis, 1997). The changes also create ambiguity concerning the role of managers, because they are caught in cross-pressure between politicians and customers. Hollowing out the state also tends to erode political responsibility (Rhodes, 1997a, p. 54).

NPM has helped to broaden the options of people trying to influence the public authorities and participate in public decision-making processes through market mechanisms and customer orientation. Whether this is a good thing from a democratic point of view is, however, debatable. There is a need to strengthen the sense of trusteeship and the development of a polity with a common purpose based on trust, but NPM does not seem to include values of this kind in the various models of governance. Even if NPM has a participatory character, it represents a shift in focus concerning accountability, from a broadly defined public interest to a more narrowly defined set of personal interests. It is a paradox that while one goal of NPM is to open public administration to the public, it may ultimately reduce the level of democratic accountability (Peters, 1999b).

The Further Transformation of Government?

Based on the studies reported in this book, what kind of further development of government can one expect? The experience of NPM reforms in the last 15 years can be interpreted in terms of three different scenarios (Christensen and Lægreid, 1998a; Olsen, 1992).

The first is the idea of a linear process towards more market, management and efficiency. If one interprets some of our main findings as evidence that the main NPM ideas and practices have become dominant, a possible future trend would be the continuing and increasing dominance of the new administrative orthodoxy. In other words, there is no alternative to the main tenets of the NPM reforms and they will become even more dominant in the future, making isomorphic and global trends more evident.

Some arguments for this interpretation are: The economic theories and economic-oriented reforms are superior and necessary instruments for combating pathological tendencies in the core public sector and ensuring its survival (Pollitt and Bouckaert, 2000, p. 16). The reforms implemented have been a success and have acquired such momentum that this type of reform is being applied broadly and spreading all over the world. Important parts of the reforms have become irreversible, as shown, for example, by the way British Prime Minister Tony Blair has handled the devolution and privatisation introduced by his predecessor Margaret Thatcher. These reforms have been institutionalised in various ways. Added to this is the apparent success of the rhetoric of NPM reforms. The globalisation of NPM has been helped by the emergence of a common vocabulary of reform concepts, stressing efficiency, rationality and modernity. This creates the often misleading impression of uniformity in reforms of this type (Pollitt and Bouckaert, 2000, p. 189).

Counter-arguments of a general kind are that history is seldom only linear and deterministic. Central political and administrative actors may always choose other directions or adjust the path chosen when decision-making constraints change and experience of reforms is gathered. Another way to say this is that particular types of reforms have their time – a window of opportunity is opened for certain actors, problems and solutions but it is later closed again (Kingdon, 1984). One major disadvantage of reforms like NPM, if they should continue to spread widely, is that they are relatively ineffective because they are not integrated and consistent, but rather inconsistent and piecemeal (Peters, 1996a, pp. 16–17). Moreover, reforms are often susceptible to the law of entropy – i.e., in the initial phase they are applied zealously but they 'burn out' as they spread more widely (Røvik, 1998).

The second scenario is that after a period of NPM there will be a reaction to the norms and values that the reform is built on and a return to some of the main features of the 'old civil service'. In pluralistic societies, uneven institutional change is likely to generate countervailing forces (Olsen, 1997a). Administrative reforms have a tendency to occur in cyclical processes (Barley and Kunda, 1992). It may be fashionable to be old-fashioned again. The general argument behind this is that history moves in cycles: a period of centralisation is followed by a period of decentralisation; specialisation once again gives way to co-ordination; and after a period when the economic aspects of public activities are emphasised, non-economic values come back into the foreground (Peters, 1996a, p. 17). The ideas behind reforms will change over time, in accordance with changing political and ideological trends, as will the driving forces and coalitions behind specific NPM-related reform elements.

But are history and its driving forces really so clear-cut that it can be divided into periods when dyadic and opposing sets of norms and values are alternately dominant? Or are reform processes more complex and ambiguous? Could it not be that there is always an element of turning back to the norms and values of the 'old administration', even as reforms proceed? Or are the public sector and the civil service continuously changing in more complicated ways?

A third interpretation, and the one underlying this book, is that NPM has contributed to making the public sector more complex and that this development will become more evident in the new millennium. Political-administrative systems in Western democracies are at a historical juncture in which a new synthesis between the old public administration and new public management is taking place as part of a dialectical process. Rather than a linear or cyclical process there is a co-evolution of reform ideas, administrative practice and theory (Lægreid and Roness, 1999; March and Olsen, 1989). One element of this is that NPM is creating a multi-structured public apparatus and more hybrid structural solutions, owing to more complex considerations and a confrontation between different structural design principles (Peters, 1996a, p. 17). Market-oriented reforms can, for example, create new organisational forms that blur the differences between the public and private sector and thereby make the features of public organisations less distinct (Pollitt and Bouckaert, 2000, p. 181). Another element is that NPM is leading to more cultural 'creolisation' – i.e., new, economically oriented cultural norms and values fuse with traditional, administrative norms and values, creating qualitatively new cultures (Hannerz, 1996). A third element is that the symbols and myths of public life seem to be more important then before. This may reflect the increasing complexity of the public apparatus and the need to develop simple guidelines for action (Meyer and Rowan, 1977), but it may also be due to the fact that NPM has generally lead to a qualitative change in leadership roles with more emphasis on image management. NPM seems to be an example of an increasing tendency to package and repackage public reforms to sell them to the public, with special prominence being given to the rationality and efficiency symbols of the reforms (Downs and Larkey, 1986; March, 1984).

The conclusion is that this book gives more support to the hypothesis of divergence than to the hypothesis of convergence. The transformation of NPM implies the development of hybrid organisational forms and substantial organisational variety and heterogeneity that challenges the generic tradition in organisational theory (Ferlie et al., 1996). There is a need to go beyond the new orthodoxy of the NPM doctrines and to develop a more differentiated view of the problems of governing the public sector.

Bibliography

Aberbach, J.D. and Christensen, T. (2000), 'Radical Reform in New Zealand: Crisis, Windows of Opportunity, and Rational Actors', Center for American Politics and Public Policy, UCLA and Department of Political Science, University of Oslo.

Aberbach, J.D. and Rockman, B.A. (1999), 'The Reinvention Syndrome: Politics by Other Means?' Paper presented at the ECPR Joint Workshops, March 26-31, Mannheim.

Abrahamson, E. (1996), 'Technical and Aesthetic Fashion', in B. Czarniawska and G. Sevón (eds), *Translating Organizational Change*, DeGruyter, Berlin, pp. 117-138.

Administrasjonsdepartementet (1996), 'Statens lederlønnsordning', Rapport fra evaluering, Oslo.

Almond, G.A. (1990), *A Discipline Divided: Schools and Sects in Political Science*, Sage, Beverly Hills, California.

Arendt, H. (1958), *The Human Condition*, University of Chicago Press, Chicago.

Aristoteles (1987), *The Nicomachean Ethics*, Oxford University Press, London.

Arter, D. (1999), *Scandinavian Politics Today*, Manchester University Press, Manchester.

Ashton, T. (1999), 'The Health Reforms: To Market and Back', in J. Boston, P. Dalziel and S. St John (eds), *Redesigning the Welfare State in New Zealand*, Oxford University Press, Auckland, pp. 134-153.

Assmann, R. (1997), 'Fra kornblanding til gryn: Statkorn fra forvaltningsbedrift til statseid aksjeselskap: En analyse av omleggingsprosessen og dens effekter', Thesis, Department of Political Science, University of Oslo.

Atkinson, J. (1997), 'The Media and MMP', in R. Miller (ed.), *New Zealand Politics in Transition*, Oxford University Press, Auckland, pp. 234-244.

Aucoin, P. (1990), 'Administrative Reform in Public Management: Paradigms, Principles, Paradoxes and Pendulums', *Governance*, vol. 3 (2), pp. 115-137.

Australian Government (1983), *Reforming the Australian Public Service,* Australian Government Publishing Service.

Bäckström, H. (1999), 'Den krattade manegen: Svensk arbetsorganisatorisk utveckling under tre decennier', Dissertation no. 79, Department of Business Studies, Uppsala University, Uppsala.

Baier, V.E., March, J.G. and Sætren, H. (1986), 'Implementation and Ambiguity', *Scandinavian Journal of Management*, vol. 2 (3/4), pp. 197-212.

Bakvis, H. (1997), 'Advising the Executive: Think Tanks, Consultants, Political Staff and Kitchen Cabinets', in P. Weller, H. Bakvis and R.A.W. Rhodes, *The Hollow*

313

314 New Public Management

Crown: Countervailing Trends in Core Executives, Macmillan, Basingstoke, pp. 84–125.

Baldersheim, H. (1993), 'Kommunal organisering: Motar sel, men ressursar avgjer?', in P. Lægreid and J.P. Olsen (eds), *Organisering av offentlig sektor. Perspektiver –reformer –erfaringer –utfordringer*, Tano, Oslo, pp. 155–170.

Bamber, G.J. and Davis, E.M. (1992), 'Australia', in M. Rothman, D.R. Briscoe and R.C.D. Nacamulli (eds), *Industrial Relations Around the World*, de Gruyter, Berlin, pp. 11–30.

Barberis, P. (1998), 'The New Public Management and a New Accountability', *Public Administration*, vol. 76 (Autumn), pp. 451–470.

Barley, S.R. and Kunda, G. (1992), 'Design and Devolution: Surges of Rational and Normative Ideologies of Control in Managerial Discourse', *Administrative Science Quarterly*, vol. 37 (September), pp. 363–399.

Bateson, G. (1979), *Mind and Nature*, Bantam Books, Toronto.

Bayliss, L. (1994), *Prosperity Delayed: Economic Failure in New Zealand and What Should Be Done about It*, GP Publications, Wellington.

Benhabib, S. (1994), 'Deliberative Rationality and Models of Democratic Legitimacy', *Constellations*, vol. 1 (1), pp. 26–52.

Bennett, C. and Ferlie, E. (1996), 'Contracting in Theory and in Practice: Some Evidence from the NHS', *Public Administration*, vol. 74 (1), pp. 49–66.

Bentham, J. (1830/1983), 'Constitutional Code', vol. 1, in *The Collected Works of Jeremy Bentham*, Oxford University Press, Oxford.

Berger, P. and Luckmann, T. (1966), *The Social Construction of Reality*, Penguin, London.

Bergström, T. (1999), 'Importing New Models and Ideas: Compliance, Resistance and Persistence in Swedish Public Organisations', Paper presented at NOPSA 99, 19–21 August, Uppsala.

Blau, P. (1963), *The Dynamics of Bureaucracy*, University of Chicago Press, rev. ed., Chicago.

Blindheim, B.-T. (1999), 'Posten: Fra forvaltningsbedrift til særlovsselskap', Thesis, Department of Political Science, University of Oslo.

Blomgren, M. (1999), 'Pengarna eller livet? Sjukvårdande professioner och yrkesgrupper i mötet med en ny ekonomistyrning', Doctoral thesis No. 78, Department of Business Studies, Uppsala University, Uppsala.

Bobbio, N. (1987), *The Future of Democracy*, Polity Press, Oxford.

Boli, J. and Thomas, G.M. (1999), 'INGOs and the Organization of World Culture', in J. Boli and G.M. Thomas (eds), *Constructing World Culture. International Nongovernmental Organizations since 1875*, Stanford University Press, Stanford, pp. 13–49.

Bollard, A. (1994), 'New Zealand', in J. Williamson (ed.), *The Political Economy of Policy Reform*, Institute for International Economics, Washington D.C.

Boréus, K. (1994), *Högervåg. Nyliberalism och kampen om språket i svensk offentlig debatt 1969-1989*, Tidens förlag, Stockholm.

Borins, S.F. (1988), 'Public Choice: 'Yes Minister' Made it Popular, But Does Winning the Nobel Prize Make it True?', *Canadian Public Administration*, vol. 31 (1), pp. 12–26.

Boston, J. (1991), 'Chief Executives and the Senior Executive Service', in J. Boston et al. (eds), *Reshaping the State*, Oxford University Press, Auckland, pp. 81–113.

Boston, J. (1994a), 'On the Sharp Edge of the State Sector Act: The Resignation of Perry Cameron', *Public Sector*, vol. 17 (4), pp. 2–7.

Boston, J. (1994b), 'Purchasing Policy Advice: The Limits to Contracting Out', *Governance*, vol. 6 (1), pp. 1–30.

Boston, J. (1995a), 'Inherently Governmental Functions and the Limits to Contracting Out', in J. Boston (ed.), *The State Under Contract*, Bridget Williams Books, Wellington, pp. 78–111.

Boston, J. (ed.) (1995b), *The State Under Contract*, Bridget Williams Books, Wellington.

Boston, J. (1999), 'The New Zealand Case', *Samfundsøkonomen*, (5), pp. 5–13.

Boston, J. (2000), 'The Challenge of Evaluating Systemic Change: The Case of Public Management Reform', Paper prepared for the IPMN Conference, Learning from Experiences with New Public Management, Macquarie Graduate School of Management, 4–6 March, Sydney.

Boston, J. and Dalziel, P. (eds) (1992), *The Decent Society? Essays in Response to National's Economic and Social Policies*, Oxford University Press, Auckland.

Boston, J., Dalziel, P. and St John, S. (1999), *Redesigning the Welfare State in New Zealand*, Oxford University Press, Auckland.

Boston, J., Martin, J., Pallot, J. and Walsh, P. (eds) (1991), *Reshaping the State: New Zealand's Bureaucratic Revolution*, Oxford University Press, Auckland.

Boston, J., Martin, J., Pallot, J. and Walsh, P. (1996), *Public Management: The New Zealand Model*, Oxford University Press, Auckland.

Boston, J. and Pallot, J. (1997), 'Linking Strategy and Performance: Developments in the New Zealand Public Sector', *Journal of Policy Analysis and Management*, vol. 16 (3), pp. 382–404.

Boston, J. and Uhr, J. (1996), 'Reshaping the Mechanics of Government', in F. Castles, R. Gerritsen and J. Vowles (eds), *The Great Experiment. Labour Parties and Public Policy Transformation in Australia and New Zealand*, Auckland University Press, Auckland, pp. 48–67.

Bouckaert, G. (1997), 'Performance, Governance and Management in the Public Sector: Comparative Experiences', in J.J. Hesse and T.A.J. Toonen (eds), *European Yearbook of Comparative Government and Public Administration*, vol. III, Nomos Verlag, Baden-Baden, pp. 469–483.

Bourdieu, P. (1977), 'The Production of Belief. Contribution to an Economy of Symbolic Goods', *Media, Culture and Society*, vol. 2 (3), pp. 261–293.

Bovens, M. (1998), *The Quest for Responsibility. Accountability and Citizenship in Complex Organizations*, Cambridge University Press, Cambridge.

Bowker, G.C. and Star, S.L. (1999), *Sorting Things Out. Classification and its Consequences*, MIT Press, Cambridge, MA.

Bradshaw, D. (1993), 'Standards of Professionalism: The Community and the Public Interest', Paper presented at the Public Service Senior Management Conference, September, Wellington.

Bramble, T. and Heal, S. (1997), 'Trade Unions', in C. Rudd and B. Roper (eds), *The Political Economy of New Zealand*, Oxford University Press, Auckland.

Bray, M. and Neilson, D. (1996), 'Industrial Relations Reform and the Relative Autonomy of the State', in F. Castles, R. Gerritsen and J. Vowles (eds), *The Great Experiment. Labour Parties and Public Policy Transformation in Australia and New Zealand*, Auckland University Press, Auckland, pp. 68–87.

Bray, M. and Walsh, P. (1998), 'Different Paths to Neo-Liberalism? Comparing Australia and New Zealand', *Industrial Relations*, vol. 37 (3), pp. 358–387.

Bridgman, P. and Davis, G. (1998), *Australian Policy Handbook*, Allen and Unwin, Sydney.

Brorström, B. and Rombach, B. (1996), 'Lugnet efter stormen – om storslagna reformer och brist på förändringsförmåga i kommuner', *Økonomistyring & Informatik*, vol. 12 (2, October), pp. 111–125.

Brunsson, N. (1989), *The Organization of Hypocrisy. Talk, Decisions and Actions in Organizations*, Wiley, Chichester.

Brunsson, N. (1998), 'Homogeneity and Heterogeneity in Organizational Forms as the Result of Cropping-Up Processes', in N. Brunsson and J.P. Olsen (eds), *Organizing Organizations*, Fagbokforlaget, Bergen, pp. 259–278.

Brunsson, N., Forssell, A. and Winberg, H. (1989), *Reform som tradition. Administrativa reformer i Statens Järnvägar*, Handelshögskolan i Stockholm/EFI, Stockholm.

Brunsson, N. and Jacobsson, B. (eds) (1998), *Standardisering*, Nerenius & Santerus, Stockholm.

Brunsson, N. and Olsen, J.P. (1993), *The Reforming Organization*, Routledge, London and New York.

Brunsson, N. and Sahlin-Andersson, K. (2000), 'Constructing Organizations: The Example of Public Sector Reform', *Organization Studies*, vol. 21 (4), pp. 721–746.

Buchanan, J. (1991), *The Economics and the Ethics of the Constitutional Order*, The University of Michigan Press, Ann Arbor.

Burns, T. and Stalker, G.M. (1961), *The Management of Innovation*, Oxford University Press, rev. ed. 1994, New York.

Campbell, C. (2000), 'Democratic Accountability and Models of Governance: Purchaser/Provider v Owner/Trustee', in R.A. Chapman (ed.), *Ethics in Public Service for the New Millennium*, Ashgate, Aldershot, UK.

Campbell, C. and Halligan, J. (1992), *Political Leadership in an Age of Constraint: The Experience of Australia*, University of Pittsburgh Press, Pittsburgh.

Castles, F.G. (1989), 'Big Government in Weak States: The Paradox of State Size in English-Speaking Nations of Advanced Capitalism', *Journal of Commonwealth and Comparative Studies*, vol. 27, pp. 267–293.

Castles, F.G. (1993), 'Changing Course in Economic Policy: The English-Speaking Nations in the 1980s', in F.C. Castle (ed.), *Families of Nations*, Dartmouth, Aldershot, pp. 3–34.

Castles, F.G., Gerritsen, R. and Vowles, J. (eds) (1996a), *The Great Experiment. Labour Parties and Public Policy Transformation in Australia and New Zealand*, Auckland University Press, Auckland.

Castles, F., Gerritsen, R. and Vowles, J. (1996b), 'Introduction: Setting the Scene for Economic and Political Change', in F. Castles, R. Gerritsen and J. Vowles (eds), *The Great Experiment. Labour Parties and Public Policy Transformation in Australia and New Zealand*, Auckland University Press, Auckland, pp. 1–21.

CCMAU (1996), 'Corporate Profile', Crown Company Monitoring Advisory Unit.

CCMAU (1999), 'Letter Concerning Information on Recent Developments in the SOE Sphere', Crown Company Monitoring Advisory Unit.

Cheung, A.B.L. (1997), 'Understanding Public-Sector Reform: Global Trends and Diverse Agendas', *International Review of Administrative Sciences*, vol. 63 (4), pp. 435–458.

Christensen, T. (1991), 'Bureaucratic Roles: Political Loyalty and Professional Autonomy', *Scandinavian Political Studies*, vol. 14 (4), pp. 303–320.

Christensen, T. (1995), 'The Scandinavian State Tradition and Public Administration – the Case of Norway', Paper presented at the Annual Meeting of APSA, Aug. 31–Sep. 3, 1995, Chicago.

Christensen, T. (1997), 'Structure and Culture Reinforced – The Development and Current Features of the Norwegian Civil Service System', Paper presented at Conference on Civil Service System in Comparative Perspective, 5–8 April, Indiana University, Bloomington.

Christensen, T. (1999), 'Administrative Reform – Transforming the Relationship Between Political and Administrative Leaders?' Paper presented at the Structure and Organization of Governance Conference , November 17–19, Tokyo.

Christensen, T. and Egeberg, M. (1997), 'Sentraladministrasjonen – en oversikt over trekk ved departementer og direktorater', in T. Christensen and M. Egeberg (eds), *Forvaltningskunnskap*, Tano Aschehoug, Oslo, pp. 85–118.

Christensen, T. and Lægreid, P. (1998a), *Den moderne forvaltning,* Tano Aschehoug, Oslo.

Christensen, T. and Lægreid, P. (1998b), 'Administrative Reform Policy: The Case of Norway', *International Review of Administrative Sciences*, vol. 64 (3), pp. 457–475.

Christensen, T. and Lægreid, P. (1998c), 'Public Administration in a Democratic Context – A Review of Norwegian Research', in N. Brunsson and J.P. Olsen (eds), *Organizing Organizations*, Fagbokforlaget, Bergen, pp. 47–172.

Christensen, T. and Lægreid, P. (1999a), 'New Public Management – Design, Resistance, or Transformation', *Public Productivity & Management Review*, vol. 23 (2, December), pp. 169–193.

Christensen, T. and Lægreid, P. (1999b), 'New Public Management: The Trade-Off Between Political Governance and Administrative Autonomy', Paper presented at International Research Symposium on Public Management, Aston University, March, Birmingham, UK.

Christensen, T. and Lægreid, P. (2000), 'New Public Management – Puzzles of Democracy and the Influence of Citizens', Paper presented at the IPSA World Congress, August 1–6, Quebec.

Christensen, T. and Lægreid, P. (2001), 'New Public Management: The Effects of Contractualism and Devolution on Political Control', *Public Management* (forthcoming).

Christensen, T. and Peters, B.G. (1999), *Structure, Culture and Governance. A Comparative Analysis of Norway and the United States*, Rowman & Littlefield, Maryland.

Clark, M. (ed.) (1999), *The Roberts Report: Writings About and By John Roberts*, Victoria University Press, Wellington.

Codd, M. (1991), 'Federal Public Sector Management Reform – Recent History and Current Priorities', Senior Executive Staffing Unit, Occasional Paper No. 11, AGPS, Canberra.

Considine, M. and Painter, M. (eds) (1997), *Managerialism. The Great Debate*, Melbourne University Press, Melbourne.

Controller and Auditor-General (1999), *Third Report for 1999*, Audit Office, Wellington.

Council of Australian Governments (COAG) Task Force on Health and Community Services (1995), 'Health and Community Services: Meeting People's Needs Better', Discussion Paper.

Crainer, S. (1997), *Corporate Man to Corporate Skunk: The Tom Peters Phenomenon*, Capstone, Oxford.

Crick, B. (1962), *In Defence of Politics*, Weidenfeld & Nicolson, London.

Czarniawska, B. (1997), *Narrating the Organization: Dramas of Institutional Identity*, University of Chicago Press, Chicago.

Czarniawska, B. and Joerges, B. (1996), 'Travels of Ideas', in B. Czarniawska and G. Sevón (eds), *Translating Organizational Change*, DeGruyter, Berlin, pp. 13–48.

Czarniawska, B. and Sevón, G. (eds) (1996), *Translating Organizational Change*, de Gruyter, New York.

Dabscheck, B. (1995), *The Struggle for Australian Industrial Relations*, Oxford University Press, Melbourne.

Dahl, R.A. (1989), *Democracy and its Critics*, Yale University Press, New Haven.

Dahl, R.A. and Lindblom, C.E. (1953), *Politics, Economics, and Welfare*, Harper & Row, New York.

Dahl, R.A. and Tufte, E.R. (1973), *Size and Democracy*, Stanford University Press, Stanford.

David, P. (1985), 'Clio and the Economics of QWERTY', *American Economic Review*, vol. 75 (2, May), pp. 332–337.

Davis, G. (1995), *A Government of Routines: Executive Coordination in an Australian State*, Macmillan, Melbourne.

Davis, G. (1997), 'Toward a Hollow State? Managerialism and its Critics', in M. Considine and M. Painter (eds), *Managerialism. The Great Debate*, Melbourne University Press, Melbourne, pp. 208–223.

Day, P. and Klein, R. (1987), *Accountability. Five Public Services*, Tavistock Publishers, London.

DiMaggio, P.J. and Powell, W.W. (1983), 'The Iron Cage Revisited: Institutional Isomorphism and Collective Rationality in Organizational Fields', *American Sociological Review*, vol. 48 (2), pp. 147–160.

DiMaggio P.J. and Powell, W.W. (1991), 'Introduction', in W. Powell and P. DiMaggio (eds), *New Institutionalism in Organizational Analysis*, University of Chicago Press, Chicago, pp. 1–38.

Douglas, R.O. (1993), *Unfinished Business*, Random House, Auckland.

Downs, G.W. and Larkey, P.D. (1986), *The Search for Government Efficiency. From Hubris to Helplessness*, Temple University Press, Philadelphia.

Dryzek, J.S. (1990), *Discursive Democracy*, Cambridge University Press, Cambridge.

Dryzek, J.S. (1992), 'Discursive Designs: Critical Theory and Political Institutions', *American Journal of Political Science*, vol. 31 (3), pp. 656–679.

Duncan, I. (1996), 'Public Enterprises', in B. Silverstone, A. Bollard and R. Lattimore (eds), *A Study of Economic Reform. The Case of New Zealand,* Elsevier, pp. 389–424.

Duncan, I. and Bollard, A. (1992), *Corporatization and Privatization: Lessons from New Zealand*, Oxford University Press, Oxford.

Dunleavy, P. (1995), 'Policy Disasters: Explaining the UK's Record', *Public Policy and Administration*, vol. 10 (2), pp. 52–70.

Dunleavy, P. (1997), 'Globalization of Public Service Production: Can Government be Best in the World?', in A. Massey (ed.), *Globalization and Marketization of Government Services: Comparing Contemporary Public Sector Developments*, MacMillan Press, London, pp. 16–46.

Dunleavy, P. and Hood, C. (1994), 'From Old Public Organization to New Public Management', *Public Money & Management*, (July–September), pp. 9–16.

Dunn, D.D. (1997), *Politics and Administration at the Top. Lessons from Down Under*, University of Pittsburgh Press, Pittsburgh.

Dunphy, D. and Stace, D. (1990), *Under New Management: Australian Organisations in Transition*, McGraw-Hill Book Company, Sydney.

Easton, B. (1994), 'Royal Commissions as Policy Creators', in P. Weller (ed.), *Royal Commissions and the Making of Public Policy*, Macmillan, Melbourne, pp. 230–243.

320 *New Public Management*

320 *New Public Management*

Easton, B. (1995), 'The Rise of the Generic Manager', in S. Rees and G. Rodley (eds), *The Human Costs of Managerialism: Advocating the Recovery of Humanity*, Pluto Press, Leichhardt, NSW.

Easton, B. (1997), *The Commercialisation of New Zealand*, Auckland University Press, Auckland.

Easton, B. and Gerritsen, R. (1996), 'Economic Reform: Parallels and Divergences', in F. Castles, R. Gerritsen and J. Vowles (eds), *The Great Experiment. Labour Parties and Public Policy Transformation in Australia and New Zealand*, Auckland University Press, Auckland, pp. 22–47.

Edelman, M. (1988), *Constructing the Political Spectacle*, University of Chicago Press, Chicago.

Edwards, M. and Henderson, A. (1995), 'COAG: A Vehicle for Reform', in P. Carroll and M. Painter (eds), *Microeconomic Reform and Federalism*, Federalism Research Centre, ANUTECH, Canberra.

Egeberg, M. (1984), *Organisasjonsutforming i offentlig virksomhet*, TANO, Oslo.

Egeberg, M. (1989a), 'Effekter av organisasjonendring i forvaltningen', in M. Egeberg (ed.), *Institusjonspolitikk og forvaltningsutvikling. Bidrag til en anvendt statsvitenskap*, TANO, Oslo, pp. 75–93.

Egeberg, M. (1989b), 'Om å organisere konkurrerende beslutningsprinsipper inn i myndighetsstrukturer', in M. Egeberg (ed.), *Institusjonspolitikk og forvaltningsutvikling. Bidrag til en anvendt statsvitenskap*, TANO, Oslo, pp. 94–113.

Egeberg, M. (1994), 'Bridging the Gap Between Theory and Practice: The Case of Administrative Policy', *Governance,* vol. 7 (1), pp. 83–98.

Egeberg, M. (1995), 'Bureaucrats as Public Policy-Makers and Their Self-Interests', *Journal of Theoretical Politics*, vol. 7 (2), pp. 157–167.

Egeberg, M. (1997), 'Verdier i statsstyre og noen organisatoriske implikasjoner', in T. Christensen and M. Egeberg (eds), *Forvaltningskunnskap*, Tano Aschehoug, Oslo, pp. 405–422.

Elmbrant, B. (1993), *Så föll den svenska modellen*, T. Fischer & Co, Stockholm.

Elster, J. (1997), 'The Market and the Forum: Three Varieties of Political Theory', in J. Bohman and W. Rehg (eds), *Deliberative Democracy. Essays on Reason and Politics*, The MIT Press, Cambridge, pp. 3–33.

Elvander, N. (1988), *Den svenska modellen. Löneförhandlingar och inkomstpolitik 1982–1986*, Allmänna Förlaget, Stockholm.

Engeset, B.H. (1994), 'Lønspolitisk modernisering. Ein studie av statlege lønspolitiske reformforsøk i Danmark og Sverige', Report 9402, LOS-Centre, Bergen.

Eriksen, E.O. (1993), *Den offentlige dimensjon, Verdier og styring i offentlig sektor*, Tano, Oslo.

Eriksen, E.O. (1994), 'Deliberative Democracy and the Politics of Pluralist Society', Working Paper no 6, ARENA, Oslo.

Eriksen, E.O. (1995), *Deliberativ politikk. Demokrati i teori og praksis*, Tano, Oslo.

Eriksen, E.O. and Weigård J. (1993), 'Fra statsborger til kunde: Kan relasjonen mellom innbyggerne og det offentlige reformuleres på grunnlag av nye roller?', in E.O. Eriksen, *Den offentlige dimensjon. Verdier og styring i offentlig sektor*, Tano, Oslo, pp. 133–155.

Erixon, O. (2000), *Marknadsöppningen fortsätter*, SAF (Union of Swedish Employers), Stockholm.

Erlingsdóttir, G. (1999), 'Kvalitetssäkringars översättning: Recentralisering av kontroll', in E.Z. Bentsen, F. Borum, G. Erlingsdóttir and K. Sahlin-Andersson (eds), *Når Styringsambitioner Møder Praksis*, Copenhagen Business School Press, Copenhagen, pp. 57–86.

Evans, L., Grimes, A.,Wilkinson, B. and Teece, D. (1996), 'Economic Reform in New Zealand 1984–95: The Pursuit of Efficiency', *Journal of Economic Literature*, vol. XXXIV (December), pp. 1856–1902.

Farazmand, A. (1996), 'Introduction: The Comparative State of Public Enterprise Management', in A. Farazmand, *Public Enterprise Management. International Case Studies*, Greenwood Press, Westport, pp. 1–27.

Ferlie, E. et al. (1996), *The New Public Management in Action*, Oxford University Press, Oxford.

Finnemore, M. (1992), 'Science, the State, and International Society', Dissertation, Stanford University, CA.

Finnemore, M. (1996), *National Interests in International Society*, Cornell University Press, Ithaca.

Forssell, A. (1994), 'Företagisering av kommuner', in B. Jacobsson (ed.), *Organisationsexperiment i kommuner och landsting*, Nerenius & Santérus, Stockholm, pp. 22–37.

Forssell, A. (1999), 'Offentlig reformation i marknadsreformernas spår', *Kommunal Ekonomi och Politik*, vol. 3 (3), pp. 7–23.

Forssell, A. and Jansson, D. (2000), *Idéer som fängslar. Recept för en offentlig reformation*, Liber ekonomi, Malmö.

Foster, C.D. and Plowden, F.J. (1996), *The State Under Stress*, Open University Press, Buckingham.

Fredrickson, H.G. (1996), 'Comparing the Reinventing Movement with the New Public Administration', *Public Administration Review*, vol. 56 (3, May–June), pp. 263–270.

Fredriksson, B. and Gunnmo, A. (1981), *Våra fackliga organisationer*, Rabén & Sjögren, 4th. ed., Stockholm.

Frendreis, J.P. (1983), 'Explanation of Variation and Detection of Covariation: The Purpose and the Logic of Comparative Analysis', *Comparative Political Studies*, 16, pp. 255–272.

Fudge, C. and Gustavsson, L. (1989), 'Administrative Reform and Public Management in Sweden and the United Kingdom', *Public Money & Management*, vol. 9 (Summer), pp. 29–34.

Fujimura, J.H. (1996), *Crafting Science: A Sociohistory of the Quest for the Genetics of Cancer*, Harvard University Press, Cambridge, Mass.

Furre, B. (1993), *Vårt hundreår 1905–1990*, Samlaget, Oslo.

Furusten, S. and Lerdell, D. (1998), 'Managementisering av förvaltningen', in G. Ahrne (ed.), *Stater som organisationer*, Nerenius & Santérus, Stockholm, pp. 99–122.

Galison, P. (1997), *Image & Logic*, Chicago University Press, Chicago.

Giddens, A. (1990), *The Consequenses of Modernity*, Stanford University Press, Stanford.

Giddens, A. (1998), *The Third Way. The Renewal of Social Democracy*, Polity Press, Oxford.

Goldfinch, S. (1998), 'Remarking New Zealand's Economic Policy: Institutional Elites as Radical Innovators 1984–1993', *Governance*, vol. 11 (2), pp. 177–207.

Greenwood, R. and Hinings, C.R. (1996), 'Understanding Radical Organizational Change: Bringing Together the Old and the New Institutionalism', *Academy of Management Review*, vol. 21 (4), pp. 1022–1054.

Greenwood, R., Suddaby, R., and Hinings, C.R. (1998), 'The Role of Professional Associations in the Transformation of Institutionalised Fields', Paper presented at the Scancor Conference 'Samples of the future', September 1998, Stanford.

Gregory, R. (1987), 'The Reorganization of the Public Sector: The Quest for Efficiency', in J. Boston and M. Holland (eds), *The Fourth Labour Government: Radical Politics in New Zealand*, Oxford University Press, Auckland, pp. 111–133.

Gregory, R. (1995a), 'Accountability, Responsibility and Corruption: Managing the 'Public Production Process'', in J. Boston (ed.), *The State Under Contract*, Bridget Williams Books, Wellington, pp. 56–77.

Gregory, R. (1995b), 'The Peculiar Tasks of Public Management: Toward Conceptual Discrimination', *Australian Journal of Public Administration*, vol. 54 (2), pp. 171–183.

Gregory, R. (1995c), 'Post-Reform Attitudes of New Zealand's Senior Public Servants: A Follow-Up Study', *Political Science*, vol. 47 (2), pp. 161–190.

Gregory, R. (1995d), 'Bureaucratic 'Psychopathology' and Technocratic Governance: Whither Responsibility', *Hong Kong Public Administration*, vol. 4 (1), pp. 17–36.

Gregory, R. (1997), 'After the Reforms: Some Patterns of Attitudinal Change among Senior Public Servants in Canberra and Wellington', *Australian Journal of Public Administration*, vol. 56 (1), pp. 82–99.

Gregory, R. (1998a), 'The Changing Face of the State in New Zealand: Rolling Back the Public Service?', Paper presented at the Annual Meeting of the American Political Science Association, September 3–6, Boston.

Gregory, R. (1998b), 'Political Responsibility for Bureaucratic Incompetence: Tragedy at Cave Creek', *Public Administration*, vol. 76 (Autumn), pp. 519–538.

Gregory, R. (1998c), 'New Zealand as the 'New Atlantis': A Case Study in Techno-cracy', *Canberra Bulletin of Public Administration*, vol. 90 (December), pp. 107–112.

Gregory, R. (1998d), 'A New Zealand Tragedy: Problems of Political Responsibility', *Governance*, vol. 11 (2), pp. 231–240.

Gregory, R. (1999), 'Social Capital Theory and Administrative Reform: Maintaining Ethical Probity in Public Service', *Public Administration Review*, vol. 59 (1), pp. 63–75.

Gregory, R. and Hicks, C. (1999), 'Promoting Public Service Integrity: A Case for Responsible Accountability', *Australian Journal of Public Administration*, vol. 58 (4), pp. 3–14.

Grønlie, T. (1995), 'Styrenes styring, et mangfold av styreroller', in Ø. Grøndahl and T. Grønlie (eds), *Fristillingens grenser*, Fagbokforlaget, Bergen, pp. 105–124.

Grønlie, T. (1998), 'Drømmen om en konkurransetilpasset stat – Ytre fristilling som styringspolitisk redskap – 1945–1995', in T. Grønlie and P. Selle (eds), *Ein stat? Fristillingas fire ansikt*, Samlaget, Oslo.

Grønlie, T. and Selle, P. (eds) (1998), *Ein stat? Fristillingas fire ansikt*, Samlaget, Oslo.

Gulick, L. (1937), 'Notes on the Theory of Organization', in L. Gulick and L. Urwick (eds), *Papers on the Science of Administration*, A.M. Kelley, New York.

Gustafson, B. (1997), 'New Zealand Politics 1945–1984', in R. Miller (ed.), *New Zealand Politics in Transition*, Oxford University Press, Auckland, pp. 3–12.

Gustavsson, L. and Svensson, A. (1999), *Public Sector Reform in Sweden*, Liber Ekonomi, Lund.

Guthrie, J. and Parker, L.D. (1998), 'Managerialism and Marketisation in Financial Management Change in Australia', in O. Olson, J. Guthrie and C. Humphrey (eds), *Global Warning! Debating International Developments in New Public Financial Management*, Cappelen Akademisk Forlag, Oslo, pp. 49–75.

Haas, P. (1992), 'Introduction: Epistemic Communities and International Policy Coordination', *International Organization*, vol. 46 (1), pp. 1–35.

Habermas, J. (1981), *Theorie des kommunikativen Handelns*, Band 1–2, Suhrkamp, Frankfurt.

Habermas, J. (1992), *Faktizität und Geltung*, Suhrkamp, Frankfurt.

Hagen, T. and Sørensen, R. (1997), *Kommunal organisering*, Tano, Oslo.

Hall, P.A. (1993), 'Policy Paradigms, Social Learning, and the State: The Case of Economic Policymaking in Britain', *Comparative Politics*, vol. 25 (3, April), pp. 275–296.

Halligan, J. (1994), 'The Art of Reinvention: The United States' National Perfor-mance Review', *Australian Journal of Public Administration*, vol. 53 (2), pp. 135–143.

Halligan, J. (1995), 'Policy Advice and the Public Service', in B. Guy Peters and D.J. Savoie (eds), *Governance in a Changing Environment*, McGill-Queens Press, Montreal, pp. 138–172.

Halligan, J. (1996), 'Learning from Experience in Australian Reform: Balancing Principle and Pragmatism', in J.P. Olsen and B.G. Peters (eds), *Lessons from Experience*, Scandinavian University Press, Oslo, pp. 71-112.

Halligan, J. (1997a), 'New Public Sector Models: Reform in Australia and New Zealand', in J.-E. Lane (ed.), *Public Sector Reform: Rationale, Trends and Problems*, Sage, London, pp. 17-46.

Halligan, J. (1997b), 'Reforming the Public Sector in Western Europe: An Antipodean Perspective', in J.J. Hesse and T.A.J. Toonen (eds), *European Yearbook of Comparative Government and Public Administration*, vol. III, Nomos Verlag, Baden-Baden, pp. 375-389.

Halligan, J. (1997c), 'Paradoxes in Reform: Australia', Paper for 'Project on Paradoxes in Public Sector Reform', 25-27 September, Berlin.

Halligan, J. (1998), 'Comparing Public Service Reform in OECD Countries', in J. Halligan (ed.), *Public Service Reform*, Center for Research in Public Sector Management, University of Australia, in collaboration with International Association of Schools and Institutes of Administration, pp. 151-168.

Halligan, J. (forthcoming), 'Politicians, Bureaucrats and Public Sector Reform in Australia and New Zealand', in G. Peters and J. Pierre (eds), *Politicians and Bureaucrats under Public Sector Reform*, Routledge, London.

Halligan, J. and Power, J. (1992), *Political Management in the 1990s*, Oxford University Press, Melbourne.

Halvorsen, T.E. (1996), 'Arbeidsgiverorganiseringen for de fristilte statlige virksomhetene. Fra tarifforening til etableringen av NAVO 1946-1995', Report 9611, LOS-Centre, Bergen.

Hanisch T. J., Søilien, E. and Ecklund, G. (1999), *Norsk økonomisk politikk i det 20. århundre*, Høyskoleforlaget, Kristiansand.

Hannerz, U. (1996), *Transnational Connections*, Routledge, London and New York.

Hansson, L. and Lind, J-I. (1998), *Marknadsorientering i kommuner och landsting*, Nerenius & Santérus, Stockholm.

Harris, S. (1990), 'Administrative Reform, Democratic Responsibility and Bureaucratic Efficiency', *Canberra Bulletin of Public Administration*, vol. 61, pp. 26-33.

Harrison, R.J. and Mungal, S. (1990), 'Harmonisation', in A.J.R. Groom and P. Taylor (eds), *Frameworks for international cooperation*, Pinter Publishers, London.

Hart, J. (1998), 'Central Agencies and Departments: Empowerment and Coordination', in B.Guy Peters and D.J. Savoie (eds), *Taking Stock: Assessing Public Sector Reforms*, McGill-Queen's University Press, Montreal, pp. 285-309.

Hazledine, T. (1998), *Taking New Zealand Seriously: The Economics of Decency*, Harper Collins, Auckland.

Held, D. (1987), *Models of Democracy*, Polity Press, Oxford.

Henning, R. (1996), *Att följa trenden*, Nerenius & Santérus, Stockholm.

Henriksson, S. and Svensson, Å. (1998), *Nya Zeeland: Vad händer med välfärden?*, Socialdepartementets skriftserie Välfärdsprojektet, no. 13, Nordstedts, Stockholm.

Hesse, J.J., Hood, C. and Peters, B.G. (2001), 'Paradoxes in Public Sector Reform: Soft Theory and Hard Cases', in J.J. Hesse, C. Hood and B.G. Peters (eds), *Paradoxes in Public Sector Reform*, Duncker & Humbolt, Berlin (forthcoming).

Hobbs, T. (1651/1968), *Leviathan*, (edited by C.B. Macpherson), Penguin, Harmondsworth.

Hood, C. (1990), 'De-Sir Humphreyfying the Westminster Model of Bureacracy: A New Style of Governance?', *Governance*, vol. 3 (2), pp. 205–214.

Hood, C. (1991), 'A Public Management for All Seasons?', *Public Administration*, vol. 69 (Spring), pp. 3–19.

Hood, C. (1995a), 'The New Public Management in the 1980s. Variations on a Theme', *Accounting, Organization and Society*, vol. 20 (2–3), pp. 93–109.

Hood, C. (1995b), 'Contemporary Public Management: A New Paradigm?', *Public Policy and Administration*, vol. 10 (2), pp. 104–117.

Hood, C. (1996a), 'Exploring Variations in Public Management Reform of the 1980s', in H.A.G.M. Bekke, J.L. Perry and T.A.J. Toonen (eds), *Civil Service Systems*, Indiana University Press, Bloomington, pp. 268–287.

Hood, C. (1996b), 'United Kingdom: From Second Chance to Near-Miss Learning', in J. P. Olsen and B.G. Peters (eds), *Lessons From Experience,* Scandinavian University Press, Oslo, pp. 36–112.

Hood, C. (1998a), *The Art of the State: Culture, Rhetoric and Public Management*, Clarendon Press, Oxford.

Hood, C. (1998b), 'Individualized Contracts for Top Public Servants: Copying Business, Path-Dependent Political Re-Engineering – or Trobriand Cricket?', *Governance*, vol. 11 (4), pp. 443–462.

Hood, C. and Jackson, J. (1991), *Administrative Arguments*, Dartmouth, Aldershot.

Hood, C. and Peters, B.G. (eds) (1994a), *Rewards at the Top*, Sage, London.

Hood, C. and Peters, B.G. (1994b), 'Understanding RHPOs', in C. Hood and B.G. Peters (eds.), *Rewards at the Top*, Sage, London, pp. 1–24.

Hood, C. and Peters, B.G. (2000), 'Towards Paradox-Free Public Management Reform?', Paper to Conference on 'Public Management and Governance in the New Millenium', January 10–11, City University of Hong Kong.

Hugemark, A. (1994), *Den fängslande marknaden. Ekonomiska experter om välfärdsstaten*, Arkiv förlag, Lund.

Hughes, O.E. (1994), *Public Management and Administration: An Introduction*, St. Martin's Press, New York.

Håkansson, A. (1997), 'Systemskiftet som kom av sig. Förändringsarbete och medborgerliga reaktioner i 90-talets svenska kommuner', *Kommunal Ekonomi och Politik*, vol. 1 (1), pp. 41–52.

Ingraham, P.W. (1993), 'Of Pigs and Pokes and Policy Diffusion: Another Look at Pay-for-Performance', *Public Administration Review*, vol. 53 (4), pp. 340–356.

Ingraham, P.W. (1996), 'The Reform Agenda for National Civil Service Systems: External Stress and Internal Strain', in H.A.G.M. Bekke , J.L. Perry and T.A.J. Toonen (eds), *Civil Service Systems*, Indiana University Press, Bloomington, pp. 247-267.

Ingraham, P.W. (1998), 'Making Public Policy: The Changing Role of Higher Civil Service', in B.G. Peters and D.J. Savoie (eds), *Taking Stock. Assessing Public Sector Reforms*, McGill-Queen University Press, Montreal, pp. 164-186.

Jacobsen, D.R. (1996), 'Personalorganisasjoner og forvaltningspolitikk i Norge', in P. Lægreid and O.K. Pedersen (eds), *Integration och decentralisering*, Jurist- og Økonomforbundets Forlag, Copenhagen, pp. 157-180.

Jacobsen, D.R. (1998), 'Omstilling under trygghet. Institusjonaliseringen av et nytt rammeverk for reformer i staten', Working Paper 9824, LOS-Centre, Bergen.

Jacobsen, K. Dahl (1960), 'Lojalitet, nøytralitet og faglig uavhengighet', *Tidsskrift for Samfunnsforskning*, vol.1, pp. 231-248.

Jacobsson, B. (1994), 'Ideer, praktik och förnyelse', in B. Jacobsson (ed.), *Organisasjonsexperiment i kommuner och landsting*, Nerenius & Santèrus, Stockholm, pp. 226-238.

Jacobsson, B. (2000). 'Standardization and Expert Knowledge', in N. Brunsson, B. Jacobsson and associates, *A World of Standards*, Oxford University Press, Oxford.

Jacobsson, B. and Sahlin-Andersson, K. (1995), *Skolan och det nya verket. Skildringar från styrningens och utvärderingarnas tidevarv*, Nerenius & Santèrus, Stockholm.

Jacobsson, B. and Sundström, G. (1999), 'Invävd i Europa: En undersökning av den svenska statsförvaltningens EU-arbete', Report 1999:10, Score, Stockholm University.

James, C. (1998), 'The State Ten Years On from the Reforms', State Service Commission, Occasional Paper, no. 6, Wellington.

Jensen, T.M. (1998), 'Forvaltningspolitisk samarbeid på sporet. En studie av tjenestemannsorganisasjonenes deltakelse og medvirkning i omorganiseringen av NSB til et særlovselskap', Thesis, Department of Administration and Organization Theory, University of Bergen, Bergen.

Jenssen, S. (1995), 'Hierarki, spill eller deliberasjon?', in E.O. Eriksen (ed.), *Deliberativ politikk. Demokrati i teori og praksis*, Tano, Oslo, pp. 130-149.

Jervis, P. and Richards, S. (1997), 'Public Management: Raising Our Game', *Public Money and Management*, vol. 17 (April-June), pp. 9-16.

Johansson, L. (1995), 'Från statstjänarkartell till SEKO – Statsanställdas förbund 25 år', SEKO, Stockholm.

Johansson, P. and Johnsson, M. (1994), *Är kommunerna slavar under modetrenderna?*, Förvaltningshögskolan, University of Göteborg, Göteborg.

Johansson, P. and Johnsson, M. (1995), *Kommunernas sökande i reformernas labyrint*, Förvaltningshögskolan, University of Göteborg, Göteborg.

Kanter, R.M. (1987), 'From Status to Contribution: Some Organizational Implications of the Changing Basis for Pay', *Personnel*, vol. 64, pp. 12–36.

Keating, M. and Holmes, M. (1990), 'Australia's Budgetary and Financial Management Reforms', *Governance*, vol. 3 (2, April), pp. 168–185.

Kellough, J.E. and Lu, H. (1993), 'The Paradox of Merit Pay in the Public Sector', *Review of Public Personnel Administration*, vol. 13 (2), pp. 45–64.

Kelsey, J. (1995), *The New Zealand Experiment: A World Model for Structural Adjustment?*, Auckland University Press/Bridget Williams Books, Auckland.

Kerauden, P. and Van Mierlo, H. (1998), 'Theories of Public Management Reform and their Practical Implication', in T. Verheijen and D. Coombes (eds), *Innovation in Public Management*, Edward Elgar, Cheltenham, pp. 39–58.

Kettl, D.F. (1997), 'The Global Revolution in Public Management: Driving Themes, Missing Links', *Journal of Policy Analysis and Management*, vol. 16 (3), pp. 446–462.

Kettner, M. (1993), 'Scientific Knowledge, Discourse Ethic, and Consensus Formation in the Public Sphere', in E.R. Winkler and J.R. Coombs (eds), *Applied Ethics: A Reader*, Blackwell, Oxford.

Kingdon, J. (1984), *Agendas, Alternatives, and Public Policies*, Little, Brown, Boston.

Kjellberg, A. (1983), *Facklig organisering i tolv länder*, Arkiv, Lund.

Kjellberg, A. (1997), *Fackliga organisationer och medlemmar i dagens Sverige*, Arkiv, Lund.

Klausen, K.K. and Ståhlberg, K. (eds) (1998), *New Public Management i Norden*, Odense Universitetsforlag, Odense.

Knight, J. and Johnson, J. (1994), 'Aggregation and Deliberation: On the Possibility of Democratic Legitimacy', *Political Theory*, vol. 22 (2), pp. 277–296.

Kotter, J.P. (1995), 'Leading Change: Why Transformation Efforts Fail', *Harvard Business Review*, (March–April), pp. 59–67.

Krasner, S. (1988), 'Sovereignty: An Institutional Perspective', *Comparative Political Studies*, vol. 21, pp. 66–94.

Laffin, M. (1995), 'The Public Service', in M. Laffin and M. Painter (eds) *Reform and Reversal*, Macmillan, Sydney.

Lane, J.-E. (1997), 'Public Sector Reform in the Nordic Countries', in J.-E. Lane (ed.), *Public Sector Reform: Rationale, Trends and Problems*, Sage, London, pp. 188–208.

Lane, J.-E. (1999), 'Contractualism in the Public Sector: Some Theoretical Considerations', *Public Management*, vol. 1 (2), pp. 179–193.

Laughlin, R. and Pallot, J. (1998), 'Trends, Patterns and Influencing Factors: Some Reflections', in O. Olson, J. Guthrie and C. Humphrey (eds), *Global warning! Debating International Developments in New Public Financial Management*, Cappelen Akademisk Forlag, Oslo, pp. 376–399.

Lerdell, A. and Sahlin-Andersson, K. (1997), 'Att lära over grenser', *SOU*: 33, Stockholm.

Levine, S. and Roberts, N.S. (1997), 'MMP: The Decision', in R.Miller (ed.), *New Zealand Politics in Transition*, Oxford University Press, New Zealand, Auckland, pp. 25–36.

Lijphart, A. (1971), 'Comparative Politics and the Comparative Method', *American Political Science Review*, vol. 65 (3, September), pp. 682–693.

Lijphart, A. (1975), 'The Comparable-Case in Comparative Research', *Comparative Political Studies*, vol. 8, pp. 158–177.

Lijphart, (1984), *Democracies. Patterns of Majoritarian and Consensus Government in Twenty-One Countries*, Yale University Press, New Haven.

Lindquist, E. (1999), 'Preconceiving the Centre: Leadership, Strategic Review and Coherence in Public Sector Reform', OECD/PUMA/S6F(99) 5, Paris.

Linz, J.J. and de Miguel, A. (1966), 'Within-Nation Differences and Comparisons: The Eight Spains', in R.L. Merritt and S. Rokkan (eds), *Comparing Nations: The Use of Quantitative Data in Cross-Country Research*, Yale University Press, New Haven, pp. 267–320.

Lipson, L. (1948), *The Politics of Equality: New Zealand's Adventures in Democracy*, University of Chicago Press, Chicago.

Locke, J. (1690/1984), *Two Treatises of Government*, Dent, London.

Logan, B. (1991), *Review of State Sector Reforms*, Steering Group, Wellington.

Lounamaa, P.H. and March, J.G. (1987), 'Adaptive Coordination of a Learning Team', *Management Science*, vol. 33, pp. 107–123.

Lüder, K. (1998), 'Towards a New Financial Management for Germany's Public Sector: Local Governments Lead the Way', in O. Olson, J. Guthrie and C. Humphrey (eds), *Global warning! Debating International Developments in New Public Financial Management*, Cappelen Akademisk Forlag, Oslo, pp. 114–129.

Lundström, T. and Wijkström, F. (1997), *The Non-Profit Sector in Sweden*, Manchester University Press, Manchester.

Lægreid, P. (1994), 'Going against the Cultural Grain: Norway', in C. Hood and B.G. Peters (eds), *Rewards at the Top*, Sage, London, pp. 133–145.

Lægreid, P. (ed.) (1995), *Lønnspolitikk i offentlig sektor*, TANO, Oslo.

Lægreid, P. (1997),'Pay Reform for Top Civil Servants in Norway: Towards Market and Performance Pay, or Business as Usual?', Working Paper 9703, LOS-Centre, Bergen.

Lægreid, P. (1999a), 'Administrative Reforms in Scandinavia – Testing the Cooperative Model', Working Paper 9903, LOS-Centre, Bergen.

Lægreid, P. (1999b), 'Top Civil Servants Under Contract: Experiences from New Zealand and Norway', Paper presented at the Structure and Organization of Government Conference, November 17–19, Tokyo.

Lægreid, P. and Mjør, M. (1993), 'Toppsjefar og leiarlønsreform i staten', Report 9303, LOS-Centre, Bergen.

Lægreid, P. and Olsen, J.P. (1978), *Byråkrati og beslutninger*, Universitetsforlaget, Bergen.

Lægreid, P. and Olsen, J.P. (1984), 'Top Civil Servants in Norway: Key Players on Different Teams', in E.N. Suleiman (ed.), *Bureaucrats and Policy Making*, Holmes & Meier, New York, pp. 206–242.

Lægreid, P. and Olsen, J.P. (eds) (1993), *Organisering av offentlig sektor*, TANO, Oslo.

Lægreid, P. and Pedersen, O.K. (1994), *Forvaltningspolitik i Norden*, Jurist- og Økonomforbundets forlag, København.

Lægreid, P. and Pedersen, O.K. (1996), *Integration og desentralisering*, Jurist- og Økonomforbundets forlag, København.

Lægreid, P. and Pedersen, O.K. (1999), *Fra opbygning til ombyging i staten*, Jurist- og Økonomforbundets forlag, København.

Lægreid, P. and Roness, P.G. (1998), 'Frå einskap til mangfald. Eit perspektiv på indre fristilling i staten', in T. Grønlie and P. Selle (eds), *Ein stat? Fristillingas fire ansikt*, Samlaget, Oslo, pp. 21–65.

Lægreid, P. and Roness, P.G. (1999), 'Administrative Reform as Organized Attention', in M. Egeberg and P. Lægreid (eds), *Organizing Political Institutions: Essays for Johan P. Olsen*, Scandinavian University Press, Oslo, pp. 301–329.

Lægreid, P. and Roness, P.G. (2001), 'Administrative Reform Programmes and Institutional Response in Norwegian Central Government', in J.J. Hesse, C. Hood and B.G. Peters (eds), *Paradoxes in Public Sector Reform*, Duncker & Humbolt, Berlin (forthcoming).

Lægreid, P. and Savland, T.E. (1996a), 'Individuell lederlønn i staten', Working Paper 9630, LOS-Centre, Bergen.

Lægreid, P. and Savland, T.E. (1996b), 'Lederlønnsreform og mobilitetsmønster', Working Paper 9614, LOS-Centre, Bergen.

Löwstedt, J. (1991), 'Structures and Processes in Administrative Change. A Reply to Brunsson's Reform and Change Discourse', *Scandinavian Journal of Management*, vol. 7, pp. 143–150.

McDonald, P. and Sharma, A. (1994), 'Toward Work Teams Within a New Zealand Public Service Organization', Paper presented at 1994 International Conference on Work Teams, September, Dallas, Texas.

McIntosh, K., Shauness, J. and Wettenhall, R. (1997), *Contracting Out in Australia: An Indicative Story*, Center for Research in Public Sector Management, University of Canberra.

McLeay, E. (1995), *The Cabinet and Political Power*, Oxford University Press, Auckland.

Mansbridge, J.J. (1992), 'A Deliberative Theory of Interest Representation', in M.P. Petracca (ed.), *The Politics of Interests*, Westview Press, Boulder, pp. 122–139.

Maor, M. (1999), 'The Paradox of Managerialism', *Public Administration Review*, vol. 59 (1), pp. 5–18.

March, J.G. (1981), 'Footnotes to Organizational Change', *Administrative Science Quarterly*, vol. 26 (December), pp. 563–577.

March, J.G. (1984), 'How We Talk and How We Act: Administrative Theory and Administrative Life', in T.J. Sergiovanni and J.E. Corbally (eds), *Leadership and Organizational Cultures*, University of Illinois Press, Urbana, pp. 11–29.

March, J.G. (1991), 'How Decisions Happen in Organizations', *Human-Computer Interaction*, vol. 6, pp. 95–117.

March, J.G. (1994), *A Primer on Decision-Making,* The Free Press, New York.

March, J.G. (1995), 'Learning Processes are Powerful Tools of Organizational Adaptation', *Tvön Tumuli Aikakauskirja* (Helsinki), pp. 28–37.

March, J.G. (1998), 'Administrative Practice, Organization Theory, and Political Philosophy: Ruminations on the Reflections of John M. Gaus, 1997 John M. Gaus Lecture', *PS: Political Science and Politics*, vol. XXX (4, Dec.), pp. 689–698.

March, J.G. and Olsen, J.P. (1976), *Ambiguity and Choice in Organizations*, Scandinavian University Press, Oslo.

March, J.G. and Olsen, J.P. (1983), 'Organizing Political Life: What Administrative Reorganization Tells Us About Government', *American Political Science Review*, vol. 77 (2), pp. 281–296.

March, J.G. and Olsen, J.P. (1989), *Rediscovering Institutions: The Organizational Basis of Politics,* The Free Press, New York.

March, J.G. and Olsen, J.P. (1995), *Democratic Governance,* The Free Press, New York.

Martin, J. (1995), 'Contracting and Accountability', in J. Boston (ed.), *The State Under Contract*, Bridget Williams Books, Wellington, pp. 36–55.

Martin, J. (1997a), 'Changing Accountability Relations: Politics, Customers and the Market', OECD, PUMA/PAC(97)1, Paris.

Martin, J. (1997b), 'Advisers and Bureaucrats', in R.Miller (ed.), *New Zealand Politics in Transition*, Oxford University Press, Auckland, pp. 108–116.

Martin, J. (1998), *Reorienting a Nation: Consultants and Australian Public Policy*, Ashgate, Aldershot.

Mascarenhas, R.C. (1990), 'Reform of Public Service in Australia and New Zealand', *Governance*, vol. 3 (1), pp. 75–95.

Mascarenhas, R.C. (1996a), *Government and the Economy in Australia and New Zealand*, Austin & Winfield, San Francisco.

Mascarenhas, R.C. (1996b), 'The Evolution of Public Enterprise Organisation: A Critique', in J. Halligan (ed.), *Public Administration under Scrutiny. Essays in Honour of Roger Wettenhall*, Centre for Research in Public Sector Management, University of Canberra, Institute of Public Administration Australia, pp. 59–76.

Mascarenhas, R.C. (1999), 'Reform of Public Enterprise: Commercialisation, Corporatisation and Privatisation in New Zealand', unpublished paper, Victoria University of Wellington, Wellington, NZ.

Massey, P. (1995), *New Zealand. Market Liberalization in a Developed Economy*, St. Martins Press, New York.

Mattsson, S. and Forssell, A. (1998), 'Med konkurrensutsättning som ledstjärna. Statligt företagande på 90-talet', in G. Ahrne (ed.), *Stater som organisationer*, Nerenius & Santérus, Stockholm, pp. 285–308.

Mellbourn, A. (1986), *Bortom det starka samhället*, Carlssons, Stockholm.

Melleuish, G. (1998), *The Packaging of Australia: Politics and Culture Wars*, University of New South Wales Press, Sydney.

Merton, R.K. (1952), 'Bureaucratic Structure and Personality', in R.K. Merton et al. (eds), *Reader in Bureaucracy*, The Free Press, Glencoe, Ill., pp. 361–371.

Meyer, J.W. (1994), 'Rationalized Environment', in W.R. Scott and J.W. Meyer (eds), *Environment and Organizations*, Sage, London.

Meyer, J.W. (1996), 'Otherhood: The Promulgation and Transmisson of Ideas in the Modern Organizational Environment', in B. Czarniawska and G. Sevón (eds) *Translating Organizational Change*, DeGruyter, Berlin, pp. 241–252.

Meyer, J.W., Boli, J., Thomas, G.M. and Ramirez, F.O (1997), 'World Society and the Nation-State', *American Journal of Sociology*, vol. 103 (1), pp. 144–181.

Meyer, J.W. and Rowan, B. (1977), 'Institutionalized Organizations: Formal Structure as Myth and Ceremony', *American Journal of Sociology*, vol. 83 (Sept.), pp. 340–363.

Meyer, J.W. and Scott, W.R. (1983), *Organizational Environments: Ritual and Rationality*, Sage, Beverly Hills, CA.

Milgrom, P. and Roberts, J. (1992), *Economics, Organization and Management*, Prentice-Hall, New York.

Mill, J.S. (1859/1975), *On Liberty, Three Essays*, Oxford University Press, Oxford.

Miller, D. (1989), *Market, State and Community*, Claredon Press, Oxford.

Miller, P. (1994), 'Accounting as a Social and Institutional Practice: An Introduction', in A.G. Hopwood and P. Miller (eds), *Accounting as a Social and Institutional Practice*, Cambridge University Press, Cambridge, pp. 1–39.

Minogue, M., Polidano, C. and Hulme, D. (1998), *Beyond the New Public Management. Changing Ideas and Practices in Governance*, Edward Elgar, Cheltenham.

Minson, J. (1998), 'Ethics in the Service of the State', in M. Dean and B. Hindess (eds), *Governing Australia. Studies in Contemporary Rationalities of Government*, Cambridge University Press, Cambridge, pp. 47–69.

Mjør, M. (1994), 'Maskulinitet og management', Working Paper 9425, LOS-Centre, Bergen.

Montin, S. (1997), 'New Public Management på svenska', *Politica*, vol. 29 (3), pp. 262–278.

Morgan, G. (1986), *Images of Organization*, Sage, Beverly Hills, CA.

Mosher, F.C. (ed.) (1967), *Governmental Reorganizations: Cases and Commentary*, Bobbs-Merrill, New York.

Mörth, U. (1996), 'Vardagsintegration – La vie quotidienne – i Europa. Sverige i EUREKA och EUREKA i Sverige', Dissertation, Departement of Political Science, Stockholm University.

Mulgan, R. (1992), 'The Elective Dictatorship in New Zealand', in H. Gold (ed.), *New Zealand Politics in Perspective*, Longman, Auckland, pp. 513–532.

Musselin, C. (1997), 'State/University Relations and How to Change Them: The Case of France and Germany', *European Journal of Education*, vol. 32 (2), pp. 145–164.

Nagel, J.H. (1997), 'Radically Reinventing Government: Editor's Introduction', *Journal of Policy Analysis and Management*, vol. 16 (3), pp. 349–356.

Nagel, J.H. (1998), 'Social Choice in a Pluralitarian Democracy: The Politics of Market Liberalization in New Zealand', *British Journal of Political Science*, vol. 28, pp. 223–267.

Naschold, F. (1996), *New Frontiers in Public Sector Management*, de Gruyter, Berlin.

Nergaard, K. (1999), 'Organisasjonsgrad og tariffavtaledekning målt ved AKU 2. kvartal 1998', Working Paper 1999:5, FAFO, Oslo.

North, D.C. (1990), *Institutions, Institutional Change and Economic Performance*, Cambridge University Press, Cambridge.

NOU 1989:5, 'En bedre organisert stat', Forvaltningstjenestene, Statens tryknings-kontor, Oslo.

NOU 1991:8, 'Lov om statsforetak', Forvaltningstjenestene, Statens trykningskontor, Oslo.

O'Brien, J. and Hort, L. (1998), 'Introduction: The State of State Employment', *Australian Journal of Public Administration*, vol. 57 (2), pp. 46–48.

OECD (1993), *Public Management: Country Profiles*, OECD, Paris.

OECD (1995), *Governance in Transition: Public Management Reforms in OECD Countries*, OECD, Paris.

OECD (1996a), *Globalization: What Challenges and Opportunities for Governments?*, OECD/PUMA, Paris.

OECD (1996b), *Ministerial Symposium on the Future of Public Services*, OECD, Paris.

OECD (1996c), *Pay for Performance: The Record in Four Countries*, OECD (PUMA), Paris.

OECD (1997), *Performance Pay Schemes for Public Sector Managers*, OECD (PUMA), Occasional Paper, no. 15, Paris.

OECD (1999a), 'Synthesis of Reform Experiences in Nine OECD Countries: Government Roles and Functions and Public Management', Document presented at the PUMA conference 'Government of the future: Getting from here the there', September 1999, Paris.

OECD (1999b), 'Government Reform: Of Roles and Functions of Government and Public Administration. New Zealand – Country Paper', Document presented at the PUMA conference 'Government of the future: Getting from here to there', September, Paris.

Offe, C. (1984), *The Contradictions of the Welfare State*, Hutchinson, London.

Olsen, J.P. (1978), 'Folkestyre, byråkrati og korporativisme', in J.P. Olsen (ed.), *Politisk organisering*, Universitetsforlaget, Bergen, pp. 13–114.

Olsen, J.P. (1983), 'The Dilemmas of Organizational Integration in Government', in J.P. Olsen, *Organized Democracy. Political Institutions in a Welfare State – the Case of Norway*, Universitetsforlaget, Bergen, pp. 148–187.

Olsen, J.P. (1984), 'Representativitet og politisk organisering', in O. Berg and A. Underdal (eds), *Fra valg til vedtak*, Aschehoug, Oslo, pp. 86–124.

Olsen, J.P. (1988a), 'Administrative Reform and Theories of Organization', in C. Campbell and B. Guy Peters (eds), *Organizing Governance: Governing Organizations*, University of Pittsburgh Press, Pittsburgh, pp. 233–254.

Olsen, J.P. (1988b), 'Nyinstitusjonalismen og statsvitenskapen', in J.P. Olsen (ed.), *Statsstyre og institusjonsutforming*, Universitetsforlaget, Oslo, pp. 29–46.

Olsen, J.P. (1988c), *Statsstyre og institusjonsutforming*, Universitetsforlaget, Oslo.

Olsen, J.P. (1991), 'Modernization Programs in Perspective. Institutional Analysis of Organizational Change', *Governance*, vol. 4 (2), pp. 121–149.

Olsen, J.P. (1992), 'Analyzing Institutional Dynamics', *Staatswissenschaften und Staatspraxis*, vol. 3 (2), pp. 247–271.

Olsen, J.P. (1993), 'Et statsvitenskapelig perspektiv på offentlig sektor', in P. Lægreid and J.P. Olsen (eds), *Organisering av offentlig sektor*, TANO, Oslo, pp. 17–42.

Olsen, J.P. (1996), 'Norway: Slow Learner — or Another Triumph of the Tortoise?', in J.P. Olsen and B.G. Peters (eds), *Lessons from Experience*, Scandinavian University Press, Oslo, pp. 180–213.

Olsen, J.P. (1997a), 'Civil Service in Transition – Dilemmas and Lessons Learned', in J.J. Hesse and T.A. Toonen (eds), *European Yearbook of Comparative Government and Public Administration*, vol III, Nomos, Baden-Baden, pp. 389–407.

Olsen, J.P. (1997b), 'Institutional Design in Democratic Context', *Journal of Political Philosophy*, vol. 5 (3), pp. 203–229.

Olsen, J.P. and Peters, B.G. (eds) (1996a), *Lessons from Experience*, Scandinavian University Press, Oslo.

Olsen, J.P. and Peters, B.G. (1996b), 'Learning from Experience?', in J.P. Olsen and B.G. Peters (eds), *Lessons from Experience*, Scandinavian University Press, Oslo, pp. 1–35.

Olsen, J.P., Roness, P.G. and Sætren, H. (1982), 'Norway: Still Peaceful Coexistence and Revolution in Slow Motion', in J.J. Richardson (ed.), *Policy Styles in Western Europe*, Allen & Unwin, London, pp. 47–79.

Olson, O., Guthrie, J. and Humphrey, C. (eds) (1998), *Global Warning: Debating International Developments in New Public Financial Management*, Cappelen Akademisk Forlag, Oslo.

Olson, O. and Sahlin-Andersson, K. (1998), 'Accounting Transformation in an Advanced Welfare State: The Case of Sweden', in O. Olson, J. Guthrie and C. Humphrey (eds), *Global warning! Debating International Developments in New Public Financial Management*, Cappelen Akademisk Forlag, Oslo, pp. 241–275.

Osborne, D. and Gaebler, T. (1992), *Reinventing Government: How the Entrepreneurial Spirit is Transforming the Public Sector*, Addison-Wesley, Reading, MA.

Painter, M. (1987), *Steering the Modern State: Changes in Central Coordination in Three Australian State Governments*, Sydney University Press, Sydney.

Painter, M. (1988), 'Public Management: Fad or Fallacy?', *Australian Journal of Public Administration*, vol. 47 (1, March), pp. 1–3.

Painter, M. (1990), 'Values in the History of Public Administration', in J. Power (ed.), *Public Administration in Australia: A Watershed*, Hale & Iremonger/ RAIPA, Sydney, pp. 75–93.

Painter, M. (1996), 'Economic Policy, Market Liberalism and the 'End of Australian Politics'', *Australian Journal of Political Science*, vol. 31 (3), pp. 287–300.

Painter, M. (1997), 'Reshaping the public sector', in B. Galligan, I. McAllister and J. Ravenhill (eds), *New Developments in Australian Politics*, Macmillan Education Australia, South Melbourne, pp. 148–166.

Painter, M. (1998a), 'Public Sector Reform, Intergovernmental Relations and the Future of Australian Federalism', *Australian Journal of Public Administration*, vol. 57 (3), pp. 52–63.

Painter, M. (1998b), *Collaborative Federalism: Economic Reform in Australia in the 1990s*, Cambridge University Press, Cambridge.

Pallot, J. (1998), 'The New Zealand Revolution', in O. Olson, J. Guthrie and C. Humphrey (eds), *Global Warning! Debating International Developments in New Public Financial Management*, Cappelen Akademisk Forlag, Oslo, pp. 156–184.

Palmer, G. and Palmer, M. (1997), *Bridled power: New Zealand Government Under MMP*, Oxford University Press, Auckland.

Peetz, D. (1998), *Unions in a Contrary World. The Future of the Australian Trade Union Movement*, Cambridge University Press, Cambridge.

Perry, J.L. (1986), 'Merit Pay in the Public Sector: The Case for a Failure of Theory', *Review of Public Personnel Administration*, vol. 7 (1), pp. 57–69.

Perry, J.L. (1992), 'The Merit Pay Reforms', in P.W. Ingraham and D.H. Rosenbloom (eds), *The Promise and Paradox of Civil Service Reform*, University of Pittsburgh Press, Pittsburgh, pp. 199–216.

Perry, P. and Webster, A. (1999), *New Zealand Politics at the Turn of the Millennium: Attitudes and Values about Politics and Government*, Alpha Publications, Auckland.

Peters, B.G. (1994), 'New Visions of Government and the Public Service', in P.W. Ingraham and B.S. Romzek (eds), *New Paradigm for Government*, Jossey-Bass, San Francisco, pp. 295–321.

Peters, B.G. (1996a), *The Future of Governing. Four Emerging Models*, University Press of Kansas, Lawrence.

Peters, B.G. (1996b), 'Contracts as a Tool for Public Management: Their Surprising Absence in North America', Paper prepared for presentation to a meeting of the European Group of Public Administration, August, Budapest.

Peters, B.G. (1998a), 'Tailoring Change Strategies: Alternative Approaches to Reform', in P. Ingraham, J.R. Thompson and R.P. Sanders (eds), *Transforming*

Government: Lessons from the Reinvention Laboratories, Jossey-Bass, San Francisco, pp. 173–189.

Peters, B.G. (1998b), 'Administration in the Year 2000: Serving the Client', *International Journal of Public Administration*, vol. 21 (12), pp. 1759–1776.

Peters, B.G. (1999a), *Institutional Theory in Political Science. The New Institutionalism*, Pinter, London.

Peters, B.G. (1999b), 'Is Democracy a Substitute for Ethics? Administrative Reform and Accountability in Post-Reform Government', unpublished paper, Department of Political Science, University of Pittsburgh.

Peters, B.G. and Hood, C. (1994), 'Conclusion: What Have We Learned?', in C. Hood and B.G. Peters (eds), *Rewards at the Top,* Sage, London, pp. 215–227.

Peters, B.G. and Hood, C. (1995), 'Erosion and Variety in Pay for High Public Office', *Governance*, vol. 8 (2), pp. 171–194.

Peters, B.G. and Pierre, J. (1998), 'Governance Without Government? Rethinking Public Administration', *Journal of Public Administration Research and Theory*, vol. 8 (2), pp. 223–243.

Peters, B.G. and Savoie, D.J. (eds) (1995), *Governance in a Changing Environment*, McGill-Queens University Press, Montreal.

Peters, B.G. and Savoie, D. (1998), *Taking Stock: Assessing Public Sector Reforms*, McGill-Queen's University Press, Montreal.

Peters, B.G. and Wright, V. (1996), 'Public Policy and Administration, Old and New', in R.E. Goodin and H.-D. Klingemann, *New Handbook of Political Science,* Oxford University Press, New York, pp. 628–641.

Petersson, O. (1994), *The Government and Politics of the Nordic Countries*, Publicia, Stockholm.

Petersson, O. and Söderlind, D. (1992), *Förvaltningspolitik*, Publica, Stockholm.

Petrie, M. (1998), *Organisational Transformation: The Income Support Experience*, Department of Social Welfare, Wellington.

Pitkin, H.F. (1972), *The Concept of Representation*, University of California Press, Berkeley.

Podder, N. and Chatterjee, S. (1998), 'Sharing the National Cake in Post-Reform New Zealand: Income Inequality in Terms of Income Sources', Paper presented to the New Zealand Association of Economists Conference, August.

Pollitt, C. (1990), *Managerialism and the Public Services. The Anglo-American Experience*, Basil Blackwell, Oxford.

Pollitt, C. (1995), 'Justification by Works or by Faith', *Evaluation*, vol. 2 (2), pp. 133–154.

Pollitt, C. (1998), 'Managerialism Revisited', in B.G. Peters and D.J. Savoie (eds), *Taking Stock: Assessing Public Sector Reforms*, Canadian Centre for Management Development, Montreal and Kingston, pp. 45–77.

Pollitt, C., Birchall, J. and Putman, K. (1998), *Decentralizing Public Service Management*, Macmillan, London.

Pollitt, C. and Bouckaert, G. (2000), *Public Management Reform. A Comparative Analysis*, Oxford University Press, Oxford.

Pollit, C., Hanney, S., Packwood, T., Rothwell, S., and Roberts, S. (1997), 'Trajectories and Options: An International Perspective on the Implementation of Finnish Public Management Reforms', Ministry of Finance, Helsinki.

Polsby, N.W. (1984), *Political Innovation in America*, Yale University Press, New Haven.

Powell, W.E. and DiMaggio, P. (eds) (1991), *The New Institutionalism in Organizational Analysis*, The University of Chicago Press, Chicago.

Power, J. (1994), 'Styles of Discourse about Public Service Reform: Political Executive, Central Agency and Parliamentary Committees', Paper presented to the 1994 conference, Frontiers of Reform: Issues in Redesigning Public Sectors, Australian National University, Canberra.

Power, M. (1994), *The Audit Explosion*, Demos, London.

Power, M. (1997), *The Audit Society*, Oxford University Press, Oxford.

Premfors, R. (1991), 'The 'Swedish Model' and Public Sector Reforms', *West European Politics*, vol. 14 (3), pp. 83–95.

Premfors, R. (1998), 'Reshaping the Democratic State: Swedish Experiences in a Comparative Perspective', *Public Administration*, vol. 76 (2), pp. 141–160.

Premfors, R. (1999), 'Organisationsförandringar och förvaltningspolitik – Sverige', in P. Lægreid and O.K. Pedersen (eds), *Fra opbyging til ombyging i staten*, Jurist- og Økonomforbundets forlag, København, pp. 145–168.

Przeworski, A. and Teune, H. (1970), *The Logic of Comparative Social Inquiry*, John Wiley, New York.

Pusey, M. (1991), *Economic Rationalism in Canberra: A Nationbuilding State Changes its Mind*, Cambridge University Press, Sydney.

Rainey, H.G. (1998a), 'Ingredients for Success: Five Factors Necessary for Transforming Government', in P.W. Ingraham, J.R. Thompson and R.P. Sanders (eds), *Transforming Government: Lessons from the Reinvention Laboratories*, Jossey-Bass, San Francisco, pp. 147–172.

Rainey, H.G. (1998b), 'Assessing Past and Current Personnel Reforms', in B.G. Peters and D.J. Savoie (eds), *Taking Stock: Assessing Public Sector Reforms*, McGill-Queen's University Press, Montreal, pp. 187–220.

Rawson, D.W. (1978), *Unions and Unionists in Australia*, Allen & Unwin, Sydney.

Rawson, D.W. and Wrightson, S. (1980), 'A Handbook of Australian Trade Unions and Employees' Associations', 4th. ed., Occasional Paper no. 15, Department of Political Science, Research School of Social Sciences, Australian National University, Canberra.

Rhodes, R.A.W. (1994), 'The Hollowing Out of the State: The Changing Nature of the Public Service in Britain', *Political Quarterly*, vol. 65 (2), pp. 138–51.

Rhodes, R.A.W. (1997a), *Understanding Governance: Policy Networks, Governance, Reflexivity and Accountability*, Open University Press, Buckingham.

Rhodes, R.A.W. (1997b), ''Shackling the Leader?': Coherence, Capacity and the Hollow Crown', in P. Weller, H. Bakvis and R.A.W. Rhodes (eds), *The Hollow Crown: Countervailing Trends in Core Executives*, Macmillan, Basingstoke, pp. 198–222.

Rhodes, R.A.W. (1999), 'Traditions and Public Sector Reform: Comparing Britain and Denmark', *Scandinavian Political Studies*, vol. 22 (4), pp. 341–370.

Roberts, J. (1987), *Politicians, Public Servants and Public Enterprise: Restructuring the New Zealand Government Executive*, Victoria University Press for the Institute of Policy Studies, Wellington.

Rokkan, S. (1966), 'Comparative Cross-National Reserach: The Context of Current Efforts', in R.L. Merritt and S. Rokkan (eds), *Comparing Nations: The Use of Quantitative Data in Cross-National Reserach*, Yale University Press, New Haven, CT, pp. 3–26.

Rombach, B. (1997), *Den marknadslika kommunen*, Nerenius & Santérus, Stockholm.

Romzek, B.S. (1998), 'Where the Buck Stops. Accountability in Reformed Public Organizations', in P. Ingraham, J.R.Thompson and R.P. Sanders (eds), *Transforming Government*, Jossey Bass, San Francisco, pp. 193–219.

Roness, P.G. (1993), 'Tenestemannsorganisasjonane si rolle i omforminga av offentleg sektor', *Nordisk Administrativt Tidsskrift*, vol. 74 (3), pp. 264–278.

Roness, P.G. (1994), 'Tenestemannsorganisasjonar og forvaltningsreformer: Påverknadsmuligheter og handlingsrom', *Norsk Statsvitenskapelig Tidsskrift*, vol. 10 (1), pp. 25–39.

Roness, P.G. (1996), 'Institusjonell orden – Norge', in P. Lægreid and O.K. Pedersen (eds), *Integration och decentralisering*, Jurist- og Økonomforbundets Forlag, Copenhagen, pp. 59–92.

Roness, P.G. (1997), *Organisasjonsendringar. Teoriar og strategiar for studiar av endringsprosessar*, Fagbokforlaget, Bergen.

Roness, P.G. (1999), 'Historisk arv, gradvis tilpassing og radikal endring', Working Paper 9930, LOS-Centre, Bergen.

Roness, P.G. (2000), 'Historiske forklaringar i institusjonelle analysar innafor statsvitskap', *Norsk Statsvitenskapelig Tidsskrift*, vol. 16 (2), pp. 181–195.

Roper, B. (1997), 'New Zealand's Postwar Economic History', in C. Rudd and B. Roper (eds), *The Political Economy of New Zealand*, Oxford University Press, Auckland, pp. 3–21.

Rose, N. and Milller, P. (1992), 'Political Power Beyond the State: Problematics of Government', *British Journal of Sociology*, vol. 43 (2), pp. 173–205.

Roth, H. (1973), *Trade Unions in New Zealand. Past and Present*, Reed Education, Wellington.

Rothstein, B. and Bergström, J. (1999), *Korporatismens fall och den svenska modellens kris*, SNS Förlag, Stockholm.

Royal Commission on Australian Government Administration (Chairman: H. C. Coombs) (1976), *Report*, Australian Government Publishing Service, Canberra.

Rudd, C. (1997), 'The Welfare State', in C. Rudd and B. Roper (eds), *The Political Economy of New Zealand*, Oxford University Press, Auckland, pp. 237–255.

Røvik, K-A. (1992), 'Institusjonaliserte standarder og multistandardorganisasjoner', *Norsk Statsvitenskapelig Tidsskrift*, vol. 8 (4), pp. 261–284.

Røvik, K.A. (1996), 'Deinstitutionalization and the Logic of Fashion', in B. Czarniawska and G. Sevón (eds), *Translating Organizational Change*, de Gruyter, Berlin, pp. 139–172.

Røvik, K.A. (1998), *Moderne organisasjoner. Trender i organisasjonstenkningen ved tusenårsskiftet*, Fagbokforlaget, Bergen.

Røvik, K.A. (forthcoming), 'The Secrets of the Winners: Towards a Theory of Management Ideas that Flow', in K. Sahlin-Andersson and L. Engwall (eds), *Carriers of Management Knowledge: Ideas and their Circulation*, Stanford University Press, Stanford.

Sabatier, C.A. (1991), 'Two Decades of Implementation Research: From Control and Guidance to Learning', in F.X. Kaufman (ed.), *The Public Sector. Challenges for Coordination and Learning*, de Gruyter, Berlin, pp. 257–270.

Sahlin-Andersson, K. (1996), 'Imitating by Editing Success: The Construction of Organizational Fields', in B. Czarniawska and G. Sevón (eds), *Translating Organizational Change*, de Gruyter, New York, pp. 69–92.

Sahlin-Andersson, K. (2000), 'Arenas as Standardizers', in N. Brunsson, B. Jacobsson and associates, *A World of Standards*, Oxford University Press, Oxford.

Savoie, D.J. (1998), 'Fifteen Years of Reform: What Have We Learned?', in B.G. Peters and D.J. Savoie (eds), *Taking Stock: Assessing Public Sector Reforms*, Canadian Centre for Management Development, Montreal and Kingston, pp. 394–414.

Scharpf, F. (1997), *Games Real Actors Play: Actor-Centred Institutionalism in Policy Research*, Westview Press, Boulder, Colorado.

Schick, A. (1996), 'The Spirit of Reform: Managing the New Zealand State Sector in a Time of Change', A report prepared for the State Services Commission and the Treasury, Wellington.

Schick, A. (1998), 'Why Most Developing Countries Should Not Try New Zealand's Reforms', *The World Bank Research Observer*, vol. 13 (1), pp. 121–131.

Schwartz, H. (1994), 'Small States in Big Trouble. State Reorganization in Australia, Denmark, New Zealand and Sweden in the 1980s', *World Politics*, vol. 46 (July), pp. 527–555.

Scott, G. (1996), 'Government Reform in New Zealand', Occasional Paper no. 140, International Monetary Fund, Washington D.C.

Scott, G., Bushnell P. and Sallee, N. (1990), 'Reform of the Core Public Sector: The New Zealand Experience', *Governance*, vol. 3 (2), pp. 138–167.

Scott, W.R. (1995), *Institutions and Organizations*, Sage, Thousand Oaks.

Scott, W.R (1998), *Organizations. Rational, Natural and Open Systems*, Prentice Hall, 4th. ed., New Jersey.

Sejersted, F. (1983), 'Politikk som interessekamp eller styringsproblem', in T. Bergh (ed.), *Deltakerdemokratiet*, Universitetsforlaget, Oslo.

Self, P. (2000), *Rolling Back the Market: Economic Dogma and Political Choice*, St Martin's Press, New York.

Selznick. P. (1957), *Leadership in Administration*, Harper & Row, New York.

Sevón, G. (1996), 'Organizational Imitation and Identity Transformation', in B. Czarniawska and G. Sevón (eds), *Translating Organizational Change*, de Gruyter, Berlin, pp. 49–68.

Shaw, R. (1999), 'Rehabilitating the Public Service – Alternatives to the Wellington Model', in S. Chatterjee et al., *The New Politics: A Third Way for New Zealand*, Dunmore Press, Palmerston North, pp. 187–218.

Shergold, P. (1997), 'The Colour Purple: Prescriptions of Accountability Across the Tasman', *Public Administration and Development*, vol. 17 (3), pp. 293–306.

Sieber, S. (1981), *Fatal Remedies*, Plenum, New York.

Simon, H. (1957), *Administrative Behavior*, Free Press, 2nd ed., New York.

Sjølund, M. (1996a), 'Lönepolitik och institutionell orden – Sverige', in P. Lægreid and O.K. Pedersen (eds), *Integration och decentralisering,* Jurist- og Økonom-forbundets Forlag, Copenhagen, pp. 93–127.

Sjølund, M. (1996b), 'Lokal lön i Sverige', in P. Lægreid and O. K. Pedersen (eds), *Integration och decentralisering*, Copenhagen, pp. 231–256.

Sjöstedt, G. (1973), *OECD-samarbetet: Funktioner och effekter*, Political Science Studies 3, Stockholm University, Stockholm.

Slotnes, A. (1994), 'Kontinuitet eller brudd? En sammenlignende studie av sentral administrative endringsvedtak i Norge og New Zealand i 1980-årene', Report 26, Department of Administration and Organization Theory, University of Bergen, Bergen.

Smelser, N.J. (1973), 'The Methodology of Comparative Analysis', in D. Warwick and S. Osherson (eds), *Comparative Research Methods*, Prentice Hall, Engle-wood Cliffs, NJ.

Smith, V. (1997), *Reining in the Dinosaur. The Remarkable Turnaround of New Zealand Post*, New Zealand Post, Wellington.

Spann, R.N. (1979), *Government Administration in Australia*, Allen & Unwin, Sydney.

Spicer, B., Bowman, R., Emanuel, D. and Hunt, A. (1991), *The Power to Manage. Restructuring the New Zealand Electricity Department as a State-Owned Enterprise. The Electricorp Experience*, Oxford University Press, Auckland.

Spicer, B., Emanuel, D. and Powell, M. (1996), *Transforming Government Enter-prises*, Centre for Independent Studies, St. Leonards, Australia.

SSC (1997), 'Strategic Human Resource Capability Issues in the Public Service', State Service Commission, Wellington.

SSC (1998a), 'Annual Report of State Service Commission. For the year Ended 30 June 1998', State Service Commission, Wellington.

SSC (1998b), 'Assessment of the State of the New Zealand Public Service', State Service Commission, Occasional Paper no.1, Wellington.

SSC (1999a), 'Improving Accountability: Setting the Scene', Occasional Paper no. 10, State Services Commission, Wellington.

SSC (1999b), 'Briefing for the Minister of State Services, 10 December', State Services Commission, Wellington.

Stace, D. and Norman, R. (1997), 'Re-Invented Government: The New Zealand Experiment', *Asia Pacific Journal of Human Resources*, vol. 35 (1), pp. 21–36.

Stace, H. (1998), 'Janet Fraser – Making Policy as Well as Tea', in M. Clark (ed.), *Peter Fraser: Master Politician*, Dunmore Press, Palmerston North.

Statskonsult (1998), 'I godt selskap? Statlig eierstyring i terori og praksis', Report, Statskonsult, Oslo.

Statskontoret 1996:20, 'Organisation och kostnader i kommunerna', Stockholm.

Statskontoret, 1997:15, 'Staten i omvandling', Stockholm.

Stephens, R. (2000), 'The Social Impact of Reform: Poverty in Aotearoa/New Zealand', *Social Policy and Administration*, vol. 34 (1).

Stewart, J. and Kimber, M. (1996), 'The Transformation of Bureaucracy? Structural Change in the Commonwealth Public Service 1983–93', *Australian Journal of Public Administration*, vol. 55 (3), pp. 37–48.

Stewart, J. and Walsch, K. (1992), 'Change in the Management of Public Services', *Public Administration*, vol. 70, pp. 499–518.

Stortingspreposisjon nr. 1 (1996–97), Administrasjonsdepartementet, Oslo.

Strang, D. and Meyer, J.W. (1993), 'Institutional Conditions for Diffusion', *Theory and Society*, vol. 22, pp. 487–511.

Strømsnes, D. (1999), 'OECD – Strategic Review and Reform – Norway', Document presented at the PUMA conference 'Government of the future: Getting from here to there', September 1999, Paris.

Svedberg Nilsson, K. (2000), 'Marknadens decennium. Gränsomdragande reformer i den offentliga sektorn under 1990-talet', in *Välfärd, vård och omsorg, SOU 2000:38*, pp. 1–23, Stockholm.

Svensen, S. and Teicher, J. (1999), 'Restructuring the Australian State? A Bipartisan Agenda', *Public Management*, vol. 1 (3), pp. 329–348.

Sørlie, J. (1997), 'Tjenestemannsorganisasjoner og endring av tilknytningsform', Report 9704, LOS-Centre, Bergen.

Tarschys, D (1979), *Den offentliga revolutionen*, Kontenta/Liber förlag, Stockholm.

Task Force on Management Improvement (1993), *The Australian Public Service Reformed: An Evaluation of a Decade of Management Reform*, Australian Government Publishing Service for the Management Advisory Board, Canberra.

Thomas, P.G. (1998), 'The Changing Nature of Accountability', in B.G. Peters and D.J. Savoie (eds), *Taking Stock: Assessing Public Sector Reforms*, Canadian Centre for Management Development, Montreal, pp. 348–393.

Thompson, D.F. (1980), 'Moral Responsibility of Public Officials: The Problem of Many Hands', *American Political Science Review*, vol. 74, pp. 905–16.

Thompson, J.R. (1967), *Organizations in Action*, McGraw-Hill, New York.

Thompson, J.R. and Sanders, R.P. (1998), 'Reinventing Public Agencies: Bottom-Up Versus Top-Down Strategies', in P. Ingraham, J.R. Thompson and R. P. Sanders (eds), *Transforming Government: Lessons from the Reinvention Laboratories*, Jossey-Bass, San Francisco, pp. 97–121.

Thornthwaite, L. and Hollander, R. (1998), 'Two Models of Contemporary Public Service Wage Determination in Australia', *Australian Journal of Public Administration*, vol. 57 (2), pp. 98–106.

Trebilcock, M. (1995), 'Can Government Be Reinvented?', in J. Boston (ed.), *The State Under Contract*, Bridget Williams Books, Wellington.

Uhr, J. (1999), 'Three Accountability Anxieties: A Conclusion to the Symposium', *Australian Journal of Public Administration*, vol. 58 (1), pp. 98–101.

Uhr, J. and Mackay, K. (eds) (1996), *Evaluating Policy Advice: Lessons from Commonwealth Experience*, Federalism Research Centre, Canberra.

Upton, S. (1999), 'The Role of the State', *IPS Policy Newsletter*, vol. 56 (February), Institute of Policy Studies, Victoria University of Wellington, pp. 8–15.

Vathne, K.E. (1998), 'Fra indre omstilling til ytre fristilling. En studie av Postverket 1986–1996', Thesis, Department of Administration and Organization Theory, University of Bergen, Bergen.

Verheijen, T. (1998), 'Public Management Reform in New Zealand and Australia', in T. Verheijen and D. Coombes (eds), *Innovation in Public Management*, Edward Elgar, Cheltenham, pp. 255–281.

Von Wright, G.H. (1993), *Myten om framsteget*, Albert Bonniers förlag, Stockholm.

Vowles, J. (1992), 'Business, Unions and the State: Organising Economic Interests in New Zealand', in H. Gold (ed.), *New Zealand Politics in Perspective*, Longman Paul, 3rd ed., Auckland, pp. 342–364.

Vrangbaeck, K. (1999), 'Markedsorientering i sygehussektoren', Thesis, Institute of Political Science, University of Copenhagen.

Walsh, P. (1991), 'The State Sector Act 1988', in J. Boston, J. Martin, J. Pallot and P. Walsh (eds), *Reshaping the State: New Zealand's Bureaucratic Revolution*, Oxford University Press, Auckland, pp. 52–80.

Walsh, P. (1998), 'From Uniformity to Diversity? Reinventing Public Sector Industrial Relations in New Zealand', *Australia Journal of Public Administration*, vol. 57 (2), pp. 55–59.

Walsh, P. and Brosnan, P. (1999), 'Redesigning Industrial Relations: The Employment Contracts Act and Industrial Relations', in J. Boston et al. (eds), *Redesigning the Welfare State in New Zealand*, Oxford University Press, Auckland, pp. 117–133.

Walsh, P., Harbridge R. and Crawford, A. (1997), 'Restructuring Employment Relations in the New Zealand Public Sector', (unpublished conference paper), Victoria University of Wellington, Wellington.

Walzer, M. (1983), *Spheres of Justice*, Basil Blackwell, Oxford.

342 *New Public Management*

Weaver, R.K. and Rockman, B.A. (eds) (1993), *Do Institutions Matter?*, Brookings, Washington, D.C.

Weber, M. (1971), *Makt og byråkrati*, Gyldendal, Oslo.

Weller, P. (1996), 'Commonwealth-State Reform Processes: A Policy Management Review', *Australian Journal of Public Administration*, vol. 55 (1), pp. 95–110.

Weller, P., Bakvis, H. and Rhodes, R.A.W. (1997), *The Hollow Crown: Countervailing Trends in Core Executives*, Macmillan, Basingstoke.

Weller, P. and Stevens, B. (1998), 'Evaluating Policy Advice: The Australian Experience', *Public Administration*, vol. 76 (3), pp. 579–89.

Westney, D.E. (1987), *Imitation and Innovation. The Transfer of Western Organizational Patterns to Meiji Japan*, Harvard University Press, Cambridge, MA.

Wettenhall, R. (1995), 'Corporations and Corporatisation: An Administrative History Perspective', *Public Law Review*, vol. 6, (1), pp. 7–24.

Wettenhall, R. (1998a), 'Privatization in Australia: How Much and What Impact?', Paper for 45th Executive Council Meeting and Seminar – Workshop on Administration in Transition, Eastern Regional Organization for Public Administration, 26–30 October, Macau.

Wettenhall, R. (1998b), 'The Rising Popularity of the Government-Owned Company in Australia: Problems and Issues', *Public Administration and Development*, vol. 18, pp. 243–255.

Whitecombe, J. (1990), 'The New Zealand Senior Executive Service', *Canberra Bulletin of Public Administration*, vol. 61, pp. 153–157.

Wilenski, P. (1986), *Public Power and Public Administration*, Hale & Iremonger, Sydney.

Wilson, J.Q. (1989), *Bureaucracy: What Government Agencies Do and Why They Do It*, Basic Books, New York.

Wilson, M. (1989), *Labour in Government*, Allen & Unwin, Wellington.

Wise, L.R. (1994), 'Implementing Pay Reforms in the Public Sector: Different Approaches to Flexible Pay in Sweden and the US', *International Journal of Public Administration*, vol. 17, pp. 1937–1959.

Wise, L.R. and Sjöström, A. (2000), 'Changing Values and Notions of Pay Equity in the Swedish Civil Service', in A. Farazmand (ed.), *Handbook of Comparative and Developmental Adminsitration*, Marcel Dekker, 2nd. ed., New York (forthcoming).

World development report (1997), *The State in a Changing World*, Oxford University Press for the World Bank, Washington, DC.

Wærness, M. (1990), 'Treårsbudgetering som rationalisering', in N. Brunsson and J.P. Olsen (eds), *Makten att reformera*, Carlssons, Stockholm, pp. 143–170.

Yates, B. (1998), 'Workplace Relations and Agreement Making in the Australian Public Service', *Australian Journal of Public Administration*, vol. 57 (2), pp. 82–90.

Yeatman, A. (1987), 'The Concept of Public Management and the Australian State in the 1980s', *Australian Journal of Public Administration*, vol. XLVI (4), pp. 339–353.

Yeatman, A. (1997), 'The Reforms of Public Management: An Overview', in M. Considine and M. Painter (eds), *Managerialism: The Great Debate*, Melbourne University Press, Melbourne.

Yeatman, A. (1998), 'Interpreting Contemporary Contractualism', in M. Dean and B. Hindess (eds), *Governing Australia. Studies in Contemporary Rationalities of Government*, Cambridge University Press, Cambridge.

Yin, R. (1994), *Case Study Research: Design and Methods*, Sage, 2nd. ed., London.

Zifcak, S. (1994), *New Managerialism: Administrative Reform in Whitehall and Canberra*, Open University Press, Buckingham.

Zifcak, S. (1997), 'Managerialism, Accountability and Democracy: A Victorian Case Study', *Australian Journal of Public Administration*, vol. 56 (3), pp. 106–119.

Zuna, H.R. (1998), 'Demografi og beslutninger', Thesis, Department of Political Science, Oslo.

Ørnsrud, I. (2000), 'Mye fristilling men lite kontroll', Report 0001, LOS-Centre, Bergen.

Åkerstrøm Andersen, N. (1995), *Selvskabt forvaltning: Forvaltnings-politikkens og centralforvaltningens udvikling i Danmark fra 1900–1994*, Nyt Fra Samfunds-videnskaberne, København.

Subject Index

Name Index